HISTORY AS WONDER

History as Wonder is a refreshing new take on the idea of history that tracks the entanglement of history and philosophy over time through the key idea of wonder.

From ancient Greek histories and wonder works, to Islamic curiosities and Chinese strange histories, through to European historical cabinets of curiosity and on to histories that grapple with the horrors of the Holocaust, Marnie Hughes-Warrington unpacks the ways in which historians throughout the ages have tried to make sense of the world, and to change it. This book considers histories and historians across time and space, including the ancient Greek historian Polybius, the medieval texts by historians such as Bede in England and Ibn Khaldun in Islamic Historiography, and more recent works by Martin Heidegger, Luce Irigaray and Ranajit Guha among others. It explores the different ways in which historians have called upon wonder to cross boundaries between the past and the present, the universal and the particular, the old and the new, and the ordinary and the extraordinary. Promising to both delight and unsettle, it shows how wonder works as the beginning of historiography.

Accessible, engaging and wide-ranging, *History as Wonder* provides an original addition to the field of historiography that is ideal for those both new to and familiar with the study of history.

Marnie Hughes-Warrington is a professor of history at the Australian National University. She is the author of several historiography books, including *Fifty Key Thinkers on History* (three editions), *History Goes to the Movies* (2007) and *Revisionist Histories* (2013).

HISTORY AS WONDER

Beginning with Historiography

Marnie Hughes-Warrington

LONDON AND NEW YORK

First published 2019
by Routledge
2 Park Square, Milton Park, Abingdon, Oxon OX14 4RN

and by Routledge
711 Third Avenue, New York, NY 10017

Routledge is an imprint of the Taylor & Francis Group, an informa business

© 2019 Marnie Hughes-Warrington

The right of Marnie Hughes-Warrington to be identified as author of this work has been asserted by her in accordance with sections 77 and 78 of the Copyright, Designs and Patents Act 1988.

All rights reserved. No part of this book may be reprinted or reproduced or utilised in any form or by any electronic, mechanical, or other means, now known or hereafter invented, including photocopying and recording, or in any information storage or retrieval system, without permission in writing from the publishers.

Trademark notice: Product or corporate names may be trademarks or registered trademarks, and are used only for identification and explanation without intent to infringe.

British Library Cataloguing in Publication Data
A catalogue record for this book is available from the British Library

Library of Congress Cataloging-in-Publication Data
Names: Hughes-Warrington, Marnie, author.
Title: History as wonder : beginning with historiography / Marnie Hughes-Warrington.Description: London ; New York, NY : Routledge/Taylor & Francis Group, 2019. | Includes bibliographical references and index. | Identifiers: LCCN 2018030489 (print) | LCCN 2018031025 (ebook) |
Subjects: LCSH: Historiography.
Classification: LCC D13 (ebook) | LCC D13 .H7517 2019 (print) | DDC 907.2–dc23LC record available at https://lccn.loc.gov/2018030489

ISBN: 978-1-138-84621-0 (hbk)
ISBN: 978-1-138-84622-7 (pbk)
ISBN: 978-0-429-42716-9 (ebk)

Typeset in Bembo
by Taylor & Francis Books

Printed and bound in Great Britain by
TJ International Ltd, Padstow, Cornwall

Thank you to the person who threw out the multi-volume *Child's Book of Wonder* from St Brendan's Primary School Library, Flemington, in the early 1970s. It was a remarkable gift.

CONTENTS

Acknowledgements ix
Introduction xi

1 Sense and non-sense in Ancient Greek histories: Plato | Herodotus | Thucydides | Phlegon | Polybius | Aristotle   1

2 Wonderful and curious histories in pre-modern Europe: Gerald of Wales | Bede | Gervase of Tilbury | Augustine of Hippo | Thomas Aquinas | Roger Bacon   21

3 The wonders of history in the pre-modern Islamic world: Al Tusi | Al Qazwini | Al Tabari | Ibn Khaldun | Ibn Sina | Ibn Rushd   42

4 Wonder against ritual: strange Chinese histories: Sima Qian | Confucius | Duan Chengshi | Pu Songling | Yuan Mei | Ji Yun   62

5 Historical cabinets of curiosity in early modern Europe: Jean Bodin | Francis Bacon | Walter Ralegh | Nathaniel Wanley | René Descartes | Thomas Hobbes   81

6 Spirited histories in modern Europe: Immanuel Kant | George William Frederick Hegel | Daniel Defoe | William Howitt | Sarah Josepha Hale | Leopold von Ranke   100

7 Seeing the wonder trick in histories of the moving image: Lynne Kirby | Tom Gunning | Walter Benjamin | Roland Barthes | Jonathan Crary | Mary Anne Doane | 120

8 History's others, history's ethics: Joan Wallach Scott | Lynn
   Hunt | Merry Wiesner-Hanks | Luce Irigaray | Jacques
   Derrida | Hélène Cixous | Marguerite La Caze   139

9 Renewing wonder in postcolonial histories: Ranajit Guha |
   Gayatri Spivak | Romila Thapar | Rabindranath Tagore |
   Kalidāsā | Abhinavagupta   158

10 The banality of history: Martin Heidegger | Hannah Arendt   178

Conclusion: I wonder as I wander: everyday historiography,
everyday metaphysics?   189

Bibliography   *192*
Index   *206*

ACKNOWLEDGEMENTS

Books are carried to publication with thanks to the caring and thoughtful hands of many colleagues, friends and family members.

I would like to acknowledge the opportunity to write this book in my role at the Australian National University. In particular, I would like to thank Roxanne Missingham and the staff of the ANU libraries for making it possible for me to explore so many ideas from around the world, and for standing with such resolve in favour of open access. Their resilience at the destruction by flood of copies of many of the texts that I used to shape this book has been an inspiration to me.

I would also like to acknowledge the support of colleagues and students from the ANU Research School of History and beyond both because of their wise advice in seminars, and because of all the annotated draft chapters that are a historiographer's delight. Karen Downing and Tania Colwell gave me a great head start on the literature review. Frank Bongiorno was an insightful reader and generated much thought with his own writings. Rae Frances and Bruce Scates were generous with their support for the ideas in the book and eagle-eyed in spotting opportunities for improvement. Jennifer Frost at the University of Auckland provided wise thoughts on chapters seven and eight. Merry Wiesner-Hanks at the University of Wisconsin-Madison was both gracious and enormously helpful with suggestions for chapter eight. Troy Larkins read the manuscript in speedy and thorough fashion and helped with the identification of opportunities to be clearer. Thanks go also to Paul Kiem at the History Teacher's Association of Australia for responding to my ideas all the way along, and for so tirelessly promoting the value of studying the past.

Mark Donnelly and Claire Norton at the Centre for the Philosophy of History at St Mary's Twickenham were patient with early ideas about this book, and I am immensely grateful to both of them and to the audience of my first talk about it. Towards the end of writing, I felt fortunate to be able to share some of the ideas in the introduction at a seminar organised by Anna Clark at the University of Technology Sydney. I am thankful to her, Tamson Pietsch, Mary Spongberg, Stuart MacIntyre and Stefan Berger for the opportunity to play with ideas in the midst of days that are often dominated by one meeting after another. I also owe great thanks to Robbert Dijkgraaf, Marian Zelanzy and the staff at the Institute for Advanced Study (IAS) at Princeton for their generosity in hosting me at the beginning and end of this book project, in 2014 and 2018. Quiet, punctuated by lunches buzzing with ideas, are priceless, as are the digital copies of many of the histories from chapter six they were able to make with the generous support of the Hathi Trust.

As always, I am grateful for the help of everyone above, but acknowledge responsibility for any errors in the book.

I would also like to thank Rita, Ewan and Felicity for the everyday ways in which they have helped to make this book possible.

Finally, as always, it is family that make research possible. Thank you to the Hughes and the Warrington families, and to A and B, my heroes.

INTRODUCTION

Beginning with history as wonder

The idea of history is weird. It seems odd, and perhaps even paradoxical, that we use a general label to describe the study of particular phenomena and change over time. An interest in individual people, events and things is hard to square with an abstract concept. Yet despite this, the idea of history has been with us for a long time, and it persists. It does so for reasons that are not always appreciated. This book offers an appreciation of the idea of history told through a history of history, and it is an unsettling story.

I am not the first person to offer a history of history. Far from it. Credit for that rests with people who long ago wrote, sang or drew acknowledgements of other people's stories about the past. But I do want us to think again about how we might have settled into particular ways of telling the story of history's past. To start that journey, I want you to think of a thaumascope, a nineteenth-century label given to an object that has been with us for arguably thousands of years. It's a small disc that you can cup in the palm of your hand. One side depicts one image—a deer with legs extended, for example—and the other another image such as a deer with legs contracted. Suspend the disk with two pieces of deer gut, string, or wire, and then spin it. Spin the disk fast enough and the images combine to suggest movement or synthesis. The deer appears to move; or a bird fills what was an empty cage. The nineteenth-century billed this as a wonder, and that seems a fair label. The science is simple, but the effect is attention grabbing and even enthralling.

The history of history is like a thaumascope. Its components are individual histories which are connected by writers and readers in ways that generate the effect of a deer running or a bird being caged. The narrative generated can make so much sense that it is hard to bring the individual pieces and the gaps in the story to mind. Change the selection of histories and the outline of the narrative might change, but the smoothness of the generated effect of the narrative remains. This new narrative can also make so much sense that its components and gaps feel elusive. How can that be? It seems like there must be a kind of 'historyness' that lurks within this story making, helping us to join the dots and to fill in the gaps, and to make sense of what we encounter. It could be that the human brain is hard wired to think historically, and this may lead us to imagine alien or artificial forms of intelligence that are history-less. But that is not the argument of this book. My claim is a much simpler one, that historians since Herodotus (484–425 BCE) have engaged with or responded to the efforts of thinkers who attempt to make general sense of the world. Metaphysicians.

Metaphysics, wonder

It will be little comfort for you to hear that metaphysics is notoriously difficult to define, and that not everyone thinks it is a good idea or worth doing. It is a slippery beast, as elusive as the moving deer of a motionless thaumascope. One of the first metaphysicians that we know about—Aristotle (384–322 BCE)—didn't call himself by that label, and he arguably didn't set about to explain how it works. Yet as we shall discover in this book, his *Metaphysics* is the means by which many histories make sense, move if you like in the manner of a running deer. He set down a kind of blueprint which encouraged the authors of the earliest written histories to make sense of the world by discerning universals through sensory perception of particular phenomena. In this way, they thought of the universal as immanent or inherent in phenomena. They looked for the general in the particular and set down rules of engagement that they saw as dividing their efforts from those of other or lesser writers such as paradoxologists or wonder writers, as I shall call them in this book. Those attempts at distinction failed, for history was already entangled with philosophy, and philosophy helped all kinds of writers to make sense of the world. This is not to suggest that history has always been simply a part of philosophy, and that this book should therefore be a history of philosophy. Historians ask questions that are not always of interest to philosophers, and the other way around. But historians took a steer from philosophical ways of thinking about existence, knowledge and categories, and their endeavours to make the most general sense of the world.

History remains indebted to philosophy in ways that are not always understood, or even desired. That debt has been described as a 'prison' by Martin Davies, a 'haunting' by Jacques Derrida, and as generative of idle talk by Martin Heidegger.[1] Knowing about and refusing that debt, in their eyes, makes it possible to make sense of the world in different, less settled ways; ways that might be fairer to people that have not been treated well by the idea of history. Indeed, some people may even insist that we dispense with the idea of history altogether for the sake of a fairer world. To take this point back to my opening analogy: the thaumascope must be broken apart if history—or a successor discipline—is to generate new ways of thinking.

I do not agree with the most extreme of these views, for it is not the case that historians have sleepwalked with Aristotle since Polybius (200–118 BCE), or that Aristotelian metaphysics has been our only option. As the variety of histories and philosophies canvassed in this book will show, people around the world have looked to the past to make general sense of things. Islamic, Indian and Chinese histories cannot be collapsed into an Aristotelian metaphysical frame, and some European writings show wilful and wonky appropriations of Aristotelian and other approaches to metaphysics. Other writers have diagnosed important gaps in metaphysical thought and drawn upon ideas in philosophy of knowledge (epistemology), philosophy of being (ontology), ethics and aesthetics to refine or even to reconfigure our general sense of things. It is easy to believe that you are imprisoned by history when you ignore the global range and the weirdest texts produced in its name. Sometimes the thaumascope wobbles. History bears the imprint of metaphysics, but that imprint is not always neatly constructed.

Metaphysics, like history, persists, but it is neither simple nor singular. That does not mean, however, that attempts to describe it are futile. Adrian W. Moore very helpfully defines metaphysics as 'the most general attempt to make sense of things'.[2] He also takes care to step through the three major components of his definition.

First, metaphysicians are interested in categories or concepts, and some are more specific in confining their interest to universals or what is necessary to make sense of the world. Examples can include 'time', 'change', and 'causation'. This is the 'most general' component of his definition, and we find it from the earliest days of metaphysics. Aristotle's interest in the study of being in his *Metaphysics* signals this. Moore's 'general' qualifier is also important for reasons that I intimated earlier and which will become more fully apparent in this book: it is no easy feat to separate the idea of history from say, the idea of literature or science, and it is no easy feat to separate histories from other histories. In the first written histories, we see writers struggle to draw and to hold the line between their efforts and those of writers that they saw as different or even as less worthy. In chapter one, for example, we will see Polybius set down the written motifs and conventions (*topoi*) of a history, only for them to be appropriated and even parodied by paradoxologists or wonder writers. Arguably, too, we see the reverse movement of historians appropriating the *topoi* of paradoxologists in medieval Europe in chapter two. Furthermore, as the example of the Chinese strange histories I will explore in chapter four shows, the appropriation of historical *topoi* can be sharpened into the edge of political criticism. Examples like these demonstrate the futility of defining history by form and provide the justification for my inclusion of works well beyond the range of texts typically covered in histories of history. Philosophy, paradoxological wonder works, literature and film are canvassed, with the last of these providing the major focus of chapter seven. Indeed, in chapter nine, we will find in the examples of Ranajit Guha's (1922–) and Rabindranath Tagore's (1861–1941) writings an invitation to experience the world through 'everyday historicality'.

Moreover, their works remind us to think twice about the claim that the twentieth century ushered in the democratization or fragmentation of history making and thereby a fatal challenge to totalizing 'master narrative' metaphysics. All kinds of people have made histories for a long time, and it is not simply the case that they were worthy writers ignored by the prejudices of their day. Sometimes they produced texts that neither their contemporaries nor we feel comfortable describing as history, even though they bear the form or the label. It is hard to know what to do with a history that reports giant singing earthworms or Bulgarian dwarf pirates, to give just two examples. That is an ongoing challenge for the history of history.

We could of course argue that earlier historians just weren't very good at historiography—thinking about history—and that we now have the expert testimony of writers like Richard Evans in the successful defence of Penguin Books and Deborah Lipstadt against David Irving to thank for defining what an historian is.[3] I think, however, that Moore's argument is different, because his suggestion that metaphysicians attempt to make *general* sense of things will make it difficult or perhaps even futile to disentangle it from other considerations like history. Put clumsily, metaphysics is the framework, blueprint or DNA for history. It is what gives a history shape. This is important because it signals that we might not be able to make sense of the idea of history without metaphysics, or to draw neat boundaries around history, literature, art, and so on.

Second is to note that the use of the word 'attempt' makes it clear that metaphysics is a human endeavour and that it may be impossible to make general sense of things. Metaphysics is not a simple discipline or science, and its knowledge is not a done deal. That doesn't mean that it isn't worth doing, however, for nearly everyone would grant that some notion of time is necessary for making sense of the past. If you find it hard or even impossible to think of what a history would be like without a notion of time, then you can see how deep-seated metaphysical considerations can be.

Third, Moore notes that rendering things intelligible or understanding the 'why' of them is a broad endeavour. It can encompass understanding the idea of history or figuring out how Ikea instruction diagrams work. But the use of the word 'things' reminds us that it is not about articulating self-contained abstract systems. Again, Aristotle grounded his *Metaphysics* in being, suggesting that it is not the study of abstract logic.[4] This suggests again that history and metaphysics will be intertwined.

Having set his definition, Moore prioritises three questions:

Are there 'transcendent' things and can we make sense of them;
Can we make sense of things in ways that are radically new; and
Are we restricted to looking for the sense that things already make?

All of these are important questions for understanding the idea of history, because they challenge us to think about whether, for example, histories reveal universals or whether they describe or create the past. None of these are easy questions, and as the case of the question of whether historians create the past or simply describe it shows, they can also be challenging and even uncomfortable. I therefore see Moore's ideas as a useful starting point for revealing the entanglement of history and metaphysics in the history of history. In selecting the texts that make up this history, I have looked to histories and philosophies that either constitute an attempt to make general sense of things, or that show evidence of an engaged, reflexive, self-conscious exercise in making sense of history and or metaphysics.[5]

Moore is the first to admit that his study of metaphysics is limited.[6] It is confined to European texts from the early modern period onwards (1500–) and turns on his three questions. He does not, for example, position metaphysics—as Aristotle did—as the 'first' philosophy. This is an interesting and important idea, challenging us to think about whether the idea of history will not make sense until we have grappled with metaphysics first. This, as we shall see in chapter eight of this book, was one of Jacques Derrida's most persistent arguments, and the basis of his ethics of how we ought to live.[7] Other thinkers go even further with their interpretation of 'first', insisting as Martin Heidegger did that we need to return to Aristotle to historicise metaphysics. His ideas, and the counter ideas of Hannah Arendt, are the focus of chapter ten.

Nor does Moore offer a view on the nature of metaphysical thinking, its epistemology. That is, how do we do metaphysics? This again turns out to be an important consideration for the idea of history. Hegel once said that 'the owl of Minerva spreads its wings only with the falling of the dusk', meaning that we make general sense of things historically.[8] For him, historical thinking was necessary for metaphysics. This sets up a potentially complicated sequence: we think historically in order to understand metaphysics, in order to understand the idea of history. Unsurprisingly, therefore, Hegel saw history and philosophy as intertwined, but not quite in the way that I suggested was the case for the earliest historians like Polybius. One of the more ambitious ends of Hegel's line of thinking is R.G. Collingwood's claim that historical-philosophical thinking has primacy as a 'mode' of thought. I am not proposing to explore Collingwood's idea in this book, as it was the major subject of one of my earlier books.[9]

It will of course be argued that I am simply following Hegel's view by opening this book on the history of history with a discussion on metaphysics. In response, I note that Aristotle had a different view, one which turns out to be important for a history of history. Aristotle saw the first philosophy—metaphysics—as starting with wonder, an activity of mind. As he explains in the first section of *Metaphysics*:

> It is through wonder that men now begin and originally began to philosophize; wondering in the first place at obvious perplexities, and then by gradual progression raising questions about the greater matters too, e.g. about the changes of the moon and of the sun, about the stars and about the origin of the universe. Now he who wonders and is perplexed feels that he is ignorant (thus the myth-lover is in a sense a philosopher, since myths are composed of wonders); therefore, if it was to escape ignorance that men studied philosophy, it is obvious that they pursued science for the sake of knowledge, and not for

any practical utility. The actual course of events bears witness to this; for speculation of this kind began with a view to recreation and pastime, at a time when practically all the necessities of life were already supplied. Clearly then it is for no extrinsic advantage that we seek this knowledge; for just as we call a man independent who exists for himself and not for another, so we call this the only independent science, since it alone exists for itself (1.982b).

Plato wrote about wonder ahead of Aristotle, noting that Socrates' questions and talk of general concepts made Theaetetus' head swim. Aristotle takes a different tack, arguing that we do not need a philosopher to lead us to philosophy. Rather, Aristotle sees the start of the first philosophy in our wonder at changes that we perceive in the world. Wonder is initiated by us, it is perceptual, and it takes flight in 'obvious perplexities'. Moreover, it arises in recreation and pastime, when our every thought is not turned to survival.

That Aristotle saw our perplexity at changes in the world as the basis for wonder and then philosophy deserves pause. That is not least because the first historians also saw their work as focused on the recording of perceptual changes and as the elucidation of universals. Indeed, they too were highly interested in wonder; enough so that they sought to refine the boundaries between legitimate acts of wonder by historians and the illegitimate attempts of other writers that they unsuccessfully tried to dismiss. Significantly, too, wonder also plays a key role in Islamic and Indian metaphysics, as this book will show. How it arises, though, and what it leads to are not easily assimilated to the Aristotelian tradition. In the case of Islamic thought, for example, wonder arises from appreciation of the aesthetic form of writing and generates an enhanced sense of rational responsibility; in Indian thought, wonder arises not from the apprehension of change or of novelty, but from repetition, and it enhances metaphysical 'attunement'.

It is the key argument of this book that wonder plays a critical part in the history of history because it is a historiographically and metaphysically rich concept. The earliest historians stressed the location of wonder at boundaries, thresholds and limits of time, thought, feeling, experience and reality. That location has been persistent and continues today. Wonder takes us from one understanding of the world to another. It takes us from present to past. It takes us from the physical world to the spiritual world. It takes us from the specific to the universal and vice versa; from the habitual to the historical; from the old the new; from understanding things to understanding ourselves; from exclusion to inclusion and thereby the unethical to the ethical. If you want to know where the cross-beams, connection points and limits of history's blueprint or thaumascope are, to put it crudely, look at wonder. It is in this sense that I see wonder as the beginning of historiography. Moreover, I believe that a greater appreciation of these features in histories makes it possible to think of new ways of doing history. It is in this sense also that I see wonder as the beginning of history.

Despite this rich tradition of thought, wonder has barely rated a mention in contemporary research. In philosophy, Howard Parsons, Ronald Hepburn and

John Sallis have offered definitional accounts,[10] but wonder is generally treated as a marginal concept that takes form at the hand of Descartes and then disappears at the rise of modern epistemology. Wonder is collapsed into curiosities and relegated to the sideshow, vaudeville performance or cinema, only to come back in science, and in particular the entertainments of the Exploratorium or Questacon. Philosophy and history are too rational, old or straitlaced, perhaps, to do wonder now. This was much to Heidegger's lament. If it has made a comeback, it is thanks to feminist philosophers such as Luce Irigaray and Marguerite La Caze. The implications of their work for the idea of history are outlined in chapter eight of this book, although I note that their reading of wonder begins with Descartes.

In history, it is wonders that have captured our attention, rather than wonder, as with Lorraine Daston and Katherine Park's highly-acclaimed *Wonders and the Order of Nature*. Theirs is a narrative that it is all too easy to connect to the themes of globalisation and possession. As I argue in chapters five, eight and nine of this book wonder is not just an object in history, it is also a disposition exercised by people in different times and places. Their thoughts and experiences remind us that historiography and metaphysics are not just conservative, descriptive thought games. History and metaphysics can be revised and reinscribed, and they can be in ways that acknowledge peoples who are often treated as objects rather than subjects. It can empower those people to make histories and to challenge whether we need history in the ways in which the West has understood it. It can be, and arguably ought to be, unsettling.

An unsettling history of history

So how to begin? I have decided to set this work in motion by revisiting contemporary histories of history. In combination, they contribute a narrative that is so much in agreement as to be highly unusual in the field. Hence my description of the history of history as a smooth running thaumascope. They align in at least four major ways: first, they present developments in strict chronological order until the twentieth century is reached, when thematic approaches take over; second, they turn on the analysis of works by historical thinkers (roughly 'great books by great men', or more unusually, 'great books by overlooked women'); third, they begin with philosophical histories made during the Enlightenment, or at a pinch, go back to Herodotus; and fourth, they suggest the professionalization of the field in the nineteenth century and then its democratization or disintegration at the hands of gender, postcolonial or postmodern thinkers. An analysis of recent introductory contributions by Ernst Breisach, Eileen Ka-May Cheng, Michael Bentley, Roger Spalding and Christopher Parker, Georg G. Iggers and Edward Q. Wang and Anna Green and Kathleen Troup confirms these four features and generates a master list of topics like this:

- Ancient Greek and Ancient Roman historians
- Christian Medieval historians

- European Renaissance and Reformation historians
- European Enlightenment and Philosophical historians
- National and Scientific historians
- Economic historians
- *Annales*, social and cultural historians
- Marxist historians
- Gender historians
- Postcolonial historians
- Postmodern historians

I have used the same list of topics for this book, but I have shaken up the sense that they make in combination in three ways. First, I have interrupted the narrative with an analysis of Islamic, Chinese and Indian histories and metaphysics. I have done so, as I noted above, to ensure that history is not seen as a simple derivation from ancient Greek thought. Moreover, these traditions of thought suggest ways of making general sense of things that can fruitfully enrich our understanding of the idea of history today.

Second, in line with the discussion on the general nature of metaphysics earlier in this introduction, I have not attempted to draw a strict boundary around history and therefore to separate it from other kinds of writing or thought tradition. Wonder writing, histories, philosophies, literature and film jostle together. Moreover, I have also tried to include a range of historians, from those you would expect to see in an introductory work on historiography—such as Leopold von Ranke—through to the writers of fine histories that have previously been neglected, through again to works that we might be less proud to call our own. These are books that flopped at market or which were sensationally successful on account of contents that would not be out of place in a Buzzfeed quiz or a Reddit forum today. To borrow an example from Edward Feser to explain this, if thinkers have produced the abstract notion of a Euclidean triangle, then they have also produced the hastily drawn triangle on the plastic seat of a moving bus.[11] Finding these histories has been fun and reading them has been at turns amusing, disturbing, challenging and even trying. Regardless, they are worthy of inclusion because they suggest the same disposition towards general sense making that we see in the books that customarily serve as shorthand for the history of history. They reflect the imprint of metaphysics, and sometimes even its wilful and playful appropriation. Historiography is all the richer for their consideration, as is the history of metaphysics.

Third, and finally, I have rethreaded the narrative by means of a focus on wonder. That, in itself, has been a revelation. As I have acknowledged in this book, I did not notice the dragons in the *Shiji* of Sima Qian or von Ranke's *Ahnen* or intuitive cognition until I started researching this book. Once you notice details like this, though, you begin to see the history of history in a different way, and as I argued above, you appreciate wonder as the beginning of history and of historiography.

Chapter One opens with Polybius' unsuccessful attempt to steer history clear of the 'unworthy and unmanly' efforts of paradoxologists or wonder writers. His *Histories*, we will discover, argues for the discernment of universals in particular phenomena, thereby showing his mutual interest with Plato and Aristotle in understanding what is knowable and what is unknowable. Moreover, like Plato and Aristotle, he argues for wonder in his account of how historians make sense of phenomena. But he also calls upon wonder to highlight when he is not sure about the knowledge claims of other historians. In the *Histories* and in Ancient Greek historiography a double function for wonder was thereby established, applying to knowledge in good faith and knowledge not in good faith. In signalling the second in the manner of literary or rhetorical conventions or *topoi*, Polybius opened the door to overlap with, and parody by, the writers of paradoxologies or wonder works.

In Chapter Two I argue that the kinds of judgements that Polybius made about the idea of history continued in medieval Europe. Historians Gerald of Wales, Bede (682–735 CE) and Gervase of Tilbury (1150–1228 CE) attempted to make general sense of things in the light of the metaphysical writings of Augustine of Hippo (354–430 CE), Thomas Aquinas (1225–75 CE) and Roger Bacon (1214–94 CE). They saw history as a means for discerning universals, which like Aristotle they considered to be immanent, in things. Additionally, they still set boundaries between the knowable and the unknowable. But they also expanded the lines of thought that Polybius set down, by drawing upon medieval metaphysics to chart a detailed account of wonder as rational and as a form of mental restraint. And they saw themselves as having solved Polybius' dilemma of judging claims to knowledge by asserting that while some things are unknowable to us, nothing is unknowable to God. This, I will argue, provided them with the opportunity to emphasise ethics as well as epistemology in the pursuit of metaphysics, for if an historian could not judge if a claim to knowledge was in good faith, God certainly could. Chapter Three sees us take a twist in our tale. I bring Aristotle's *Poetics* to the forefront, and with it, affective and physiological notions of wonder at work in the pre-modern Islamic world. I appreciate that in some ways, 'Islamic world' is a clumsy coverall title for a broad and sophisticated range of Arabic, Berber, Syriac and Persian works that emanated from North Africa through to the East Mediterranean, through to the courses of the Euphrates and the Tigris rivers and beyond. I have, however, used it as it has most currency still in histories of history. I will argue that the Arabic translation of *Poetics* from a Syriac intermediary text epitomises the 'the strange and the transferred' uses of language that Ibn Rushd (also known as Averroes) (1126–1198) pinpointed as triggers for wonder. This will be new territory in English-language historiography, taking us from Ibn Khaldun's (1332–1406) well-known thoughts on history as both form and substance to his assertion of affective and charismatic experiences of wonder in prophecy. Ibn Khaldun's thoughts on wonder, I will argue, help us to relocate him in a world in which paradoxographers, historians and metaphysicians not only saw the experience of wonder as the means of revealing the universal in the particular, but as the main means for judging the beauty of speech in histories such as Muhammad ibn Jarir al Tabari's (838–923 CE) *History of the Prophets and Kings*. In this way, I will argue that Islamic historiography is generative, rather than conservative, as commentators have been inclined to see it.

Chapter Four opens with dragons and scans official and unofficial Chinese histories to highlight the interest of historians in being in harmony with an immanent world, and of growing into an understanding of that world by speaking, but more importantly, by being silent and therefore being open to and a part of it. We will also, however, see historians speak out when harmony ossifies into social and political practices that suggest close mindedness to the immanent world. We will see them speak out obliquely, as Sima Qian (145–86 BCE) did in his *Shiji*, and we will see them speak out through wonders, as authors of 'strange histories' like Duan Chengshi (ca. 800–63 CE), Pu Songling (1640–1715), Yuan Mei (1716–97) and Ji Yun (1724–1805) did. Therefore, we will see a historiographical tradition that is interested in the immanent, which expresses views on how to discern the immanent, and which assumes it has a role in opening peoples' minds to an appreciation of the general sense of things.

Early-modern historians continued ancient Greek traditions of using sense perception to discern universals. But as I argue in Chapter Five, they also enhanced those earlier conjunctions of history and metaphysics by insisting upon the exhaustive categorisation of the most basic kinds of things in our world, including emotions. Jean Bodin's (1529/30–1596 CE) *Method for the Easy Comprehension of History* provides a clear example of this. Bodin wrote history not just for the sake of describing what he took to be the actual structure of the world, or to possess that world, but because he saw categorisation through history as necessary for the rightful operation of mind, the self, and society. This, as it will be argued through an analysis of the historical works of Walter Ralegh (c. 1552–1618) and Nathaniel Wanley (1638–80), and the philosophers Francis Bacon (1568–1621), René Descartes (1596–1650) and Thomas Hobbes (1588–1679), established what I call a 'triple skip' from metaphysics to epistemology to ethics via history.

Chapter Six unfolds Leopold von Ranke's (1795–1886) and G.W.F. Hegel's (1770–1831) thoughts on the interconnection between history and philosophy and illustrates how their interleaving of wonder, intuition and thought was also expressed in a much wider range of works than is typically acknowledged, from the metaphysical universal histories of Immanuel Kant (1724–1804) and Sarah Josepha Hale (1788–1879), to the paradoxological histories of Daniel Defoe (1684–1731), and William Howitt (1792–1879). This interest in interconnection, I argue, stems from their desire to explain how we might gain an understanding of the universal from concrete, particular, historical phenomena and their varying determinations to see the 'leap' from one to the other through the more or less rational experiences of the sublime, intuition, and spirit. In the case of von Ranke, there is an argument for the superiority of history over philosophy in explaining the universal. But this argument, it will be shown, bears fewer radical implications than the historical embodiment of intuition as female in Hale's world, or its realisation in the ghosts, revenants and poltergeists of Defoe and Howitt's spirited histories.

What happens to our attempts to make general sense of things if sensory perception changes? Chapter Seven charts the rise of scepticism about perception in written and filmic histories, and tests whether there was a knock-on effect to wonder. All of the thinkers canvassed in this chapter—Lynne Kirby (1952–), Tom Gunning (1949–), Jonathan Crary (1951–), Mary Ann Doane (1952–), Walter Benjamin (1892–1940) and Roland Barthes (1915–1980)—argued that modernity ushered in seismic shifts in seeing and knowing. Yet I will also show that in their hands, wonder maintained a relatively stable metaphysical function as the gateway to the consideration of the contingent. This, I will conclude, generated new thinking about the historicisation of metaphysics ushered in by Hegel, where the speed of change for immanent universals may vary.

The ethical implications of our attempts to make general sense of things through history is the focus of Chapter Eight. It picks up from Chapter Seven in highlighting the interest of writers such as Merry Wiesner-Hanks (1952–), Joan Wallach Scott (1941–), Lynn Hunt (1945–), Jacques Derrida (1930–2004), Hélène Cixous (1937–), Luce Irigiray (1930–) and Marguerite La Caze (1964–) in revisionary, rather than descriptive metaphysics. That is, they seek to move from outlining the most basic features of things to making sense of things in new ways. The driver in this case is the question of how we *ought* to make sense of the world, as seen in the examples of gender history and gender metaphysics, and in historiographical and philosophical reflections on the uncomfortable implications of 'un homing' ourselves through wonder to acknowledge others and to show them hospitality.

Chapter Nine considers whether the acknowledgement of what some post colonialists call the subaltern—the traces of peoples 'without history' within the evidence record of the coloniser—implies the need to walk away from historiography as we know it and towards an aesthetic 'historicality' in which the possibility of wonder is reclaimed. Ranajit Guha lays this path by showing the affinity of Aristotle's *Metaphysics* with the philosophy of Abhinavagupta (950–1015 CE, also known as Abhinava) in Rabindranath Tagore's (1861–1941) idea of passing through the threshold limit of wonder to experience latent historicality. Romila Thapar (1931–) navigates to a sense of historicality via very different means: her idea of a Western 'scientific' idea of history. As we shall see, the key explanation for this difference of route is her professed need for protection from historiographical interference from the state, violent threats, and colonial portrayals of India as a timeless land of Europeanised wonder. I will argue that the common link between these two writers—and Tagore—could be their refraction of classical Indian metaphysics, and in particular the metaphysics of light developed from various sources such as Kalidāsā (fl. 5th century CE) by Abhinavagupta. That metaphysics argues for immanence in all things, including history, and ourselves, as discerned by attunement to wonder.

In Chapter Ten, I ask whether Martin Heidegger's (1889–1976) and Hannah Arendt's (1906–1975) different approaches to the connection of history and metaphysics provide us with the means to deal with extraordinary events such as the Holocaust. I will argue that they do not, on the grounds that Heidegger's reading of the opening of Aristotle's *Metaphysics* as an invitation to dwell apart with the ordinary and to make it inscrutable, and Arendt's recuperation of responsibility in a philosophical-political realm through consensus metaphysics, prioritise the ordinary over the extraordinary. They, like many thinkers before them, treat the extraordinary as the edge case or as the focus of a curiosity that at least generates what Heidegger calls 'idle talk' and at worst, eternal damnation. I therefore ask whether the Holocaust might be seen as a new beginning for wonder, and therefore for historiography.

Finally, in a very brief conclusion, I reiterate that the corpus of works in this book are not an example of 'everyday' historiography or 'everyday' metaphysics, but a demonstration of the variety of forms of entanglement of history and metaphysics and of the historiographical and metaphysical richness of wonder.

Notes

1 Martin L. Davies, *The Prison-House of History: Investigations into Historicized Life*, London: Routledge, 2009. For Derrida and Heidegger, see chapters eight and ten in this book.
2 Adrian W. Moore, *The Evolution of Modern Metaphysics: Making Sense of Things*, Cambridge: Cambridge University Press, 2014, p. 1. For other introductions to metaphysics, see Michael J. Loux, and Thomas M. Crisp, *Metaphysics: A Contemporary Introduction*, 4th edn., London: Routledge, 2017; Peter Van Inwagen, *Metaphysics*, 4th edn., London: Routledge, 2014; and Alyssa Ney, *Metaphysics: An Introduction*, London: Routledge, 2014.
3 Irving v Penguin Books Ltd and Anor [2001] England and Wales Court of Appeal ((Civil Division) Decision 1197, 20 July 2001), online at: www.bailii.org/ew/cases/EWCA/Civ/2001/1197.html <accessed 25 March 2018>.
4 Adrian W. Moore, *The Evolution of Modern Metaphysics*, pp. 2–6.
5 Adrian W. Moore, *The Evolution of Modern Metaphysics*, p. 12.
6 Adrian W. Moore, *The Evolution of Modern Metaphysics*, p. 1.
7 See also Ethan Kleinberg, *Haunting History: For a Deconstructive Approach to the Past*, Stanford, CA: Stanford University Press, 2017.
8 G. W. F. Hegel, *Elements of the Philosophy of Right*, ed. Allen W. Wood, trans. H. B. Nisbet, Cambridge: Cambridge University Press, 1991, p. 23.
9 M. Hughes-Warrington, '*How Good an Historian Shall I Be?*': *R. G. Collingwood, the Historical Imagination and Education*, Thorveton, UK: Imprint, 2003.
10 See for example Howard Parsons 'A Philosophy of Wonder', *Philosophy and Phenomenological Research*, 1969, vol. 30(1), pp. 84–101; Ronald Hepburn, *Wonder and Other Essays*, Edinburgh: Edinburgh University Press, 1984; and John Sallis, 'The Place of Wonder', in *Double Truth*, New York: SUNY, 1995, pp. 191–210.
11 Edward Feser, 'Being, The Good, and the Guise of the Good', in *Neo-Aristotelian Perspectives in Metaphysics*, eds. D.D. Novotny and L. Novák, London: Routledge, 2014, pp. 84–103.

References

Aristotle, *Metaphysics*, trans. H. Tredennick, London: Heinemann, 1933.
Bentley, Michael, *Modern Historiography: An Introduction*, London: Routledge, 1999.

Breisach, Ernst, *Historiography: Ancient, Medieval, and Modern*, 3rd edn, Chicago, IL: University of Chicago Press, 2007.
Cheng, Eileen Ka-May, *Historiography: An Introductory Guide*, London: Bloomsbury, 2012.
Green, Anna, and Troup, Kathleen (eds), *The Houses of History: A Critical Reader in Twentieth-Century History and Theory*, New York: New York University Press, 1999.
Iggers, Georg G., and Wang, Edward Q., *A Global History of Modern Historiography*, London: Routledge, 2012.
Moore, Adrian W. *The Evolution of Modern Metaphysics: Making Sense of Things*, Cambridge: Cambridge University Press, 2014.
Spalding, Roger, and Parker, Christopher, *Historiography: An Introduction*, Manchester, UK: Manchester University Press, 2007.

1

SENSE AND NON-SENSE IN ANCIENT GREEK HISTORIES

Plato | Herodotus | Thucydides | Phlegon | Polybius | Aristotle

The ancient Greek writer Polybius (200–118 BCE) had a very clear idea of what historians should not do. Surely, he writes:

> ... an historian's object should not be to amaze his readers by a series of thrilling anecdotes; nor should he aim at producing speeches which *might* have been delivered, nor study dramatic propriety in details like the writer of a tragedy: but his function is above all to record with fidelity what was actually said or done, however commonplace it may be.
>
> (The Histories, 2.56)

They should not try to enthral their readers, they should not make things up and they should not give people and events a dramatic backstory. They should tell it like it was, no matter how ordinary or even insignificant the resulting narrative.

Polybius' stern words seem a long way from the engaging and even epic beginning given to the study of history in books such as Ernst Breisach's *Historiography: Ancient, Medieval and Modern*:

> The Homeric epics, now innocuously enshrined in the treasure house we all call Great Literature, were in centuries past sources of inspiration and pride. The ancient Greeks found them endlessly fascinating, edifying, and particularly useful for the educating of the young.[1]

This past for history as 'heir to epic poetry' is woven with mythical heroes and guides for good or moral living.[2] It sounds like a fitting start for a discipline: 'fascinating, edifying, and particularly useful'. But as historians today appreciate, the past is rarely a straightforward story of heirs and successors. Myth and epic poetry were part but not all of an ancient world in which texts, images, performances, memories and accounts of geography were exchanged and circulated.[3] People told stories, recited poetry, sang and recounted events for understanding and entertainment and to keep track of relationships, victories, offences and even debts. Those stories shifted in form and content as the languages and cultures of Europe, Africa and Asia collided and coalesced in the Hellenistic world that emerged from the wake of Alexander's conquests. It was in this world that the western idea of historians and of histories emerged.[4]

The historians of the Hellenistic world did not have university history departments, school syllabuses, or historiography texts to guide them in their work. What they did have were images, oral accounts and other texts upon which they could comment. In writing history, they often told their readers what they thought about the efforts of their predecessors and contemporaries. They made judgements about whether other works were good histories or even histories at all.

It was by judgement that historians worked to define their discipline. This in itself was a significant act, for it is not beyond the bounds of possibility to believe in a world in which everything that is called a history is accepted as a history. This, as we already know, was not Polybius' world. He discriminated between histories and other written works, and between good and bad histories. How he did so marks what is arguably the beginning of our story of the relationship between history and metaphysics. In this chapter we trace that beginning to three particular judgements that Polybius made about history: first, that it is concerned with the universal; second, that we can discern universals through rigorous acts of sensory perception; and third, that while our own sensory perceptions are to be trusted more than the claims of others, our perceptions have limits. So far so good, until we get to wonder. Polybius, as we shall see, did not see all experiences of wonder as equal. Plato (c. 427–347 BCE) and Aristotle (384–322 BCE) might have positioned wonder as the beginning of philosophical thinking, but their scanty descriptions of the nature of wonder left a lot to be desired. In their wake, Polybius struggled not only to discriminate between legitimate and illegitimate claims to wonder—thereby making it extremely difficult to divide history off from 'idle and unprofitable' paradoxology or 'wonder writing' (*Histories* 1.14)— but also to pin down when he thought it was right for him to seek recourse in wonder in his own writing. In so doing, he encountered both the sheer difficulty and slipperiness of metaphysics in ways that exceeded the experiences of his predecessors, Herodotus and Thucydides. This chapter charts that struggle, and in so doing exposes the mutual interest of historians and philosophers of the ancient Greek world in finding the limits of our attempts to make the most general sense of things. In particular, it introduces questions about what is knowable and what is unknowable, what is accessible and inaccessible to sensory perception, what is natural and what is supernatural, and what is universal and what is particular. In short, it introduces Polybius to us as an historian who was interested in transcendence.

Historiography begins with history, or philosophy?

Polybius' description of how not to write history is one of many examples of historiographical judgement from the Hellenistic world. Polybius was not the first Western historian: we give credit to Herodotus (c. 484–c. 424 BCE) for that achievement. Polybius' *Histories* were, however, important in explaining the transition of Rome from republic to empire to a Greek world that had developed from the conquests of Alexander.[5] Moreover, his work is distinguished by the sheer number and range of comments he offers about the works of earlier and contemporary historians, many of which do not survive today. His *Histories* are a compendium of historiographical shadows.

Polybius' views about other historians are not concentrated in an introduction or what we might call a literature review. They are peppered throughout *The Histories* in a way that suggests that history is defined via the aggregation of arguments for and against other historians. The quote that I opened this chapter with, for instance, can be found towards the end of his account of the first Punic War between Rome and Carthage (264–241 BCE). The prompt for his comments is the need to explain to his readers why the histories of Aratus and Phylarchus diverge, and why he places more credence on the claims of the former than the latter. The problem with Phylarchus' account, he tells us, is that it is driven by the 'unworthy and unmanly' purpose of bringing the past 'vividly before his readers' (2.56).

Yet Polybius' work is not simply an aggregation of snipish judgements, carried by the assumption that argument by volume is a winning strategy. He knew what he liked and what he didn't like, and those preferences reflected three key judgements about the idea of history that I introduced at the start of the chapter. The first of these, we recall, was that history concerns the study of universals; the second that discernment of universals is best achieved via rigorous acts of sensory perception; and third that sensory perception has limits. If *The Histories* is a compendium of historiographical shadows, it is also a reflection of philosophical shadows. My grounds for claiming this, as we will see below, is that the substance of his claims owes more to Aristotle—whom he does not credit—than to a Plato he credits for a revolution in thinking.

Polybius' interest in universals is first declared in book one, chapter three, with the claim that his predecessors had presented world history as 'a series of disconnected transactions, as widely separated in their origin and results as in their localities'. They see only parts, when there is the whole to be understood:

> … it has always seemed to me that men, who are persuaded that they get a competent view of universal history from episodal history, are very like persons who should see the limbs of some body, which had once been living and beautiful, scattered and remote; and should imagine that to be quite as good as actually beholding the activity and beauty of the living creature itself … some idea of a whole may be got from a part, but an accurate knowledge and clear comprehension cannot (1.3).

This is a significant set of claims by Polybius, and it is worth unpacking. History, he suggests, is not singular. While particular individuals engage in particular acts, and particular phenomena come into being, or change, or disappear, historians do not just describe those particularities. This is more than just the observation that we use words like 'horse' or 'soldier' to describe particular phenomena; what he wants historians to do is to discern the ways in which phenomena reflect or suggest universals. That Polybius saw universals as in things was not a given. He could have opted to argue—following Plato in *Republic*—that universals are separate from particular objects, and that philosopher kings—not historians—are needed to tell us about their existence. But he didn't, opting instead for the Aristotelian view that universals exist *in re*, in things. Moreover, the excerpt above suggests that they can exist in things that appear to be quite different to one another. This is therefore not a simple case of us, for example, applying the label 'soldier' to two different men. Quite different events can be like the parts of a body, and Polybius wants us to see the whole body.

The universal or 'body of history' that Polybius discerns, which makes all phenomena 'incline in one direction', is *Tyche* or fortune. This does not mean that Polybius is a predeterminist: a believer that historical outcomes are controlled by fate (1.63; and 18.28). Rather, his claim is that we can see fortune at work when we step back and consider the broad sweep of events, just as we can see the skills and decisions of individuals at work when we consider smaller-scale events (1.4; 2.35). He is, consequently, quite critical of historians who automatically see fortune at work in smaller-scale events because they fail to give credit for human skill. This is seen, for instance, in his acknowledgment of the achievements of the Roman general Scipio Africanus in book ten, and of the wider Roman leadership in book eighteen:

> Now all other writers represent [Scipio Africanus] as a man favoured by fortune, who succeeded in his undertakings contrary to rational expectation, and by the mere force of circumstances. They consider apparently such men to be, so to speak, more godlike and worthy of admiration, than those who act in every case by calculation. They do not seem to be aware of the distinction between credit for good fortune and credit for good conduct in the case of such men; and that the former may be assigned to any one however commonplace, while the latter belongs to those alone who act from prudent calculation and clear intelligence: and it is these last whom we should look upon as the most god-like and god-beloved. (10.2)
>
> … it will be, I think, a useful and worthy task to investigate their differences, and discover why it is that the Romans conquer and carry off the palm from their enemies in the operations of war: that we may not put it all down to Fortune, and congratulate them on their good luck, as the thoughtless of mankind do; but, from a knowledge of the true causes, may give their leaders the tribute of praise and admiration which they deserve. (18.28)

Polybius' clever play between historical scales secures a place for human will and thought in writing about the past. Here we arrive at his second judgement about the idea of history, which concerns sensory perception. Universals are not beyond particulars and not beyond our understanding of them. But how does that understanding arise? Socrates' interlocutors got there as a consequence of his 'midwifery', and Plato consequently suggested that philosopher kings are needed to help us discern more than the shadows of universal forms. Polybius, like Aristotle, holds that we can get there on the basis of our own thought. We do not need the philosopher kings. And like Aristotle, again, Polybius sees that thought as taking shape from perceptual sensations (see Aristotle, *De Sensu*, 1.436b.10–12, 16–17; also *De Anima* ii.2.413b.4–7; ii.3.414b6–9, 434a30–b4). Indeed, Aristotle's and Polybius' writings share an interest in empirical description, with the key distinction between their writings turning on the former's interest in natural phenomena and the latter's interest in human action.

Polybius does not offer an account of how sensory perception works physiologically, as Aristotle does in works like *De Sensu*. His interest, rather, is in the senses, and more specifically, what he sees as the three perceptual bases for historical knowledge: that which is seen, that which is heard, and that which is read (12.27.1–4). Moreover, he holds that there is a hierarchy of the senses in historical research. That which is seen provides the most accurate and certain knowledge while that which is read provides the least accurate and least certain knowledge. This hierarchy of ways of knowing is no less significant a revolution in thought, Polybius tells us, than Plato's claim that 'human affairs will not go well until philosophers become kings or kings become philosophers'. This is because the achievement of 'proper' historical knowledge will require historians to break their dependency on written reports and thus on other historians' claims to knowledge (12.28). Historians will need to see things for themselves, as witnesses, and to use their previous experiences to actively make sense of what they see (20.12; 7.25.4; 27.28). Reading about the past, on the other hand, is equivalent to seeing the shadows in Plato's allegory of the cave: whatever glimpse we gain of events is dependent on the skill and judgment of the writer in telling us about them. His point is that our knowledge ought not be dependent on that of others. To settle for less than our own sense making and judgement in the writing of history is to settle for history 'without eyes', as he explains in book one:

> For as a living creature is rendered wholly useless if deprived of its eyes, so if you take truth from History what is left is but an idle unprofitable tale. Therefore, one must not shrink either from blaming one's friends or praising one's enemies; nor be afraid of finding fault with and commending the same persons at different times. For it is impossible that men engaged in public affairs should always be right, and unlikely that they should always be wrong. Holding ourselves, therefore, entirely aloof from the actors, we must as historians make statements and pronounce judgement in accordance with the actions themselves (1.14).

Polybius' commitment to the idea of historical knowledge as perceptual sense making is reflected in his decision to write about a period that he experienced and about places to which he travelled (4.2; 29.14; 10.9; 30.4; 3.26). At the same time, however, he acknowledges that he has provided a somewhat ideal picture of the acquisition of knowledge. Historians cannot always be in the right place and the right time to witness events and regions can be too remote or too dangerous to access. They cannot also be expected to be fluent in all of the world's languages. This is where sense making by hearing comes in. If historians are unable to witness an event, then they can build up an account of what happened by critically interviewing witnesses. If that is not possible, it is only at that point that the historian resorts to sense making by reading, but they must think carefully about the plausibility of what they read to achieve as accurate an understanding of the past as possible (3.58; 12.28;12.25; 27.5).

Just as there are limits to the experiences of historians, so too there are limits to sense making and therefore to historical knowledge. This is Polybius' third judgement about the idea of history. This is not simply an acknowledgment that historians might not have the background or linguistic skills to account for what they see. Polybius has a more fundamental point to make: some phenomena seem to defy understanding and rational explanation. So far, so reasonable, but this is where Polybius strikes serious difficulties in trying to explain the historian's craft. Those difficulties arise, as we shall see, from Polybius' faith in his own visual perceptions as certain and his use of wonder to denote the limit of the knowable rather than the beginning of the knowable.

Polybius' first call upon wonder is to signal the boundary of his ability to explain his visual perceptions. He trusts what he sees, but he does not know why he has seen what he has seen. He writes:

> Those things of which it is impossible or difficult for a mere man to ascertain the causes, such as a continuous fall of rains and unseasonable wet, or, on the contrary, droughts and frosts, one may reasonably impute to God and Fortune in default of any other explanation; and from them come destruction of fruits, as well as long-continued epidemics, and other similar things, of which it is not easy to find the cause (37.9).

In the context of Polybius' account of knowledge, this is historical non-sense. Then he does something very interesting: he labels this experience as wonder and characterises it as being 'overwhelmed with astonishment', horrified and even 'struck dumb' by the scale and the strangeness of some events (1.63; 31.4; 7.17). These are events that cannot be rendered sensible by *any* prior experience. They mark the limits of historical explanation. Or do they?

Wonder as beginning: philosophy

One person's limit can be another person's beginning. Both Plato and Aristotle tell us that wonder marks the beginning of philosophy. Plato's most extensive statement on wonder can be found in *Theaetetus*, his dialogue between Socrates and a young student of mathematics whose name is captured in the title. The dialogue turns on the question 'what is knowledge?', to which *Theaetetus* makes four attempts at an answer. His first attempt is to suggest that knowledge can be defined by reference to examples of it. Socrates rejects this view as a diversion, because examples presuppose an understanding that a definition of knowledge is intended to offer. The second to fourth attempts propose that knowledge is sense perception; that knowledge is true judgement; and that knowledge is true judgement with an account. No resolution about a 'right' definition of knowledge is achieved by the end of the text.

The discussion on the second definition of knowledge is significant, for it is in here that we see the designation of wonder not as a last resort in sense making, but as the point of departure for philosophical thought. The problem with sense perception, Socrates informs us, is that it is not infallible. We can be mistaken in conclusions about what we see, hear, smell and feel. Eyewitness accounts can differ, and even be irreconcilable. This point forms the backdrop for Theaetetus' declaration in section 155c that 'I am lost in wonder when I think of all these things, and sometimes when I regard them it really makes my head swim'. Socrates' reply takes the form of an affirmation that says some interesting things about the nature of knowing:

> this feeling of wonder shows that you are a philosopher, since wonder is the only beginning of philosophy, and he who said that Iris was the child of Thaumas made a good genealogy. (155d)

Here we see wonder as connecting the human with the divine—denoted by the use of the term *thaumazein* and its connection with Iris, the messenger of the gods[6]—which was also the case in Polybius' *Histories*. But the discovery of the divine is not through phenomena that no-one understands. Rather, Theaetetus' head swims because he realises that he cannot get a grip on a concept that people appear to use with ease every day. Wonder can be prompted by objects, events or experiences that are at hand, familiar, or that are so commonplace as to be taken for granted. Here Plato highlights the potential for a lack of mental effort with the familiar, and not just things that are new to us. Polybius thought that we should work hard to establish an understanding of events and phenomena from other times and cultures; Plato also wants us to labour just as hard on the things that we appear to take for granted.

The idea of the familiar made strange in Plato's writings applies by extension to our own thoughts. Wonder arises in our everyday experiences, and is thus a part of our present. But it also aids our thinking about our own past experiences and thought. As Socrates explains in *Cratylus*:

> I myself have long been wondering at my own wisdom, and I distrust it. So it seems to me that we must re-examine what I am saying. For being deceived by oneself is the most terrible thing of all: when the deceiver is not absent

even for a little while, but is always there, how could that not be fearful? Hence one must, as it seems, frequently turn around to what has been said before, and try, as that famous poet has it, to 'look forward and backward at the same time'. (428d1–8)

Wonder is a remedy against the orthodoxy of everyday thought, and against being enchanted by our own thoughts. Wonder is thus an aid for knowledge and a form of protection against reliance on the thoughts of others and the comfort of assuming that our own knowledge is certain.

Plato's account of wonder is such that the unknowable is not necessarily implied. Wonder can be triggered by the familiar or the strange. This is not the case for Polybius, who restricts his discussion of wonder to unknown, but also potentially unknowable phenomena. Recall Polybius' examples of rains that are *difficult* or *impossible* to explain. Difficulty suggests that it is possible, albeit with more effort, information, or assistance. What Polybius means by *impossible* is harder to discern. It could mean unknowable, or it could mean not knowable with certainty. As Polybius connects this sense of impossibility with being awestruck, this does not seem to be a case where certainty is at stake. It is, I believe, an encounter with the unknowable. This is not a case of Meno's paradox, of searching for something that you do not know about (Plato, *Five Dialogues: Euthyphro, Apology, Crito, Meno, Phaedo*). We know about the rains in his example, we just may not ever be able to understand why they happened. This is not a scenario included in Plato's discussion of wonder, suggesting either that he did not hold perceived phenomena to be unknowable, or he did not see wonder as helping in this case. There either is no issue with Polybius' examples or there is such an issue that recourse to wonder will not solve it.

Grappling with this problem further takes us to Aristotle who, like Plato, positions wonder at the beginning of philosophical thought, as is clear from his *Metaphysics*:

It is through wonder that men now begin and originally began to philosophize; wondering in the first place at obvious perplexities, and then by gradual progression raising questions about the greater matters too, e.g. about the changes of the moon and of the sun, about the stars and about the origin of the universe. Now he who wonders and is perplexed feels that he is ignorant (thus the myth-lover is in a sense a philosopher, since myths are composed of wonders); therefore, if it was to escape ignorance that men studied philosophy, it is obvious that they pursued science for the sake of knowledge, and not for any practical utility. The actual course of events bears witness to this; for speculation of this kind began with a view to recreation and pastime, at a time when practically all the necessities of life were already supplied. Clearly then it is for no extrinsic advantage that we seek this knowledge; for just as we call a man independent who exists for himself and not for another, so we call this the only independent science, since it alone exists for itself (1.982b).

Aristotle's opening assumption is that humans desire to know, and that they desire not only knowing particular things, but also the activity of knowing itself. That is, we desire knowing as much as the known.[7] Knowledge starts with sense perception and knowledge of facts (*knowing that*) but proceeds via two kinds of wonder to consider knowledge of first principles (*knowing why something is the case*): 'obvious perplexities' (*aporiai*) and then 'greater matters'. Aristotle cites a range of examples of obvious perplexities, including soltices, automata and the mathematical case of needing a number that is both odd and even for the diagonal of a square with sides equal to one (1.983a). These examples suggest that wonder might be experienced in a range of contexts, from geometrical calculation to sense perceptions of human-made and natural phenomena. The geometry example might lead us to conclude that wonder is triggered by being confronted by illogical claims, but the examples of the soltices and automata suggest that we might also be taken aback by not being able to explain why something happens (as might be the case with soltices) or that our explanations for ourselves and the world do not stack up (as the self-movement of automata might challenge a definition of 'life').[8] Importantly, what these examples have in common is that they are not unknown to us, and there is no intimation of them being unknowable.

Aristotle's examples of greater matters are all large scale: the changes of the moon and the sun, the stars, and the origins of the universe (1.982b). They are not mutually exclusive with obvious perplexities. This is not simply the case because soltices are included in the examples for obvious perplexities: Aristotle makes it clear that we go from one to the other via a 'gradual progression'. The idea that we experience a 'gradual progression' of instances of wonder signals a distinctive decision by Aristotle about the relationship of wonder and knowledge. The experience of wonder is disruptive. Yet it *develops* in a *gradual* manner. It could be, for example, that it develops in a manner akin to Aristotle's view of how we arrive at an appreciation of universals. That is through repeated perception and the mental activities of grouping memories together and of generalising from particulars (*Metaphysics*, 980b29), as he explains somewhat cryptically in *Posterior Analytics*:

> When one of the undifferentiated things takes a stand, the first universal is in the mind for although one perceives the particular, perception is of the universal, e.g. of man but not of Callias the man. Again a stand is taken in these, until the undivided, that is, the universal stands, e.g. Such and such an animal stands, and in this same way (100a15–b3).

This suggests that the development of wonder is not itself disruptive or a form of non-sense. Rather, Aristotle presents it as a part of the development of knowledge. It is not outside of or prior to knowledge. It is a kind of knowing, and more particularly, knowing what you do not know. Conversely, the gradual development of knowledge rests upon the disruptive power of wonder. In short, sense is what it is because of non-sense.

Aristotle's account of wonder fills in epistemological details that are missing in Plato's account. But he too directs his attention to the familiar and the unknown

10 Sense and non-sense in Ancient Greek histories

but not to the unknowable. This is a problem for Polybius, who resolves in the end to credit these phenomena to Fortune or the gods. He trusts what he sees, but he cannot make sense of it. Moreover, he does not see these phenomena as providing an opportunity for learning: his job is to provide an authoritative account for his readers to learn. So he talks of wonder to signal what is unknowable. This creates a new problem for Polybius, which Plato and Aristotle do not address in their accounts of wonder. Plato and Aristotle talk about wonder in contexts of knowledge *in good faith*. Polybius, on the other hand, is clearly aware that people do not always claim knowledge in good faith. To understand this distinction, think about these three scenarios: you can credit a phenomenon to Fortune or the gods on the grounds of having made an effort to explain that phenomenon; *or* on the basis that you do not want to put in the effort to explain that phenomenon; *or on the* basis that you have included that phenomenon in your narrative for reasons other than seeking historical truth. Polybius locates his own efforts in the first scenario, but he is not sure that other historians' efforts should be similarly designated. They could, for example, be writing to Aristotle's instruction on wonder in *Rhetorics*:

> when the right moment comes, one must say, "And give me your attention, for it concerns you as much as myself"; and, "I will tell you such a thing as you have never yet" heard of, so strange and wonderful (3.14).

The distinction between these three cases matters for Polybius, and not being able to tell them apart worries him because recourse to wonder may signal surrender to various base tendencies or temptations,[9] as he explains in his account of the difficulties of writing remote histories in book three:

> And even if one did reach these countries on the confines of the world, whether compulsorily or voluntarily, the difficulties in the way of a personal inspection were only begun: for some of the regions were utterly barbarous, others uninhabited; and a still greater obstacle in way of gaining information as to what he saw was his ignorance of the language of the country. And even if he learnt this, a still greater difficulty was to preserve a strict moderation in his account of what he had seen and despising all attempts to glorify himself by traveller's tales of wonder, to report for our benefit the truth and nothing but the truth (3.58).

Historical thought is hard work, and the achievement of excellence is rare (33.6–8). Like reading, it can only be mastered through consistent effort and determination and the exercise of moderation (47.4–11).[10]

Polybius interprets moderation as a decision not only to hold back from including some information, but also as a holding back in writing style. The less thrilling or vivid a history, the more likely it is to reflect careful and critical thought worthy of a philosopher king. By this measure, he saw his own work as outstanding (20.3–4). But his work, as the example of the unknowable from above reminds us, was not devoid of wonder. So, what could he do to signal the distinction between good histories and bad ones?

What Polybius tried to do, like Herodotus and Thucydides before him, was to solve the problem stylistically. As we noted at the start of this chapter, Polybius suggested a moderation of writing style, and in sparsity of recourse to wonder as an explanation. As the next section—a comparison with the style of Herodotus and Thucydides—will show, he did exercise restraint in mentioning wonder. But all three historians took a further step and used wonder as a rhetorical convention or motif to signal their scepticism about other historians' claims. Here was an opportunity to generate clear ground for history. The problem with this approach was that it was easily parodied, however, as the final part of this chapter will show.

Wonder and the style of history

As I noted at the outset of this chapter, Polybius was not the first historian. Nor were his efforts unusual: *The Histories* lists a large number of contemporary and antecedent histories. Most of those histories have not survived, and ironically, we are reduced to understanding them through the words of Polybius alone. Two of the most extensive histories that have survived from the ancient Greek world are *The Histories* of Herodotus and the *History of the Peloponnesian War* by Thucydides (c.460–c.395 BCE), and these are the works that we will take as the focal point for our comparison with Polybius' text.

One of the most striking things that emerges from a consideration of the two *Histories* and the *History of the Peloponnesian War* is the scarcity with which wonder—*Thaumazein* and its cognate concepts—is mentioned. But it is still present. There are 97 mentions in a corpus of around 312,000 words for Polybius; 79 in a corpus of around 185,000 for Herodotus; and 21 mentions in a corpus of just over 150,000 words for Thucydides. Furthermore, of the 97 uses of *Thaumazein* in Polybius' *Histories*, fewer than 10 are typically rendered as the English word wonder by various translators. More commonly, they are presented as surprise (e.g. 1.78; 3.33; 3.57; 4.42; 15.20; 36.8); astonishment (e.g. 2.63; 3.61; 12.15; 21.38); admiration (e.g. 3.61; 4.82; 5.12; 9.8; 12.3); terror or alarm (e.g. 5.18; 6.56; 38.4); or puzzlement (11.27; 21.1). These cognates give us the sense of the novelty of wonder, of being struck, confused or puzzled by something never seen before. More importantly, wonder is something that people other than Polybius experience. The historical agents of *The Histories*, like Hamilcar, experience wonder, as do historians like Phylarchus and historians in the abstract. In 34.4, for example, we see that the poet Pytheas uses vivid detail to 'give pleasure or [to] rouse wonder', whereas in 1.63 we gain a sense of historians being rightly struck by events of a scale never seen before:

> Those therefore who have spoken with wonder of the sea-battles of an Antigonus, a Ptolemy, or a Demetrius, and the greatness of their fleets, would we may well believe have been overwhelmed with astonishment at the hugeness of these proportions if they had to tell the story of this war.

On the whole, though, we gain a sense of the wonder of others as absurd and as readily rectified by sensible consideration (e.g. 2.63).

Whereas Polybius frames wonder as resulting from a lack of mental effort by others, Herodotus describes at least ten wonders that he has experienced. As Christine Hunzinger has noted, this is just one type in a wide range of wonders in *The Histories*.[11] Wonder is used to denote the recognition of unparalleled human ingenuity, by which Herodotus means works of enormous scale or of intricate craftsmanship. Consider for example his account of the Shrine of Leto in book two and the breastplate gifted to the Lacedaemonians by King Amasis of Egypt in book three:

> In Buto there is a temple of Apollo and Artemis. The shrine of Leto where the oracle is, is itself very great, and its outer court is sixty feet high. But what caused me the most wonder among the things apparent there I shall mention. In this precinct is the shrine of Leto, the height and length of whose walls is all made of a single stone slab; each wall has an equal length and height; namely, seventy feet. Another slab makes the surface of the roof, the cornice of which is seven feet broad. (2.155)
>
> The Lacedaemonians then equipped and sent an army to Samos, returning a favour, as the Samians say, because they first sent a fleet to help the Lacedaemonians against Messina; but the Lacedaemonians say that they sent this army less to aid the Samians in their need than to avenge the robbery of the bowl which they had been carrying to Croesus and the breastplate which Amasis King of Egypt had sent them as a gift. This breastplate had been stolen by the Samians in the year before they took the bowl; it was of linen, decked with gold and cotton embroidery, and embroidered with many figures; but what makes it worthy of wonder is that each thread of the breastplate, fine as each is, is made up of three hundred and sixty strands, each plainly seen. (3.47)

Wonder also arises from contemplating the scale or diversity of natural features, as with the size of Lake Moeris (2.149) and the richness of the Scythian environment (4.53). It is seen in lands on the margins of the world (e.g. 3.101–106; 3.116), but it is also used to describe the qualities of singular individuals—the remarkably brave or audacious—who are known to us (e.g., §2.121), and instances of intervention by the gods. Wonder is for Herodotus, Hunzinger concludes, anything but ordinary.[12]

Jessica Priestley has also credited Herodotus with the view that wonder is subjective: one person's ordinary can be another person's extraordinary.[13] This view is conveyed in a distinctive stylistic feature in *The Histories* that Polybius appears to have also adopted: wonders that cannot be verified or that are not believable are a matter of what *others say*. We see this, for example, in Herodotus' description of the Corinthians recounting Arion's travels by dolphin (1.23); Chersonese stories of dried fish appearing to come back to life (9.120); Greek accounts of Heracles giving sexual favours to a half woman, half snake in order to free his horses from her (4.9); and in descriptions of the motives ascribed to Alcmeonidae in book six and Artemesia and the Telines in two chapters in book seven:

> It is a wonder to me, and I do not believe the story, that the Alcmeonidae would ever have agreed to hold up a shield as a sign for the Persians out of a desire to make Athens subject to foreigners and to Hippias; for it is plain to see that they were tyrant-haters as much as Callias (son of Phaenippus and father of Hipponicus), or even more so. (6.121)
>
> I find it a great wonder that a woman [Artemisia] went on the expedition against Hellas: after her husband died, she took over his tyranny, though she had a young son, and followed the army from youthful spirits and manliness, under no compulsion. (§7.99)
>
> Now it makes me wonder that Telines should have achieved such a feat, for I have always supposed that such feats cannot be performed by any man but only by such as have a stout heart and manly strength. Telines, however, is reported by the dwellers in Sicily to have had a soft and effeminate disposition. (§7.153)

In these examples, wonder functions as a form of scepticism about the claims of others. Herodotus uses the term to alert us to the distance between his views and those of others.

This leads us to an interesting question: if Herodotus did not believe some of the claims that he encountered, why did he nonetheless still include them in *The Histories*? Detlev Fehling answers this question by assuming that Herodotus' attribution of accounts to others is nothing more than a rhetorical device used to present his own materials in an engaging manner.[14] Whether Fehling's claim is true or not, however, the impact of Herodotus' style is such that we are steered for or against conclusions about the reality or probability of events. Herodotus expresses doubt, caution and outright scepticism about a wide range of phenomena, including those that are not described as wonders (e.g. 2.123; 4.195.2; 6.105.3; 7.37.3; 152.3). He also offers alternative versions of events on more than 125 occasions. Instances where he offers alternatives include those where there are conflicting accounts and where he offers his own thoughts on an event. Some alternatives are posed to be dismissed immediately (e.g. 3.9.2) but others are left open to the reader's judgement (e.g. 3.122.1; 5.45.2). Generally, however, he makes a choice on behalf of the reader (e.g. 2.146.1; 4.11.1; 8.94.1–4, 19). Herodotus exercises judgement, but he does so in a way that shows his readers the ways in which he works through others' claims.

In *The Histories* of Herodotus and Polybius, both the workings and the conclusions of the historian are presented for their audiences to consider. This is the case whether phenomena are described as wonders or not. Some people's claims to knowledge are not believable because it is clear that these claims stem from a desire to entertain the audiences of histories, or from a lack of effort in seeking out the truth. Other claims to knowledge cannot be sustained or dismissed outright, because they rely upon evidence from the margins of the world that is not easily corroborated. Still other claims to knowledge are legitimate, because they can be attested through sensory experience. Finally, some claims to wonder are legitimate, because the writer of the history attests that nothing of their kind has ever been seen before. Herodotus and Polybius thus share in common an acknowledgement of legitimate, illegitimate and inconclusive claims to both knowledge and wonder. Where they differ is in the balance of these kinds of wonder in their works. The far-ranging ethnographic sections of Herodotus' *Histories*, for instance, take us to wonders from the margins of the world; whereas Polybius' history of events that are close at hand allows him to minimise claims to wonder. This difference is important for Polybius: the historian is not a passive recipient of information, but an active participant in ensuring that history makes sense. He did not write history at the scale of Herodotus because he did not believe that it could rest on certain sense making. But he did not dispense with wonder, either.

The connection of the discipline of history with the mental activity of making sense is also seen in Thucydides' *History of the Peloponnesian War*. Aside from a handful of examples where Thucydides employs the idea of wonder to express his admiration for the achievements of individuals or groups (e.g. 1.138; 7.56; 2.39; and 2.41), the term more commonly denotes a state of disbelief or even anger about the unjust actions of others. This is seen in book three:

> [I] wonder at those who have proposed to reopen the case of the Mitylenians, and who are thus causing a delay which is all in favour of the guilty, by making the sufferer proceed against the offender with the edge of his anger blunted; although where vengeance follows most closely upon the wrong, it best equals it and most amply requites it. I wonder also who will be the man who will maintain the contrary, and will pretend to show that the crimes of the Mitylenians are of service to us, and our misfortunes injurious to the allies (3.38).

More importantly, wonder is associated with phenomena that are at both the margins of the world and of historical research:

> We all know that that which is farthest off and the reputation of which can least be tested, is the object of admiration ... (§6.11).

Herodotus is often assumed to be the target of comments like these, and of Thucydides' more general complaint about entertaining histories in the introduction to his work:

> To hear this history rehearsed, for that there be inserted in it no fables, shall be perhaps not delightful. But he that desires to look into the truth of things done, and which (according to the condition of humanity) may be done again, or at least their like, shall find enough herein to make him think it profitable.

And it is compiled rather for an everlasting possession than to be rehearsed for a prize (1.22)

It is not hard to see why we might assume that the focus is Herodotus, given his declaration in the first book of *The Histories* to record the '*astonishing* achievements both of our own and of other peoples' (my emphasis, 1.1.1). But Herodotus was not the only historian who had some interest in the astonishing, as Polybius' work attests. More importantly, we should not assume that they were directed solely at an historian. Historians criticised or praised the efforts of other historians, but they also criticised or praised the efforts of other kinds of writers, including paradoxology.

What others say: mocking, with geese

Paradoxography—the compilation of wondrous phenomena—originated in the Hellenistic world with writings such as Kallimachos of Cyrene's (c. 305–240 BCE) *A Collection of Wonders from the Entire Earth Arranged by Locality* and Antigonos of Karystos' (fl. 240 BCE) *Wondrous Researches*. By the third century AD, over 20 compilations of wonders had been produced, including two more extensive works that still survive: Phlegon of Tralles' *Book of Marvels* and *On Marvellous Things Heard*, which has been attributed to Aristotle with little solid evidence.[15] The format employed in these wonder works is that of a compilation of very brief reports of phenomena, and sometimes the reports are arranged thematically. Sections 25–6 and 28 of *On Marvellous Things Heard*, for example, tell us about remarkable mice:

> It is said that in the island of Gyaros the mice eat iron (25).
> Men say that among the Chalybians, in an islet situated beyond them, gold is collected by mice in large numbers: wherefore also, as it appears, they rip up those that are found in the mines. (26) ...
> Men say that in Cyrene there is not merely one sort of mice, but several kinds differing both in forms and in colours; for some are broad-faced, like mustelae, and some like hedgehogs, which they call 'echines'. (28)

As these examples suggest, paradoxographies list the wonderful qualities of the natural world, including unusual insects and animals, lakes and rivers, stones and fires, but human achievements are sometimes included as well. Two of the 178 items in *On Marvellous Things Heard*, for example, foreground human phenomena: the temporary madness of a theatre goer in Abydos and of a wine merchant in Tarentum (31–2):

> It is said that a certain man in Abydos being deranged in mind, and coming into the theatre during many days looked on (as though actors were performing a play), and applauded; and, when he was restored to his senses, he declared that that was the happiest time he had ever spent.

> Moreover they say that at Tarentum a certain wine-merchant was mad at night, but sold his wines during the day: he also kept the key of the cellar attached to his girdle, and though many tried to steal it from him and get possession of it, he never lost it.

The interesting thing about these two examples is that they foreground experiences of people moving from states of being in or out of their senses: neither man is wholly sane nor wholly mad. This is a contrast with the physical phenomena in *On Marvellous Things Heard*, which have a constancy in their wondrous features.

In Phlegon's *Book of Marvels* we see this fascination with liminal beings writ large: centaurs, revenants, mothers who give birth to animals, and hermaphrodites are the overwhelming focus of the text. Moreover, in distinction from *On Marvellous Things Heard*, we gain a sense of Phlegon positioning these phenomena as problematic. Occasional authorial interjections in descriptions of these cases indicate that Phlegon saw liminal beings as a threat to social order. The sex change of a maiden in Antioch, for example, leads the Emperor to take pre-emptive action against the possibility of evil:

> A maiden of a prominent family, thirteen years of age, was good-looking and had many suitors. She was betrothed to the man whom her parents wished, the day of the wedding was at hand, and she was about to go forth from her house when suddenly she experienced an excruciating pain and cried out .... At around daybreak of the fourth day her pains became stronger, and she cried out with a great wailing. Suddenly male genitals burst forth from her, and the girl became a man. Some time later she was brought to the Emperor Claudius in Rome. Because of the portent he had an altar built on the Capitoline to Jupiter the Averter of Evil (6.2–4).

In the case of a woman who gave birth to a two-headed baby, corrective social action is taken more rapidly:

> In Rome a certain woman brought forth a two-headed baby, which on the advice of the sacrificing priests was cast into the River Tiber (25).

Much of the *Book of Marvels* and *On Marvellous Things Heard* have the tone of what we might now call tabloid reporting or belong in Ripley's *Believe it or Not*, but the above examples show that there are intimations that they also offer instruction in social norms and boundaries.

Paradoxography has been characterised as a 'problem' for historiography in the Hellenistic world and even as a 'parasitic growth on the tree of historic and natural-scientific literature'.[16] In large part, I believe that this judgement stems from the verification conventions that overlap between history and wonder works. In *On Marvellous Things Heard*, for example, items are often introduced with the generic phrase 'Men say' or 'they say'. These phrases suggest that the author did not just make up the text: the claims originated with others and are recorded by the writer in the manner of an historian. At the same time, though, 'Men' or 'they' would be less convincing to a writer like Polybius than a named source that can be checked via interview or reading or seeing the phenomena for yourself. By his measure, the author has settled for the easy road of a vivid account over the hard toil of locking down historical evidence.

But these are not the only verification phrases used by the author of *On Marvellous Things Heard*, and this is where the clear distinction between history and wonder work begins to unravel. On the matter of a man who apparently died and came to life again after sleeping in a tomb on the Island of Aeolus (one of the Lipara Islands), for instance, the writer makes it clear that while the story is likely 'fabulous', one cannot write about the place without mentioning it (101). The author raises doubts about the account in the manner of Herodotus or Thucydides saying 'it makes me wonder' or 'I wonder at those who propose'. Moreover, in other sections of the work, the author names the sources for claims—for example, Xenophanes in item 38—and even attests personally that phenomena have taken place (130). A wonder writer can use the testimonies of others and their own acts of sense making just as an historian does.

Phlegon's approach to verification claims reinforces the overlaps in approach: he collates multiple examples of the same phenomenon (e.g. eight examples of giant skeletons in sections 11–19); declares his hand as a witness, and invites readers to inspect the evidence for themselves (e.g. the remains of a Saunian centaur in the Emperor's palace in Rome in sections 34–5). Of these kinds of verification, Phlegon's claims as witness come closest to the descriptions of historical sense making preferred by Polybius. In book one, for example, we hear him say that the appearance of the revenant Philinnion 'was quickly heard through the city and was reported to me' (1.13); and in book four he attests that in the case of the sex change of Aitete from female to male, 'I myself have seen this person' (4.9).

As Emilio Gabba expresses it, the problem with these kinds of claims is that they generate the *impression* that they are a part of a history:

> Sophisticated antiquarian learning and the citation of recondite sources conveyed to the reader an impression of scholarship, which was in many cases simply a further element of fantasy.[17]

The problem as Gabba frames it is that wonder works in some ways resemble histories and there is a risk that audiences will not be able to distinguish truth from titillation. Gabba has some grounds for this complaint. This potential confusion—and fear about audiences being duped—is exploited humourously in the Greek-speaking Assyrian writer Lucian of Samosata's 'True History' of a journey to the moon with the help of geese, written in the second century:

> … I think it does students of literature good, after hard and serious reading, to relax their minds and to invigorate them further for future efforts …. For they will be attracted [to my work] not only by the exotic subject-matter and the

charm of the enterprise, and by the fact that I have told all manner of lies persuasively and plausibly, but because all the details in my narrative are amusing and covert allusion to certain poets, historians, and philosophers of old, who have written a lot of miraculous and fabulous stuff .... So as I too was vain enough to want to leave something to posterity, and didn't want to be the only one denied the right to flights of fancy, and since I had nothing truthful to report (not having experienced anything worth recording), I turned to lying. Thus I think that by freely admitting that nothing I say is true, I can avoid being accused of it by other people. So, I am writing about things I neither saw nor experienced, nor heard about from others, which moreover don't exist, and in my case could not exist. My readers must therefore entirely disbelieve them (1.1–4).[18]

Lucian leaves us wondering whether ancient histories and philosophies are just an elaborate rhetorical ruse.

If paradoxography fed parasitically upon the form of verification claims of historians, then the option of distinction still remained through means of content. That is, historians could achieve clear ground from paradoxography by means of what they wrote about, not just how they wrote about it. Polybius' declared intent to rein history in to perceptual sense making is such an act of distinction. But he, like Herodotus and Thucydides before him, left open a place for wonder. Granted that it was restricted to phenomena that were inexplicable to everyone and that the focus of their works was not solely upon wonder. But in granting wonder any role at all, this meant that at least in theory, historians and paradoxographers could report on the same phenomenon *and* use the same verification conventions to do so. Paradoxography was not parasitic to history, feeding off it as an ancillary genre. Paradoxography and history shared an interest in wonder and an entangled set of verification conventions, and history had little hope of achieving clear disciplinary ground.

Entangled

Polybius' attempts to manoeuvre history clear of the 'unworthy and unmanly' efforts of entertainment writers such as paradoxologists failed. History and fiction were arguably entwined before Herodotus set down his *Histories*, and there is now an extensive and impressive body of research on the continuing relationship between the two fields.[19] But this chapter has also highlighted a lesser appreciated form of entanglement, between history and metaphysics. Polybius' *Histories* suggest an attempt to make general sense of the world. He did so in a way that explicitly acknowledged the efforts of Plato, but which also bore some of the same interests as Aristotle in discerning universals in things. Polybius shared a mutual interest in understanding transcendence; asking questions about the relationship between the particular; and what is knowable and what is unknowable. But he also took a steer from Aristotle in positioning perceptual knowledge as the means by which universals could be apprehended. Moreover, like Plato and Aristotle, he made a place for wonder in his account of the nature of perceptual knowledge. History and metaphysics were for him interconnected, but the connection fell short on account of wonder. Plato and Aristotle located wonder at the beginning of philosophical knowledge; Polybius positioned it as the limit of historical knowledge.

Why that happened comes down, I think, to his positioning of himself as the purveyor of certain knowledge. Polybius wanted to record the knowable, and so he restricted his *Histories* almost entirely to events that he witnessed. But he struggled to account for things that he saw as unknowable, and called upon wonder. Moreover, in not being sure about the knowledge claims of others, he called upon wonder again. A double function for wonder was thereby established, applying to knowledge in good faith and knowledge not in good faith. And in signalling the second in the manner of literary or rhetorical *topoi*, he opened the door to overlap with, and parody by, the writers of paradoxologies or wonder works.

History and fiction were reconnected, but not for reasons of shared form alone. They reconnected because of Polybius' attempts to make general sense of the world, in the manner of a philosopher. History was arguably born from literature, and so was entangled with it. But as we have also seen, a mutual interest in sense-making connected the efforts of the historian with that of the philosopher, and that mutual interest persists.

Notes

1. E. Breisach, *Historiography: Ancient, Medieval and Modern*, 3rd edn., Chicago, IL: University of Chicago Press, 2007, p. 5.
2. R. Nicolai, 'The Place of History in the Ancient World', in *A Companion to Greek and Roman Historiography*, ed. J. Marincola, Oxford: Blackwell, 2009, p. 16.
3. A. Chaniotis, 'Travelling Memories in the Hellenistic World', in *Wandering Poets in Ancient Greek Culture*, eds. R. Hunter and I. Rutherford, Cambridge: Cambridge University Press, 2011, p. 253.
4. K. Clarke, *Making Time for the Past: Local History and the Polis*, Oxford: Oxford University Press, 2008, p. 362.
5. J. Thornton, 'Polybius in Context: The Political Dimension of The Histories', in *Polybius and his World*, eds. B. Gibson and T. Harrison, Oxford: Oxford University Press, 2013, pp. 213–30.
6. T.J.D. Chappell, *Reading Plato's Theaetetus*, Sankt Augustin, Germany: Academia Verlag, 2004, p. 172.
7. D. Schaeffer, 'Wisdom and Wonder in Metaphysics A: 1–2', *The Review of Metaphysics*, 1999, vol. 52(3), p. 642.
8. A. Marr, 'Gentille curiosité: Wonder-working and the culture of automata in the late Renaissance', in *Curiosity and Wonder from the Renaissance to the Enlightenment*, eds. R.J.W. Evans and A. Marr, Aldershot, UK: Ashgate, 2006, pp. 149–70.
9. G. Schepens, 'Polybius on Phylarchus' "Tragic" Historiography', in *The Shadow of Polybius: Intertextuality as a Research Tool in Greek Historiography*, eds G. Schepens and J. Bollansée, Leuven, NL: Peeters, 2005, pp. 141–64.
10. A.M. Eckstein, *Moral Vision in The Histories of Polybius*, Berkeley, CA: University of California Press, 1995, p. 250.
11. C. Hunzinger, 'La notion de θαῦμα chez Hérodote', *Ktèma*, 1995, vol. 20, pp. 47–70.
12. C. Hunzinger, 'La notion de θαῦμα chez Hérodote', p. 51. See also F. Hartog, *The Mirror of Herodotus: The Representation of the Other in the Writing of History*, Berkeley, CA: University of California Press, 1988, pp. 230–7.

13 J. Priestley, *Herodotus and Hellenistic Culture: Literary Studies in the Reception of The Histories*, Oxford: Oxford University Press, 2014, p. 56.
14 D. Fehling, *Herodotus and his 'Sources': Citation, Invention and Narrative Art*, Leeds, UK: Leeds University, 2000.
15 For the most extensive collection of paradoxical works, see A. Giannini (ed.), *Paradoxographorum Graecorum Reliquiae*, Milan, Italy: Istituto Editoriale Italiano, 1965.
16 E. Gabba, 'True History and False History in Classical Antiquity', *Journal of Roman Studies*, 1981, vol. 71, p. 54; and W. von Christ, Geschichte der griechischen Litteratur, Munich, Germany: W. Schmid and O. Stählin, 1920–24, as cited in W. Hansen, 'Introduction', *Phlegon of Tralles: Book of Marvels*, trans. W. Hansen, Exeter, UK: University of Exeter Press, 1996, p. 9.
17 E. Gabba, 'True History and False History in Classical Antiquity', p. 54.
18 C.D.N. Costa (ed.), *Lucian: Selected Dialogues*, Oxford: Oxford University Press, 2009, pp. 203–4.
19 For recent examples, see Jerome, De Groot, *The Historical Novel*, London: Routledge, 2009; id., *Remaking Histories: The Past in Contemporary Historical Fictions*, London: Routledge, 2015; Beverley C., Southgate, *History Meets Fiction*, London: Routledge, 2009; Ann Curthoys, and John Docker, *Is History Fiction?*, 2nd edn., Ann Arbor, MI: University of Michigan Press, 2015; A. Robinson, *Narrating the Past: Historiography, Memory and the Contemporary Novel*, Basingstoke, UK: Palgrave, 2011; and J. R. Morgan, 'Fiction and History: Historiography and the Novel', in *A Companion to Greek and Roman Historiography*, Oxford: Blackwell, 2007, pp. 513–65.

References

Aristotle, *De Anima*, trans. C. Shields, Oxford: Oxford University Press, 2016.
Aristotle, *De Sensu and De Memoria*, trans. G.R.T. Ross, Cambridge: Cambridge University Press, 1906.
Aristotle, *Metaphysics*, trans. H. Tredennick, London: Heinemann, 1933.
Aristotle, On Marvellous Things Heard, in *The Complete Works of Aristotle*, ed. J. Barnes, Princeton, NJ: Princeton University Press, 1984.
Herodotus, *The Histories*, 4 vols, trans. A.D. Godley, London: Heinemann, 1926.
Phlegon of Tralles, *Book of Marvels*, trans. W. Hansen, Exeter: University of Exeter Press, 1996.
Plato, *Five Dialogues: Euthyphro, Apology, Crito, Meno, Phaedo*, trans. G.M.A., Grube, New York: Hackett, 2002.
Plato, *Republic*, trans. P. Shorey, London: Heinemann, 1930.
Polybius, *The Histories*, 2 vols, trans. E.S. Shuckburgh, intro. F.W. Walbank, Bloomington, IN: Indiana University Press, 1962.
Thucydides, *History of the Peloponnesian War*, 4 vols, trans. C.F. Smith, London: Heinemann, 1969.

2

WONDERFUL AND CURIOUS HISTORIES IN PRE-MODERN EUROPE

Gerald of Wales | Bede | Gervase of Tilbury | Augustine of Hippo | Thomas Aquinas | Roger Bacon

Gerald of Wales (1146–1223) thought that the best gift for a king was a history of prodigies and wonders. Better than any gift of gold or a falcon or hawk, that history would provide the king and his successors with an abiding glimpse of the 'secret and distant freaks' that resulted from nature tiring of making the 'true and the serious' (*The History and Topography of Ireland*, dedication). By this measure, *The History and Topography of Ireland* is a remarkable gift, replete with accounts of geese born from barnacles (1.11); incorruptible kingfishers (1.13); soil that is toxic to reptiles (1.23); islands that are deadly to women (2.4); hybrids that result from bestial acts (2.23); as well as tales of a woman with a beard and a mane (2.20); a stone that is mysteriously filled with wine every day (2.30); and a werewolf that sought communion from a priest (2.19). And it was a serious historical gift, as he explains:

> I shall have to write some accounts which will seem to the reader utterly impossible, or quite ridiculous. But, with the help of God, I will insert nothing in my book the truth of which I have not elicited with the greatest diligence either from my own firm belief or the authentic testimony of most trustworthy men ... What I have witnessed with my own eyes, that I assert firmly and without hesitation. But what has only reached my ear through others, which I am slower to believe, that I do not affirm, but only relate. (2.1)

The History and Topography of Ireland is history but not as we know it. Moreover, as Gabrielle Spiegel has argued, it does not seem to be history as we *want* it to be. Medieval histories like that of Gerald of Wales appear to have a long list of shortcomings, which Spiegel encapsulates in the following summary:

[a] low level of literary achievement, approaching at times narrative unintelligibility; a weak notion of historical evidence; lack of sense of anachronism; propagandistic intentions; substitution of symbolic interpretation for causal analysis; and vulnerability to invasion by fiction, forgery, myth, and miracle, not to mention genuine demons.[1]

Spiegel sees these features as arising from the fundamental equation of history with that of a perceptual field 'to be seen and represented instead of constructed and analysed, an object more of perception than of cognition'.[2]

If medieval historiography was a perceptual activity, then it might be considered an extension on the sense-making efforts of ancient Greek historians. In the last chapter, I outlined how historians such as Polybius worked to build up a body of history theory or historiography by documenting their acceptance or rejection of particular histories. Moreover, I noted how Polybius drew upon the ideas of philosophers like Plato and Aristotle to emphasise the importance of relying only upon only our own mental efforts and senses in understanding the past. This led Polybius to present history as based on sense making, and to reserve the use of concepts like wonder for phenomena that exhausted attempts at sense making.

Wonder marked the limits of knowledge for Polybius. But for philosophers like Aristotle, it also marked its beginning. Polybius and Aristotle shared an interest in understanding the universal, but Polybius struggled to clarify how we might discriminate between genuine and false claims to understanding. He struggled because while he knew that his own claims about the past were rigorous, other historians and wonder writers (paradoxographers) who were less rigorous by his account employed the same *topoi*: methods for making and sustaining an argument. Both, for example, authenticated accounts through the use of eyewitness rhetorical devices such as 'I saw', 'I witnessed'. That is, an historian and a paradoxographer might write exactly the same sentence, but their level of effort and intention in writing that sentence might differ markedly. Hence Polybius' resolution to treat history as a discipline in which we can only ultimately trust what we see for ourselves.

We have no evidence to conclude with any certainty that Polybius was familiar with the ideas Aristotle or Plato expressed about the role of wonder in reason. And even if he were to have been familiar with their claims, they would likely have done little to assuage his scepticism. This was to change in medieval Europe, when Aristotelian and Platonic notions of reason and wonder were adopted and adapted in the service of Christian devotion and redemption. In theory, the endpoint of philosophy and history alike became a right relationship with God that was driven by an effort of reason and will known and judged by God. Historians and philosophers had the task of seeing and understanding the universal and knew that even if they deceived others about their efforts, they would not be able to deceive God. Moreover, they had an obligation to warn others about the eternal consequences that flowed from weakness of reason or will.

The consequences of this shift in endpoint from reason to union with God through reason and strength of will were important for history. We might see medieval histories as ill-disciplined combinations of the event and the fantastic, but that combination was driven by an increasingly confident ability to discriminate devotional wonder from sinful curiosity. Vestiges of that distinction remain with us today. In this chapter, I am going to unpack these claims through an examination of the works of three British historians—Gerald of Wales, Bede (682–735 CE) and Gervase of Tilbury (1150–1228 CE)—in the light of the metaphysical writings of Augustine of Hippo (354–430 CE), Thomas Aquinas (1225–75 CE) and Roger Bacon (1214–94 CE).

Caroline Bynum has described medieval European historiographical views of wonder as cognitive, not meant to be imitable by audiences, and perspectival. Moreover she, like Axel Rüth, sees these views at play across the porous boundaries of history, philosophy and what we might call ecclesiastical paradoxology (e.g. miracle accounts and hagiographies).[3] In this chapter, I will affirm that medieval thinkers saw wonder as a rational function. Bynum's second claim—the question of whether wonder acts were not meant to be imitable by readers—is best tested by an analysis of reception, as has been done with Aviad Kleinberg's analysis of medieval canonisation depositions. There is much more work needed on sources of this kind, but Kleinberg's work is enough to show us that peasants and elites did not always hold the same views on what phenomena could be rightly designated as wonders and whether they were singular.[4] On Bynum's third claim that wonder is perspectival—I might consider something as a wonder, you might not consider it a wonder—I will chart a distinctive course by arguing that differences in opinion were not ultimately accepted by medieval philosophers and historians such as Gerald of Wales and Gervase of Tilbury. Rather, I will dig deeper into their distinctions between wonder and curiosity and note that the former was seen as a kind of epistemic constraint that promoted a rightful view of the universal. This was set against the addictive captivation of curiosity as an overconcentration on material or sensible phenomena. In so arguing, I will recognise later on in this chapter the first steps of Neil Manson's work on epistemic restraint and presentations of curiosity as a vice.[5]

Moreover, I will show that more can be said on the variations of views of wonder and curiosity within and across medieval historiography and philosophy. In particular, I will highlight differences over whether the inclusion of a wide variety of phenomena in a history promotes rational engagement, and whether wonder always operates at the beginning of rational processes. A closer inspection of medieval philosophy will also highlight how writers extended classical notions of wonder, as with Augustine's claim that wonder has social as well as individual consequences; Thomas' positioning of curiosity as an incomplete subsidiary of wonder; and Bacon's identification of wonder with particular academic disciplines. Finally, I will round out the chapter by showing through the case of miracle narratives that Polybius' problem of distinguishing legitimate claims to wonder on the basis of *topoi* persisted, but for medieval European writers judgement of difference could be achieved by God.

In simple summary, I will argue that the kinds of judgements that Polybius made about the idea of history continued in medieval Europe. Medieval historians attempted to make general sense of things. They saw history as a means of discerning universals, which like Aristotle they considered to be *in re* or present in particular phenomena. They held that rigorous sense perception was the key to discerning those universals. And they still set boundaries between the knowable and the unknowable. But they also expanded the lines of thought that Polybius set down, by drawing upon medieval metaphysics to chart a detailed cognitive account of wonder as rational and as a form of mental restraint. And they saw themselves as having solved Polybius' dilemma of judging claims to knowledge by asserting that while some things are unknowable to us, nothing is unknowable to God. This provided them with the opportunity to emphasise ethics as well as epistemology in the pursuit of metaphysics, for if an historian could not judge if a claim to knowledge was in good faith, God certainly could.

The severe discipline of history

That medieval histories like *The History and Topography of Ireland* were often framed as a gift might lead us to assume that they were ephemeral aggregations designed to entertain and affirm royal or mercantile audiences. Indeed, there are five editions of *The History and Topography of Ireland*, with versions three and five dedicated to two different patrons: William de Vere and King John respectively.[6] Recent research, however, has emphasised the role of these works in exploring larger themes such as the nature of knowledge and belief, change and social order and disorder. Two recent, notable contributions on *The History and Topography of Ireland* are Caroline Bynum's careful analysis of Gerald's werewolf story in light of medieval anxieties about shapeshifting, and Lorraine Daston and Katharine Park's account of Gerald's distinction between wonders as the result of nature acting 'against her own laws' (1.2) and horrors as arising from immorality and social disorder.[7]

Daston and Park designate *The History and Topography of Wales* as a travel narrative on the grounds that Gerald preferred to write only about things that he had seen for himself.[8] At first sight, this is a reasonable conclusion given Gerald's declaration reproduced at the opening of this chapter to 'assert firmly and without hesitation' by only reporting on the things that he had witnessed on his travels to Ireland as royal clerk and chaplain for Henry II (Second Preface). Eyewitness claims ground Gerald's account of contemporary natural phenomena such as geese born from barnacles and the ability of ospreys to hover:

> I have often seen with my own eyes more than a thousand minute embryos of birds of this species on the seashore, hanging from one piece of timber, covered with shells, and already formed (1.11)
>
> It is wonderful how these birds—and I have often witnessed it myself—hover in the air over the waves supported by their wings … (1.12).

But a common feature of both of these claims is the idea of their veracity stemming from Gerald having observed them more than once, over a period of time. This suggests that his observations of even natural phenomena are not just contemporary, but are historically grounded.

Gerald's preference for multiple observations helps his audience to rule out the possibility that his conclusions depend on particular environmental or human conditions, such as poor light or a fever. They also allow Gerald to dispel doubts and to speak 'without hesitation' about the past. Written evidence, by contrast, only allows the historian to speak with probability as it offers only 'precious stones among the sands on the seashore' (First Preface; 2). It does not provide us with anything more than that which we can outline, as he argues of the flood described in the Bible:

> ... it appears to be a matter of doubt how, if nearly all perished in the flood, the memory of these events and of their arrival could have been preserved. However, those who first committed to writing these accounts must be answerable for them. For myself, I compile history; it is not my business to impugn it. Perhaps some record of these events was found, inscribed on a stone or a tile, as we read was the case with the art of music before the flood. (3.1)

So too, the oral accounts of others are perishable, for there is 'nothing so firmly fixed in the mind', Gerald argues, 'that it is not lost by neglect and the lapse of time' (3.3). Witnessing means being able to check and to verify; listening and reading leave us vulnerable to the gaps and shortfalls in knowledge of others.

Gerald's insistence that only our own eyewitness claims can provide certain knowledge does suggest that *The History and Topography of Ireland* is more of a contemporary travel or geographical work than a history. As we saw in the last chapter, though, eyewitness evidence also played a critical role in histories of the ancient Greek world. We recall in particular Polybius' argument that the sense of seeing provides the basis for the most accurate and certain historical knowledge. This was coupled with a call for restraint in claims to wonder unless all other attempts at explanation had been exhausted.

Like Polybius, Gerald saw himself as the purveyor of a strenuous and austere approach to the writing of history. This is evidenced in his insistence in 3.25:

> There are some things which shame would prevent my relating, unless the course of my subject required it. For a filthy story seems to reflect a stain on the author, although it may display his skill. But the severity of history does not allow us either to sacrifice truth or affect modesty; and what is shameful in itself may be related by pure lips in decent words.

This claim to serve the severe discipline of history might be hard for us to reconcile with the many wondrous phenomena that Gerald describes, including the description of the bestial acts that follows the quote above. Indeed, it is not difficult to imagine Polybius condemning *The History and Topography of Ireland* as an idle and unprofitable paradoxographical or wonder work. So how do we make sense of his claims to authenticity and certainty, made throughout the work (e.g. 2; 2.13; 2.33)? Useful clues are provided in the words translated as 'required' and 'severe'. Required connotes a compelling demand; severity connotes gravity and austerity rather than geniality or elaborateness. Gerald feels that the demand of his work is such that he has no choice but to outline Irish acts of bestiality. His and our shame and modesty have to be put aside to meet this demand.

That demand is not the same as that underpinning Polybius' *Histories*: the use of rationality to discern the work of the universal idea of fortune at play in the material world. Gerald was also interested in the work of the universal in the world, but his universal was God, not fortune. God, he tells us, possesses 'universal knowledge and freedom from error' (1.5) and it should not surprise us 'that wonders should be discovered, related, and written concerning his works, who made all things according to his will; and with whom nothing is impossible' (2). It is by the privileges of reason and intellect that we are able to gain some inkling of God's designs, even when they appear to be monstrous (1.9). This, for Gerald, was demonstrated by the metaphysician and theologian Augustine of Hippo in *City of God*, who argues that the varying and even monstrous appearances of humans belie the hand of one creator who is not confused by material differences in phenomena (*City of God*, 16.8). We humans, however, understand only material intimations of the universal, and we must demonstrate the strength of will in rational constraint to appreciate that. As Gerald explains in 1.9:

> Beware then, lest in thus employing your intelligence you become as though you had no understanding. Beware, lest abusing the privileges of reason and intellect, through which, by the merciful goodness of the Creator, you excel all beings under the sun, you justly forfeit them .... The Lord knoweth the thoughts of man, that they are but vain ... search not into things that are above thee, nor inquire into those that are mightier than thee; but meditate always on what the Lord hath commanded thee, and in many of his works be not too curious....
>
> ... Why is your heart so lifted up, and your eyes raised on high, that you are conversant with wonders and with miracles which are above you? Does your pride so separate you from the love of God, that while you are wise in that which is above knowledge, and aspire to still higher attainments, you turn aside from the path of the humble?

At stake here is redemption from sinful pride that stems from us not being able—as Gerald again refers to Augustine—to resist 'a foe within' that 'confirms our propensity to evil' (1.8).

History for Gerald finds its basis in sense perception and in severe restraint from intellectual overreach. In short, he is interested in the role that history can play in answering questions about transcendence, but its answers lie within boundaries. Importantly for our purposes, the touchstone test of intellectual overreach plays out in Gerald's use of the words 'curiosity', 'wonder' and 'miracle' in the passages from 1.9 reproduced above. Curiosity, we sense, is something to be avoided because it entails a form of unconstrained inquisitiveness that leads to error and to sin (see also 1.11), whereas wonders and miracles are from God. This distinction is important because it marks a turn from Polybius' claim that legitimate and illegitimate claims to wonder can be distinguished solely on the basis of intellectual effort. For Polybius, genuine appeals to wonder are made only after every other explanation has been exhausted, and they mark the limits of knowledge. Wonder also marks the limits of knowledge in Gerald's history, but that limit is one that we impose upon ourselves. More specifically, it suggests an ability to develop the right kinds of knowledge: not second guessing the mind of God and not getting carried away by material appearances. This is seen in his discussion of the example of geese born from barnacles on branches to highlight our predilection to get caught up with anomalous or rare phenomena. If you read carefully, one can see the imprint of Aristotle's thoughts on wonder at work:

> The first creature was begotten of clay; this last is engendered of wood. The one, proceeding from the God of nature for once only, was a stupendous miracle; the other, though not less admirable, is less to be wondered at, because imitative nature often performs it. But human nature is so constituted, that it holds nothing to be precious and admirable but what is uncommon and of rare occurrence. The rising and setting of the sun, than which there is nothing in the world more beautiful, nothing more fit to excite our wonder, we pass by without any admiration, because they are daily presented to our eyes; while an eclipse of the sun fills the whole world with astonishment, because it rarely occurs (1.11).

What flows from these passages is a signal that glimpses of the universal are to be marked with the term wonder (*admiratio*) or miracle (*miracula*) and, and that a mistaken focus on the surface differences in phenomena are to be marked with the term curiosity (*curiositas*). In distinction from Polybius, therefore, Gerald had terminology to distinguish legitimate and illegitimate claims to wonder.

Against curiosity, for wonder

Gerald's references to Augustine of Hippo suggest that his distinction between wonder and curiosity might not have been novel or even confined to the discipline of history. To establish whether Gerald's views are novel, I begin by looking at authors whom he cites as historical sources: Gaius Julius Solinus (fl. 357 CE), the author of a chronological and geographical account of wonders called *Polyhistor*; Orosius (385–420 AD), contemporary of Augustine and author of *Seven Books of History against the Pagans*; Isidore of Seville (560–636 CE), author of the *summa* of all things known, *Etymologiae*; and Bede (672–735), author of *Ecclesiastical History of the English People*. As a second step, I will look to the metaphysical philosophies of Augustine, Thomas Aquinas and Roger Bacon, before assessing whether medieval histories were simply a form of miracle or devotional narrative.

Of these four sources, Solinus and Bede provide us with some comment on the nature of wonder. Before I outline their views, however, it is worth noting that the other sources are not devoid of interest. Orosius' *Seven Books of History Against the Pagans* includes an account of a serpent's skin nearly 37 metres in length, which 'for a time remained a wonder to all' in Rome (4.8.15). In addition, Orosius indicates that the start of his research was marked by a 'confusion' that stemmed from his assumption that 'the disasters of our present time seemed to rage beyond what could have been expected' (1.1.12).[9] So too, in Isidore of Seville's *Etymologies* we find not only a reassertion of the ancient Greek view of history as things seen—'history is about times which we see, and annals are about years unfamiliar to our age' (1.44.4)—but also a distinction of fable from history—on the grounds that their contents are 'contrary to nature'—that would seem to rule out much of Gerald's work as history (1.44.5).[10]

Things being contrary to nature is the focus of much of Solinus' *Polyhistor*.[11] His stated aim is to gloss things known and to tarry 'in things more strange' in order to achieve a variety of content that will 'ease the weariness of readers' (Preface). This is not to lift the burden of reason from readers, for Solinus sees it as a mark of the human to exceed all other animals in understanding and capacity of wisdom. The operating assumption here is that variety enhances audience engagement, rather than diminishing it. Moreover, he aims to hold audience attention through greater—rather than lesser—wonders, as he explains in the case of likenesses between people who are not related:

> Now who so bends his mind to consider the causes of likenesses, shall perceive the wonderful disposition of the workmanship of nature. For sometimes such likenesses belong to some stocks, and descend from issue to issues, into the succession .... But this is the lesser wonder if we consider those things that have been seen between mere strangers (4).

This highlights Solinus' interest in the sensible world of appearances. There is, however, no universal at play in the sense of Fortune in Polybius' history or the revelation of God in Gerald's *The History and Topography of Ireland*, just the prevailing assumption that variety engages readers.

This brings us to Bede. Over 300 years before Gerald dedicated *The History and Topography of Ireland* to Henry II, Bede narrated a history of the English church and the Anglo Saxon people in which remarkable events abound. Prayers quell fires and epidemics (1.19; 4.14), people and horses are cured of maladies in the places where saints have died (3.9) and the martyrdom of saints is described in forensic detail (1.7). People, objects and places evoke wonder in the author and others who witnessed them first hand (1.7; 2.10; 3.8; 3.9; 3.10; 3.13; 3.17; 3.25; 4.9; 4.10; 4.12; 5.22). Consider, for example, the 'favours and miracles' associated with the bones of Oswald, a King of 'wonderful piety':

> The water in which the bones had been washed was poured away in a corner of the cemetery, and from that time on the very earth that had received this venerated water has the saving power to expel devils from the bodies of those who were possessed .... The abbess [Queen Osthryd] ... asked that she might be given some of this healing dust; and when it had been given her, she tied it up in a cloth, and she put it into a little casket which she took away with her .... Some while later, a guest visited her abbey who was often horribly tormented by an evil spirit during the night hours .... he was suddenly possessed by the devil and began to cry out, grind his teeth, foam at the mouth, and toss his limbs in wild contortions .... a priest therefore employed exorcism and did all he could to allay the sufferer's frenzy; but all his efforts were useless. When there seemed no hope left of easing his frenzy, the abbess suddenly remembered this dust, and told a maidservant to go at once and fetch the casket containing it. As soon as she returned from her errand and entered the porch of the house where the possessed man lay writhing, he immediately became silent, laying down his head as though to sleep, and relaxing his whole body .... saying 'I am now restored to health and in my right mind' (3.11–12).

Dust cures for demonic possession are not a feature of histories as we know them today. Nor does it escape our attention that the power of dust exceeds that of a priest, which is surprising given Bede's status as the author of a number of Christian devotional texts. It could be that the point of the passage is to highlight the wonders of the natural world, as with Gerard of Wales' history. Bede, like Gerard of Wales, attested to the faith-driven efforts of his labours, noting in his preface to the *History* that any inaccuracies stemmed from a shortfall in the efforts of others:

> ... from the period at which this volume begins until the time when the English nation received the Faith of Christ, I have drawn extensively on the works of earlier writers gathered from earlier sources.... With regard to events in the various districts of the province of the Northumbrians, from the time that it received the Faith of Christ up until the present day, I am not dependent on any one author, but on countless faithful witnesses who either know or remember the facts, apart from what I know myself .... Should the reader discover any inaccuracies in what I have written, I humbly beg that he will not impute them to me, because, as a true law of history requires, I have laboured honestly to transmit whatever I could ascertain from common report for the instruction of posterity.

Regardless of what we might think about Bede's motives for transferring the burden of accuracy to others, his claims do reinforce the Ancient Greek view that the claims of others cannot be viewed with certainty.

Bede's views on the nature of wonder—as distinct from descriptions of wonders—are seen most clearly in his inclusion of a letter from Pope Gregory to Augustine of Canterbury in which we are warned of the pride that takes root in the frail mind after the performance of multiple wonders:

> My very dear brother, I hear that almighty God has worked great wonders through you for the nation which He has chosen. Therefore let your feeling be one of fearful joy and joyful fear at God's heavenly gifts—joy that the souls of the English are being drawn through outward miracles to inward grace; fear lest the frail mind becomes proud because of these wonderful events. (1.31)

Here we find the suggestion echoed in Gerald's work that repeated recourse to wonders might challenge our strength of will and generate sinful vanity. So too, there is the contrast drawn between 'outward miracles' and 'inward grace', the former lowering our sights from the universal to 'private and temporal joys' (1.31). Unlike Gerald, though, Bede encapsulates his reflections under the rubric of wonder, without distinguishing it from sinful curiosity.

This leads us to consider whether the distinction between wonder and curiosity presented by Gerald emanates from a roughly contemporaneous history, or whether it is philosophy, theology or some other approach to writing that we have to thank for its origin. On the question of history, a promising candidate is provided in Gervase of Tilbury's extensive *Otia Imperialia* ('Recreation for an Emperor') which dates from around 1209–14, roughly ten years before Gerald's death. Dedicated to the Holy Roman Emperor Otto IV, *Otia Imperialia* is divided into three sections, focused on history, geography, and marvels and miracles. Gervase's interest in wonder, though, is not confined to the third section, as the example of his claim for a sea in the sky in section one attests:

> A strange event in our own time, which is widely known but none the less a cause of wonder, provides proof of the existence of an upper sea overhead. It occurred on a feast day in Great Britain, while the people were struggling out of their parish church after hearing high mass. The day was very overcast and quite dark on account of the thick clouds. To the people's amazement, a ship's anchor was seen caught on a tombstone within the church wall, with its rope stretching up and hanging in the air … (1.13).

So too we learn of the claim 'not to be repudiated' of women transforming into serpents and men into wolves (1.15); pygmies that are old by the age of seven, five-metre high giants who fight griffins, one-footed sciapodes, and Scythian women who have boars' tusks, hair down to their ankles and cows' tails (2.3–4). It is in section three that Gervase explains the inclusion of these accounts, noting that his is not an idle work:

> our primary purpose is to present the marvels of every province to our discerning listener, in order that His Imperial Highness may have a source of refreshment for his thoughts when a clear interval of leisure is his, according to the dictum: 'Interrupt your cares with gladness now and then'. To be sure, it is not proper that an emperor's leisure should be contaminated with the prating babbling of players; on the contrary, the crude falsehoods of idle tales should

be spurned, and only those things which are sanctioned by the authority of age, or confirmed by the authority of scripture, or attested by daily eye-witness accounts, should be brought to his venerable hearing in his leisure hours. And since the human mind is always keen to hear and lap up novelties, the oldest things will have to be presented as new, natural things as miraculous, and things familiar to us all, as strange (3, preface).

Wonders are presented not as an idle distraction, but as triggers for departure from habitual patterns of thought. In the manner of Solinus, Gervase views variety as a way of enhancing engagement and not as a way of being excused from rational deliberation. He is also careful to stress the rigour and Christian sanction underpinning his selection of materials, which sets them aside from 'prattling' and 'idle' chatter. Effort of research is important for him as it was for Polybius, but he has Christian scripture as a guide in addition to reason. Significantly, his view of marvels also builds upon his distinction between miracles and marvels in 2.23:

… both result in wonderment. Now we generally call those things miracles which, being preternatural, we ascribe to divine power, as when a virgin gives birth, when Lazarus is raised from the dead, or when diseased limbs are made whole again: while we call those things marvels which are beyond our comprehension, even though they are natural: in fact the inability to explain why a thing so constitutes is a marvel.

Miracles are of God and explicable to God alone. This point is reinforced with a reference to Augustine of Hippo in 3.2 in an account of the weakness of the human mind and will:

We have recorded these things concerning the properties of stones in order that our limited understanding may marvel at what we are unable to explain, due to the ignorance of our weak nature. For, as Augustine says, when we talk about divine miracles, past or future, which we do not have the power to demonstrate to them in practice, unbelievers demand an explanation from us which we are not able to give. Miracles, indeed, are beyond the capacity of the human intellect.

These views are roughly in alignment with those of Gerald in *The History and Topography of Ireland*, but again there is no distinction between curiosity and wonder, simply a distinction between marvels and miracles. Gervase's reference to Augustine, as well as the use of Gerald as a source for a description of barnacle geese in 3.123, suggests that he was unlikely to have been the progenitor of the distinction between wonder and curiosity in Gerald's *The History and Topography of Ireland*. To gain some traction in answering the question of whether this distinction was particular to medieval historiography, therefore, the logical next step is to consider the views of the thinker to which both Gerald and Gervase refer: Augustine of Hippo.

Reason, wonder and the universal: metaphysics

The fifth century writer Augustine of Hippo was a key driver of medieval efforts to adapt ancient Greek philosophy to Christian thought. He was the author of over 100 titles, 200 letters and 400 sermons which ranged from contemplation of the relationship between the sensible world of ephemeral phenomena to the intelligible world of permanent realities to a consideration of the embodiment of the soul in humans. As part of his reflections on the relationship between the sensible, material world and the universal, Augustine noted that it was appropriate to consider the role of wonder because God in the human form of Jesus saw and wondered at the faith of believers (*Two Books on Genesis against the Manichees*, 1.8.14; cf. Matthew 8:10).

Augustine believed that we are susceptible to focus on the sensible world of material phenomena at the expense of contemplation of the universal (*Confessions* 4.15.24). This is a form of moral danger, because our belief that the material world provides us with everything we need to navigate life casts us adrift from knowledge of God (*City of God*, 13.14–15). This moral danger is played out every day in even very simple acts of seeing. In a manner akin to Polybius, Augustine considers seeing as a path to either the contemplation of the universal or of entertainment in the fleeting. Moreover, like Polybius, Augustine sees the destination of our perceptions as determined by the degree of intellectual effort that we invest. Sight of the universal thus hinges on rational engagement. In a refinement to ancient Greek thought, though, Augustine also considers the endpoint of sight as reflecting mental and moral restraint: we do not give in to temptations such as laziness, lust or vanity.

Augustine's distinction between the two endpoints for seeing is clearly reflected in his use of the terms wonder (*admiratio*) and curiosity (*curiositas*). Augustine uses the latter term more than the former in *Confessions* and *City of God*, and associates it with adjectives such as unlawful, sacrilegious, illicit, pernicious, excessive, diseased, idle and impious. This is because curiosity, as he explains in *Confessions* 10.35, results from a lack of restraint and mental effort. It is worth quoting the passage at length:

> ... there pertains to the soul, through the same senses of the body, a certain vain and curious longing, cloaked under the name of knowledge and learning, not of having pleasure in the flesh, but of making experiments through the flesh. This longing, since it originates in an appetite for knowledge, and the sight being the chief among the senses in the acquisition of knowledge, is called in divine language, the lust of the eyes (1 John 2:16) .... pleasure follows after objects that are beautiful, melodious, fragrant, savoury, soft; but curiosity, for experiment's sake, seeks the contrary of these—not with a view of undergoing uneasiness, but from the passion of experimenting upon and knowing them. For what pleasure is there to see, in a lacerated corpse, that which makes you shudder? ... From this malady of curiosity are all those

strange sights exhibited in the theatre .... Hence, too, with that same end of perverted knowledge we consult magical arts. Hence, again, even in religion itself, is God tempted, when signs and wonders are eagerly asked of Him—not desired for any saving end, but to make trial only ... in how many most minute and contemptible things is our curiosity daily tempted, and who can number how often we succumb? How often, when people are narrating idle tales, do we begin by tolerating them, lest we should give offense unto the weak; and then gradually we listen willingly! ... It is one thing to get up quickly, and another not to fall, and of such things is my life full; and my only hope is in Your exceeding great mercy.

In this passage we see curiosity depicted as both an active experiment of mind and a passive surrender to the 'idle tales' of others and to other daily temptations. These characteristics are not incompatible, because while all humans seek knowledge, they are also called upon to exercise mental restraint in the face of impulses such as voyeurism. Curiosity is thus a kind of knowledge, but a privative or incomplete kind that speaks of weakness of will—called *akrasia* in ancient Greek philosophy— or disobedience to the self. As Augustine explains in *City of God*:

There is nothing else that now makes a man more miserable than his own disobedience to himself. Because he would not do what he could, he can no longer do what he would. It is true that even in the Garden, before man sinned, he could not do everything; but he could still do all he desired to do, since he had no desire to do what he could not do. It is different now .... In too many ways not to mention, man cannot do what he desires to do, for the simple reason that he refuses to obey himself; that is to say, neither his spirit or his body obeys his will (11.15).

All of these points would indicate that Augustine or an intermediary commentary are likely the source for Gerald's views on curiosity and wonder. Importantly, this suggests a closer connection between metaphysics and history than we saw in the first chapter. This makes sense given that philosophy was *Christian* philosophy, and historiography, *Christian* historiography. But Augustine and Gerald are not completely in lock step on the matter of wonder. Augustine extends the analysis of curiosity further by characterising it as addictive, 'entangling the minds of men' (20.8) and setting them on a destructive path in the manner of the Emperor Julian:

... whose gifted mind was deceived by a sacrilegious and detestable curiosity, stimulated by the love of power. And it was because he was addicted through curiosity to vain oracles, that, confident of victory, he burned the ships that were laden with the provisions necessary for his army, and therefore, engaging with hot zeal in rashly audacious enterprises, he was soon slain, as the just consequence of his recklessness ... (5.21)

Conversely, we reach the whole and highest object of thought—knowledge of God—through constraint from impulses and rational consideration at God's wonders (*City of God*, 9.45). When we give in to curiosity, we are less than we are able to be, and on the path to nothingness: 'no longer to be in God but to be in oneself in the sense of to please oneself is not to be wholly nothing but to be approaching nothingness' (*City of God*, 14.13).

Additionally, Augustine suggests that curiosity is not only a problem for individuals; it is also potentially a social problem. This is because he sees our own addictive surrender to weakness of will as entailing the temptation to encourage others to do the same. My *akrasia* is thus also a social *akrasia*, and with this step, Augustine transposes epistemology into social philosophy in a way that will be picked up and further developed by Thomas Hobbes' suggestion of an addictive, politically destabilising view of curiosity. Even God is not protected from our desire to seek signs and wonders, as we saw from the passage in *Confessions* above: 'even in religion itself, is God tempted, when signs and wonders are eagerly asked of Him'. Yet there is no indication that God succumbs, and this opens up the possibility that not everything we take as a sign or wonder is taken as such by God.

Augustine's suggestion that not everything is a wonder to God reflects the wider medieval distinction between *mirabilia* (marvels) and *miracula* (miracles), as echoed in Gervase's *Otia Imperialia*.[12] Miracles stem from God; marvels do not. In his *Summa contra Gentiles*, for example, the Italian philosopher and theologian Thomas Aquinas (1225–74) designated monsters as being apart from the intention of God and of nature (3.6.11), and evil as an accidental falling short of the good arising from God (3.10.18; 3.14.3). As Thomas writes in *Summa contra Gentiles* 3.7.8:

> The births of monsters are the result of lack of assimilation on the part of the matter. Nor may this be attributed to some defect in the agent, if it fail to convert poorly disposed matter into perfect act. There is a determinate power for each natural agent, in accord with its type of nature, and failure to go beyond this power will not be a deficiency in power; such deficiency is found only when it falls short of the measure of power naturally due to it.

That deficiency finds expression not only in monsters of nature and of humanity, but in a lack of effort to understand the causes of those phenomena.

Thomas, like Augustine, played a key role in disseminating and assimilating ancient Greek philosophy—particularly that of Aristotle—for Christian contemplation. He too sees wonder as an activity of thought, but he also qualifies that proper wonder is a metaphysical search for causes and the 'first cause', God, as metaphysics was the first philosophy for Aristotle:

> ... there is naturally present in all men the desire to know the causes of whatever things are observed. Hence, because of wondering about things that were seen but whose causes were hidden, men first began to think philosophically; when they found the cause, they were satisfied. But the search did

not stop until it reached the first cause .... Therefore, man naturally desires, as his ultimate end, to know the first cause. But the first cause of all things is God. Therefore, the ultimate end of man is to know God (*Summa contra Gentiles* 3.25.11).

In seeking the first cause, God bestows *beatitudo* or a blessedness upon us that allows us to achieve a happiness in which we see God and all things in God (*Summa Theologicae, prima secundae* Q11.3–4). Curiosity, on the other hand, is a lesser form of happiness that can lead us to assume that our needs are met by consideration of subsidiary causes or sensible phenomena. In tune with Augustine, this settling for a lesser kind of happiness reflects weakness of will. Curiosity, we learn, is a form of sensual sloth as opposed to a form of rational engagement (*Summa Theologica, prima secundae* Q35.4).

Importantly, Thomas also sees curiosity as incomplete knowledge. This suggests that there is the opportunity for someone who rashly, lazily or ignorantly declares something to be a wonder—Thomas cites the example of a peasant's view of an eclipse of the sun—to develop a fuller understanding, will permitting. In the *prima secundae* of *Summa Theologica*, Thomas sets out in careful detail the ways in which intellect, will and wonder coalesce in reason. As a first step, the intellect apprehends a phenomenon. If the intellect does not know the cause of that phenomenon, wonder triggers the desire for inquiry (*Summa Theologica, prima secundae* Q3.8). This is in alignment with the metaphysical views of Plato and Aristotle. Wonder also quells pleasure because the intellect does not know the cause of the phenomenon (Q32.8). In a second step, the inquiry of intellect apprehends the phenomenon as good and wills it. This does not mean that the intellect will pursue action as a consequence of this willing: it still has to be judged whether the action would be sinful, or whether there are a range of actions available before any action is pursued.

Complexities of this process description aside, it is significant for our purposes because it clearly presents wonder as a part of rational deliberation and as a constraint on pleasure. Curiosity, conversely, is the result when the will gives in to pleasure. As the operation of will follows intellectual apprehension, curiosity is not of equal mental status to wonder. Rather, it is a result that can follow an experience of wonder. Thus, curiosity is subordinate to wonder.

In his account of reason, Thomas does not specify whether some intellectual pursuits or approaches to education are better than others in holding the temptations of curiosity at bay. That was to be more the focus of a contemporary of Thomas, the English philosopher and theologian Roger Bacon. Bacon's application of Aristotle's ideas was to be found primarily in the fields of mathematics, the natural sciences and linguistics. Bacon was heavily critical of the lack of commitment of academics to the practical improvement of society and their slavish conformity to conventional approaches to thought. These failings left the masses ignorant, and worse, tempted by the vanity of pseudo wisdom. Bacon outlined these concerns in general in his *Opus Maius*, but in the letter *Concerning the*

Marvellous Power of Art and Concerning the Nullity of Magic (hereafter *Concerning the Marvellous Power of Art*) he takes specific aim at wonder as the refuge of the lazy and the tool of the fraudulent and deceitful. As he argues:

> There are those who, by quickness of movement and by the appearance of the members, or by variations of the voice, or by subtlety of instruments, or by shadows, or by playing upon popular opinion, propound to mortals many wonders which do not have the truth of existence (p. 15).

Here we gain a sense of people performing in ways that aim deliberately to hold others in thrall. These performative acts include forms of writing as well as non verbal gestures: 'in order that no one shall suspect them, with allusions they build up high-sounding style and construct their mendacity under the form of a text' (*Concerning the Marvellous Power of Art*, p. 19). Wonder comes to be associated thus with stupefaction and obfuscation and is socially stratified. Peasants wonder, and the educated—who are often not wise—like to keep things that way:

> In this discussion distinction ought to be made between the common rabble and the wise who are sharply set off from it. For, whatever is believed by all is true, and similarly whatever is believed by wise men and examined carefully. Therefore beliefs which are held by the many, beliefs which are commonly held by the rabble, must necessarily be false—and I am speaking here of the rabble which is distinguished from the wise in this discussion .... In the common conceptions of the mind the crowd is in accord with the wise, but in the proper principles and conclusions of the arts and sciences it is discordant, and labouring with appearances runs off into sophisms and subtleties which the wise reject altogether. Thus the crowd is in error in its opinions of proper and secret qualities, and so is divided from the wise (*Concerning the Marvellous Power of Art*, p. 39).

The root of the problem, as Bacon saw it, was a tendency to rely on authority and on reason alone. The problem with authority is that it is a form of belief, not understanding, and reason alone cannot help us to discriminate between true claims and claims that *appear to be true* (*Compendium Studii Philosophiae*, 1.396). This, we recall, was Polybius' *topoi* problem. Bacon's proposed solution is threefold: start with the study of simple phenomena and progress to more complex matters; use and create texts with very simple and straightforward language; and be satisfied only with certainty that includes no doubt. The result is that we will begin to appreciate the causes of phenomena, and to filter through appeals to wonder (*Concerning the Marvellous Power of Art*, p. 26), much in the manner of Abelard of Bath (fl. 1116–42) in *Quaestiones naturales*:

> For the soul, imbued with wonder and unfamiliarity, when it considers from afar, with horror, the effects of things without causes, has never shaken off its

confusion. Look more closely, consider the circumstances, propose causes, and you will not wonder at the effects.[13]

Bacon explains this through his dissection of the apparently wonderful case of a long-lived farmer:

> A farmer who was tilling his field plowed up a golden flask filled with noble liquor, and, judging it to be the dew of heaven, he washed his face and drank with the result that he was renewed in body and spirit and in the goodness of wisdom—and from a ploughman he was made porter to the king of Sicily (p. 33–4)

Bacon navigates through the elements of the story, concluding that the prime cause for the farmer's long life was care for his health, not ancillary activities such as the discovery of a golden flask in a field. Long life thus arises from individual responsibility and is open to us all. Indeed even Aristotle would have lived longer, Bacon quips, had 'he not occupied himself with base pursuits' (*Concerning the Marvellous Power of Art*, p. 37).

Attention to scientific observation and cause and effect, however, does not necessarily mean the dissipation of all claims to wonder. Rather, Bacon proposes a new approach to wonder writing, one that respects the ingenuity of scientific thought in inventions such as nautical instruments, telescopes, perpetual lamps, gunpowder (*Concerning the Marvellous Power of Art*, p. 30). Bacon's examples might seem to hark back to Aristotle's example of an automaton in his *Metaphysics* (983a12–15) but each is included because they are understood rather than not understood. Wonder here is thus fundamentally associated with an understanding of the operations of reason, not its beginnings or its limits.

Across the writings of Augustine, Thomas, and Bacon we see agreement on the association of wonder with the intellect rather than the passions and the splitting off of curiosity as an incomplete operation of rationality that stems from weakness of will. I also noted, though, differences in their views on whether wonder is associated with the beginnings of the operations of reason. Importantly, too, I have suggested that each amplified the concept of wonder: arguing that its operation might have social as well as individual consequences (Augustine); that curiosity is rightfully considered as an incomplete subsidiary of wonder (Thomas); and that some academic activities are more likely to result in wonder than others (Bacon).

Although I have not offered a complete appraisal of medieval philosophies of practical reason, the highlights I have sketched above suggest that it was Augustine's positioning of wonder as a legitimate operation of intellect and as distinguished from curiosity that was relayed in the histories of Gerald and Gervase. This is not to say that their thoughts were in lock step with Augustine or indeed even with one another. In particular, I noted the divergence between Gerald and Gervase on the matter of whether the presentation of a variety of wonderful phenomenon and thus the assumption of singularity engages the intellect or fires curiosity. This leaves us to reconsider Bede.

Interior authenticity: ecclesiastical paradoxology

As Rüth has argued, hagiographies and miracle collections were not so much a standalone genre in medieval Europe as a functional element across a wide range of writings. Bede's *Ecclesiastical History of the English People*, for example, contains enough in the way of hagiographical elements to suggest that it functioned as a devotional as well as an historical work. An important question is to ask why, and to test whether there are any views on wonder in histories that were not transposed across to the wider functional element of hagiography and miracle collection or the other way around.

We recall from the previous chapter Polybius' difficulty in clearing space between history and paradoxography or wonder writing. A key part of this difficulty stemmed from paradoxographers employing similar or the same authenticity phrases such as 'I saw', 'I have often seen', or 'I have read'. This led Polybius to seek refuge through the interiorisation of wonder as an expression of mental effort. This was not particularly successful, because the signs of mental effort cannot always be reliably discerned.

In medieval Europe, the overlap in *topoi* between histories and Christian wonder works not only remained, but was kindled by ecclesiastical reforms contemporary with Gerald of Wales' *The History and Topography of Ireland*. These set out standard, judicial criteria for Church recognition of miracles and canonisation.[14] Satisfaction of these criteria was determined on the basis of witness interviews and written submissions. This shift prioritised manifest signs (*signa*) that an inexplicable, faith affirming phenomenon had been observed with wonder by observers. These changes were designed to shift recognition of saints and their wonders from local practices to those set by Rome. Canonisation became a slow, expensive and often quite political process, as Ronald Finucane has shown. But as Finucane has also noted, sworn depositions about miracles suggest that peasants and the elite had varying notions of how a miracle might be deemed authentic.[15] Moreover, by the time that canonisation processes were formally codified by Rome, it was already the case that written accounts of miracles reflected well-established *topoi* or methods that were used to construct and sustain argument. This meant that even if the formal process of canonisation was slow or even ultimately unsuccessful, miracle narratives could still be circulated and deemed authentic by their audiences.

Bede's *Ecclesiastical History of the English People* reflected and accentuated these *topoi* long before Papal reforms in the thirteenth century. We first see this in the preface, where he informs King Ceowulf that:

> In order to remove all occasions of doubt about these things written, either in your mind or in the minds of any others who listen to or read this history, I will make it my business to state briefly from what sources I have gained my information (Preface).

This is largely followed through in the body of the work, with just over half of the 76 miracle stories referring to written, eyewitness or unnamed sources. Other *topoi* include a description of location, the inclusion of any objects pertinent to the acts of the holy person (e.g. a staff, a church buttress) and a description of the wonder of others at the events. These markers of authenticity all have in common the assumption that the audience can go to the location, the sources, the objects, and the witness and check that the phenomena occurred in the way described.

What stands out about these methods of argument is that they function just as well in an historical work as they do in an ecclesiastical work. This is why Bede's work works as both. It might be argued therefore that historiography was ecclesiastical in the middle ages. But in so arguing, we find ourselves back at the dilemma experienced by Polybius. This is because it is possible to find these *topoi* used in non-miracle stories in medieval histories, such as Gervase's account of the bearded women of Scythia. A further exterior mark of function might be seen in the Papal acceptance of an account, but not all miracle stories were given such a mark of authenticity.

So we again find ourselves at the interiorisation of authenticity, which in the case of philosophy and the histories of Gerald and Gervase was marked out through the terms wonder and curiosity. Finding the signs of wonder versus curiosity was no less difficult for the audiences of medieval histories than it was for the audiences of ancient Greek histories and paradoxographies. The difference in this case, though, is that a judge in the form of God was able to sort the devotional from the sinful.

Still entangled

Medieval historians, like ancient Greek historians, saw history as an activity of sense making. Within that activity of sense making, the cognitive function of wonder assisted in the revelation and contemplation of the universal. In this way, the pursuit of metaphysical answers emphasised understanding of mind, or epistemology. Wonder also came to be seen as a restraint from the sinful interest of curiosity in sensible phenomena. There were, though, differences of opinion about whether inclusion of a wide range of 'strange' phenomena in histories would stimulate rational engagement or test the weakness of will that led to curiosity. Significantly, too, philosophers added to ancient Greek views on wonder, highlighting its social as well as individual implications, the steps in rational processes that determined whether wonder or curiosity would be achieved, and opportunities for developing rightful senses of wonder in the academic world. Finally, the overlap in *topoi* deployed in histories and paradoxologies from the ancient Greek world persisted, with recourse to God being the determinant of whether a writer had displayed rigorous, rational judgement.

In short, the metaphysical path that Polybius and ancient Greek historians charted was sustained in medieval historiography. History was concerned with universals, rigorous sense perception discerned those universals, and there were boundaries between the knowable and the unknowable. What differed was an enhanced interest in epistemology to detail how wonder worked, and to address the problem of judging other historians' claims that had left Polybius so perplexed.

Notes

1 Gabrielle Spiegel, *The Past as Text: The Theory and Practice of Medieval Historiography*, Baltimore, MD: Johns Hopkins University Press, 1999, p. 100.
2 Spiegel, *The Past as Text*, p. 101.
3 Caroline W. Bynum, *Metamorphosis and Identity*, New York: Zone Books, 2001, pp. 37–76; and A. Rüth, 'Representing Wonder in Medieval Miracle Narratives', *Modern Language Notes*, 2011, vol. 126(4), pp. 89–114.
4 Aviad Kleinberg, 'Proving Sanctity: Selection and Authentication of Saints in the Later Middle Ages', *Viator*, 1989, vol. 20, pp. 183–205.
5 Neil Manson, 'Epistemic Restraint and the Vice of Curiosity', *Philosophy*, 2012, vol. 87, pp. 239–59.
6 Amelia Lynn Borrego Sargent, 'Gerald of Wales' Topographical Hibernica: Dates, Versions, Readers', *Viator*, 2012, vol. 43(1), pp. 293–92. The online York text translated by Forester and Wright is referred to in this chapter as it provides a fuller version of the work than the Penguin translation.
7 Caroline W. Bynum, *Metamorphosis and Identity*, pp. 77–111; and L. Daston and K. Park, *Wonders and the Order of Nature 1150–1750*, New York: Zone Books, 2001, p. 27.
8 Lorraine Daston and Katharine Park, *Wonders and the Order of Nature 1150–1750*, pp. 25–7.
9 Orosius, *Seven Books of History Against the Pagans*, trans. A.T. Fear, Liverpool, UK: Liverpool University Press, 2010.
10 Isidore of Seville, *Etymologies*, trans. S.A. Barney and W.J. Lewis, J.A. Beach, O. Berghof, Cambridge: Cambridge University Press, 2006.
11 Solinus, *The Excellent and Pleasant Worke of Iulius Solinus Polyhistor contayning the noble actions of humaine creatures, the secretes and providence of nature, the description of countries, the manners of the people: with many mervailous things and strange antiquities, seruing for the benefit and recreations of all sorts of persons*, trans. A. Golding, London: I. Charlewoode for Thomas Hacket, 1587. This remains the most recent English translation of this work and I have modernised the English in quotations. Quotation numbers refer to chapter numbers.
12 Axel Rüth, 'Representing Wonder in Medieval Miracle Narratives', p. S93.
13 Abelard of Bath, *Adelard of Bath, Conversations with His Nephew: On the Same and the Different, Questions on Natural Science and On Birds*, trans. and ed. C. Burnett, Cambridge: Cambridge University Press, 1999.
14 Jacques Le Goff, *The Medieval Imagination*, Chicago, IL: University of Chicago Press, 1988; and M. Goodrich, *Miracles and Wonders: The Development of the Concept of Miracle 1150–1350*, Aldershot: Ashgate, 2007.
15 Ronald C. Finucane, *Contested Canonizations: The Last Medieval Saints, 1482–1523*, Washington, D.C.: Catholic University of America Press, 2011, pp. 14–15.

References

Aquinas, Thomas, *Summa Theologica, prima secundae*, Ottawa, Canada: University of Ottawa Press, 1944.
Aquinas, Thomas, *Summa Contra Gentiles*, trans. V.J. Bourke, Notre Dame, IN: University of Notre Dame Press, 1975.
Augustine of Hippo, Two Books on Genesis against the Manichees, in *Saint Augustine on Genesis*, trans. R.J. Teske, Washington, D.C.: Catholic University of America Press, 1991.
Augustine of Hippo, *City of God Against the Pagans*, trans. R.W. Dyson, Cambridge: Cambridge University Press, 1998.
Augustine of Hippo, *Confessions*, trans. H. Chadwick, Oxford: Oxford University Press, 2009.

Bacon, Roger, *Concerning the Marvelous Power of Art and of Nature and Concerning the Nullity of Magic*, London: Williams and Norgate, 1923.
Bede, *Ecclesiastical History of the English People*, trans L. Sherley-Price and R.E. Latham, Harmondsworth: Penguin, 1990.
Gerald of Wales, *The History and Topography of Ireland*, trans T. Forester and T. Wright, full text available online at: www.yorku.ca/inpar/topography_ireland.pdf <accessed 21 September 2014>.
Gervase of Tilbury, *Otia Imperialia*, trans S.E. Banks and J.W. Binns, Oxford: Oxford University Press, 2002.

3

THE WONDERS OF HISTORY IN THE PRE-MODERN ISLAMIC WORLD

Al Tusi | Al Qazwini | Al Tabari | Ibn Khaldun | Ibn Sina | Ibn Rushd

'Abd-ar-Rahman Abu Zayd Muhammad Ibn Khaldun (1332–1406) has long been celebrated as a theorist of history with few or no equals. His is a well-established reputation built upon arguments in the *Muqaddimah* for systematic thinking over 'blind trust in tradition' and a refusal to allow history to 'move or charm the reader', 'moralise or convince', or to 'serve any administration or government' (*Muqaddimah*, I:78, 79). Yet Ibn Khaldun can still surprise us. This capacity for surprise stems in part from the relative neglect of the much larger work for which the *Muqaddimah* serves as an introduction: the *Kitab al-'Ibar* ('History of the World'). Ibn Khaldun was not only a theoretician; he also applied that theory in an extensive description of historical phenomena. Yet reflections on Ibn Khaldun's *Kitab* are sparse. Moreover, as this chapter will also show, analyses of the *Muqaddimah* are also quite selective. Ibn Khaldun is not just the progenitor of a cyclical theory of civilisational growth and decline, and of a rational, critical approach to the writing of history. The *Muqaddimah* also outlines for us an account of wonder (*'ajab*) as an affective and physiological experience which connects the sensible, particular world with that of the universal realm of God.

What role is there for surprise or even wonder in writing the history of historiography? In chapter one, we followed Polybius as he set down three judgements about the idea of history that intersected with the interests of metaphysicians. History concerned universals, those universals were discerned through rigorous sensory perception, and there was a boundary between the knowable and the unknowable set by the limits of his visual perception. We saw him struggle to deal with the question of whether claims made by historians were made in good or in bad faith, and he opted for a plain writing style, infrequent recourse to wonder for his own claims, and the application of a claim of wonder against the ideas of others which he did not trust. He shared a mutual interest in the questions of metaphysicians and worked himself into a tangle with wonder writers via his adoption of wonder *topoi*. Chapter two outlined some subtle shifts in medieval historiography and metaphysics that presented devotional acts of wonder as a means of accessing the universal. Polybius' call for self-regulation in historical knowledge claims was still needed, but God became the judge of whether it had been achieved in good faith. We might not be able to discriminate between the efforts of an historian and a paradoxographer, but God can. Historiography changed, but not in a way that would have made Theaetetus' 'head swim'.

Still, there was a sense of the relationship between history and metaphysics as generative, of authors in both fields introducing and addressing questions that suggested an enhanced, more detailed or even better understanding of how to make general sense of things. Some of these writers saw themselves as describing the actual structure of our thought about the world, whilst others had a more playful take on recounting the past. Regardless, metaphysics and historiography iterated. In this chapter we turn to pre-modern Islamic historiography (roughly pre-1500 CE), which is rarely, if ever, explored in introductory histories of history or general historiographical texts. An obvious explanation lies with translation: few Islamic histories of the pre-modern world have been translated out of Arabic, let alone translated into English. Even better known texts have only been translated in part. It is for this reason that the introductory bibliography for this chapter contains textual fragments and one translation into German rather than English. These translations are invaluable, and this valuable work is finally gathering some pace in the English-speaking world. But there might be another, more substantive reason why Islamic historiography is neglected in Western texts, which has to do with its having been characterised as fundamentally conservative rather than innovative. Consider, for example, the judgement of Chase Robinson in *Islamic Historiography*:

> Put very schematically, traditionalist cultures such as medieval Islam and Rabbinic Judaism hold that knowledge is better conserved than it is created. In particular, they hold that the best kind of knowledge is the wisdom of pious and inspired forefathers, which, whether recorded in their day or generated retrospectively by subsequent generations, can validate and guide the experience of the present. As distrustful of creativity as they are convinced of the inerrancy of those who came before them, traditionalists are generally critical about the present and nostalgic about a 'golden age' when men, acting in accordance with fresh truths, accomplished great things. They do not revere the past; they revere a past, and although the length and character of this past differs from culture to culture, there is always an ever-widening gap between the time of inspiration (or revelation) on the one hand, and the present time of decay, on the other.[1]

It appears that on the basis of this appraisal that this will be a reiterative chapter on the relationship between history and metaphysics, or at least a disappointing read beyond a consideration of Ibn Khaldun's contribution. Robinson's judgment needs further scrutiny, however, because it turns on an underlying assumption about the relative importance of what is called *hadith* in Islamic historiography. *Hadith* refers to the corpus of knowledge we have of Muhammad's ideas, including the chains of transmission (*isnads*) through which that knowledge has passed, the transmitters themselves, and the styles of transmission. This is more than a Biblical 'x begat y', as might be found in the medieval Christian histories explored in the last chapter. The introduction to Muhammad ibn Jarir al Tabari's (838–923 CE) 39 volume *History of the Prophets and Kings* provides us with a stark example. Here is one part of a twenty-page *isnad* which outlines the views of Muhammad on the comparatively short lifetime of individuals compared to that of nations:

> According to Khallad b. Aslam—al-Nadr b. Shumayl—Shu'bah—Qatadah—Anas b. Malik: The Messenger of God said: When I was sent, I and the Hour were like these two. We were told by the same Mujahid b. Musa—Yazid—Shu'bah—Qatadah—Anas b. Malik—the Prophet, with the addition in this hadith: and he pointed with the middle and index fingers.
> According to Muhammad b. 'Abdallah b. 'Abd al-Hakam—Ayyub b. Suwayd—al-Awza'i—Isma'il b. 'Ubaydallah: When Anas b. Malik came to al-Walid b. 'Abd al-Malik, al-Walid asked him: What have you heard the Messenger of God mention about the Hour? Anas replied: I heard the Messenger of God say: You (pl.) and the Hour are like these two—pointing with his two fingers (I: 178).

Over and over again we explore variations of interpretation of Muhammad's words, culminating with al Tabari's summary judgment on the most persuasive chain of transmission.

Al Tabari's apparent predilection for *isnads* results in a history of the world that Robinson appraises as preserving rather than as generative.[2] It does not advance knowledge of the past; it secures knowledge of the most acceptable version of a past. This description of al Tabari's work does suggest that Ibn Khaldun's *Muqaddimah* might be an outlier in Islamic historiography. Ibn Khaldun not only uses far fewer *isnads*; he also criticises mistakes that arise from uncritical acceptance of *isnads*.

We must remember, however, that the *Muqaddimah* is simply the methodological preface to an historical work that does contain *isnads*. Moreover, *hadith* is not the sole means by which we can judge the efforts of Islamic historians. There is another story about transmission that this chapter seeks to tell. Given the direction of the narrative in this book so far, which has emphasised the role of sensory perception in discerning universals, it is a surprising one. That story has as its focus not the corpus of knowledge we have of Muhammad's ideas, but the corpus of knowledge we have of Aristotle's ideas. As I will argue, Ibn Khaldun's account of wonder in the *Muqaddimah* locates him in a pre-modern world in which ancient Greek and Islamic ideas coalesced. The first major meeting of these two traditions followed the absorption of Hellenistic colonies in the Umayyad empire (661–750 CE). By the time of the Abbasid empire (750–1258 CE), nearly all of Aristotle's texts had been translated into Arabic. A well known exception to this was

Aristotle's *Politics*, with the reason for its exclusion from the translated corpus still being unknown.[3] A lesser known exception, but a critical one for our purposes, was the first half of the first book of Aristotle's *Metaphysics*. This book, we recall from chapter one, introduced the idea of philosophy as beginning with wonder. Seven, or possibly even eight renderings of the *Metaphysics* were produced in the major waves of Arabic translation between the ninth and tenth centuries. None of these translations include the first half of the first book, which means that it was not considered by key Islamic philosophers such as Abu Nasr al Farabi (872–950 CE), Abu 'Ali al-Husayn Ibn Sina (also known as Avicenna) (980–1037 CE) and Abu I-Walid Muhammad Ibn 'Ahmad Ibn Rushd (also known as Averroes) (1126–1198). Nor is there evidence of it being available through other intermediaries, whether they were philosophers or any other kinds of writers. As Amos Bertolacci has observed, the focus of Arabic translators and commentators on Aristotle's *Metaphysics* was on the sections in which Aristotle set out his views on natural theology and Plato's forms. These sections aligned most closely with contemporary Arabic discussions on theology and Platonism.[4]

If the opening sections of Aristotle's *Metaphysics* were not available to philosophers, this means they were also not available to other writers such as historians and paradoxologists. Nor is there any evidence to suggest that Islamic thinkers arrived at a similar view of wonder independently. Pre-modern Islamic histories simply do not consider the idea of philosophy as beginning with wonder. Yet pre-modern Islamic historiography, paradoxology and metaphysics do not lack for references to wonder. As we shall see in this chapter, Ibn Khaldun establishes a place for wonder in the apprehension of God's creation. For his, as for other pre-modern Islamic accounts of wonder, we have to give primary credit to Arabic translations of another work by Aristotle, the *Poetics*.

Up until now, Aristotle's *Poetics* has lurked behind the scenes of this book, taking a back seat to a consideration of the general sense of things articulated in *Metaphysics*. Indeed it might be argued that I dismissed poetry all too abruptly in chapter one. In this chapter I bring the *Poetics* to the forefront, and with it, affective and physiological notions of wonder. Moreover, I will argue that the Arabic translation of *Poetics* from a Syriac intermediary text epitomises 'the strange and the transferred, the altered, and the foreign' uses of language that Ibn Rushd pinpointed as triggers for wonder.[5] This is largely uncharted territory in historiography, taking us from Ibn Khaldun's well-known thoughts on history as both form and substance to his assertion of affective and charismatic experiences of wonder in prophecy. Ibn Khaldun's thoughts on wonder, I will argue, help us to relocate him in a world in which paradoxographers, historians and metaphysicians not only saw the experience of wonder as the means of revealing the universal in the particular, but as the main means for judging the beauty of speech. In these ways, I hope to show that Islamic historiography is not an act of conservation, but rather a wonder of creation, and one that guides our attention towards European views of wonder as a passion needing to be controlled.

In summary, in pre-modern Islamic historiography we will discern the same interest in history as a means for discerning universals. We'll see a different take on sensory perception, one that inverts Polybius' hierarchical arrangement of knowledge by certainty for earthly experiences, but one that upholds it in the case of prophets who gain access to universal knowledge in connection with God. We'll see a permeable boundary between the knowable and the unknowable, made possible by the argument that some individuals can get closer to God's will via a rapturous, affective experience of wonder. And we'll learn that wondrous forms of writing—as seen in poetry—help us learn not only about what is, but also about what might be. That's probably different enough from the previous chapters to make all of our heads swim, but it reinforces the picture I have been building of history and metaphysics as intertwined.

Blades with scabbards: history as form and substance

Ibn Khaldun's *Kitab* is made up of three books: the first treats the nature of history and society, the second the history of the Arabs and the third the history of the Berbers. In the foreword to the first book, the *Muqaddimah*, Ibn Khaldun stakes his claim to a systematic analysis of history and society:

> I chose a remarkable and original method. In the work, I commented on civilisation, on urbanisation, and on the essential characteristics of human social organisation, in a way that explains to the reader how and why things are as they are. … As a result, he will wash his hands of any blind trust in tradition. (I:11)

Other works of history are 'absurd' by comparison, reflecting 'partisanship for opinions and schools', uncritical 'reliance upon transmitters', 'unfounded assumptions as to the truth of a thing', and a fawning attitude towards people of wealth and rank (I:9–71). This is because historians are tempted by the 'idle talk of storytellers' or rhetoricians (I:75). By this, Ibn Khaldun means a lazy satisfaction in the literal, sensible appearances of phenomena—including the claims of earlier historians—over a relentless search for the 'essence' of civilization that is 'inspired by God' (I:77, 83). The result is history as form without substance, like a blade without a scabbard:

> [Historians disregard] the changes in conditions and in the customs of nations and races that the passing of time had brought about. Thus, they present historical information about dynasties and stories of events from the early period as mere forms without substance, blades without scabbards, as knowledge that must be considered ignorance, because it is not known what of it is extraneous and what is genuine. (I:9)

These historians, Ibn Khaldun argues, have forgotten to 'pay attention to historiography's purpose', which is to get to the 'inner meaning' of historical events (I:63). This entails, as he explains:

speculation and an attempt to get at the truth, subtle explanation of the causes and origins of existing things, and deep knowledge of the how and why of events. History, therefore, is firmly rooted in philosophy. It deserves to be accounted a branch of philosophy. (I:6)

In order to get to the truth, historians must look to the social, political, economic, cultural and physical conditions that explain the rise and fall of *'umran* or civilisations (I: 11). When they look at *'umran* in this way, history ceases to be a branch of rhetoric and takes on the interest of metaphysical philosophy in universals.

Ibn Khaldun's invitation for us to consider universals is backed up with an extensive analysis of how we can achieve knowledge of God's creation. Much of this analysis is found in chapter six of the *Muqaddimah*, but there are also passages of particular interest to us in the sixth prefatory discussion. In agreement with Aristotle, Ibn Khaldun sees it as being in the nature of humans to seek knowledge. In distinction from Aristotle, however, Ibn Khaldun does not see knowledge as arising from the rendering of the familiar as strange through wonder. Rather, he sees us as building upon the knowledge claims of those before us, or those who know more than us. This means *hadith*, including consideration of chains of transmitters (*isnads*), the transmitters themselves (*ruwat*) and the *topoi* and technical nomenclature of acts of transmission (*istilahat*) (II:448–9). Respect for *hadith* does not entail blind acceptance, though, for Ibn Khaldun sees us as only achieving knowledge when we appraise transmission in a critical fashion.

As chains are only as strong as their links, so *isnads* are only as strong as the knowledge claims from which they are built. Strong *isnads* use multiple, independent knowledge claims for each link. Weaker *isnads* have missing links or links that rest on dubious or unverifiable claims. An *isnad* is therefore not automatically authoritative, and nor is the length of an *isnad* an indication of authenticity or certainty. Neither the historian nor the historian's reader can accept knowledge that has been handed down. Through acts of 'disparaging and authenticating', they learn to discern the truth of *isnads* by critically analysing the approach, probity, accuracy, thoroughness and care of transmitters (II:449).

In chapter one, we learnt of Polybius' insistence that we should trust only knowledge seen with our own eyes. This reduced the scope of history to an activity in which we make sense of contemporary or recent events. Ibn Khaldun's view of history differs markedly in that he is prepared to consider the knowledge claims of others, past and present. This is because the methods of *hadith* include the search for multiple accounts of the same event, testing whether a writer is reliable across a range of claims, and a consideration of the form *and* content of claims. Claims put through this level of scrutiny could provide a more certain account of events than our own unexamined perceptual experiences. As Plato cautioned, we place our own knowledge claims beyond question at our own peril. Moreover, while Ibn Khaldun sees some forms of knowledge as being more certain than others, his hierarchy does not culminate with eyewitness evidence of sensible, worldly events. His view is the inverse of that promoted by Polybius: perceptual sense making focused on worldly phenomena is only seen as a preliminary step in understanding (II:412–3). The highest form of knowledge is that achieved through a direct, prophetic connection with God (I: 184, 196). Prophetic connection with God is beyond the reach of most of us: only some individuals of naturally good and innocent character are chosen to know the universal and to instruct others in salvation (I: 184–5).

Apprehension of the universal is attained via what Ibn Khaldun characterises as a 'leap' into the angelic realm (I: 199). That leap, though, is not one into inimitability, for God has to bring the universal 'down to the level of human perceptions' and translate inner perception to external sense perceptions (I: 184; 192–3; 196) which take the form of

> some speech sound the person (who receives the revelation) hears and is able to understand, or in the [visual] form of an individual delivering the message to him. (I: 185; 200)

Of these sense perceptions, vision lends itself to more perfect knowledge than hearing in that it is clearer to the prophet and thus more readily transmitted to others (I: 216). God communicating through sound, however, is more readily understood by humans (I: 200). None of the senses are ultimately suited for the perfect apprehension of the universal, however, because of their corporeality. This is because the body is subject to fatigue (I: 210). Vision is thus not the pinnacle of knowledge making, but more of a reminder of our limitations in trying to discern the designs of God.

Wonder also plays a role in the transmission of prophetic knowledge. This is not wonder in the Polybian sense of us having exhausted all other attempts at explanation, or even the cognitive search for first causes favoured by Aquinas. Rather, it is an affective, physiological state of inspiration in which we see the prophet faint, swoon, choke, sweat or fall into a state of catatonia:

> In the state of inspiration, they seem to be removed from those who are present. This is accompanied by a feeling of being choked that looks like swooning or unconsciousness but has nothing to do with either. In reality, it is an immersion in (and) encounter with the spiritual kingdom …. During that (process, the person that receives the revelation) shows inexplicable signs of strain and choking (I:185; see also 201–2).

All of these physiological signs highlight not mastery of, but removal from the ordinary, material world. In this state of immersion, prophets are able to work wonders that reinforce the truthfulness of their claims at connection with God.

Wonders are defined as actions that are non-customary and impossible for other humans to achieve, and are interchangeable with the idea of miracles (I: 188; 190). The wonders of prophets are unusual, such as 'ascending to heaven, passing through solid bodies, reviving the dead, conversing with angels, and flying through the air' (I: 191). False wonders are by Ibn Khaldun's reckoning impossible, because wonders imply 'confirmation of truthfulness and right guidance' (I: 190). Beyond this circular suggestion, the idea of false claims to wonder are given no brook. Nor can the miracles of the inspired person be confused with the claims of the insane, for the latter have corrupt humours and are not deeply immersed in the senses or are completely removed from sensory perception (I: 218).

Reconciling Ibn Khaldun's critical view on 'disparaging' *isnads* with his appreciation of the wonders of prophetic immersion in the angelic realm seems difficult. An understandable temptation for those trying to reconcile these views is to note that Ibn Khaldun's views on wonder and prophetic knowledge are confined to the sixth prefatory discussion of the *Muqaddimah*. This makes it all too easy to dismiss the views as marginal to the work, or conversely, to argue for a rational Ibn Khaldun and a religious Ibn Khaldun. In so arguing, we miss an important point raised by Ahmad: that the interplay of philosophical and religious thought is a hallmark of pre-modern Islamic writing.[6]

Ahmad's conclusion is that Ibn Khaldun's efforts ultimately tip in the direction of religious affirmation. It is important to note, though, that Ahmad's view is based on an analysis of chapter six of the *Muqaddimah* alone. A wider textual analysis rewards us with insight into a critical feature shared across Islamic history, paradoxography and metaphysics: that the relation of religion and philosophy is the ultimate responsibility of the reader, not the writer. This view, which will be unpacked in the remainder of this chapter, provides an interesting counterpoint to the all-seeing, judgemental God that was needed in the European medieval histories to provide a caution against the shift from wonder to unconstrained, sinful curiosity. This makes me question whether wonder can be explained epistemologically without recourse to metaphysics. Do we need something like Plato's forms, or God, or an angelic realm to achieve a level of comfort in seeking recourse to wonder? Or, put more simply, do we need something other than ourselves to achieve certain knowledge? This is the point at which we note that the absence of Aristotle's metaphysical claim for wonder is not a lack in Islamic thought, but a great opportunity to be surprised three chapters into this story.

A poetic turn

Our starting point for considering Ibn Khaldun in context is the Persian historian who appears to be his conservative inverse: al Tabari. While much has been written in praise of Ibn Khaldun's views on history, al Tabari has attracted very little scholarly attention. Moreover, what little has been written about him is hardly complimentary: we recall Robinson's judgement that he sought to conserve a particular view of the past, rather than to create one.

Robinson's appraisal is understandable. The introduction to al Tabari's 39 volume *History of the Prophets and Kings* hardly inspires confidence that we are in the presence of a creative or even prophetic thinker:

The reader should know that with respect to all I have mentioned and made it a condition to set down in this writing of ours I rely upon traditions and reports which I have transmitted and which I attribute to their transmitters. I rely only very exceptionally upon what is learned through rational arguments and deduced by internal thought processes. For no knowledge of the history of men of the past and of recent men and events is attainable by those who were not able to observe them and did not live in their time, except through information and transmission provided by informants and transmitters. This cannot be brought out by reason or deduced by internal thought processes. This writing of mine may [be found to] contain some information, mentioned by us on the authority of certain men of the past, which the reader may disapprove of and the listener may find detestable, because he can find nothing sound and no real meaning in it. In such cases, he should know that it is not our fault that such information comes to him, but the fault of someone who transmitted it to us. We have merely reported it as it was reported to us (I: 170).

Sentence by sentence, al Tabari appears to position himself as the servant of his transmitters. He is a reporter rather than a judge, relying on a world created by others.

Or is he? The absence of a prefatory discussion to *History of the Prophets and Kings* makes it all too easy to conclude that al Tabari did not have—or want to have— command over the claims in his work. On this measure, the *History of the Prophets and Kings* is clearly not the *Muqaddimah*. Yet al Tabari's work is not constructed without care, and it does not lack for deliberation. It is simply the case that we have to read all of *History of the Prophets and Kings* to discern al Tabari's views. This was one of the salient lessons of chapter one: that historiography is not a prefatory activity alone. One of the things that Polybius taught us is that you have to look throughout a work of history to gain a sense of an author's stance on the discipline. This is the idea of historiography by examples.

A close reading of *History of the Prophets and Kings* rewards us with a view of wonder quite unlike anything we have seen in this work so far. While there are only seventeen substantive references to wonder (*'ajab*) across the 39 volumes, they are very unevenly distributed. Half are to be found in volumes one to six, and the other half are to be found in volumes 29 to 32. The references to wonder in volumes one to six align reasonably well with Ibn Khaldun's idea of prophetic knowledge. As al Tabari puts it in volume four, God shows us wonders 'only to complete the proofs of his [manifest existence] for you' (4: 806). These are exceptional phenomena such as eclipses (1: 68) and the parting of the sea (3: 418, 421) and they serve to take us from 'eavesdropping to overhear God's inspiration' to direct revelation. We gain the sense that questioning these phenomena amounts to questioning the existence of God. This would explain in part al Tabari's deference to his sources in his prefatory comments and would likely see us conclude that he opted for religious apprehension over rational deliberation. These are views on wonder that are not unexpected given our earlier analysis of Ibn Khaldun. From volume 29, though, a textual transformation occurs: the *History of the Kings and Prophets* takes a turn towards the poetic. The frequency of poetic segments increases, and those segments include claims to wonder. Consider these poetic extracts from volumes 29, 31 and 32, which are worth quoting at length given how unknown al Tabari's work is today:

> What a wonder is the changing of affairs
> pleasing and unpleasing.
> Time plays with men
> and has running occurrences.
> Because of Ya'qub b. Dawud,
> the ropes of Mu'awiyah are fraying.
> The disasters from 'Afiyah have infringed upon Ibn 'Ulathah the qadi.
> Say to the wazir Abu 'Ubaydallah,
> "Do you have a future?"
> Ya'qub is looking into affairs, and you are looking sideways.
> You introduced him, and he rose above you.
> That is the real inauspiciousness. (29: 464–5)
> Why should we weep for you? Why?—because of [your] raptures,
> Abu Muss [alAmin]? because of [your] promoting of amusement?
> Because of [your] omission of the five [prayers] in their times,
> in your eagerness for the juice of the grape?
> For Shanif I do not weep;
> as for Kawthar, the thought of his death gives me no grief.
> You did not know what was the measure of [God's] pleasure,
> nor did you know the measure of [His] wrath.
> You were not fit to rule,
> and the Arabs did not grant you obedience as ruler.
> You who weep for him, may the eye
> of whoever caused you to weep have wept only for wonder!
> Why should we weep for you?—because you exposed us
> to manjaniqs, and at times to being plundered,
> And to people who made us their slaves—
> because of them the tail seeks to gain power over the head—
> In torment and wasting siege
> that blocked the roads, so that there was no way to [obtain]
> one's needs? (31: 939)
> Praise be to God for the authority which he has given to you since you departed from your specified purpose!
> Indeed, we and all our dependents remind ourselves with pride of your conduct in engaging in battle and granting peace, and we show immense wonder at the qualities bestowed on him ['Abdallah] [by God] of severity and leniency in their appropriate places.

> We do not know of any ruler over a body of soldiers or subjects who acts so equitably between them as you do, nor of
> anyone who grants forgiveness, to persons who have
> caused harm or shown rancor towards him, from a position of superior strength as you do. How rarely do we see a
> nobly descended person who does not give up control of
> his affairs [that is, throw away his own personal talent or potential], relying rather upon what his forefathers have
> passed on to him! And the one who is given good fortune, material sufficiency, ruling authority and governmental
> power does not simply cleave
> what has fallen to his
> share in abundant quantity, so that he falls short in being able to cope with what is before him. (32: 1097)

The first extract—from volume 29—suggests a view of the past akin to Polybius' historical sense making. In this case, we look beyond the experiences of particular individuals and discern how changes in leadership can influence the fortunes of groups. The final line also makes it clear that antecessors can overshadow predecessors. Neither of these claims indicates a conservative disposition: the historian is capable of discerning the universal across sequences of particulars, and the future may overshadow the past. The second and third extracts—from books 31 and 32 respectively—make it clear that wonder is rightfully used to describe exceptional events. To be clear, these uses of wonder do not mark a bold departure from those of the ancient Greek philosophers in chapter one of this book. What is unusual is their appearance in poetry. Some of these poems are by other authors, but some reflect the hand of al Tabari. Moreover, it is important to note that wonder makes its appearance *only* in poetry in the later volumes of *History of the Prophets and Kings*. Is it by accident that wonder is clothed in verse?

The wonders of creation

Al Tabari does not explain his use of poetic extracts to account for contemporary events in the *History of the Prophets and Kings*. It is a textual shift that only becomes apparent when you look at the work as a whole. As such, it is a salutary reminder of how little we might be able to conclude about Ibn Khaldun's views of history by reading the *Muqaddimah* alone. Moreover, the lack of explanation for this shift within the *History of the Prophets and Kings* encourages us to look to other text types to see if we can discern whether this was something al Tabari did on his own, or as part of a wider body of thought. A good place to start are the intertwined interests of paradoxologists and then metaphysicians.

Persis Berlekamp has demonstrated that there was an outpouring of Arabic, Persian and Turkish paradoxologies or wonder works between the thirteenth and nineteenth centuries that worked to induce wonder (*'ajab*) as a sense of astonishment at the Divine.[7] How wonder connects—if at all—to the nature, scope, certainty and sources of knowledge—is something that Berlekamp leaves us to discern from a contemplation from the texts themselves. The best known of these works is the *Wonders of Creation and Oddities of Existence* (hereafter *Wonders*) by the thirteenth-century Persian writer Abu Yahya Zakariya' ibn Muhammad al Qazwini (1203–83). Al Qazwini's work, in turn, appears to have been influenced by Muhammad ibn Mahmud ibn Ahmad al Tusi's text of the same name.[8]

Al Qazwini's carefully structured account of the universe opens with four prefaces on the key terms of the title. In al Qazwini's muqaddimah, wonder is defined as 'the astonishment that befalls a person because he lacks knowledge about the cause of a thing or knowledge of its effects' (p. 26).[9] This he explains through the example of a beehive, the geometric properties of which seem remarkable given that bees do not have a knowledge of mathematics or make use of a compass or ruler. The efforts of bees are a sign of God's work in the world—they are a wonder of God's creation—and our wonder is an avenue to contemplation of God. All of creation may evoke wonder, from the actions of people to stars, rocks and trees, animals and insects. Phenomena do not need to be what Qazwini calls 'oddities': unusual or unheard of phenomena such as monsters or different kinds of angels to stimulate contemplation of God (pp. 234–42). The only limit to our ability to wonder at God's creation comes from our treatment of phenomena as familiar: for example, as al Qazwini notes in the case of camels, we see them so often that they are no longer considered strange. The limits of wonder are thus not limits of explanation, but limits in our capacity to be struck by the remarkable works of God.

Travis Zadeh has seen in al Qazwini's *Wonders* an affinity with ancient Greek paradoxographical wonder works.[10] Although an interesting idea, Qazwini's work diverges in approach from the ancient Greek texts in at least two significant ways. First, his definition of wonder is far more inclusive than the unusual and unique items highlighted by Greek writers. This difference is deliberate and important: Qazwini sees the limits of wonder as set only by the reader's capacity for astonishment, not by the judgement of the author about which particular phenomena are to be explained by recourse to wonder. All phenomena reflect the work of God, therefore all phenomena can trigger the experience of wonder. Second, Qazwini's account of the features of the known universe is prefaced by comments on the nature, reliability and limits of knowledge. It is not simply a list of phenomena of the kind we see in ancient Greek texts. Consequently, his use of textual markers—*topoi*—to signal the source and quality of the information is part of a more systemic consideration of the nature of knowledge. His prefatory remarks outline preferences for the acquisition of knowledge, and underline the chief message of the work: that contemplation of God flows from the sight of the reader.

As with Ibn Khaldun and al Tabari, Qazwini's reflections on knowledge stem from a consideration of *hadith*, but they also reflect the preference of Ibn Khaldun and ancient Greek historians for evidence attained by sight. Sight can be spiritual as well as literal, as al Qazwini explains:

> The inner eye of insight opens to him and he sees every aspect of wonder, the mention of which is impossible to articulate completely, for even if he expressed just a bit of it to someone else, this other person would not believe him (p. 27).

Here we see sight positioned as preferential to speech. This preference for sight, though, does not stem from the insistence of ancient Greek writers like Polybius that we can trust only the things that we see. Rather, al Qazwini and Ibn Khaldun prefer sight on the grounds that it is the most effective means for God to communicate to humans. This makes it clear that the way that the reader sees the text is critical, as he explains:

> I call God the Almighty as witness that there is nothing from these [marvels], which I have invented. Rather, I have written everything down as I have come across them. If you look at these [marvels] with an accepting eye, then [the eye] would be dimmed to every defect. But if you viewed [them] with an eye of indignation, then the shortcomings would be many. The eye of the generous is blind to the blemishes and his ear is deaf to the shortcomings (p. 5).

While al Qazwini's commitment to accuracy is a necessary condition for the contemplation of the works of God, this extract suggests that his work serves as a base condition for the efforts of the reader. The reader is not passive; the same text may be considered with an 'accepting eye' or with an 'eye of indignation'. This is an interesting point: we can well imagine being struck by one passage in one reading of a text, and by another passage in a subsequent reading. Such a variation in experience lends weight to the view more explicitly articulated in Ibn Khaldun's *Muqaddimah* that any dependence on corporeality will mean that human knowledge of God is not inimitable.

If reader engagement is the primary determinant for the experience of wonder, then we might well expect that al Qazwini treats the reliability of other's claims to knowledge—like his own—as a background or even ancillary consideration in the development of knowledge. This is the case, with him clearly telling us not to get caught up on trying to verify everything we read or hear. If God is capable of anything, then our minds have to be open to the possibility of encountering anything. Think about it rationally, he instructs us:

> I have mentioned matters which the disposition of a negligent idiot might reject, but that the soul of a rational man could not deny. Although these affairs may be far from well-known customs and ordinarily witnessed events, nothing should be deemed too great for the power of the Creator or the cunning of creation and everything therein. They are the marvels of the art of the Creator, which are either perceivable by the senses or intelligible by the intellect, for which there can be no doubt or imperfection concerning them;

or they are elegant tales ascribed to transmitters, for which I have no responsibility concerning their authenticity; or they are strange properties for which a lifetime would not be enough to test them, and thus it would make little sense to ignore all of them, since there is doubt concerning just some of them (pp. 4–5).

You could expend a lifetime trying to explain a phenomenon, worry about the accuracy of reports of phenomena from distant places and quibble with the rhetorical flourishes of historians, or you could appreciate rationally that God is remarkable. This does not mean that al Qazwini is skeptical about the knowledge claims of others, or that he has no respect for *hadith*. His thoughts are simply a reminder that the experience of wonder in God's creation is our responsibility.

Al Qazwini's views on knowledge set out contours of argument that are also present in Ibn Khaldun. Both suggest that all manner of phenomena may be explained by recourse to wonder on the grounds that they are the work of God. Both privilege sight as a means of contemplating the acts of God, and both see corporeality as ruling out the inimitability of human knowledge. Yet al Qazwini and Ibn Khaldun also diverge on at least two points that are of interest to us. First, where al Qazwini's preface positions us all as being capable of wonder, Ibn Khaldun makes it clear that prophets wonder at the universal with a level of skill far beyond that of most people. This sets up an instructional role for prophets, which means that the experience of wonder is not the responsibility of al Qazwini's reader alone. As we see in the excerpt from the *Muqaddimah* that opens this chapter, God has chosen certain individuals, and those individuals are to acquaint us with God's work in the world.

Second, Ibn Khaldun is much more taxed by the certainty of the knowledge claims of transmitters. This is because mental acts of 'disparaging and authenticating', and the discernment of the truth of *isnads* by critically analysing the approach, probity, accuracy, thoroughness and care of transmitters (II:449), are not separate or ancillary to our wonder at God. The active, seeing, reader does not accept the claims of others: they need to engage themselves in order to achieve the mental virtuosity needed to appreciate the universal. These differences suggest that Ibn Khaldun's work is without precedent. Such a conclusion, though, rests on a tenuous knowledge of contemporary and earlier paradoxological, historical and philosophical thought.

Diagnostic work by Zadeh suggests al Tusi's *Wonders of Creation and Oddities of Existence* (hereafter *Wonders*) as a precedent for Qazwini's *Wonders*, and in particular the passage on the validity and certainty of knowledge reproduced above. Al Tusi's prefatory comments on knowledge are as follows:

We have gathered this book from what we have seen hidden in books and from what we have heard from globe-trotters and world-travellers. Some of this is such that it is not necessary for anyone to stand as witness to it, for it is self-evident, such as the heavens, the moon, and the sun—which is greater than all the wonders. On the margins of these, we have set down a *"za"* for *"zahir"* self-evident. Some of these are in need of proof (*burhan*), which can be reached in only a long period of time, such as the talismans of Byzantium and al-Andalus. Next to these, we have placed on the margins *"ba" "ayn"* for *"ba'id"*, remote. Some of these the Quran and the sayings of the Prophet discuss; for these we have placed a *"sad dal"* for *"sidq"*, authentic. The mention of some of these wonders is transmitted through established authorities (*mutawatir*) in books. On the margins of these, we have marked a *"mim 'ayn"* for *"ma'ruf"*, well-known. Some of these marvels we have heard of by way of world-travellers, for which we have no decisive (*"qati'"*) proof and thus they cannot be said to be blatant lies (*durugh*). On the margins of these we have marked *"shin ba' ha'"* for *"shubha"*, uncertain. For to deny such a thing is an evil characteristic. When somebody reports on the wonders of Byzantium, al-Andalus, Qandahar, or Multan, if you were to request proof of their authenticity, it would be impossible to verify (*"tashih"*) it all in one lifetime.[11]

The similarities between the two texts are apparent: both stress the existence of self-evident knowledge, note the challenges of verifying reports from distant places and conclude by noting that proof for some phenomena would require more than a lifetime of work. But the two passages are not identical, and there are two differences worth highlighting at this point in our discussion. First, al Qazwini explicitly positions God as capable of creating anything. This is an important prefatory comment in a book on wonders, as it legitimises all of the phenomena included and suggests and other phenomena may also be considered. There is no legitimation akin to this in al Tusi. Second, al Tusi's work presents a scale of certainty for hadith: *zahir* (self-evident); *burhan* (in need of proof), *ba'id* (remote); *sidq* (authentic); *ma'ruf* (well-known); *qati* (lacking in decisive proof); *durugh* (blatant lies) *shubha* (uncertain); and *tashihit* (open to correction or verification). Here there is a tighter connection with Ibn Khaldun, although the latter presents a much simpler scale of three points: sound *sahih* (sound); *hasan* (good); and *da'if* (weak). Ibn Khaldun's scale, we note, lacks a reference to the self-evident. This is likely in keeping with his emphasis on the mental effort of knowledge and contemplation of God. Nothing is to be taken for granted. This might indicate a diminished role for wonder in the *Muqaddimah*; a suspicion further compounded by the restriction of discussion of wonder to the prefatory section on those with prophetic powers.

What al Tusi and al Qazwini do have in common is the assumption that the burden of responsibility for contemplating God does not rest with the author alone. Their judgement that verification can sometimes take more than a lifetime reminds us that we can sometimes let ourselves become tangled in chains of isnads at the expense of respecting God's creative hand in the world. If something is wonderful, we should appreciate it as such without wringing our hands at the technical deficiencies in descriptions of that phenomenon. This casts an interesting light on Ibn Khaldun's *Muqaddimah* as a technical text in which the desire to disparage authorities might be seen as a failure to distinguish the wood from the trees. Or, more bluntly, Ibn Khaldun may be guilty of writing history as form without substance. Moreover, it may lead us away from reading al Tabari's description of his efforts of 'mere' reporting (I: 170) as a disavowal of responsibility and towards the more generous reading of it as recognition of the responsibility of the reader.

We have ascertained that there may be some alignment between al Tabari and paradoxographical views of reader responsibility. What we still do not have, though, is an explanation for why al Tabari included poetry in his *History of the Prophets and Kings*, and why Ibn Khaldun provided an affective and physiological account of wonder.

The key to filling these two explanatory gaps is the power that al Tusi and al Qazwini ascribe to the form of a text in either guiding or distracting a reader from the contemplation of God. Theirs is an important insight, for we recall the difficulties that Polybius had in discriminating the efforts of historians and paradoxographers because of overlapping *topoi*. This was left unresolved until the insertion of an overseeing, judging God, in medieval histories.

The poetics of wonder

Polybius wrote in a world in which Aristotle set down a role for wonder in his *Metaphysics*. The *Metaphysics*, however, is not the only text in which Aristotle contemplated a role for wonder. *Poetics* is also an important source for Aristotle's views, and in the case of the pre-modern Islamic world, it provides the primary explanation for an affective view of wonder that recognises the power of textual forms.

The *Poetics* provides an explanation of the nature and impact of verse. A key observation of the text is that poetry is imitation. By this, Aristotle does not mean to relegate the role of the poet to that of cipher. Rather, poets create worlds which exercise our cognitive powers of recognition. In this way, poetry is like philosophy, and unlike history, for '[p]oetry tends to express universals, and history particulars' (51a).[12] Importantly, this distinction does not turn on form, for 'it would be possible to turn the works of Herodotus into verse, and it would be a history in verse just as much as in prose. The distinction is this: the one says what has happened, the other the kind of thing that would happen' (51b).

Yet form is not unimportant, because Aristotle sees rhythm and melody as naturally pleasurable to people (48b), and the experience of wonder is important if a verse is to impact on its readers or auditors (52a). That experience of wonder is emotional. Two things are likely to evoke that emotional experience of wonder. The first is reversal—the presentation of ideas or events that are the opposite of our expectation—and the second is the illusion that the ideas or events in a verse hang together regardless of any reversals (52a). Here we see the assembly of materials for general sense making (the illusion of connection) amplified in its effectiveness by us encountering something unexpected (reversal). Importantly, there is no suggestion that a reversal turns on an oddity, as al Qazwini would describe strange or unique phenomena. Indeed, a reversal can involve the novel juxtaposition of two conventional phenomena in a way that triggers contemplation of the universal.

At the opening of this chapter, I noted Bertolacci's work in highlighting the absence of the opening part of Aristotle's *Metaphysics* and the presence of his *Poetics* in pre-modern Islamic thought. This is borne out when we consider the works of Ibn Sina (Avicenna) and Ibn Rushd (Averroes). The work of these two writers, it turns out, provide the keystone for explaining Ibn Khaldun's affective view of prophetic wonder, and al Tabari's notion of poetic citation of wonder.

Ibn Sina's *Commentary on the Poetics of Aristotle* (hereafter *Commentary*) provides more than a simple restatement of ancient Greek views on knowledge and wonder. Ibn Sina's *Poetics* builds on his wider philosophical presentation of thought as the movement from things present or realised in our mind to things not present or yet to be realised in our mind (*Remarks and Admonitions*, 5:5:340) and evil as arising from a deficiency or incompleteness of thought (*The Metaphysics of Avicenna (Ibn Sina)*, 37). Wonder strikes us in poetry when an image prompts our recognition of a universal or we encounter a strange phenomenon (*Commentary*, 62). Poetry thus needs to be 'deflected from the usual' and 'congenial to the soul' if impact is to be achieved (*Commentary*, 63). Importantly, Ibn Sina connects Aristotle's thoughts on wonder with those of poetic genres, noting that the experience of wonder can be positive and negative, 'leav[ing] in the soul an astonishing effect of distress or pleasure (*Remarks and Admonitions*, 6.1.362). Consequently, we must be open to contemplation of the universal via the praiseworthy and pleasant and the abominable and horrifying. All of this gives us the sense of wonder as stimulated by what Ibn Khaldun calls 'substance'. But in accordance with Aristotle, Ibn Sina also sees wonder as elicited by what he calls 'poetic artifice': internal rhyme, metrical proportion, decoration and inversion (*Commentary*, 64). As he puts it:

> The wonder-evoking in either sound or sense is of two types: (1) it may be, without artifice, and in this case the wording itself is eloquent and yet without "art", or the meaning itself is unusual not through art but due to the strangeness of its imitation and imaginative representation; or (2) the wonder may originate in a simple or composite artifice in either wording or meaning' (*Commentary*, 64).[13]

This opens the way for us to recognise the effect of the way in which universals are presented to readers, which Ibn Khaldun would describe as form. Form and substance are not therefore mutually exclusive or an inhibitor in the contemplation of the universal.

Ibn Rushd echoes many of Ibn Sina's ideas but extends the idea of wonder through the concept of *taghyir* or alteration. When a poet aims at clarity, he tells us, 'he brings forth the familiar nouns; and when he wants wonder and pleasure, he brings forth the other sorts of nouns (*Averroes' Middle Commentary on Aristotle's Poetics*, 124). These 'other sorts of nouns' are 'the strange and the transferred, the altered, and the foreign' (*Averroes' Middle Commentary on Aristotle's Poetics*, 124). By this he means ambiguous terms, unusual words, foreign or loanwords, and even invented words or neologisms. To explain this, he uses the analogy of foreign visitors:

> just as the inhabitants of a town experience awe and reverence when seeing foreigners come upon them, so is the case with strange words when they happen upon the ears of the listener. Therefore, he who desires to succeed in these two arts [—rhetoric and poetry—] must make their speech strange. The beauty of altered words [...] depends on the degree of their strangeness.[14]

Use of the unfamiliar has to be moderated, though, suggesting an optimal middle course between the banal and the strange. His advice for all of us is that:

> the poet must not so indulge in his use of unfamiliar nouns that he is on the verge of making a riddle or so indulge in familiar nouns that he moves away from the path of poetry to trivial discourse. (*Averroes' Middle Commentary on Aristotle's Poetics*, 124)

This reinforces an observation from the previous two chapters, that frequent recourse to wonder suggests a lack of mental discipline, and even a predilection towards sin.

Ibn Rushd also builds out Aristotle's and Ibn Sina's views on kinds of reversal, noting that we can be struck by new insights when we combine two familiar phenomena, and when we combine real with fantastic phenomena. This intimates at the opportunity to contemplate the universal through the combination of 'what is' and 'what might be', or as Aristotle might have put it, history and poetry.

The idea of wonder arising from a combination of history and poetry provides us with a way of making sense of the later books of al Tabari's *History of the Prophets and Kings*. His juxtaposition of verse and prose is striking, and perhaps he meant for this approach to elicit a sense of wonder in his readers. So too, Aristotle's careful distinction between the form and the focus of history and poetry leaves open the possibility that al Tabari, al Qazwini and al Tusi's insistence on the contemplation of God over the particulars of isnads—and Ibn Khaldun's argument for history as philosophy—make their works poetic. Here we see the wisdom of dividing history from paradoxography or philosophy on the basis of its *topoi* questioned. A text doesn't have to look like a history in order to be a history: the status of a history simply turns on whether it contemplates the world as it is, rather than as what it might be. This provides a strong counterpoint to Polybius' use of *topoi* to navigate history away from some of the metaphysical problems he struck in considering knowledge generated not in good faith.

More radically, the acknowledgement of poetic form as a trigger for an emotional experience of wonder opens this text up to the idea of wonder without metaphysics. We might not need Aristotle's universals in things, or God, or an angelic realm to achieve a level of comfort in seeking recourse to wonder. Wonder can simply be a response to fine writing. As Lara Harb has observed, this complicates the conventional view of pre-modern Islamic thought as conservative.[15] Lest we gallop away with this idea, though, we have to remember why poetry was written in the pre-modern Islamic world. We may experience wonder at the beauty of a verse, but we contemplate that verse in order to see the hand of God at work in the world. Poetry may be beautiful, but it is a wonder of God's creation, and elevation of specific expression over universal contemplation may leave our knowledge incomplete. As with medieval Christian historiography, Ibn Sina reminds us incomplete knowledge is sinful (*The Metaphysics of Avicenna (Ibn Sina)*, 37).

Still, there is something tantalising at work in the idea of history transforming into beautiful poetry, and of us acknowledging the emotional and physiological impact of facing the beautiful and the horrifying. Ibn Khaldun's prophetic discourse with angels and al Tabari's verse quotes beckon us to leave off with pinning history down to its *isnads* and invite us to imagine the world as it might be, and not—as scholars typically conclude about Islamic historiography—the world as it was or is. And all of this we might credit to the failure to translate the first half of the first book of Aristotle's *Metaphysics* and the 'translation'—as Ibn Rushd would describe it—of Aristotle's poetics via a Syriac intermediary, Ibn Sina, and Ibn Rushd.

Entangled, retangled

It is tempting to think that Polybius and other ancient Greek historians established a relationship between history and metaphysics in the manner of an unstoppable billiard ball. The remainder of this book would therefore simply have charted the course of that ball, diversions and wobbles included. But as I noted in the first chapter, history rarely offers a straightforward story of heirs and successors. This is because, firstly, the transmission of ideas is never perfect. Texts and ideas are lost, translated in ways that are intelligible to their new readers, or even partly translated. We have the pre-Islamic world to thank for the survival of much of Aristotle's writing. But as we noted in this chapter, the translation of his *Metaphysics* was partial, and that provided an excellent opportunity to assess the translation, adoption and adaptation of Aristotle's metaphysics without wonder. We found evidence of wonder reconnected to metaphysics, but via another of Aristotle's texts, his *Poetics*. The relationship between history and metaphysics was partially re-wrought in ways that emphasised the importance of both the form *and* the content of histories in making general sense of the world, and which liberated the historian from writing to strict fidelity with the past. God still presided as judge on those efforts, but it generated the firm possibility of creativity as a part of the historiographical endeavour to make general sense of the world.

Notes

1 Chase Robinson, *Islamic Historiography*, Cambridge: Cambridge University Press, 2002, pp. 85–6.
2 Chase Robinson, *Islamic Historiography*, p. 96.

3 Hans Daiber, *Islamic Thought in the Dialogue of Cultures*, Leiden: Brill, 2012, p. 60.
4 Amos Bertolacci, 'The Arabic Translations of Aristotle's Metaphysics', *Arabic Sciences and Philosophy*, 2005, vol. 15(2), pp. 241–75.
5 Ibn Rushd, *Averroes' Middle Commentary on Aristotle's Poetics*, trans. Charles E. Butterworth, Princeton, NJ: Princeton University Press, 1986, p. 12.
6 Zaid Ahmad, *The Epistemology of Ibn Khaldun*, London: Routledge, 2002.
7 Persis Berlekamp, *Wonder, Image, and Cosmos in Medieval Islam*, New Haven, CT: Yale University Press, 2011, p. ix.
8 Travis Zadeh, 'The Wiles of Creation: Philosophy, Fiction and the 'Aja'ib Tradition', *Middle Eastern Literatures*, 2010, vol. 31(1), pp. 21–48.
9 Al Qazwini, *Die Wünder des Himmels und der Erde*, trans. A. Giese, Berlin: Goldmann, 1986, p. 26, translation is my own.
10 Travis Zadeh, 'The Wiles of Creation', p. 23.
11 As quoted in Travis Zadeh, 'The Wiles of Creation', p. 27.
12 References are to the Bekker pagination in Aristotle, *Poetics*, trans. M. Heath, Harmondsworth, UK: Penguin, 1996.
13 Translation as modified by Lara Harb, *Poetic Marvels: Wonder and Aesthetic Experience in Medieval Literary Theory*, unpublished PhD thesis, New York University, 2013.
14 Khataba, as quoted in Lara Harb, *Poetic Marvels*, p. 48.
15 Lara Harb, *Poetic Marvels*, p. 1.

References

Al Qazwini, *Die Wünder des Himmels und der Erde*, trans. A. Giese, Berlin: Goldmann, 1986.

Al Tabari, *The History of Al Tabari, 39 vols.*, various translators, New York, Albany: State University of New York Press, 1989–1998.

Ibn Khaldun, *The Muqaddimah, 3 vols.*, trans. F. Rosenthal, Princeton, NJ: Princeton University Press, 1958.

Ibn Rushd, *Averroes' Middle Commentary on Aristotle's Poetics*, trans Charles E., Butterworth, Princeton, NJ: Princeton University Press, 1986.

Ibn Sina, *The Metaphysics of Avicenna (Ibn Sina)*, trans. P. Morewedge, London: Routledge and Kegan Paul, 1973.

Ibn Sina, *Avicenna's Commentary on the Poetics of Aristotle*, trans. I. M. Dahiyat, Leiden: Brill, 1974.

Ibn Sina, *Remarks and Admonitions*, trans. S. C. Inati, Toronto: Pontifical Institute of Medieval Studies, 1984.

4

WONDER AGAINST RITUAL: STRANGE CHINESE HISTORIES

Sima Qian | Confucius | Duan Chengshi | Pu Songling | Yuan Mei | Ji Yun

I noticed the dragons on my fourth reading of Sima Qian's (145–86 BCE) *Shiji*. Previous readings had seen me acknowledge the ambitious scope of the work, and Sima Qian's clever use of a thematic structure to revisit and render ambiguous the achievements of prominent figures from the Qin (221–206 BCE) and the Han (206 BCE–220 CE) dynasties. In all honesty, I did not expect the *Shiji* to canvas the strange and the wonderful. Sima Qian, in my mind, was set to play the role of the 'serious' historian in this chapter on Chinese strange histories. Yet there are dragons in the *Shiji* (Han 1:10, p. 303; 6, p. 59; Han 2:28, pp. 5, 22, 37), along with a man with the body of a swallow (Qin 5, p. 2); 'weird beings' (Han 1: 55, p. 113); omens (Qin 6, pp. 36, 53; Han 2:28, p.5); and supernatural roosters (Han 2: 28, p. 8).[1] Consider, for example, this story of the son of Dame Liu:

> Dame Liu was one day resting on the bank of a large pond when she dreamed she encountered a god. At this time the sky grew dark and was filled with thunder and lightning. When Gaozu's father went to look for her, he saw a scaly dragon over the place when she was lying. After this she became pregnant and gave birth to Gaozu. Gaozu had a prominent nose and a dragon-like face, with beautiful whiskers on his chin and cheeks; on his left thigh he had seventy-two black moles …. When he got drunk and lay down to sleep, the old women, to their great wonder, would always see something like a dragon over the place he was sleeping. Also, whenever he would drink and stay at the shops, they would sell several times as much wine as usual. Because of these strange happenings, when the head of the year came around the old women would always destroy Gaozu's credit slips and clear his account. (1:8, pp. 51–2)

Esther Klein has noted the respect with which modern scholars have treated the structural and stylistic innovations at play in the *Shiji*.[2] A good example is Grant

Hardy's appraisal of the work as an adept rendering of the 'world in miniature', and of Sima Qian as holding 'notions of accuracy, consistency, evidence and rationality [that are] similar to ours'.[3] Yet Klein has also noted that the structural complexity of the *Shiji* and modes of transmission for the text after Sima Qian's death complicate any methodological celebration we wish to make of it. For every instance in which we may see our own methodological likings at work in the *Shiji*, there are others that appear to render Sima Qian strange. This situation is compounded by the availability of only abridged and rearranged English translations.

Klein's conclusion that Sima Qian seems to defeat us is nowhere more evident than in her silence about wonder in the *Shiji*. 'For modern readers', she tells us, phenomena like the swallow man Qi 'are easily understood by reference to the features of comparative mythology, such as the miraculous births of heroes, and so forth'. Qi's birth, Sima Qian tells us, is connected with his mother ingesting a swallow's egg:

> Qi of Yin's mother was Jian Di, who was one of the daughters of Yousong and the secondary wife of Emperor Ku. She was going with her two sisters to bathe, when she saw a dark bird drop its egg. Jian Di picked it up, and swallowed it, and thus being with child gave birth to Qi (Qin 5).

The important question, Klein notes, is what Sima Qian made of Qi. Klein answers by noting simply that Sima Qian remained silent on the matter.[4]

Silence is the focus of this chapter. It purportedly explains why, as Xupeng Zhang has argued, Chinese historiography is generally passed over in histories of history. As he argues, and it is worth quoting at some length:

> Theory seems never to have been prominent in Chinese historiographical traditions. Sima Qian (c. 145–85 BCE), the father of Chinese historiography, voiced the foundational claim that history serves as a human effort "to explore the relationship between Heaven and humanity and to comprehend the changes of past and present." This could be taken as meaning that he insisted on a comprehensive view of history and its laws, yet in actual practice he did nothing more than intersperse his chronologically ordered stories with a few comments, intending the latter to pinpoint his understanding of particular historical personages and events. Likewise, generations of Chinese historians after him have stuck to the historiographical position of "never ever talking of principles separately from affairs," that is, they don't fashion general concepts or universal laws from specific cases. Thus, in spite of their strong historical consciousness, Chinese historians have never been keen on viewing history from a purely theoretical perspective.[5]

Not speaking can be interpreted as not theorising. Ruth Wajnryb reminds us, however, that sometimes when we remain silent, we speak volumes. She noticed how things left unsaid can have a powerful impact on the lives of the descendants of Holocaust survivors.[6] Moreover, it is not clear that understandings of silence are stable and agreed over time. Silence is significant in Chinese historiography, as we shall discover in this chapter. In order to grant that point, we have to become acquainted with Chinese metaphysics because it plays a critical role in explaining why Sima Qian did not speak out, and why—as we shall discover later in this chapter—so many writers have produced what are called 'strange histories'. Political carefulness certainly plays a role, but making general sense of things by being in harmony matters even more. This chapter will highlight the interest of Chinese historians in being in harmony with an immanent world, and of growing into an understanding of that world by speaking, but more importantly, by being silent and therefore being open to and a part of it. Conversely, we will also see historians speak out when harmony ossifies into social and political practices that suggest close mindedness to the immanent world. We will see them speak out obliquely, as Sima Qian did, and we will see them speak out through wonders, as the thousands of authors of 'strange histories' did. Therefore, we will see a historiographical tradition that is interested in the immanent, which expresses views on how to discern the immanent, and which assumes it has a role in opening peoples' minds to an appreciation of the general sense of things.

We begin this chapter by needing to become reacquainted with metaphysics. This is not metaphysical reacquaintance of the kind we experienced in the last chapter, where the pre-modern European and Islamic worlds shared an engagement with the ideas of Aristotle. This is something altogether different, but not so different that we do not see historians trying to make general sense of things. If anything, this chapter is an important reiteration of a point I made in the last chapter: the history of the entanglement of history and metaphysics is not an Aristotelian ball set rolling throughout world history. It is, however, a reiteration of my overall argument that the history of history bears the imprint of a persistent engagement with metaphysical questions. Importantly, this reacquaintance needs to happen early in this chapter lest we all read Chinese histories with a Western metaphysical frame of mind, and assume that historiography will only take flight when the West gifts its texts and metaphysical traditions.

Chinese 'metaphysics': immanence, harmony, silence

While Chinese philosophers have long worked on questions designed to make general sense of things, there is no label equivalent to 'metaphysics' that sits comfortably over their efforts. A key tenet of Confucian (551–479 BCE) thought is that the universal is immanent, but this is not immanence in the Aristotelian sense. This is because this immanent sense of things is generative and without tense: we contemplate an approach to the natural order of things (*dao*) in the manner of being on a path or being on a way. And *dao* is in everything, including ourselves. When we look to make general sense of things, we must also look to ourselves and understand that we too are on a path to understanding the natural order of things. It is a dynamic inclination within us which we can embrace through the removal of obstacles, giving up striving or lack of action or fasting of the heart or mind.[7] This includes learning to refrain from speech and to embrace silence. So far from being an absence of speech, silence is the decision not to speak.

Confucius was reluctant to speak, as we learn in *Analects* 17.19:

The Master said, 'I am thinking of giving up speech.' Zigong said 'If you did not speak, what would there be for us, your disciples to transmit?' The Master said, 'What does Heaven ever say? Yet there are four seasons going round and there are the hundred things coming into being. What does Heaven ever say?'

Not speaking is an important idea in Confucian thought, and not simply because silence might appeal to our notions of self-restraint. It is also the case that we *do not need* to speak to discern the seasons going round; in the harmony of nature Heaven shows us much about how to live and to act. Katrin Froese's characterisation of speaking as a kind of marking aside or separateness of the self that displaces the showing of heaven helps us here. Speaking is not needed because being open to heaven showing us is the way to learn (*Analects* 7.2).[8] Speaking interrupts that showing, and if not checked, there is the risk that our speaking becomes habitual, obsessive, and empty. This is in line with a view of ethics in which we learn to be moral in acts of harmonisation that draw upon the immanent potential of nature. The ethical is in us and our world. There are no separate, abstract universals, but our experiences are not entirely subjective either. We find harmony in the natural order of the world and in social order or harmony. Hence Confucius' suggestion in *Analects* 4.10 that 'Exemplary persons in making their way in the world are neither bent on nor against anything; rather they go with what is appropriate.'.

Confucius did not just offer advice on universal silence. He also offered advice on not speaking about particular things. Of most relevance for this chapter are the ideas in *Analects* 7.21: 'Subjects the Master did not discuss: strange occurrences, feats of strength, rebellion, the spirits'. In explaining this passage, Michael Puett, David Hall and Roger Ames and Erin Cline hone in on the final item in Confucius' list: spirits. Puett's sense is that spirits are powerful and that we should focus on our own ethical journey rather than trying to influence them, whereas Hall and Ames read it as a call for respectful detachment by an a-theist. Cline disagrees with this interpretation, opting to align with Puett's notion of neither rejecting nor accepting practices concerning spirits in Confucian thought.[9] Yet none of these interpretations acknowledge the range of phenomena covered in the clause, which looks like a summary of the items you might expect to find in a paradoxology or a history.

We have no grounds to believe that Confucius' misgivings stem primarily from critical judgement of those who are enamoured by telling entertaining tales. We should therefore be careful about reading his thoughts as akin to those of Polybius. We do, however, get the sense that the eloquent speaker is not necessarily a good speaker. This is seen in *Analects* 5.5, in which it is claimed that 'an agile speaker creates many enemies'. Something more of a hint at Confucius' ethical view is seen in 1.3, in which we hear that 'clever talk and affected manners are seldom signs of goodness'. At work in this saying is the suggestion that mannered talk is empty talk: there can be an assumption that form delivers the good, which may lead us only to empty agreement and empty action. Again, it is useful to be reminded of speech as separation or abstraction out, and the more eloquent, the more we lose our sense of the way. This returns us to the fundamental idea of harmony, and also takes in the idea of ritual. Action that ossifies and thus separates from the harmony of the world cannot lead us to rightful action. Rather, rightful action flows from 'constant perseverance and application', as we are reminded in the opening of the *Analects* (1.1).

We do not speak of the strange, the strong, the rebellious and the spirits because doing so sets them apart from the order of nature. They, like the normal, are part of nature. It makes no sense to separate the strange from the normal in speaking, because nothing is purely transcendentally strange. The strange is immanent in the world, and has to be appreciated as entangled in the order of nature along with us and all other manner of phenomena. And so it is also that nothing is purely transcendentally normal, strong, rebellious, or even historical. The history that we write or read ritually, without perseverance and application, risks separating us from appreciating the order of the world that heaven shows us in a variety of phenomena. Silence, speaking, separation and ritual, as we shall see, were the key drivers behind both Sima Qian's silence and the profusion of speaking in what are called strange Chinese histories.

Sima Qian having nothing to say about Qi the swallow man locates him in a Confucian world in which not speaking about 'strange happenings' (*Analects* 7:21) is part of living a harmonious ethical life. Paradoxically, the ideas of harmony and community are also needed to make sense of a body of over 4000 strange histories that Robert Campany estimates were written in China between 206 BCE and 618 CE, and a further two thousand stories that Sing-Chen Francis notes as having been added in a Qing dynasty revival between the seventeenth and early nineteenth centuries.[10] Chinese historiography abounds with tales of fox spirits, revenants, strange births, gender shifts, and the consequences of human shortcomings. My first step in making sense of this silence-breaking will be to note that Chinese paradoxography is presented as transmission rather than as creation, written in the past tense, and supported by a range of *topoi* in common with history such as '*x* told me' and 'I learned when travelling'. Moreover, I will observe that the comingling of history and paradoxography in Chinese strange histories was not seen as a problematic union in need of reversal, but as a necessary ethical demand.

In distinction from Francis, though, I will not advance the argument that strange histories arose simply as a 'safety zone within which... dominant [Qing] cultural values might be toyed with, temporarily suspended, or even subverted'.[11] Strange histories are a persistent feature of Chinese historiography, even though the volume produced during the reign of the Qing is notable. Nor will this chapter provide a simple affirmation of Rania Huntington's argument that '[b]y imagining the alien, we establish the boundaries of the human'.[12] Confucian China is not one in which our ethical abstractions and notions of self and other play out neatly, and we should not expect that in experiencing the strange that we can abstract the normal via logical inversion. There are no dipoles of normal/abnormal, man/woman, alien/human, for example, for distinguishing and setting opposites are acts of separating out. The recognition of ethics at play in our daily interactions means refraining from separating out and establishing those dipoles. As the histories of Duan Chengshi (ca. 800–63 CE), Pu Songling (1640–1715), Yuan Mei (1716–97) and Ji Yun (1724–1805) show us, the wonderful is the ordinary and the human the alien. Theirs are stories in which people and spirits transition from one form to another, seamlessly, in ways that cast a stern light on habitual forms of moral judgement. Moreover, they point to and even mock the ways in which state-sponsored authors work to split out history from other kinds of writing. What these texts invite us to consider is our potential to mistake habitual approaches to the writing of history as an expression of harmony. Official, state-sponsored histories were, in their eyes, expressions of hollow ritual that formed obstacles to harmony, and the strange was needed to remove them.

In summary, we will find in Chinese historiography an interest in immanence. This will provide us with another instance of the interrelation of history and metaphysics in this book. As we will also discover, though, the discernment of the immanent, and the treatment of the knowable and the unknowable, will play out in a manner quite unlike views we have previously considered. This will not be another rehearsal of sense making that enshrines active, critical perception, thought and feeling. Rather, restraint, silence and being open will be seen as critical to making general sense of things.

History as saying many different things, and then holding silence

The arresting structure of Sima Qian's *Shiji* makes it easy for readers to miss the dragons. It is not so much a history as at least five different kinds of history: basic annals (*benji*, 12 chapters), chronological tables (*biao*, 10 chapters), treatises (*shu*, 8 chapters), hereditary houses (*shijia*, 30 chapters) and memoirs (*liezhuan*, 70 chapters). The basic annals outline the history of dynastic houses and emperors. These are followed by the chronological tables, which present events in the form of lists. Next come treatises on a range of topics of contemporary and historical interest, from economics to music and religious affairs. Following the treatises are the hereditary houses, which identify prominent hereditary office-holding families. The final section, the biographies, is dedicated to the lives of individuals, foreign peoples and peoples of similar disposition, social status or profession such as assassins, harsh officials, jesters, diviners and tycoons.

Within each of these sections, the chapters are arranged hierarchically or chronologically. This combination of thematic, hierarchical and chronological approaches allowed Sima Qian to describe the same individual or event multiple times. As commentators such as Hardy have noted, this provided Sima Qian with the means to describe the achievements of individuals and groups in slightly different ways, and thus to provide an oblique criticism of influential figures.[13]

One of Sima Qian's stated reasons for writing the *Shiji* was to provide a comprehensive and true record (*shilu*) of past events. This purpose is not only articulated in the last *Shiji*—130—but also throughout the work. Sima Qian tells us about major sources that he used such as the *Zuozhan*, the *Guoyu* or *Discourses of the States* and the *Zhan Guo Ce* or *Intrigues of the Warring States* (Han 2:123); visits to historical sites (Han 1:92, Han 2:29); meetings with key individuals or their descendants (Han 1:102, 104; Han 2:108, 109, 124); and his own participation in events (Han 2:28). These declarations are in keeping with Sima Qian's official role as historian of the court of Wu-di, a position that he inherited from his father, Sima Tan. On the evidence of *Shiji* 130, Sima Tan determined to bring together records of the various rulers, officials and events of the known Chinese world together in a single history and Sima Qian completed the work out of filial piety. In this way, Sima Qian exemplifies wider Confucian belief in the importance of historiographical harmony, as Roger Ames explains:

> In this traditional paradigm, a figure achieves prominence not from standing out in contrast to his historical inheritance but rather from the degree to which he embodies, expresses, and amplifies his tradition. It is for this reason that from the earliest times there has been such an extraordinary emphasis on historical records in China. The records represent a repository of the past cultural tradition out of which the new can emerge.[14]

While we have already observed the conjoining of history and harmony in Confucianism, it is important to note for the present that Sima Qian's deference towards family tradition did not prevent him from achieving innovations in the scope and structure of his history.

The scale and textual variety of the *Shiji* was novel. So too was the extent of Sima Qian's critical stance towards earlier attempts at history making. He did not assume that historians had to accept their sources. This scepticism stemmed from his recognition—much like that of Polybius—that texts reflect a variety of motives and levels of understanding. Nowhere is this view clearer than in his comments on the source 'Basic Annals of the Five Emperors' in *Shiji* 1, which is worth quoting at length:

> Scholars have often referred to the great antiquity of the Five Emperors. However, the Book of Documents begins only with Emperor Yao. As for the hundred schools that speak about the Yellow Emperor, their accounts are implausible and extravagant, and it is difficult for a person of refinement and learning to speak about them. What Confucius is supposed to have passed on—the questions of Zai Yu on 'The Virtues of the Five Emperors' and the 'Genealogies of Emperors'—are sometimes rejected (as spurious) even by Confucian scholars. I have traveled west to Kong Tong, north past Chou-lu, east almost to the ocean, south along the Jiang and Huai Rivers. Where I went, the elders without exception referred to the places associated with [the names of] the Yellow Emperor, Emperors Yao and Shun: the customs and ethos of those places are actually different. In sum, that which does not depart

from the canonical writings in ancient script is close to the truth. I have examined the Spring and Autumn Annals and the Discourses of the States, which elaborate (ideas from) the Virtues of the Five Emperors and the Genealogies of Emperors, yet people do not pay [this derivation] much attention. Only love of learning and sustained reflection can bring intuitive understanding: this is difficult to explain to those of shallow perception and scanty knowledge. I thus sort out the sources, and choose the most plausible and responsible accounts to place at the beginning of the 'Basic Annals'.[15]

Here we see Sima Qian reject speaking of the extravagant, irresponsible and implausible in favour of the intrinsic pursuit of 'sustained reflection' and 'intuitive understanding'. This stance, he explains, arises from checking sites and sources for inconsistencies against canonical writings and 'implausible' claims. Sima Qian's historian does not follow the extrinsic desire of wishing to please others; rather, they hold back and contemplate, thinking about whether the sources justify speech. This would seem to accord neatly with the sense making view of history promoted by Polybius in chapter one, but as we noted earlier, Confucius was also circumspect about speaking at all. Importantly, the extract suggests a further meaning for 'intuitive', which is hinted at in his claim in *Shiji* 28 that he will present the 'inside and outside' of phenomena (Han 2:28).[16] Here, Sima Qian points to a desire to help others to understand Confucian thought, as he explains more explicitly in *Shiji* 130: 'I wanted to convey Confucius' concerns through abstract, conceptual language, but it would not be as profound, compelling, and clear as embodied and seen through past events and actions'.[17] History reveals the universal in the context of the particular; or to put it another way, the 'inside' through the 'outside'. Philosophy is immanent in the concrete particulars of history, and not the other way around. This is an important observation to make at this stage of the book, and indicates that wonder at the past might not be a rationally or morally deficient activity. If it entails awe or speechlessness, it may even support our journey on the way.

Whether Sima Qian himself achieved an understanding of the immanence he described has long been a matter of dispute. One of the most interesting complaints about his work can be found in the *Yangzi Fayan* of the Han scholar Yang Xiong. To Yang Xiong's mind, Sima Qian fell prey to his own charge of shallow perception due to an unseemly interest in *guai* (the strange):

Having many interests and not content to leave out anything—that was Sima Qian. Confucius had many interests, but his interests all revolved around *yi* [the different]. Sima Qian had many interests, but he was interested in *guai* [the strange].[18]

How *yi* differs from *guai* is something we will explain when we look to the wider tradition of strange histories in the next section of this chapter. What is apparent to us at this stage is that Yang Xiong's complaint suggests an imbalance in writing in favour of the particular over the universal. This seems to arise not simply from the historian's desire to entertain others—as Sima Qian suggested—but also from the historian's own captivation by the entertaining. The song writer Ouyang Xiu also presents Sima Qian as being overly interested in the strange, but his explanation for that interest focuses not on the desire to entertain but on an inability or unwillingness to judge. He writes:

> As for curiosity-loving gentlemen of broad learning, they set to work on the abundant hearsay and so thought themselves the most accomplished. Thus did they exhaustively compile all kinds of discourse, but from the very start, they did not discriminate in what they selected, and only feared leaving things out—such a work was Sima Qian's Records of the Historian.[19]

What Sima Qian's critics highlight for us is a distinction between wonder at the world, and writing about wonder at the world. There is nothing to indicate that the former is problematic; rather, it is the precarious activity of achieving harmony in writing that we have to be wary about. Too much interest or too little judgment are likely to land us with a text that Sima Qian's person of refinement would have trouble speaking about. To adapt Confucius' thought: a person's writing, is 'neither bent on nor against anything; rather [it goes] with what is appropriate' (*Analects* 4.10).

These judgements appear to be out of keeping with the Sima Qian we know in translation. Burton Watson's English translation of the *Shiji* suggests that Sima Qian was not much interested in the strange, and there are fewer than a dozen mentions of wonder across the three volumes, including the examples in the opening of this chapter. This makes us realise, however, how susceptible we might be to the translator's vision and understanding of Sima Qian. Even noting this point, though, the small number of mentions of wonder and the strange in the *Shiji* cannot be explained away, even if we believe William Nienhauser's portrait of Sima Qian as a time poor bureaucrat who became overwhelmed by his work.[20] Nor are we helped by Sima Qian's paradoxical handling of not mentioning strange phenomena by mentioning them, as seen in his appraisal of the *Shanhaijing* (*Classic of Mountains and Seas*) and *Yu Benji* (*Annals of Yu*):

> As for anomalous creatures (*guaiwu*) found in the *Yu Benji* and *Shanhaijing*, I dare not even mention them (Han 2: 123).[21]

Not mentioning something can mean that it is beneath contempt. On this reading, the *Yu Benji* and *Shanhaijing* are simply bad histories. It is important to note, though, that Qian's conclusion stems from his prefatory statement about there being 'anomalous creatures' in the two texts. It is not so much the texts that should not be mentioned, but the anomalous within them. If anomalous creatures are the focus of Qian's criticism, though, what are we to make of anomalous in the *Shiji*? Our analysis of Confucian thought earlier in the chapter highlights the parallels between Sima Qian's claim and Confucius' avowal to remain silent on the strange, but it would have been logical on that account not to have mentioned them at all. Some other dynamic is at play, and that, as we shall see in the next section, concerns the need to speak out against ritualistic historiography.

Strange history and ritualistic histography

Understanding the anomalous in the *Shiji* begins with a return to Ames' idea of historiographical harmony, and with the appreciation that harmony suggests alignment with both successors and predecessors. Sima Qian's *Shiji* was a continuation of the work commenced by his father Sima Tan, and purportedly a true record (*shilu*) of past events. It was also the progenitor for the 24 standard or official histories (*Zhengshi*), which ranged over the period from 3000 BCE to the Ming dynasty (1368–1644) and comprised around 40 million words. These reflected the output of the bureau of historiography, which located historians in the imperial court. These historians were positioned to record events with absolute fidelity, serving not only to memorialise but also to make rulers think twice about their actions, as the later Han historian Ban Gu (32–92 CE) explains in his official *Han shu* (*History of the Han Dynasty*):

> Kings of ancient times, in generation after generation, had scribal officials. The sovereign's every act had to be written down. This was the reason why he was cautious in word and deed and clarified his rule and model. The scribe of the left recorded words; the scribe of the right recorded events. Events were [the basis of] the *Springs and Autumns*; words were [the basis of] the *Esteemed Documents* [*Shang shu*]. Of rulers and kings, there were none who did not act in the same way.[22]

This account positions the historian at a triple intersection of restraint. First, the historian as observer encourages self-control on the part of the sovereign. On this logic, the knowledge that I am being observed encourages me to be 'cautious in word and deed'. Second, the historian's record of the court is assumed to reveal ethical principles that might shape the nature and limits of a good life for the wider community. In this case, the behaviour—and restraint—of the emperor is taken to be a model for community restraint. Here we see the contribution of history to making general sense of things. Third, the historian records only phenomena connected to the imperial court and refrains from distraction by a wider field of phenomena. Importantly, too this practice is seen as maintaining a harmony of approach, as seen in the phrase 'there were none who did not act in the same way'. This phrase not only applies to rulers, but also to the historians who record their actions.

These assumptions appear to present a very tightly-bound role for historians, including the range of sources that they might use. In a way, they work at the extreme end of Polybius' idea of history as only recording that which the author saw. Yet Ban Gu did not want to see the anecdotes and accounts of 'woodcutters and madmen' passed over. While he noted Confucius' advice that too much of an interest in the 'hearing from the highroad and retelling in the lane' proved a hindrance to reason, he also conceded that as they might contain even one expression of wisdom they ought to be preserved.[23] This is, fundamentally, a recognition of ethics as immanence: any description of the world that falls short generates the risk of an incomplete, abstracted or even distorted account of the virtues in action. Moreover, we cannot be sure that accounts of imperial events are certain, as he concedes in his *Jinshu*:

> Although we can examine what was formerly set down in records and collect excluded fragments that have come down to the present, I suppose these are not matters which were heard and seen with one person's own eyes and ears . ... As for what I have herewith collected, when it sets forth what has been received from earlier accounts, any fault that might be found is not my own; if there are vacuous or erroneous places in what has been garnered from inquiries into more recent events, then I wish to share the ridicule and criticism with former worthies and scholars.[24]

Ban Gu's comments acknowledge a world in which wonder as the experience of the strange and ethics were never apart. Moreover, they indicate the struggle of knowing what to record and whether other peoples' records can be trusted. Restraint only works, it seems, when you know where and when the ethical is at work. The particular challenge of Confucian ethics is the assumption that it is at work in daily phenomena, rather than in the crystallisation of abstract concepts. This may be seen as predisposing the historian towards the recording of more phenomena rather than fewer, and thus as being susceptible to Ouyang Xiu's complaint about the absence of historiographical judgement.

This opens the way for histories of the strange, which number in the thousands in China, and which pre- and post-date the *Shiji*. Helpful explanations of the nature and purpose of these texts can be found in the works of writers like Robert Campany, Judith Zeitlin, Sing-chen Lydia Francis and Rania Huntington. Campany designates these texts as histories on the grounds that they share three key features with *Zhengshi*. First, both sets of authors position themselves as harmonious transmitters rather than as creators; second, both present descriptions in the past tense; and third, both are underpinned by the same kinds of *topoi* or methods for making and sustaining an argument such as eyewitness rhetorical devices like 'I heard' and 'I saw in my travels'.[25] Looking in more detail at a smaller range of texts, Zeitlin reminds us that strange histories are not a homogenous text type: she suggests a threefold subdivision into literature that focuses on *yi* (the different, departure from the norm); the *guai* (the anomalous, the weird, freakish or unfathomable as distinct from the normative); and the *qi* (the marvellous, the rare, the wonderful as distinct from the canonical).[26] Of these, *qi* is the most common focus of strange histories, and *guai* the least common focus. So too, she highlights how these three terms might be conjoined with their opposites—different with same;

aberrant with normative; exceptional with canonical—in stories that emphasise the crossing of various social boundaries. In crossing the boundary between male and female, or being awake or dreaming, she suggests, we see in play the social mores that set the boundaries and paths of our lived order of the world. Zeitlin thus asks us to pause in assigning positive value to the demarcation of history and paradoxology. It is in the ambiguous boundary between history and fiction, sense and nonsense that the virtues dwelling in our world are thrown into sharp focus. This idea is extended by Francis, who suggests a role for strange histories in providing a 'safety zone within which ... dominant [Qing] cultural values might be toyed with, temporarily suspended, or even subverted', and by Huntington's idea of extrapolating the human through inversion of the alien.[27]

As appealing as these ideas might be to our notions of self and other, and contemporary western ethics, they ignore an important feature of their Confucian context, as expressed by the Eastern Jin author Guo Pu (276–324 CE) in his commentary on the *Shanhaijing*:

> What the world calls 'anomalous' it does not know by virtue of what it is anomalous; what the world calls 'non-anomalous' it does not know by virtue of what it is non-anomalous. How is this so? Things are not intrinsically anomalous; they wait upon a self and only then are 'anomalous'. 'Anomalousness' is therefore located in a self; it is not things in themselves that are anomalous. (Campany, *Shanhaijing*, 274).

Guo Pu's simple yet powerful point is that there are no fixed, transcendent poles of anomalous and non-anomalous. They are concepts that we come to know through the concrete and particular features of the world and via understanding ourselves. Inversion from the anomalous to the non-anomalous is therefore not a straightforward matter of abstraction. The very act of abstracting may distract us from seeing how much of the alien is at work in the ordinary—including in ourselves—and the other way around.

The co-presence of the strange and the normal is a feature of the 500 stories in the Qing text, *Strange Tales from a Classical Studio*, which was the work of the self-titled 'historian of the strange', Pu Songling. The *Strange Tales* range the boundaries between the dead and the living, spirits and humans, dreams and consciousness, animals and humans and male and female. These boundary crossings are lively and detailed, with fox spirits conjuring up mansions for humans who cannot discriminate between dreaming and consciousness ('The Marriage of the Fox's Daughter', 39–42); a man's soul taking rest in a parrot's body ('Miss Abao, or Perseverance Rewarded', p. 124); and a terrestrial man falling for a beautiful sea woman in a tale not unlike Guillermo del Toro's film *The Shape of Water* ('The Luocha Country and the Sea Market', 245–54). On Campany's view, these stories should be designated as histories because they are cast in the past tense and are preceded or closed by the use of eyewitness or secondary source *topoi* such as 'The story was fully related to me...' ('Mr Zhu, the Considerate Husband', p. 107); 'I learned the above when travelling…' ('Miss Lianxiang, the Fox Girl', p. 120); and *x* 'told me' ('The Singing Frogs', p. 136; and 'The Performing Mice', p. 137). Moreover, there are instances where—as we discovered in chapter one—the use of ambiguous *topoi* might suggest the attempt of authors to distance themselves from the claims reported. Take for example Pu Songling's closing thoughts for 'The Man who Changed into a Crow':

> The person who told me this story did not recollect from what department or district he came. (p. 171)

This claim might function as an empty marker: a necessity to make the claims in the story 'historical' in the style promoted by Sima Qian. It is also worth considering whether the claim is not so much inadequate as ambiguous and therefore a parodic or even mocking comment on the veracity of the story or even our belief in the authority of historical accounts.

In this way, the *Strange Tales* may be an exposé of our trust in histories. As you may recall from the account of Lucian of Samosata's 'True History' in chapter one, paradoxographical works can function to highlight scholastic practices that are seemingly hollow. On this account, wonder works are not poor histories but indictments against blind historiographical trust. In Pu Songling's world, the doubt generated is significant because it might be seen as undercutting the authority of the functions and activities of the imperial court and the assumption that history is *the* way to discern the lived order of the world.

This tantalising glimpse of strange histories as a destabilising force is not isolated, for the preface to *Strange Tales* establishes an inversion of the historian traveller model employed in Sima Qian's *Shiji* and Polybius' *Histories*. Those from the margins of the known world came to Pu Songling to recount wonders, not the other way around:

> What I have heard, I committed to paper, and so this collection came about. After some time, like-minded men from the four directions dispatched stories to me by post, and because 'things accrue to those who love them', what I have amassed became even more plentiful. (preface).

In this way, Pu Songling tells us that the wonderful and the strange are not only found in distant places, but also with us. The profound point at work here is that the strange is not something that we seek out in distant parts of the world: it comes to us, and it is a part of us. Knowledge is not 'out there' separate or abstracted from our experiences: it is accrued to and in us. This is the immanence of the strange.

The authority of the *Strange Tales* will rest upon sources that would have troubled Polybius mightily—things that Pu Songling has not seen, things recounted without sources, stories that have passed through many hands—and Pu Songling is in no way troubled by this. As if to sharpen the point against discriminating fidelity, Pu Songling also positions himself as an indiscriminate, obsessive collector. In this way, the historian is part of the *Strange Tales* of individuals who succumb to gambling, book collecting, pigeon chasing, the love of rocks and the excessive consumption of alcohol. Yet this form of obsession is not necessarily a bad thing, because absorption is seen as necessary for the development of expert knowledge. As he explains:

> If one's nature is 'foolish', then one's resolve will be firm: thus those who are foolish in their love of books are sure to excel in composition, and those who are foolishly devoted to the arts are bound to have excellent technique, whereas those people who make no progress and achieve nothing are always those who claim that they are not foolish (2.239).

Obsession entails commitment, and commitment is necessary to develop expertise. On this count, the historian is a fool, and the writing of history is a foolish pursuit. This runs against the advice on avoiding curiosity laid out in our chapter on medieval European histories. But it also highlights the difference between initial commitment and detainment of interest, as explained well by the song writer Su Shi (1037–1101) in 'On Wang Shen's Hall of Precious Paintings':

> A gentleman may temporarily 'lodge' his interest in things, but he must not 'detain' his interest in things. For if he lodges his interest in things, then even trivial objects will suffice to give him joy and even 'things of unearthly beauty' will not suffice to induce mania in him. If he detains his interest in things, then even trivial objects will suffice to induce mania in him, and even things of unearthly beauty will not suffice to give him joy.[28]

In this account, detained interest is a form of mania, even a pathology. The emerging sense of mental activity we have here is that captivation is good, but that persistent pursuit means a susceptibility to forgetting other possibilities and to a habitual going through the motions. We may be so fervently devoted to the writing of history that we cannot remember why we do it and lose joy in the experience. This is no better than gambling, excessive drinking or hoarding. It does not take much interpretation to see, for example, how Pu Songling's description of money hoarding—'money is properly a circulating medium, and is not intended for a man to lie upon and keep all to himself' ('The Stream of Cash', 300)—might be translated into the ossified obsessions of official historians. Historical expertise might be necessary in imperial China, but our habitual dependency on it is also potentially a problem.

Sima Qian might have positioned history as a 'profound, compelling and clear' vehicle for understanding Confucian thought (*Shiji*,130), but any investment of belief in it as a reliable and stable foundation for knowledge sees us forego the persistent struggle for ethical enlightenment. That investment is fair game to Duan Chengshi, a financially independent imperial official whose *Chinese Chronicles of the Strange* appear to be far from the idea of historiographical harmony in the Tang world. Sparrows perform good deeds and are promoted to higher ranks (1.14.534);

a silkworm as big as a cow is reported (Xuji, 2.1: 1); a man exorcises himself (2.1.10); a baby drops from the sky and then turns into a broom (2.2.35); a man eats a supernatural fish and turns into a shapeshifter (2.2.40); and perhaps most intriguingly of all, a spirit morphs from a walnut to wasps, leaving the author to conclude 'There is no telling what strange thing it was' (1.14.560; see also 1.15.597). Yet all of these stories are written in the past tense, and nearly all end in the manner of the *Shiji*, with the author summarising the point of the tale and its source. All of them make sense in historiographical form, and because of that, we grasp at straws to reject accounts like his imperial record of giant singing earthworms:

> In the upper capital ... grew a small cassia tree in which there is a hole the size of a coin. Every night, after the clouds had passed from the face of the moon, (on this tree) there would appear an earthworm like a giant arm, more than two feet long, with white neck and red spots. This earthworm would go in advance of several hundred earthworms that looked like ropes encircling the branches and twigs of the tree. In the morning they would all cry out, and the sound was always melodious. According to the student Zhang Cheng, when Hun Jian was Secretariat Director, in front of the hall a tree suddenly sprang up from the ground, and it was covered with earthworms hanging on its branches. There was a source for this information, but he said he had forgotten the name of the book. (2.18)

As with Pu Songling's tale of a man who changed into a crow, the account is simultaneously detailed and historiographically ambiguous. It emanates from the imperial court, but the name of the book is forgotten. Duan Chengshi hereby mocks our obsession with knowing precisely where historical stories come from. If, he teases us, we can accept the accounts of emperors based on less than certain sources, why not accept an account of earthworms based upon a forgotten book?

Even more pointed is Yuan Mei's *Censored by Confucius* (1788), which includes just under 750 tales of revenants, 10-foot high hairy giants from the hills, gender shifts, sightings of reincarnation and an old man who resembles a prawn (36). Yuan Mei's financial independence provided an opportunity not only to contribute to a critical picture of history but also to comment on the Chinese judicial system and behavioural norms. Justice is frequently served in the firm but fair courts of the underworld but found wanting on earth; just as the behaviour of fox spirits highlights the shortcomings of humans (e.g. Zhang Guangxiong, 100–3).

That we might read Duan Chengshi and Yuan Mei's texts as an oblique attack on both the imperial court, and more specifically the historiographical function within that court, comes from our interpretation of particular stories. This leaves us open to the charge of seeking out the kinds of historiographical scepticism which feature in our times, akin to some criticisms of Hardy's reading of Sima Qian. Yet these texts are challenging to our views because they do not square evenly with our attempts to split out the form and content of history, or the strange and the normal. History and paradoxography are entangled, and explicitly so, as Ji Yun tells us in his *Shadows in a Chinese Landscape*. The 1200 stories of the *Shadows* are presented in the order recalled by Ji Yun (1789 preface, 149) and are far from a certain corpus of knowledge, as he explains in the preface:

> When others include stories about my family, I can know when they diverge from the truth. Others cannot know this. Similarly, when I include stories about other people's families, I based them on what I have heard and produce narratives right away. Sometimes they might be false; sometimes they might be true; sometimes they might be incomplete. The others will know which it is, but there is no way for me to know …. My writings have always been true and tolerant. They encourage what is good and discourage what is bad.' ('Corrections', p. 24)

His writings are 'true and tolerant' despite some of them being based on sources that might be false. They are also able to 'encourage what is good' despite such uncertainty. This is not Ames' idea of historiographical harmony played out in the passive acceptance of sources that might be false. This is because Ji Yun echoes Pu Songling's connection of histories and history makers with a foolish obsession:

> Those mired in the past are fools …a former teacher of mine, once said to me: 'When your guts are filled with nothing but books it can be dangerous—just as dangerous as if your guts are filled with nothing.' The most skilful chess players in the empire do not discard the ancient treatises, nor do they adhere to them blindly. The most skilful physicians in the empire are not stuck in the methods of ancient times, nor do they abandon them. ('By the Book', p. 31).

Ji Yun's call is for wariness about any one source of knowledge, which would include histories. He also warns us about the difference between consuming books and understanding them, as highlighted in a tale in which a servant seeks to study the ideas of Confucius:

> That servants read books is arguably a good thing. Nevertheless, one reads books to grasp principles. And one grasps principles in order to apply them in actual situations. Consuming knowledge without digesting it may lead to confusion and stupidity, causing endless pain. ('The Neo-Confucian Conscience', p. 123).

Similarly, a fox spirit fails to grasp the principles of Confucius because he confuses fervent reading over careful deliberation ('A Fox on Sagehood', p. 50).

Never apart: immanence

Like Ban Gu, Ji Yun held that 'the anecdotes and opinions of the alleyways may … be useful in encouraging good and discouraging evil' (p. 149). On the reading of Francis and Huntington, this is an invitation to consider not only how the strange shapes the normal, but also how the anomalous may highlight the shortcomings of the normal. This is a reasonable interpretation when we see tale after tale in which fox spirits lay bare human shortcomings such as greed, intemperance and resort to violence. The subjects of strange histories impugn us, reminding us of the need to restrain our impulses.

Yet such is the historical spread of strange histories in China that Francis' characterisation of them as a safety zone for exploring the social mores of the Qing is not right, or at least an incomplete idea. Strange histories are a far more persistent feature of Chinese historiography. This is, however, not my only departure from prevailing explanations of strange histories. In the above section, I have suggested that the ethical indictment of authors like Ji Yun and Pu Songling is even deeper, with them both providing pointed reminders of the risk of a detained belief in the certainty of histories as a source of knowledge, including ethical knowledge. History, we learned, can be the obsession of the foolish. Characterising history as the obsession of the foolish might be seen as politically destabilising given the formal function of historiography in the imperial court. Going through the motions in historiography—either as a writer or a reader—means that you cannot spot your emperor for your earthworms. As I also pointed out, however, it also destabilises the assumption set out by Sima Qian in *Shiji* 130 that history provides a clear vehicle for conveying Confucius' teachings.

Reading Pu Songling, Duan Chengshi, Yuan Mei and Ji Yun requires perserverance and application: it is all too easy to dismiss the false, the ambiguous, the tale collected when the margins of the world come to the writer. Their historian also shifts from being a senior official in the imperial court to an obsessive fool, providing us with the suggestion that histories, like money, are 'a circulating medium, and ... [are] not intended for a man to lie upon and keep all to himself'. In this shift, we are delivered a blunt reminder not to mistake harmony for agreement, and not to delude ourselves that in fixing on activities that we believe to be right, we are delivered from the struggle of finding our own way.

This leaves us wondering about Sima Qian's dragons. The volume of the strange in English translations of the *Shiji* is slight, making it easy for us to conclude that this work is squarely the progenitor of the official line of histories that writers like Pu Songling question. Hardy suggests otherwise, noting that the use of multiple, conflicting accounts of the same individual may function as a form of oblique criticism. Hardy's idea can be further extended to encompass both Sima Qian's use of *topoi* and juxtaposition of the strange and apparently normal. The occasional appearance of a dragon is not simply due to lack of judgement in selecting materials, as Ouyang Xiu suggests. It can reflect both a dedication to ethics as immanence, requiring consideration of all manner of phenomena, and a critical stance on the nature and purpose of the activity of history making itself. Content, form and arrangement of materials may point to the shortcomings of individuals, but they can also point to shortcomings in the very activities that record the activities of those individuals for our consideration.

To be clear, though, there is no explicit diagnosis of the historian fool in the *Shiji* or inversion of the eyewitness model used by the historian to claim certainty.

The *Shiji* is not positioned explicitly as a set of strange tales, or even as a collection of things that Confucius would not speak about. Our search for a definitive ruling on whether Sima Qian sought to undercut the historiographical form is met only with silence. Understanding the *Shiji* clearly requires a measure of Confucian perseverance.

In sum, Chinese historiography points to, wrestles with and impugns our lack of respect for radical immanence, as against transcendence. It is radical because it shows us that making general sense of things through the assumption of universals does not necessarily imply boundaries and divisions. There is no making sense of what is outside or inside us, self or other, beyond and near, past, present or future. It unsettles any obsession we might develop in dividing out what is accessible to us through experience and what is inaccessible to us through experience. It confounds the idea of a boundary between the knowable and the unknowable, abstract and particular. And wonder is its diagnostic. Not speaking of it implies harmony in living with that radical immanence, but speaking of it means that our world is at odds. This is a world in which not writing history might be seen as good, but also in which writing and even mocking history might be necessary to help us to find our way. Arguably, Chinese history and metaphysics never needed to come together for historians to make sense of the world, because they were never apart.

Notes

1 References to the *Shiji* are from the Watson translation, with the title of the volume—Han 1 or 2, Qin—followed by the *Shiji* number. Pinyin has been used to transcribe names thoughout the chapter. In the case of excerpts using Wade Giles transcription, the Pinyin transcription is indicated in square brackets.
2 Esther S. Klein, *The History of a Historian: Perspectives on the Authorial Roles of Sima Qian*, unpublished PhD thesis, Princeton University, 2010, p. 1.
3 Grant Hardy, *Worlds of Bronze and Bamboo: Sima Qian's Conquest of History*, New York: Columbia University Press, 1999, pp. xiv; 47.
4 Esther S. Klein, *The History of a Historian*, pp. 348–9.
5 Xupeng Zhang, 'In and Out of the West: On the Past, Present, and Future of Chinese Historical Theory', *History and Theory*, 2015, vol. 54(4), p. 47 [46–63].
6 Ruth Wajnryb, *The Silence: How Tragedy Shapes Talk*, London: Allen and Unwin, 2002.
7 Chung-ying Cheng, 'Chinese Metaphysics as Non-Metaphysics: Confucian and Daoist Insights into the Nature of Reality', in *Understanding the Chinese Mind*, Robert E. Allinson, ed., Oxford: Oxford University Press, 1990, pp. 167–208; Brook Ziporyn, *Ironies of Oneness and Difference: Coherence in Early Chinese Thought: Prolegomena to the Study of Li*, Albany, NY: SUNY Press, 2013; and id., 2014, *Beyond Oneness and Difference: Li and Coherence in Chinese Buddhist Thought and Its Antecedents*, Albany, NY: SUNY Press, 2014.
8 Katrin Froese, 'The Art of Becoming Human: Morality in Kant and Confucius', *Dao*, 2008, vol. 7, pp. 257–68.
9 Michael Puett, *To Become a God: Cosmology, Sacrifice, and Self-Divinization in Early China*, Cambridge, MA: Harvard University Asia Center for the Harvard-Yenching Institute, 2002, p. 98; David L. Hall and Roger. T. Ames, *Thinking Through Confucius*, New York: SUNY Press, 1987, p. 196; and Erin M. Cline, 'Religious Thought and Practice in the Analects', in *Dao Companion to the Analects*, ed. A. Olberding, New York: Springer, 2014, pp. 277–8.

10 Robert F. Campany, *Strange Writing: Anomaly Accounts in Early Medieval China*, New York: State University of New York Press, 1996, p. ix; and Sing-Chen L. Francis, *What Confucius Wouldn't Talk About: The Fantastic Mode of the Chinese Classical Tale*, unpublished PhD thesis, Stanford University, 1997, p. 8.
11 Sing Chen L. Francis, *What Confucius Wouldn't Talk About*, p. iv; and Judith T. Zeitlin, *Historian of the Strange: Pu Songling and the Classical Chinese Text*, Stanford, CA: Stanford California Press, 1993, p. 5.
12 Rania Huntington, *Alien Kind: Foxes and Late Imperial Chinese Literature*, Cambridge, MA: Harvard University Press for Harvard University Asia Center, 2003, p. 4.
13 Grant Hardy, *Objectivity and Interpretation in the Shih Chi*, unpublished PhD thesis, Yale University, 1988, p. 96.
14 Roger T. Ames, *The Art of Rulership*, Honolulu: University of Hawaii Press, 1983, pp. xii–xiii.
15 As quoted in Wai-Yee Li, 'The Idea of Authority in the Shih Chi (Records of the Historian)', *Harvard Journal of Asiatic Studies*, 1994, vol. 54(2), p. 370.
16 Esther S. Klein, 'The History of a Historian', p. 47.
17 Wai-Yee Li, 'The Idea of Authority in the Shih chi (Records of the Historian)', pp. 345–405.
18 Yan Xiong, *Yangzi Fayan*, online at: http://ctext.org/yangzi-fayan/juan-shi-er <accessed 6 April 2015>.
19 Ouyang Xiu, *Ouyang Xiu quanji* [Complete works of Ouyang Xiu], ed. Li Yian, Beijing: Zhonghua shuju, 2001, vol. 41, pp. 591–2; as translated by Jack W. Chen, 'Blank Spaces and Secret Histories: Questions of Historiographic Epistemology in Medieval China', *Journal of Asian Studies*, 2010, vol. 69(4), p. 1075.
20 William Nienhauser, 'A Note on a Textual Problem in the Shih chi and Some Speculations concerning the compilation of the Hereditary Houses', 2003, *T'uong Pao*, vol. 89(1–3), pp. 55–6.
21 Modified translation provided by Robert Campany, *Strange Writing*, p. 37. Watson translates 'I dare not mention them' as 'I cannot accept them' (Han 2, p. 252).
22 Ban Gu, *Han shu* [History of the Han Dynasty], Beijing: Zhonghua shuju, 1962, vol. 30, p. 1715, as translated in Jack W. Chen, 'Blank Spaces and Secret Histories', p.1075.
23 Ban Gu, *Han shu*, vol. 30, p. 1745, as translated by R. F. Campany, *Strange Writing*, p.132; see also Guo Xian, *Dongmingji*, as translated by R. F. Campany, *Strange Writing*, p. 145.
24 Ban Gu, *Jinshu*, as translated by R. F. Campany, *Strange Writing*, p. 147–8.
25 Robert F. Campany, *Strange Writing*, esp. pp. 178; and 237–8.
26 Judith Zeitlin, *Historian of the Strange: Pu Songling and the Chinese Classical Tale*, Stanford, CA: Stanford University Press, 1993.
27 Sing Chen L. Francis, *What Confucius Wouldn't Talk About*, p. iv.; Rania Huntington, *Alien Kind*, p. 4.
28 Shu Shi, 'On the Hall of Precious Paintings', in Yu Jianhua, *Zhongguo hualan leibian*, vol. 1, p. 48, modified translation in Judith Zeitlin, *Historian of the Strange*, p. 67.

References

Chi Yün [Ji Yun], *Shadows in a Chinese Landscape: The Notes of a Confucian Scholar*, ed. and trans. D. L. Keenan, New York: M. E. Sharpe, 1999.
Confucius, *Analects*, trans. R. Dawson, Oxford: Oxford University Press, 2008.
Duan Chengshi, *Chinese Chronicles of the Strange*, trans. C. E. Reed, New York: Peter Lang, 2001.
Pu Songling, *Strange Tales from a Chinese Studio*, trans. H. A. Giles, Rutland, VT: Tuttle, 2010.
Sima Qian, *Records of the Grand Historian, rev. edn,* 3 vols, trans. B. Watson, New York: Columbia University Press, 1993.
Yuan Mei, *Censored by Confucius: Ghost Stories*, ed. and trans. K. Louie and L. Edwards, New York: M. E. Sharpe, 1996.

5

HISTORICAL CABINETS OF CURIOSITY IN EARLY MODERN EUROPE

Jean Bodin | Francis Bacon | Walter Ralegh | Nathaniel Wanley | René Descartes | Thomas Hobbes

No one likes dining at a banquet when the order of the courses or the seasonings are haphazardly arranged. So too, the lawyer, historian and philosopher Jean Bodin (1529/30–1596 CE) argued, all historical phenomena 'are nicely adjusted to each other and cemented into one body ... by the great industry of scholars; but by some people they are unskilfully separated' (*Methodus ad facilem historiarum cognitionem* [*Method for the Easy Comprehension of History*], 1565, hereafter *Method*, p. 20). Jean Bodin's *Method* is as much about the unskilfully made history as it is about the properly universal one. The unskilful historian, we learn first in the book's dedication, falls short in the ability to discover and collect materials; to arrange them in the 'correct order'; and to eliminate errors in earlier histories (pp. 1–2). By the time we reach chapters four and five—on the choice and evaluation of historians—Bodin's analysis of the historiographically inept peaks at the suggestion that the 'evil' writer is captive to delights, superstition, enthusiasm, zeal and a desire to entertain or to achieve fame (pp. 41, 43, 46, 57, 85).

History making was for Bodin, as it was for Polybius, a sense making activity. Diligent observation and 'taking a modest part in practical affairs' provide us with the 'most valuable fruits from history' (pp. 24–5). Moreover, that observation must have as its end the discernment of universals in a cohesive account of the past, for a history without universals Bodin tells us—using the same analogy as Polybius—is like a body without eyes (p. 61). So too, Bodin's critical choice and evaluation of historians throughout *Method* suggests a Polybian approach in which history is defined in the process of writing history itself. Yet *Method* is not simply a slavish reinscription of the ancient *Histories*. Bodin's thought represents a wider revisitation of ancient thought for moral and civil ends that is first hinted at in this extract:

> In this exercise, truly, I have appreciated the saying of Plato—nothing is more difficult or more nearly divine than to separate accurately. (p. 3)

Bodin credits Plato with the insight that separation is difficult. Plato, we recall from chapter one, argued that we make sense of particular things in the world, not abstractions: we may witness, for example, a particular act of kindness, then another particular act of kindness on a different day in a different place. He was interested in the idea that if many different acts are understood by us to be kind, then there must be something that they share in common which is 'kindness', and that this 'kindness' must exist even though we might not experience it directly through our senses. This formed the basis of his proposition that there are 'forms' or ideas, and that these forms were not only distinct from our sensory experiences of particular things, they were distinct from one another (*Phaedo*, 78b–84b). The key problems with forms, Plato intimates in the later dialogue *Parmenides*, is that we need to be able to explain how they are present in particular things, even though they are distinct from one another. Moreover, as we cannot access forms directly, it becomes a challenge to know how many forms there might possibly be (*Parmenides*, 142B5–C2). Is there, for example, a form of history, as distinct from a form of philosophy?

It is well known that Aristotle's *Metaphysics* presents an extended critique of Plato's theory of forms. Aristotle, we recall, was not at all convinced that forms exist independently of the sensible objects that are meant to be their instantiation. Yet Aristotle was not averse to the idea of providing a systematic categorisation of the most general, distinct kinds of things that are and which help us to make sense of how the world hangs together. The very point of the *Metaphysics* is to help us to understand being, and this work is not unusual in the Aristotelian corpus for that interest. In looking for the practical result of Aristotle's interest in the separation, uniqueness and distinction of different kinds of being, it is the early work, *Categories* that catches our eye. *Categories* provides a departure point for this chapter in two important ways. First, Aristotle goes one step further than Plato, specifying a list of the ten kinds of being that cannot be further reduced, including quantity, place, date, action and emotion (*Categories*, 1b25–2a1). That is, he tells us what the most basic kinds of things are, rather than just suggesting that there *are* basic kinds of things. This initiated a practical and philosophical interest in distinction, differentiation and classification that remains with us today, with writers articulating various reasons for the activity of categorisation. It is a tradition that is far removed from the themes of harmony and radical immanence we explored in the last chapter. Second, while Aristotle specified emotion as a kind of being, *Categories* breaks off unfinished after the brief observation that emotions can be experienced in varying degrees (11b1–5). This leaves us with less of an idea of how to make sense of the nature and purpose of the emotions than the other nine categories.

The incomplete state of Aristotle's thoughts on emotion as a category of being turns out to be quite important, because it provided much later writers such as Thomas Hobbes (1588–1679) and René Descartes (1596–1650) with an opportunity to flesh out theories of the emotion and affective states, which for them included wonder. This designation of wonder does not sit squarely with current theories of the emotions, because early modern European writers followed

Aristotle in treating the passions as embodied responses to the world, much like perceptions. It was their status as sensory responses that piqued Aristotle's interest in the extent to which we can control them, or whether we can control them at all. Aristotle's later work *Nicomachean Ethics* looks to the role of the passions in stimulating actions in accordance with our habits and desires as moderated by reason (*Nicomachean Ethics*, 1105b26). They are like an inhibitor that prevents our completion of an action, whether the action is good or bad. This, we recall from chapter two, is seen in the akratic weakness of will that lets curiosity drive individuals to sin. Importantly, Aristotle saw the taxonomic ordering of the emotions as an important means for understanding and controlling them (*Rhetoric*, book II).

Descartes and Hobbes shared the Aristotelian view that categorising the emotions helps us to understand and to control them. In their hands, Aristotle's basic insights provided a platform to further distinguish different kinds of emotions, including in Descartes' case some diagrams of the physiological aspects of particular emotional expressions. More significantly, though, Hobbes' identification of some emotions as concerned with future rather than present objects and Descartes' positioning of wonder as the 'first of all passions' and as prior to judgement led them to be able to extend the connection drawn by Aristotle between categorisation and rightful action. Whereas Descartes saw wonder as facilitating individual, ethical judgements, Hobbes located that rightful action in a civil society in which individuals needed to be in possession of their mental activities in order to support government. The inversion of this state is seen in the addictive tendencies of a gamester, whose addiction to hope leads them to disengage from the necessary task of being a member of civil society in the present. Wonder facilitates self-understanding and control and good government; curiosity signals a loss of self-control and that signals the end of society.

The above connection of wonder with self and social order accords with Michael Deckard's analysis of Descartes' and Hobbes' contributions to our understanding of wonder. This chapter extends his argument, though, by highlighting the role that rightful functioning of mind by historians plays in a rightfully functioning state.[1] An historical engagement with wonder, it turns out, is a pivot in the struggle for self-possession over possession by others. This highlights the limitations in the predominantly materialist and imperialist interpretations of European history and histories that loom large in contemporary historiography. Early modern historians were not bent solely on possessing others; they drew upon categorisation and wonder to ensure that they were not possessed by the limitations of ancient thought that might prevent them from thinking and acting rightfully.

Early modern European histories were far more than expressions of the rise of global mercantilism. Yet there is something beguiling about Lisa Jardine's argument in *Worldly Goods* that the dual drivers of international trade and domestic economic development birthed a consumerism in which history writing was entangled.[2] This consumerism, Stephen Greenblatt explains in *Marvellous Possessions*, connotes complex encounters of possession and rejection for which 'wonderful' first encounters provide the starting point. This locates wonder, he proposes, as:

> A central feature ... in the whole complex system of representation, verbal and visual, philosophical and aesthetic, intellectual and emotional, through which people in the late Middle Ages and the Renaissance apprehended, and thence possessed or discarded, the unfamiliar, the alien, the terrible, the desirable, and the hateful.[3]

James Bester makes a similar point when he notes that '[w]onder was recognised as overpowering when imposed from without, but empowering when possessed.'[4] Wonder is the tool of the possessor over the dispossessed. From this position it is not difficult to extend arguments about wonder and possession in the direction of James Gregory's observation that wonder works—including histories—suggest a normative expression of the normal, Lorraine Daston and Katharine Park's separation of the discriminating and refined wonder of the connoisseur and the effusive wonder of the 'vulgar stay at home' and Michel Foucault's now famous reminder in *The Order of Things* that categorisation is a cultural act designed to include and exclude:

> This book first arose out of a passage in Borges, out of the laughter that shattered ... all the familiar landmarks of my thought—*our* thought, the thought that bears the stamp of our age and geography—breaking up all the ordered surfaces and all the planes with which we are accustomed to tame the wild profusion of existing things, and continuing long afterwards to disturb and threaten with collapse our age-old distinction between the Same and the Other. This passage quotes a "certain Chinese encyclopedia" in which it is written that "animals are divided into (a) belonging to the Emperor, (b) embalmed, (c) tame, (d) sucking pigs, (e) sirens, (f) fabulous, (g) stray dogs, (h) included in the present classification, (i) frenzied, (j) innumerable, (k) drawn with a very fine camelhair brush, (l) *et cetera*, (m) having just broken the water pitcher, (n) that from a long way off look like flies". In the wonderment of this taxonomy, the thing we apprehend in one great leap, the thing that, by means of the fable, is demonstrated as the exotic charm of another system of thought, is the limitation of our own, the stark impossibility of thinking *that*.[5]

The lengthy, comprehensive and apparently eccentric contributions of early modern European historians make them an easy target for our laughter at the 'stark impossibility of thinking that', and our sense that they are easily unmasked as European imperialist acts of exclusion. This account of early modern European histories, however, underestimates the extent to which their authors worried about their European contemporaries not being in possession of their thought and actions. There is no doubt that Bodin wrote in an age of exploration, possession and consumerism, but his interest in order signals a need for Europeans to engage in rightful thought and action, and that stemmed from making general sense of the world. His oblique connection between order, ethics and civil society becomes an explicit remonstration in the writings of Francis Bacon (1561–1626), who positioned an openness to wonders and thus the activity of wonder as a necessary remedy to the foreclosure of categories of thought and action by ancient atheist writers. Comprehensive historical documentation and analysis drives our visitation and revisitation of the most basic, distinct kinds of being, and these in turn, set down the 'rules' for our individual and society actions. These themes are echoed in more empirically oriented works such as Walter Ralegh's (c. 1552–1618) *History of the World*, including a warning about the overambition and vanity at work in a mind that endlessly pursues curiosities. That warning would seem to apply to prodigiously 'eccentric' works like Nathaniel Wanley's (1638–80) *The Wonders of the Little World* (1678),[6] but in it too we will find recourse to Descartes' taxonomy of the passions and its primary positioning of wonder as prior to judgement.

The simple point here is that early modern European historians were not driven by a common imperialist or consumerist agenda; rather, they reflected variations on the Aristotelian theme that categorisation of the most distinct kinds of being is necessary if we are to understand and regulate our actions as individuals and as participants of civil society. In short, this chapter marks the start of an unravelling of the uncomplicated equation of early modern European wonder with the possession of others. Possession of self in society is also a key theme, and wonder plays a role in triggering openness to different ways of encountering the world, and thus agency. Moreover, as a secondary point, it complicates any argument we might wish to make about the emergence of history as a distinct discipline over time. In this period, as with earlier ones, the boundaries between history, philosophy and wonder writing or paradoxology are blurred. This is not by accident. While ancient writers like Polybius wanted history to part ways with paradoxology, the association of wonder with openness in early modern Europe and the need to lay bare the categories that such openness reveals meant that all three were seen as necessary for making sense of the world.

In summary, early-modern historiography continued ancient Greek traditions of looking to the past to discern universals and doing so through rigorous sense perception. But they also enhanced those earlier conjunctions of history and metaphysics by insisting upon the exhaustive categorisation of the most basic kinds of things in our world, including emotions. Moreover, they did so not just for the sake of describing what they took to be the actual structure of the world, but because they saw categorisation through history as necessarily for the rightful operation of mind, the self, and society. This, as I will come to describe it in this chapter, suggested a triple skip from metaphysics to epistemology to ethics via history.

Orderly historical comprehension

A relatively small body of research on Jean Bodin's views on history celebrates what Peter Gay describes as his 'critical rationalism'. By this, Gay—as well as other writers such as Jacob Soll and Nicholas Popper—mean a rigorous disposition towards the analysis of primary sources and other histories.[7] Soll captures this rationalist Bodin well in a quote from the fourth chapter of *Method*, on the choice of historians:

> Rather stupid are those readers who admire nothing in history but eloquence or invented speeches or pleasing digression. I have made up my mind that it is practically an impossibility for the man who writes to give pleasure, to impart the truth of the matter also—a thing which Thucydides, Plutarch, and Diodorus criticised in Herodotus. (p. 55)

The best historian is one who, like Tacitus and Polybius, presents the truth in an unpolished manner, rids themself of emotions and who works assiduously to find firsthand documents and to critique them via comparison with one another (pp. 43, 47, 52, 70). *Method* is an empirically thorough work. Five chapters on the categories, order, reading, selection and evaluation of histories precede applications of this thought in a consideration of government types, regal histories, time and chronology, the origins of peoples and an appraisal of the best historians and the order in which to read them. In so doing, Bodin demonstrates an admirable grasp of both the principles and the publications that were associated with the idea of history in his day.

Moreover, *Method* is a very appealing work to us by dint of the proximity of Bodin's views to the work practises of many present-day historians. But as Soll intimates, Bodin's views are part of a wider project to glean the universal. This is the Bodin seen in the dedication and first three chapters of *Method*, encapsulated in this passage from the dedication which Soll quotes at length:

> At the beginning I outlined in a table a form of universal law, which I have shown you, so that from the very sources we may trace the main types and divisions of types down to the lowest, yet in such a way that all members fit together. In this exercise, truly, I have appreciated the saying of Plato—nothing is more difficult or more nearly divine than to separate accurately. Next, I have established postulates, on which the entire system rests as the firmest foundation. Then I have added definitions. Afterward I have laid down as briefly as possible precepts called 'rules' according to the proposed form, as if to a norm. At one side I added, in brief notes, the interpreters of Roman law, so that from the same sources whence I have drawn, each man can take his satisfaction. (pp. 2–3)

The important thing to note about this excerpt is that Bodin does not equate the term 'universal' with the encapsulation of all phenomena and events in a written work. Rather, as with ancient historians such as Polybius, it means setting out the divisions, postulates, definitions and rules that give meaning to all past phenomena and events. Universal in this case means setting out the definitions, rules and principles that allow us to order and to understand the vast particulars of the past and to present them as history.

For Bodin as for Polybius, history without universal truths is like a body without eyes (pp. 20; 61). History is a form of sense making that helps us to see beyond the particulars of the world to the rules that drive it. Yet in distinction from Polybius, Bodin does not see the achievement of universal history as one historian's project. Polybius argued that the unity of one mind and the assiduous use of certain claims about the past—those things seen by the historian—were the key to apprehending the universal. In practical terms, this resulted in Polybius offering a largely contemporary account of things that he had experienced. He worked to shut down uncertainty by shutting out all the claims that he could not trust. Consequentially, as noted in chapter one, readers are reliant on Polybius understanding—and *wanting* to understand—past phenomena. The problem with this view was not simply that it was idealised—as Polybius himself noted—but it also presumed that the one historian's views are more certain than all others. Polybius might have succeeded in uncovering some aspects of the universal in the past but not others, or no aspects at all.

Bodin was confident that many historians could contribute to the revelation of the universal in an orderly and comprehensive way, and that their efforts could make sense to readers. This confidence turns on two principles that underpin *Method* more or less explicitly: first, that there are universal rules that shape the activities of historians; and second, that these rules are seen at work in the rightful operation of mind. The first principle is signalled in the title of the first chapter of *Method*, 'categories'. There are three historical categories, Bodin asserts with confidence: the human, the natural and the divine (p. 15). We might assume that these are Bodin's assertion of the most basic, irreducible, kinds of history there are, and that they consequently do not overlap. But there is more in store for us in the second and third chapters of *Method*, which explain how the different kinds of history can form a comprehensible universal. This order, we are told, arises from two basic rules in history making: the presentation of events in chronological order, and in order from the general to the specific.

Bodin's suggestion that chronology is basic to the idea of history seems intuitively right. While there may be thematic works on offer, it is hard to think of history as making sense without chronology. His point about proceeding from the general to the particular is far more contestable given the predominant interest of present day historians in phenomena that are sub global. The important point about both of these claims is that neither is derived logically in *Method*. Bodin is no Plato or Aristotle. Yet they are not simply bald, untested metaphysical assertions. Rather—and this brings us to see the second reason for Bodin's confidence—they are seen in all good histories. Setting the circularity of this argument aside, his point is that a history without chronology or with no sense of movement from the general to the specific is akin to dining at a banquet when all the courses and seasonings are out of place. It is what we want, and not just because a properly ordered banquet is agreeable. Bodin has a more fundamental point to make: that we cannot function mentally or in our actions unless things are in the right order.

This is seen somewhat obliquely in his suggestion that developing memory as a 'treasure chest' of sayings and deeds is needed as a guide for rightful actions (pp. 27–8). This triple skip from metaphysics to epistemology to ethics is easy for our eyes to miss because of his use of the phrase 'treasure chest'. By treasure chest, we might appraise him as suggesting the establishment of a stuffed cabinet of curiosities, and back that claim up by conjuring up Francis Bacon's contemporary definition of such a cabinet as containing:

> whatever the hand of man by exquisite art or engine has made rare in stuff, form or motion; whatsoever singularity, chance, and the shuffle of things hath produced; whatsoever Nature has wrought in things that want life and may be kept. (*Gesta Grayorum*, in *The Oxford Francis Bacon*, hereafter *OFB*, vol. 8: 335)

But this idea of a hodgepodge repository of curious or wonderful acquisitions is not what Bodin has in mind, and as we shall see below, it does not capture Bacon's complex views on mind well either. Bodin's *Method* sounds a strong argument in favour of order because disorder and the ill-disciplined collection of novelties are the marks of a superficial or insane mind and the immorality that such states imply (pp. 14, 21–9, 71).

The problem is that Bodin does not tell us directly that order is necessary for reason and moral action. We have only a route via *negativa*, the chaotic, superficial, curiosity chasing activities of the insane immoral are *not what we want*. We have to join the dots between Bodin's rules and good histories and say that orderly histories reflect and reinforce reasoned, ethical action. A good historical 'banquet' goes without saying, even if it leaves us puzzled about where that might leave wonder in the writing of history.

Overcoming the retrenchment of mind

Bodin might be forgiven for providing more of a practical primer for historians than a theoretical reflection on how the rules of history are known, make sense, and take shape in or shape activities of mind. He was not an Aristotelian logician. Nor could we fault him for echoing the medieval association of unbounded curiosity with the disordered mind and the immorality that it was assumed to generate. But it still stands that he was interested in the intersection of history and philosophy in seeking to understand categories, mind and social ethics. His writings reflect lines of thought set down by ancient and medieval approaches to metaphysics, even if he was not a metaphysician. He was not alone in these interests. Daston and Park draw our attention in *Wonders and the Order of Nature* to the contribution of writers like Walter Ralegh and Francis Bacon to late-sixteenth and early seventeenth-century challenges to ancient and medieval philosophy.[8] Theirs is a refreshing expansion of analyses that typically emphasise the increasing autonomy of the discipline of history and the role of the historian as the critical arbiter of historical evidence or, as Beverley Southgate puts it, as 'political manqués—people who would have liked to be politicians and who resorted to history as a substitute for more active and direct political involvement'.[9]

Yet Daston and Park's analysis also falls back to conventional thought in one key way. This is hinted at in the disproportionate attention given to Bacon as against Ralegh, and is more explicitly seen in their celebration of Bacon as a radical who used wonder to challenge customary lines of categorisation, and of Ralegh as providing an empirical correction to John Mandeville's account of the headless blemmyes in Guyana.[10] Put bluntly, Bacon opens up thought using wonder; Ralegh corrects accounts of wonders. But the distinction is not so clean, because Bacon's ideas provide a significant source of orientation in Ralegh's multi volume *History of the World* (1618), and thus Ralegh is a theorist as well as a practitioner. This encourages revisitation of other works of history, including those which have been passed over in histories of history-making. Nathaniel Wanley's *The Wonders of the Little World* is a strong case in point. While an examination of this work is not meant to provide an exhaustive analysis of early modern histories, a revision of its 'eccentric' pages shows a similar tendency towards categorisation and the triple skip from metaphysics to epistemology and ethics. Where it differs from the works of Bodin and Ralegh is in the use of later currents of thought to make these arguments, namely the philosophies of Descartes and Hobbes.

Wonders, Bacon argued in *Novum Organum* (1620) and *De dignitate et augmentis scientiarum* (1623), provide a corrective to principles derived solely from non-wonderful phenomena and a panacea to the human tendency to make the metaphysical leap from a tiny number of particular phenomena to abstract generalisations about them (*De dignitate et augmentis scientiarum*, hereafter *De augmentis scientiarum*, OFB, vol. 6, 2.2; *Novum Organum*, OFB, vol. 11, 1.19–1.22; 1.26–8). In this expansive view of knowledge, history functions as a 'warehouse' that we can draw upon to move backwards and forwards between the universal and the particular. History, and this constant motion of mind, are needed to reveal the order of nature (*Novum organum*, OFB vol. 11, 1.18).

History in the *Advancement of Learning* is divided fourfold, into natural, civil, ecclesiastic and literary categories. Those categories are collapsed further in *De augmentis scientiarum*, with ecclesiastic and literary history rolled into civil history—concerned with the activities of people—and distinguished only from natural history, which is concerned with acts of nature (*Advancement of Learning*, OFB, vol. 4, 2.1.2; *De augmentis scientiarum*, OFB, vol. 6, 2.2). Both categories of history result from acts of sense making, in which our perceptions are brought to memory and classified—ordered—and recalled by reason. The role of reason is important, for the simple capture by memory misses the engagement of the intellect, as Bacon explains in an account of the power of mental images in *De augmentis scientiarum*:

> ... even brutes have their memory excited by sensible impressions, never by intellectual ones. And therefore you will more easily remember the image of a hunter pursuing a hare, of an apothecary arranging his boxes, of a pedant

making a speech, of a boy repeating passages from memory, or a player acting on the stage, than the mere notions of invention, disposition, elocution, memory, and action. (*De augmentis scientiarum, OFB*, vol.6, 2.5)

Thinking back to chapter two, this quote suggests a role for mental images akin to that of curiosity in Augustine's writing. They are an active expression of memory, but the ease with which they can be recalled means that they can prevent us from engaging in the more taxing tasks of combining images or of considering and classifying non-visual ideas. We need reasoning and judgement to make prudent decisions about good and bad courses of action.

So too, wonder is both the 'seed of knowledge' and 'broken', he tells us, and a part of a world in which knowledge is 'confined and circumscribed':

> ... all knowledge and wonder (which is the seed of knowledge) is an impression of pleasure in itself: but when men fall to framing conclusions out of their knowledge... and ministering to themselves thereby weak fears or vast desires, there groweth that carefulness and trouble of mind.... for the contemplation of God's creatures and works produceth (having regard to the works and creatures themselves) knowledge, but having regard to God, no perfect knowledge, but wonder, which is broken knowledge (*Advancement of Knowledge, OFB*, vol. 4, 1.3).

The limits of our knowledge are both internal and external: internal in the sense that the limits of our will and self-control see us fall prey to fears and vanities, and external in the sense that we cannot know God directly. Thus wonder—positioned at the start of our mental activities—can generate only a 'broken' knowledge of God. We need to exercise reason to strengthen our will and to remind us not to overreach in our claims to know the universal. In this process, wonder acts as a stimulant to new knowledge in the ways suggested by Plato and Aristotle, but as we shall see below, it is also taken as the mechanism by which we open up ways of thinking and acting that go without saying.

Bacon expects us to labour at knowledge, moving constantly from memory to knowledge and back again and from the particular to the universal and back again. This means that the historian must 'examine things to the bottom; and not to receive upon credit, or reject upon improbabilities, until there hath passed a due examination' to do more to establish which accounts of phenomena are certain, dubious, and to be condemned.[11] The problem with this approach, as Bacon acknowledges, is that when we go beyond accounts derived from our own first-hand experiences, we are reliant upon the mental efforts of others (*Novum Organum, OFB*, vol. 11, 176–77). This is a familiar complaint in this book: the treatment of history as a sense making activity sees certainty connected with individual sense-making. A boundary is established between what is certain knowledge and what is not certain knowledge, with our involvement in the former as the critical discriminator between the two. This opens the way for scepticism about the sense-making of others. Bacon has two remedies for this scepticism. The first sees him employ *topoi* or textual conventions to signal not the veracity, but the dubiousness of others' claims. The second sees him remind us that wonder was not just important at the start of philosophy, but that it is constantly needed to protect us from the ossification of thought.

Phrases such as 'I heard from X' or 'I read in an account by Y' signal doubt. Certain claims, on the other hand, come with none of these riders (*Historia naturalis et experimentalis, OFB,* vol. 12, 12–17). Bacon's arguments on source claim *topoi* suggest a significant departure from some of the other approaches outlined in this book. Islamic writers, we recall for instance, see the statement of lines of source transmission—who handed a description of a phenomenon down to whom—as an important part of splitting out dubious claims from those to be trusted. As we have also noted, though, wonder writers also used source claim *topoi* either to signal the veracity of their accounts of wonders, or to criticise the approaches of historians who held state-supported positions. The strange tales we examined in the previous chapter, for example, provided oblique and even direct criticisms of the efforts of official historians. If we were to apply Bacon's view to histories generated in our own time, footnoting would be taken as a signal not of certainty but of uncertainty. The more references in a work, the more dubious its claims.

In Bacon's view, the more we say about the sources of an individual sense-making claim, the more doubt we signal about it. He also appreciated, however, that a lot of sense making activities can go without saying. In simple terms, what we take for granted as being certain can also be uncertain or even dubious. Here we might assume that Bacon got stuck in the same way as Polybius, not being able to provide us with a guide on what to trust and what not to trust. Polybius tried to resolve the problem by relying on only his own knowledge claims. Bacon, on the other hand, recalls that wonder is always available to us to ensure that we think things through and not simply rely upon the thoughts of others. Bacon's account of history thus takes aim at others' decisions of inclusion and exclusion, suggesting that we open up consideration of both the ordinary and the irregular (history of wonders) in our consideration of phenomena (*Advancement of Knowledge, OFB,* vol. 4, 4.67). In this way, he sees us as being able to address the blind spots of earlier thinkers, and to ensure possession of our own minds by constantly renewing our understanding of the world.

Nothing less than the regeneration of thought via history was what Bacon sought. This is because he saw the ancient foundations of the thought of his day as having become unquestioned. The inclusion of wonders and the experience of wonder signalled the need to re-do the work of deriving categories and descriptions of the most basic kinds of being by induction through propositions seen at work in particular phenomena. That is, he argued for us to be open to the possibility that past descriptions of the most basic categories of being are unduly limited. Bacon spent more time elaborating on this task of shifting between the particular and the universal in his various writings on natural history, but *Novum Organum* makes it clear that the inductive method is appropriate for all endeavours of mind, including human history. We need, he tells us:

histories and tables of discovery concerning anger, fear, shame and so on, and also ones to do with examples of civil business; no less than to do with the mental motions of memory, composition and division, judgment and the rest, just as much as I would of hot and cold (*Novum Organum, OFB* 11.191).

These would provide the foundations needed to assist us in making judgements about particular courses of action, as Aristotle believed was the case with the study of the affections. Moreover, the acts of the individual who uses will to make good judgement contribute to good government (*Advancement*, 4.135) and to an understanding of 'pertubations and distempers of the affections' needed to treat others suffering from weakness of will or even insanity (*Advancement, OFB,* vol. 4, 4.149–50; *De augmentis scientiarum* 1: 735, 737).

Bacon saw the ancient Roman historians Tacitus and Livy as providing some of the descriptions of phenomena upon which universal categories of the most basic kinds of being could be derived. But the work of the historian in his day was not done. Far-ranging and comprehensive accounts of past phenomena were needed to build an understanding of the universals that shape individual and social action. Exhaustiveness was thus not a sign of methodological weakness; rather, it reflected a willingness to be critical about past assumptions in order to derive a fuller, and better, account of the categories of being that shape our lives. As we recall from the past chapter, some of the same intent was at play in the critical stance strange historians took against the Chinese official histories.

Strange historians, though, needed to question official histories through a separate, unendorsed, even guerrilla approach to history making. Bacon's stance, on the other hand, signalled an invitation for the wondrous and the wonderer to be part of history as it was recognised by the state and by those who wrote other histories and who might have also called themselves historians. Combined with liberal notions of textual ownership and copyright, there was only one direction for the word totals of histories to go: up. Volumes heaped upon volumes, with a variety of authors of both genders seeking to explain the universal through the careful cataloguing and classification of what Foucault would have called 'the wild profusion of existing things'. This age also continued the tradition of the commonplace book, where authors created meta distillations of the things that students and those who wished to transact well in society ought to know.[12]

Walter Ralegh's crystallisation—while imprisoned in the Tower of London—of around five hundred texts into the five books of *History of the World* is a much noted example. This is not simply because, as Daston and Park have noted in a passing remark, Ralegh gave his readers cause to think critically about wonder claims of the travel writer John Mandeville.[13] Further, while he did as Nicholas Popper suggests, labour to illuminate the hand of providence, his was not a work simply of categorical description.[14] He, like Bacon, saw a need to be exhaustive in order to illuminate universals kept from our view by the tyranny of 'sloth and dullness' at work in philosophy. As he explains, in a fashion much like Bacon:

> ... [philosophers] have so retrenched their minds from the following and overtaking of truth, and so absolutely subjected themselves to the law of those philosophical principles; as all contrary teaching, in the search of causes, they have condemned either for fantastical or curious... that where natural reason hath built any thing so strong against itself, as the same reason can hardly assail it, much less batter it down... (*History of the World*, I:xliv).

Here we see the traditional lines of philosophical thought coming up short in the explanation of the 'fantastical' or the 'curious', which as he explains further on, may reflect the work of God. By necessity, historical research has to be opened up so that we can gain 'sense and feeling of corporeal things' (*History of the World*, I:xl; and xxxi). So too, we see in Ralegh's use of the word 'feeling' that an exhaustive account of phenomena embraces the affections in sense making.

The echo of Bacon is also seen, significantly, in Ralegh's positing of a double limit to wonder. That limit, we recall, is internal and external, reflecting the overreach we experience due to weakness of will, and the fact that we cannot apprehend God directly. Our knowledge can only be of God's works in the world. So while Bacon and Ralegh saw wonder as a necessity in reopening lines of enquiry closed down by ancient—indeed 'secular' or 'atheist'—philosophers, they made it clear that it could not be relied upon solely because it spurs endless recourse to curiosity. Here we see Ralegh echo the medieval idea that a little wonder is a good thing, but a lot of curiosity is a bad thing. Bacon describes this stretch using the rich analogy of 'flying up to the Deity by the waxen wings of the senses' (*Advancement of Learning*, OFB, vol. 4, 1.3). Ralegh opts for his own analogy, which sees us focus on the overambition of those who attempt to cross a powerful river:

> ... who, not contented with a known and safe ford, will presume to pass over the greatest river in all parts, where he is ignorant of their depths: for so doth the one lose his life, and the other his understanding (*History of the World*, I:i.xii).

Why someone switches from wonder to curiosity is not explained by Bacon and Ralegh in terms of specific mental activities. Rather, they see the switch from one to the other as reflecting both the fact that human reason is limited, as distinct from God's powers, and because the Devil 'seemeth to work his wonders by moving the cogitations and affections of men' (*History of the World*, I:ix.399). Protection comes from the humility of knowing that human knowledge is limited, and therefore that the historian must employ a critical attitude towards sources. That aim, however, runs up against the counter tendency of dismissing sources on the grounds that they suggest phenomena too remarkable to be explained by known methods of explanation.

Where Popper saw in Ralegh's *History of the World* a deliberate opting for a more extensive account of phenomena than might be trusted by rigorous source analysis, any notion of deliberation seems to fly out the window in works such as

Nathaniel Wanley's *The Wonders of the Little World* (1678).[15] What few appraisals of Wanley's *Wonders* we have seen him described as a source for 'eccentric' and 'abnormal' biographies. A surface glance at *Wonders* seems to underscore the soundness of these judgements, and Foucault's idea of us arriving at the stark impossibility of Wanley thinking such things. Six books of lives which are organised by chapter heads such as 'Of the Different and Unusual Ways by which Some Men have Come to their Deaths' (I:28); 'Of Such as Having Been Wild, Prodigal, or Debauched in their Youth, Have Afterwards Proved Excellent Persons' (III: 2); and 'Of the Signal Deformity, and Very Mean Appearance, of Some Great Persons, and Others' (I: 13). It is a great read, but read in one sitting, the detail is overwhelming, and suggests that Wanley was correct to appraise himself as a reciter and a collector, rather than an inventor or framer (Preface: vi).

Wanley saw himself as a cipher in order to position the reader as judge of the phenomena described. As he admits in the preface to *Wonders*, though, the work includes citations, and multiple citations are used to build up an account of the same phenomenon in order to fill in gaps (*Wonders*, Preface:vi). Yet *Wonders* is not without stance, as the highly critical comments on the materialism of Catholic clergy in the chapter on different and unusual deaths show (*Wonders*, I:28). More importantly, *Wonders* is not without order. Books two and three provide the most apparent evidence of this, with Wanley setting out a detailed account of all known human virtues, affections and sense making abilities through a prodigious collection of examples. *Wonders* is a catalogue of human appearances, sense making abilities and types of reason and affection.

A deeper dive rewards us with a sense of the primacy of some human virtues, forms of reason, and affection over others. Wanley's ordering of the affections is particularly striking, because of how it positions admiration, which is a cognate term for wonder. As he explains:

> ... admiration, the first of all the passions, rises in the soul before she hath considered whether the thing represented to her be good, or convenient to her, or not; so, after she has judged it to be good, there is raised in her the most agreeable and complacent of passions, love; and when she hath conceived the same to be evil, she is quickly moved to hatred, which is nothing but the soul's aversion to that which threatens pain or grief (*Wonders of the Little World*, II.9.176).

There is something more to this than Bacon and Ralegh's insistence that we need wonder to open ourselves up to new lines of thought. Wanley takes great pains to tell us that admiration is the first of all passions, and that it is prior to judgement. This view is not incompatible with Bacon's or Ralegh's views, and it certainly suggests a revisitation of the ideas of Thomas Aquinas. But the idiom of Wanley's description, and the sheer number of affections he catalogues suggests that their lines of thought are insufficient for capturing the contours of his view.

First of all the passions

Wanley did not arrive at these views of admiration on his own. As with Ralegh, his history draws upon philosophy as the source for explanations of why we categorise in particular ways, and to what ends. In *Wonders* we see two other currents of early modern European philosophy that postdate the ideas of Bodin, Bacon and Ralegh: the writings of Descartes and Hobbes on the passions.

Hobbes and Descartes both classified wonder—Hobbes also used the term admiration—as a passion or affection. This designation is not easily translated into the term emotion as we understand it. Rather, they employed the term passion to signal a reflection of Aristotle's interest in receptive—even passive—states or states of perception. They also followed Aristotle in providing an account of the most basic, distinct kinds of passions, with Descartes identifying six in a detailed physiological and philosophical taxonomy in *The Passions of the Soul* (1649) and Hobbes proposing 25 to 30 across *The Elements of Law Natural and Politic* (c. 1640, in *Human Nature and De Corpore Politico*, hereafter *Elements of Law*) and *Leviathan* (1651). Where they parted company with Aristotle was in the placement of a particular passion at the head of their taxonomies, and the choice of passion differed for the two: glory for Hobbes, wonder for Descartes. This difference in choice is significant, and stems back to differing views on social interaction and the power of will. The latter, we will see, provides a strong rebuttal to the Aristotelian idea of the passions as passive human states. Whereas Hobbesian glory is a sense of superiority that drives conflict between at least some individuals (*Leviathan*, I:13); Cartesian wonder is prior to judgements of good and bad, but the wonderer does consider attentively and either bestow scorn or esteem depending on the smallness or the greatness of the phenomenon respectively (*Passions of the Soul*, 2:70; 2.54).

The Hobbesian individual never attains what they desire, and consequently, human action is future oriented (*Leviathan*, I:6). This spurs a diffidence or even lack of trust in others, which can result in acts of harm (*Leviathan*, I:13). That distrust can extend to the state or the ruler of a state, and be fuelled by admiration or wonder at the distracting words of tricksters and false prophets (*Leviathan*, III:37). The result is addictive hope akin to that of a gambler who focuses only on the hope of bettering their own life circumstances. This analogy is seen at work in Hobbes' adaptation of Aristotle's opening to the *Metaphysics* in *Elements of Law*:

> And from this beginning is derived all philosophy: as astronomy from the admiration of the course of heaven; natural philosophy from the strange effects of the elements and other bodies. And from the *degrees of curiosity* proceed also the *degrees of knowledge* among men; for to a man in the chase of riches or authority (which in respect of knowledge are but sensuality) it is a diversion of little pleasure to consider, whether it be the motion of the sun or the earth that maketh the day, or to enter into other contemplation of any strange accident, than whether it conduce or not to the end he pursueth. Because curiosity is delight, therefore all *novelty* is so, but especially that novelty from

which a man conceiveth an opinion true or false of bettering his own estate. For in such a case they stand affected with the *hope* that all gamesters have while the cards are shuffling (*Elements of Law*, IX:18).

Philosophy begins with wonder, but without moderation, it transforms into a curiosity that endlessly seeks out novelty. What is lost in the process is an awareness of our need to submit to a powerful sovereign in a state if we are to be protected from harm by others. We see only ourselves and the hope for something different, even novel, in the future. Curiosity is thus, taken to extremes, a destabiliser of individuals and states.

Hobbes' remedy for curiosity is a shift from attraction to superficial consideration of causes to the disciplined consideration of the basic categories of cause and effect (Leviathan, I:11). That discipline comes from not treating books as the complete source of reason; not accepting established definitions as going without saying; and scrutinising the claims of historians against our own and others' experiences (*Leviathan*, I: 4; IV: 46; I:7;). In stressing the importance of not being beguiled by speech or past definitions or categories, Hobbes combines the insights of Roger and Francis Bacon, the former of which he knew by text and the latter of which he knew by a series of conversations.

Descartes also held to the importance of regulation of the passions by training (*Passions of the Soul*, I:50), and the avoidance of too much wonder in particular:

> although it is good to be born with some inclination to this passion, since it disposes us to the acquisition of the sciences, we should still try afterwards to emancipate ourselves from it as much as possible. For it is easy to supplement a deficiency of it by a particular [state of] reflection and attention to which our will can always bind our understanding when we judge that the thing presented is worth the trouble. But to prevent excessive wonder there is no remedy but to acquire the knowledge of many things, and to apply oneself to the consideration of all those which may seem most rare and unusual (*Passions of the Soul* II:76).

That we may seek a remedy for the development of too much wonder in the comprehensive consideration of wonders seems paradoxical, even if it reflects the same devotion to openness of thought promoted by Francis Bacon. How could we know when to pull back from wonder? Descartes derives his confidence from three things. First, there is his assumption that wonder loses its thrall with a loss of novelty. As he explains: 'because the more one encounters rare things one wonders at, the more one routinely ceases wondering at them and comes to think that any that may be presented thereafter will be ordinary ...' (*Passions of the Soul*, II:78). We assume in this case that as we get older, fewer and fewer phenomena will appear wonderful to us. Second, as we age and acquire more knowledge of ourselves, we are less apt to be humbled by the esteem or scorn of the wondrous phenomena we encounter, and attribute that esteem or scorn to ourselves (*Passions *of the Soul*, III:170). We possess a stronger sense of self and will from which to make judgements about the knowledge claims of others. Finally, and most fundamentally, *Meditations on First Philosophy* (hereafter *Meditations*) I and IV make it clear that Descartes holds to strong voluntarism: full, direct control over passing or withholding judgement. This strength of will makes the harnessing of wonder possible and likely also explains why wonder loses its grip over us as we age. Consider his thoughts on employing a shift towards falsehood to counteract the pull of propositions that we find so plausible as to go without saying:

> I shall never get out of the habit of confidently assenting to these opinions, so long as I suppose them to be what in fact they are, namely highly probable opinions—opinions which, despite the fact that they are in a sense doubtful, as has just been shown, it is still much more reasonable to believe them than to deny. In view of this, I think it will be a good plan to turn my will in completely the opposite direction and deceive myself, by pretending for a time that these former opinions are utterly false and imaginary (*Meditations*, in *The Philosophical Writings of Descartes*, I: 15).

Through sheer force of will, Descartes is able to open his mind to propositions that seem implausible, and thus to act with possession of mind.

Nathaniel Wanley's *Wonders* is far from the sustained examination of the passions that we find in Hobbes' and Descartes' writings. But their ideas clearly influenced his vocabulary—'admiration' from Hobbes—and his positioning of wonder as the first passion, and as prior to judgement. *Wonders* may be eccentric, but it takes its steer from a philosophical age in which Francis Bacon railed against the foreclosure of thought and both Hobbes and Descartes worked through the individual and social implications of wondering before judgement. These writings bore a confidence in the power of the human will both to prevent a slide into the addictive, sinful, path of the curious, and to make sense of, order, and act upon a wider description of phenomena than they saw in their predecessors' books.

Aristotle held that philosophy begins with wonder, but somehow, along the way, that wonder seemed to have been lost in what seem to have been exhaustive logical descriptions of the universal. Early modern European wrote of wonder in order to recapture an openness to the novel and the strange and to make sense of the world through the ordering and categorisation of phenomena. In doing so, I noted that they seemed to skip lightly from metaphysics to epistemology and to ethics, and therefore from a sense of wonder as order, to wonder as the order of an individual's mind, to wonder as the order of a good society. Their works were neither an expression of mindless consumerism nor the simple premise for possessing others through imperial expansion. Rather, the early modern European histories of Bodin, Bacon, Ralegh and Wanley were potent invitations for their readers to seek enough control over their own powers of mind to open up the positive possibilities of encountering Foucault's 'wild profusion of existing things'. Their response was not a stark realisation of the impossibility of thinking some things, but an openness to the implausible in order to drive a better understanding of the universal through the particular. That hope in wonder as the means for achieving openness to the most basic kinds of being—and to being itself—remains with us today.

Notes

1. Michael F. Deckard, 'A Sudden Surprise of the Soul: The Passion of Wonder in Hobbes and Descartes', *The Heythrop Journal*, 2008, vol. 49, pp. 948–63.
2. Lisa Jardine, *Worldly Goods: A New History of the Renaissance*, London: Macmillan, 1996, p. 10. See also Maxine Berg, 'In Pursuit of Luxury: Global History and British Consumer Goods in the Eighteenth Century', *Past and Present*, 2004, vol. 182(1), pp. 85–142 and Maxine Berg and Elizabeth Eger (eds.), *Luxury in the Eighteenth Century*, Basingstoke, UK: Palgrave Macmillan, 2003.
3. Stephen J. Greenblatt, *Marvellous Possessions: The Wonder of the New World*, Chicago, IL: University of Chicago Press, 1991, pp. 22–3. See also Lorraine Daston and Katharine Park, *Wonders and the Order of Nature 1150–1750*, New York: Zone Books, 1998, p. 305.
4. James Bester, *Lyric Wonder: Rhetoric and Wit in Renaissance English Poetry*, Ithaca, NY: Cornell University Press, 1977, p. 13.
5. James D. Gregory, 'Eccentric Lives: Character, Characters and Curiosities in Britain, c. 1760–1900', in *Histories of the Normal and Abnormal: Social and Cultural Histories of Norms and Normativity*, ed. W. Hurst, London: Routledge, 2006, pp. 73–100; Lorraine Daston and Katharine Park, *Wonders and the Order of Nature*, p. 321; and Michel Foucault, *The Order of Things: An Archaeology of the Human Sciences*, trans. Anon, London: Routledge, 1970, p. xvi.
6. James D. Gregory, 'Eccentric Biography and the Victorians', *Biography*, 2007, vol. 30(3), p. 344 [342–76].
7. Peter Gay, *The Enlightenment*, New York: Knopf, 1966, p. 298; Jacob Soll, 'Empirical History and the Transformation of Political Criticism in France from Bodin to Bayle', *Journal of the History of Ideas*, 2003, vol. 64(2), pp. 297–316; and Nicholas Popper, 'An Ocean of Lies: The Problem of Historical Evidence in the Sixteenth Century', *The Huntington Library Quarterly*, vol. 74(3), 2011, pp. 375–400.
8. Lorraine Daston and Katharine Park, *Wonders and the Order of Nature*, pp. 219–31.
9. See for example Nicholas Popper, 'An Ocean of Lies', pp. 374–400; Joseph M. Levine, *The Autonomy of History: Truth and Method from Erasmus to Gibbon*, Chicago, IL: University of Chicago Press, 1999; and Anthony Grafton, *What Was History? The Art of History in Early Modern Europe*, Cambridge: Cambridge University Press, 2007. Quote is from Beverley Southgate, *Why Bother with History?: Ancient, Modern and Postmodern Motivations*, London: Routledge, 2013, p. 60.
10. Lorraine Daston and Katharine Park, *Wonders and the Order of Nature*, for the section on Walter Ralegh, see p. 219; on Francis Bacon, see pp. 219–31.
11. Francis Bacon, *Parasceve ad historiam naturalem*, as quoted in Silvia Manzo, 'Francis Bacon's Natural History and Civil History: A Comparative Survey', *Early Science and Medicine*, 2012, vol. 17, p. 39.
12. See for example Ann Moss, *Printed Commonplace Books and the Structuring of Renaissance Thought*, Oxford: Oxford University Press, 1996; and Victoria E. Burke, 'Recent Studies in Commonplace Books', *English Literary Renaissance*, 2013, vol. 43(1), pp. 153–77.
13. Lorraine Daston and Katharine Park, *Wonders and the Order of Nature*, p. 219
14. Nicholas Popper, *Walter Ralegh's History of the World and the Historical Culture of the Late Renaissance*, Chicago, IL: University of Chicago Press, 2012, p. 69.
15. Nicholas Popper, *Walter Ralegh's History of the World*, p. 122.

References

Aristotle, *Categories*, in *The Complete Works of Aristotle* trans. J.L. Ackrill and ed. J. Barnes, Princeton, NJ: Princeton University Press, vol. 1, pp. 3–24.
Aristotle, *Nicomachean Ethics*, in *The Complete Works of Aristotle* trans. J.L. Ackrill and ed. J. Barnes, Princeton, NJ: Princeton University Press, vol. 2, pp. 1729–1867.
Aristotle, *Rhetoric*, in *The Complete Works of Aristotle* trans. J.L. Ackrill and ed. J. Barnes, Princeton, NJ: Princeton University Press, vol. 2, pp. 2152–2269.
Bacon, Francis, *The Oxford Francis Bacon, 15 vols.*, Oxford: Oxford University Press, 1996.
Bodin, *Method for the Easy Comprehension of History*, trans B. Reynolds, London: Macmillan, 1989.
Descartes, René, *Meditations on First Philosophy*, trans. J. Cottingham, Cambridge: Cambridge University Press, 2016.
Descartes, René, *The Passions of the Soul* [1649], trans S.H. Voss, Indianapolis, IN: Hackett, 1989.
Hobbes, Thomas, *Human Nature and De Corpore Politico*, trans and ed. J.C.A. Gaskin, Oxford: Oxford University Press, 1994.
Hobbes, Thomas, *Leviathan* [1668], trans and ed. E. Curley, Indianapolis, IN: Hackett, 1994.
Plato, *Parmenides*, trans M.L. Gill and P. Ryan, Indianapolis, IN: Hackett, 1996.
Plato, *Phaedo*, trans D. Gallop, Oxford: Oxford University Press, 2009.
Ralegh, Walter, *The Works, vols. 2–7*, Oxford: Oxford University Press, 1829.
Wanley, Nathaniel, *The Wonders of the Little World, or A General History of Man, 2 vols.*, London: W.J. and J. Richardson, 1678.

6

SPIRITED HISTORIES IN MODERN EUROPE

Immanuel Kant | George William Frederick Hegel | Daniel Defoe | William Howitt | Sarah Josepha Hale | Leopold von Ranke

Modern historiography means Leopold von Ranke (1795–1886). It is hard to avoid him in histories of history, for he often forms the marker point for the emergence of professional or 'scientific' history making. But he is also seen less positively, as one of the twin shoals upon which the idea of history nearly came to be wrecked in the nineteenth and twentieth centuries. In the extreme he is a writer who failed to follow his own injunction that the historian is a colourless or transparent overlay on the past.[1] His binary is George William Frederick Hegel (1770–1831), who is cast as the progenitor of 'metaphysical history' replete with 'pseudo-statements' and speculation.[2] In Hegel's hands, purportedly, metaphysics came to be seen as shorthand for a progressive narrative which ends with the triumph of the West to the exclusion of everyone else.[3] Both von Ranke and Hegel purportedly give history a bad name, and in the case of Hegel, unmask the pursuit of metaphysics as socially, politically and ethically dangerous. Making general sense of the world, on these terms, means controlling it in your lights. This chapter breaks down the Ranke-Hegel binary and shows that both were part of a wider movement that harnessed metaphysics and history in the service of creating quite diverse visions of how things make sense.

Described variously as the 'nineteenth-century's historical titan'[4] and as the progenitor of a 'critical historical science'[5], writers such as Georg Iggers, Peter Novick and John Tosh have laboured to promote a nuanced understanding of von Ranke's contribution to historical scholarship. This has meant, in the main, arguing against the collapse of his thought into a literal reading of a single passage:

> History has had assigned to it the task of judging the past, of instructing the present for the benefit of ages to come. To such lofty functions this work does not aspire. Its aim is merely to show how things actually were [*wie es eigentlich gewesen*] (*The Theory and Practice of History*, p. 85).

Careful readings of this snippet from the preface to the first edition of *Histories of the Latin and Germanic Peoples* emphasise Von Ranke's place in an Idealistic tradition dominated by Immanuel Kant (1724–1804) and Hegel. In this tradition, the aim to show 'how things actually were' is an endeavour to discern the universal in the particular, which Iggers expresses as 'how things *essentially* were'.[6] Iggers reminds us that Rankian histories were not simple mass aggregations of historical facts; they offered an account of the essential nature of phenomena as well. So too, Peter Novick has emphasised the reading of von Ranke's claim as a creed used by him and later writers to support the emerging idea of an historical profession. In that profession, the rallying cry for an objective understanding of 'how things actually were' served to broker a fragile peace between a burgeoning number of writers with very different styles, interests and political beliefs.[7]

This idea of a peace brokered in the name of objectivity is seen by some as having come at the price of wonder. Lorraine Daston and Katharine Park, for example, paint a picture of the age of Enlightenment and its wake as ushering in the diminution and even the extinction of the 'star of the marvellous'.[8] This was the age of the 'new science', a shaking free from assumed abstractions and the embrace of rational observation and testing. Wonder was laid bare as the fixation of the 'ordinary person'—often assumed to be a woman or child—with vulgar oddities and freaks. It would be a short step from there to the sideshow and to the films that form the focus of the next chapter. Wonder not only enthralled and entertained, but it was also discerned as a threat to hard fought scientific, religious and political order alike. John Spencer's *A Discourse Concerning Prodigies* (1663) seems to capture this view well:

> How mean a regard shall the issues of the severest debates, and the commands of Authority find, if every pitiful Prodigy-monger have credit enough with the People to blast them, by telling them that heaven frowns upon the laws, and that God writes his displeasure against them in black and visible Characters when some sad accident befals the complyers with them?[9]

Yet this was also the age of intuition. Iggers and Breisach remind us that von Ranke had a metaphysical interest in discerning the hand of God in events, and that this revelation of the universal was not to be achieved by rational induction from the concrete to the abstract. Rather, Ranke argued for *Ahnen*, an intuitive cognition that reveals the ideas that shape concrete phenomena.[10] As he explains in *The Idealistic Theory of State*:

> Without a leap, without a new start you never can progress from the general to the particular. The spiritual force which suddenly arises as concrete phenomenon before your eyes in unimagined uniqueness cannot be derived from a higher principle. From the particular, perhaps, you can ascend with careful boldness to the general. But there is no way leading from the general theory to the perception of the particular. (*The Theory and Practice of History*, pp. 63–4)

He was far from singular in this interest: Kant's meticulous *Logic* divides all cognitions into intuitions and concepts, and Hegel treated it in his encyclopedia *Philosophy of Mind* as the starting point for the self-realisation of rational thought.

It is important to pause and to note that writing on intuition and wonder does not imply support for either idea. John Sallis, for example, sees Hegel's writings on intuition as dealing the double blow of displacing, and then extinguishing wonder. Displacement, he argues, came with Hegel's decision to treat intuition and wonder in part three of his *Encyclopedia of the Philosophical Sciences—Philosophy of Mind* (1817), which has more of a practical, psychological focus than his other works. Philosophy might have had its beginning with wonder in Aristotle's *Metaphysics*, but it ended with its move out of metaphysics and into the new field of psychology. This meant seeing the meaning of intuition and wonder as exhausted with an understanding of mind, rather than an understanding of how everything—including mind—hangs together and makes sense. Second, he appraises Hegel as putting 'an end to wonder still more decisively' by linking it to intuition. This is a claim he supports by reference to the following excerpt from *The Philosophy of Mind*:

> Aristotle refers to its [intuition's] place when he says that all knowledge begins from *wonder* [*Verwunderung*]. Initially, the object is still loaded with the form of the irrational, and it is because it is within this that subjective reason as intuition has the certainty, though only the indeterminate certainty, of finding itself again, that its subject matter inspires it with wonder and awe. Philosophical thought, however, has to raise itself above the standpoint of wonder. (§449)[11]

On this reading, we have reached the point when the shadow cast by the opening of Aristotle's *Metaphysics* over the idea of history begins to shrink.

As you might guess from the number of pages that follow this one, I do not agree with Sallis' reading of Hegel on intuition and wonder. Rather, as with Martin Heidegger, it might be counter argued that this chapter marks the beginning of the idea of history as wonder. This Heideggerian reading celebrates Hegel as having understood the connection of history and philosophy in Aristotle's *Metaphysics* better than any writer before him. Had Sallis extended his quote from Hegel's *Philosophy of Mind* to incorporate the next few sentences, for example, we would have seen a glimpse of an account of the historical self-realisation of mind in which wonder is not left behind. Hegel writes:

> In immediate intuition, I do indeed have the entire matter before me; but only in the cognition that is unfolded in all its aspects and returns to the form of simple does the matter stand before my mind as an *internally articulated, systematic totality*. (§449)

Intuition and wonder are not left behind when higher forms of thought are developed: they are a part of them.

This chapter unfolds Hegel's thought on the interconnection between history and philosophy. To that end, it covers ground familiar to those who know something of the contribution of Hegel to the philosophy of history. In distinction from those customary accounts, however, this chapter does not celebrate Hegel—as Heidegger did—for having thought 'the philosophy of the Greeks for the first time [*zum ersten mal*]'.[12] Rather, I show that his interleaving of wonder, intuition and thought in history is expressed in a much wider range of works, from the metaphysical universal history of Kant to the empirical histories of von Ranke and Sarah Josepha Hale (1788–1879), and to the paradoxological histories of Daniel Defoe (1684–1731), and William Howitt (1792–1879). Arguably none of them present philosophy in as an historicised manner as Hegel and we may fault their logic and conclusions, but the gesture of connecting metaphysics and historical phenomena is there. This interest, I argue, stems from their desire to explain how we might gain an understanding of the universal from concrete, particular, historical phenomenon and their varying determinations to see the 'leap' from one to the other through the more or less rational experiences of the sublime, intuition, and spirit. In the case of von Ranke, there is an argument for the superiority of history over philosophy in explaining the universal. But this argument, it will be shown, bears fewer radical implications than the historical embodiment of intuition as female in Hale's world, or its realisation in the ghosts, revenants and poltergeists of Defoe and Howitt's spirited histories.

History as intuitive leap to the universal

It is not customary to think of the 'father' of the modern profession of history as being interested in intuition, or indeed any other operations of mind and meaning making. Our received understanding of von Ranke is very much that of a technically adept historian, not a theorist. Indeed, as Iggers argues, Ranke's very interest in the uniqueness of historical agents and their contexts meant a rejection of philosophical approaches like those proposed by Hegel or Kant.[13] Historical understanding demanded a critical interpretation of the evidence that points to historical agents and events. This view of von Ranke might be seen as a liberating challenge to the assumption that historians serve the philosophical cause of illuminating the universal through time. This was the moment to unshackle history from metaphysics. Ranke's vision of history is not ancillary to philosophy, but a discipline in and of itself. In this discipline, truth is not to be found in the shadows of Plato's forms or Aristotle's immanent universals realising themselves in some grand world historical narrative, but in attention to archival detail by carefully trained analysts.

Much of Ranke's writing supports this interpretation of him as a technical empiricist. History and philosophy are distinct, as he explains in an early manuscript from the 1830s:

There are two ways of acquiring knowledge about human affairs—through the perception of the particular and through abstraction. The one is the way of philosophy, the other that of history .... These two sources of knowledge are therefore to be kept clearly distinguished. ('On the Relations of History and Philosophy', in *The Theory and Practice of History*, p. 5).

So too, in the preface to his final work—*Universal History* (1884)—the limitations of history are declared:

The province of History is limited by the means at her command, and the historian would be overbold who should venture to unveil the mystery of the primeval world, the relation of mankind to God and nature. The solution of such problems must be entrusted to the joint efforts of Theology and Science. (*Universal History*, p. ix)

To von Ranke's mind, historical overstretch is there from the beginnings of history making, with some accounts being no more than legends embellished with a variety of fabulous and miraculous phenomena (*Universal History*, pp. 84, 97, 129). This judgement sharpens further as he narrows in on the examples of Herodotus and Thucydides, and the exemplar of the latter's matter of fact approach to sense making:

The miraculous, which has such charm for Herodotus, disappears in Thucydides behind the unadorned fact. The tone of his narrative is sometimes as simple as that of a chronicle; it impresses one as at once trustworthy and intelligent (*Universal History*, p. 318; see also p. 171).

Yet across the corpus of von Ranke's writings, we cannot help but notice his wrestle with the universal in history. This point is played out most clearly in his extended examination of the same two historians mentioned above: Herodotus and Thucydides. Thucydides is trustworthy and intelligent, but he is also, Ranke tells us, 'circumstantial' as a consequence of his impartiality. That is, Thucydides' provision of a detail-laden narrative leaves the matter of judging those past phenomena to readers. Herodotus' recourse to the gods and to the miraculous, on the other hand, relieves readers of some of the burden of judgement (*Universal History*, pp. 318–9). Moreover Thucydides' recourse to detail as providing certainty and authority, Ranke notes, is not consistent. He does not provide word for word accounts of speeches or letters, thus offering a 'moment in which the science of history and the science of rhetoric... unite their forces' (*Universal History*, p. 321). This appears to be quite a concession to style, and one that might lead us to revisit Ranke's judgement of Herodotus. It is no fleeting comment, for it is reinforced by a slightly earlier discussion of Thucydides' speeches in *Universal History*, which stresses their legitimacy as stemming from their encapsulation of principles at work in concrete phenomena and actions:

Alkibiades exerted all the power imparted both by his personal influence and his prestige. The noble speech which Thucydides put in his mouth cannot be regarded as an exact report of what he said, but the principles therein expressed are of the greatest importance as illustrating the political views of the period. (*Universal History*, p. 253)

Thucydides shows us how something essentially happened (*wie es eigentlich gewesen*) without relaying all of its details.

Ranke's analysis of Thucydides suggests that historians can opt to describe the principles at work in particular phenomena without labouring the details. What it does not show us, though, is a case for seeking those principles. We can discern principles in phenomena, but *ought* we do so? It might be argued in the case of Thucydides, for example, that he resorted to presenting principles in the absence of a detailed archival record. Had more archival information been available, he might not have relied so heavily on rhetoric. On this view, archival details would be preferable to principles.

In stark contrast with the time of Thucydides, Ranke lived in an archivally rich age. His work is grounded in a strong appreciation of the value of archives, and—on the logic that I set out above—there might be seen as less necessity for him to resort to principles. Yet he does present principles, and he does not see them as functioning to fill archival gaps or a back-up option. This is because principles point to the work of God. Ranke's identification of the value of principles for finding God in history date back to at least 1820, as seen in this excerpt from a letter to his brother:

In all of history God dwells, lives, can be recognised. Every deed gives testimony of him, every moment preaches His name, but most of all, it seems to me, does so the connectedness of history (*Zusammenhang der großen Geschichte*). He stands there like a holy hieroglyph, understood and preserved in His most extreme manifestation (*in seinem Äußersten aufgefaßt und bewahrt*), perhaps in order that He is not lost to more perceptive future centuries …. [L]et us do our part to unveil this holy hieroglyph! In this way too we serve God, in this way we are also priests and teachers. ('The Young Ranke's Vision of History and God' [1820s], in *The Theory and Practice of History*, p. 4; see also 'On Progress in History' [1854], in *ibid.*, p. 21).

God's universality is at work in the particular, making it possible for historians to discern it and thus to contribute to divine understanding. Importantly, too, Ranke sees spiritual discernment as not so much detected by historians as intuited (*ahnen*) through an act of spiritual apperception ('On the Character of Historical Science' [1830s], p. 15, see also p. 12; and 'On the Relations of Philosophy and History' [1830s], in *The Theory and Practice of History*, p. 6). That detection appears to be akin to the work of prophets in Ibn Khaldun's *Muqaddimah*, as discussed in Chapter Three. Closer inspection of von Ranke's discussion, though, suggests that *ahnen* is not only open to those born with prophetic skills: as he suggests, we can all be priests.

Ranke has very little to say about the nature of this historical intuition, apart from noting that it leads to certain knowledge, and—as the quote that opens this chapter suggests—that the move from the particular to the universal does not require the same leap as needed in the move from the universal to the particular ('On the Relation of and Distinction Between History and Politics' [1836], in *The Theory and Practice of History*, p. 78; and 'A Dialogue on Politics' [1836], in *Ibid.*, p. 62). These characterisations suggest that we are more likely to succeed in exercising intuition in empirical sense making activities, rather than abstract considerations. As such, they point us in the direction of suggesting that historians might be more able to educate us in the universal than philosophers. Theory proceeds from the particular, not the other way around. Lest we leap to such a conclusion, however, it should be noted that his characterisations might apply to other empirically-based disciplines. God's 'heiroglyph' might also be discerned in other empirical disciplines such as science, geography or psychology.

World history in the service of spirit

Yet history is named specifically and repeatedly by Ranke as a means of attaining universal history through a consideration of the concrete. Moreover, he saw a role for intuition in achieving that consideration. Recourse to intuition did not necessarily herald a turn from metaphysics to epistemology, or even the diminution of metaphysics by epistemology. In this sense, Ranke's writing appears to have a connection with the older currents of thought outlined in this book. We recall from chapters two and three—on pre-modern European and Islamic histories—for example, the connection of the metaphysical contemplation of history with the contemplation of God's work in the world. So too, we have to admit the possibility that if Ranke was not the progenitor of these ways of thinking about history, then there might have been other contemporary writers with similar or even more extended interests in the connection of the universal and the particular in history. In sum, Ranke might not have been the only writer of his time to see historical contemplation as providing insight into the most fundamental senses of being.

In making this point, I am not referring only to 'metaphysical historians' like Kant and Hegel. History making boomed in the eighteenth and nineteenth centuries, fuelled by the growth of institutional education, circulating libraries, cheaper forms of textual production, and liberal or even non-existent copyright laws. Even the most cursory glance highlights that Ranke was not the only writer interested in the idea that history making afforded the opportunity for intuition to support metaphysical sense making. Nor, as it turns out, were his views on historical intuition particularly radical. This is a point I am going to unpack through three examples of histories that are yet to register in introductory historiographies both by virtue of who their authors were, and the topics they took as their focus.

We begin with the apparition histories of Daniel Defoe and William Howitt: *Essay on the History and Reality of Apparitions* (1727) and its second edition *The Secrets of the Invisible World Disclosed* (1729) and *The History of the Supernatural in All Ages and Nations* (1863) respectively. Defoe is best known to us as the author of *Robinson Crusoe* (1719), but he was also a royalist pamphleteer and is acknowledged for his blend of history and fiction in his journalistic accounts of the great storm of 1703 (*The Storm*, 1704) and the great plague that ravaged London in 1665 (*Journal of the Plague Year*, 1722). William Howitt was a Quaker turned spiritualist, who wrote prolifically on religion, science, literature, magic and his experiences as a traveller to Australia (see for example *A Popular History of Priestcraft in All Ages and Nations*, 1833; and *Labour, Land, and Gold; or, Two Years in Victoria*, 1855).

Neither Defoe's nor Howitt's apparition histories have attracted significant attention by historiographers, and this is probably due to their subject matter. After all, histories of ghosts and revenants do not seem to sit comfortably with our current day notions of a discipline built upon professional standards. Professional historians don't do ghosts, paradoxologists do. Yet as we have noted throughout this book, paradoxological writers employ *topoi* or literary devices that suggest shared features with histories. On that basis, an examination might be warranted to contextualise them within that tradition. Michael McKeon and Jayne Lewis see apparition histories of the eighteenth and nineteenth centuries as having a further and particular claim to our attention: that their extensive empirical descriptions function to help us to form vivid pictures that do not have moral or metaphysical implications. In this way, they mimic the commitment to mass description birthed in the new science, and reinforce Sallis' claim that intuition functioned as a barometer of a shift from metaphysics to epistemology.[14]

Support for McKeon's and Lewis' point is easy to find, particularly in Defoe's *History and the Reality of Apparitions*. There is, for instance, Defoe's logical point that if all souls wandered the earth after life, 'the inhabited and visible world would have been continually haunted with ghosts, and we should never have been quiet' (p. 99). Apparitions are occasional, and the world can make sense without them. Moreover, there is his explicit likening of apparitions to paintings:

> [a]n apparition assumes the shape and appearance of [a] man himself, clothes himself in his likeness ... as a painter clothes the cloth he paints on with figures, postures, habits, garments, all in colours; while the passive person represented is in no way affected with or concerned in the draught representing him (p. 132).

This leads Lewis to conclude that in apparition histories we see evidence of a commitment simply to empirical description that sets 'metaphysics on the run'. She explains:

> In their emphasis on empirical verification ... the apparitionists aimed to impose new criteria of veracity on metaphysical phenomena—a gesture that in itself tolled the death knell of such phenomena as a valid and authentic order of experience.[15]

A closer look at the second edition of Defoe's work—*The Secrets of the Invisible World Disclosed*—and Howitt's *The History of the Supernatural in All Ages and Nations*, however, complicates the picture. Defoe acknowledges that apparitions can be conjured up by our imagination, but he further argues that this does not dismiss the metaphysical implications of his enquiry. He argues:

> ... it does not follow from thence that there are therefore no such Things in Nature; that there is no Intercourse or Communication between the World of Spirits, and the World we live in ... (p. 2).

There is an order of nature, constituted by the realm of God, the realm of the living, the realm of the Devil, and the realm of the spirits. The boundaries between these three realms are permeable. This turns out to be an important premise for supporting the critical observation that God has appeared to us as a voice (p. 9) and as a dove (p. 14); but also most importantly, as incarnated in Christ (p. 11). If God has appeared to humanity in the past, then appearances by those who herald from the realm of the spirits are also a worthy topic for historical examination. Moreover, the appearance of spirits is documented in the Bible, which Defoe classifies as an authentic and authoritative document (p. 45), but at the same time, he makes it clear that he is not simply a cipher or annotator of Biblical events. His own authority is built on the basis of 'authentic' written, visual and auditory evidence (see for example pp. 86; 90; 166), with the occasional qualification that he believes an account to be true (pp. 101–2; 152; 167). Moreover, he judges that evidence in accordance with his reasoned understanding of what makes sense, and that understanding—he makes clear with a reference to Plato—is based upon the reality of things, not their shadows (p. 320). In discussing Matthew 27:52, for example, he notes that the bodies of saints resurrected after Christ's ascension must have included their souls because he has no sense of a bodily apparition that has no soul (p. 49; see also pp. 198–9).

When Defoe shifts to the converse description of ignorance, he draws out implications that are very like medieval warnings about what happens when mental activities are unconstrained by reason. Ignorant people, he argues:

> ... [n]either know how or by what Rules to judge of such Things, or are capable of right Conceptions about them; who do not give themselves time to exercise that little Power of thinking that they are Masters of, and so are left to the Darkness of their own Fancies, thinking everything they see is a Devil, merely because they do not know what else to make of it ... (p. 74).

This point is reiterated in a later discussion in which he notes that feelings of guilt hinder reason to such an extent that the imagination is flooded with 'sudden and surprising' delusions (p. 110; see also p. 111; 126; 390; 394). It is not simply that delusions flood the mind of the weak. Defoe also wants us to appreciate that reason bestows an ability to judge the *rules* of phenomena, not just to describe their appearance. This suggests that we not only judge on the basis of our experience: the well-trained mind knows how the world hangs together. And this well-trained mind is needed because God will not discern the right courses of action for us. If God constantly sent apparitions warning us off courses of action, he notes, we would have only weak powers of judgement and would be not much accountable for our actions (p. 32). Moreover, he doubles back on the notion of appearances as pictures, arguing that the depictions that we have created of the Devil are so varied that he would have difficulty recognising himself (p. 364). A rational mind is needed to discriminate between these appearances and to determine if the Devil has ever crossed over into the realm of the living. On this argument, Defoe's detailed, descriptive language is not a new scientific end in itself—as Lewis holds—but part of a sustained argument about looking beyond appearances to discern universal forms.

The pictorial is the metaphysical and the moral. All of this suggests that Defoe did not simply assemble *The Secrets of the Invisible World Disclosed* as an empirical casebook in the service of the new science. Those who know Defoe's writings well sense that he is far too clever to have wrought a simple guidebook. What Defoe shows us—in his own terminology—is that our world is neither empty of wonders nor overwhelmed by them. Strength of reason and empirical sense making are needed to get to grips with reality, and to explain it by recourse to rules that reflect the invisible presence of God. *The Secrets of the Invisible World Disclosed* marks therefore not the exit of metaphysics in an age of new science, but the co-opting of belief in the value of extensive empirical observation to the service of metaphysical sense making. Nor therefore does it mark the exit of wonder; it remains a possibility given that God can appear.

The same expansionist co-opting of empirical observation to metaphysics is at play in Howitt's *The History of the Supernatural in All Ages and Nations*, but it is expressed in the form of a sharp rebuke to scientists and philosophers for rejecting the sense making claims of spiritualists who use their 'spiritual eye' (vol. 1, p. 7). Whereas Defoe argued for the prevailing use of rationality, Howitt sees that as the means by which humanity will experience its eclipse. He, like Defoe, holds to the existence of both a physical, visible world, and of a spiritual, invisible world (vol. 1, pp. ix; 227). But unlike Defoe, he views the loss of ability to discern the invisible world after the great flood of the Bible as a narrowing of sense making activities (vol. 1, p. 229; see also vol. 2, p. 1). This contraction of abilities produced a deadening of faith and the sacrilegious assumption that salvation could be achieved through rational transaction and the rebuttal of wonder. For Howitt, this approach—instantiated in the writings of Kant and to a lesser extent, Hegel—is nothing more than slavery to Aristotelian logic (vol. 1, pp. viii; 115; 79–89; vol. 2, p. 87). Howitt's history is a call to reverse the tide of thought, and that reversal, he maintains, will best come about through the contemplation of a detailed, empirical world history of appearances in all times and ages. This is because, Howitt argues:

> There is God in history as well as in metaphysics. That deep and universal idea in the human mind thus develops itself in perpetual majesty, and clothes the abstract idea, the radical and innate faith of the race, as a body clothes the spirit. (vol. 1, p. 81)

Moreover, we might harness the power of the imagination and the wonders it generates to act on that knowledge in expressions of belief that include spiritualism (vol. 2, p. 46). When we do so, we will have the ability again to know and to understand human nature (vol. 1, p. 10). This is a duty that Howitt sees us needing to embrace in order to arrest the downward trajectory of humanity caused by shallowness of rational scientific and philosophical thought (vol. 1, p. 14).

Salvation is also at stake in Sarah Hale's *Women's Record; or Sketches of all Distinguished Women, from "The Beginning" till AD 1850* (first edition 1853), but as we shall see, that salvation results from a gendered notion of intuition. Like many other pre-twentieth century women historians, Hale's work has received scant historiographical attention. She is known predominantly for being the editor of *Godey's Lady's Book* from 1837–77 and as a champion for the education of girls. *Women's Record* is a 900-page world history compiled from the biographies of over 1650 women, including Hale herself. Whilst a cursory appraisal might locate the text in the tradition of 'women's worthies'—texts that provide moral instruction via the aggregation of the biographies of 'good' and 'bad' women—the preface reveals a far more radical agenda. No previous women's world history, to her view, had provided a 'true idea of woman's nature and mission' (*Women's Record*, p. vii). Hale is happy to oblige, starting with the premise that the history of the world is a Christian narrative. This is a standard nineteenth century narrative assumption, but she extends it in an unusual direction. Women, she insists, are God's agents of morality, and this leads her to conclude that world history is the story of the progressive realisation of women into that appointed role (*Women's Record*, p. xxxv).

This is a conclusion that Hale arrives at on the basis of theology. Genesis, she argues, narrates the fall of man, not woman. Woman was created second to man, and that provided God with the chance to exercise greater care in creation and thus to wrought a finer mold (p. xxxvi). This positions woman not only as complementary to man, but also as superior:

> Woman was the crown of all,— the *last*, and must therefore have been the *best* in those qualities which raise human nature above animal life; the link which pressed nearest towards the angelic, and drew its chief beauty and strength from the invisible world. (*Women's Record*, p. xxxvi)

Woman was not made to serve man, as Paul had assumed, but to refine and to elevate his sensibilities and moral skills (*Women's Record*, p. xxxvii). That superiority is seen in women's intuitive knowledge of God's work, which puts them in closer proximity to the angelic than men (*Women's Record*, p. xxxix). Men, by contrast, are driven by thinly veiled animal propensities, which are expressed in physical feats, lust, violence, patriotism and idolatry (*Women's Record*, pp. xxxv–xxxvi). The difference is an organic one of mind, which Hale explains on multiple occasions. The first critical difference revisits the theme of the universal and particular at work in this book, but in a gendered, embodied fashion. In Hale's view, men inhabit and master the world of matter, whereas women inhabit and master the world of the spirit. Hale is in no doubt that the latter is the superior power of mind, because it draws us closer to God. This is explained in a passage that is worth quoting at length:

> That she reasons intuitively, or by inspiration, while he must plod through a regular sequence of logical arguments, is admitted by all writers on mental philosophy; but there is another difference which has not been noticed. Woman never applies her intuitive reasoning to mechanical pursuits. It is the world of life, not of things, which she inhabits. Man models the world of matter. These manifestations are precisely such as would result from the differences in the nature of the two sexes, as I have described them in Adam and Eve. And also, we here find the perfect solution of the assertion of St. Paul, that man 'is the image and glory of God; but the woman is the glory of the man.'— An image is something visible; the glory of God which men see, is in the things He has created; consequently, to create is to show forth, or be the 'glory of God.' Man is the maker or creator on earth… He, therefore, represents on earth the Creator's glory.
>
> But to create is not man's greatest glory; it is to worship God in spirit and in truth. The manifestation of this worship is moral goodness. Woman cannot create or make, like man; but, better than he, she worships God in spirit and in truth; and thus, showing forth the beauty of moral goodness, becomes 'the glory of the man.'(*Women's Record*, p. xlvi)

At the same time, though, Hale concedes that if women are to redeem men, they will have to explain the spiritual in material terms. This problem is solved if women are trained like men:

> Woman has a quicker capacity for comprehending moral truth or sentiment than man, but she cannot explain this truth, nor expose error to his comprehension, unless her intellect has been, in some measure, trained like his. Men have little sympathy with intuitive knowledge, or feeling;— 'pure Reason'— in the doctrine of Kant: hence they must have the truth set before them in its relations with 'practical Reason.' The mother who can in this intelligible manner aid the mind of her son in his pursuit of knowledge, will have over him a double control; he will honour as well as love her. And the pious woman who can give, clearly and wisely, a 'reason for her hope,' will often silence the proud infidel who scoffs at believing what is only felt to be true. (*Women's Record*, p. xlvii).

Here we see intimated the double superiority of women: they possess spiritual intuition but they can also be trained to exercise material intellect. This is a clever co-opting of the argument that women and men are distinct, but that women can also think like men. But it also provides something of a response to Ranke's positioning of the move from the particular to the universal as easier than the universal to the particular. Ranke experiences that asymmetry *as a man*; Hale contends that the 'leap' from the universal to the particular is natural to women, and that they can be taught to leap the other way around.

Hale sees her provision of a detailed, empirical history of the spirit as proving exactly this point. It is against the animal instincts of man that women enact their intuition and moral strengths, and the record of history suggests the progressive victory of women in doing so. That victory takes place both through incremental changes and large events in four ages: from the creation to the birth of Christ; from 1 CE to 1500 CE; from 1500 CE to 1800 CE; from 1800 CE to Hale's times. Within that narrative there are two critical turning points after Adam's fall. The first comes with her assertion that as Christ 'inherited his human nature entirely from his mother (*Women's Record*, p. 65), he was feminine:

> [Christ's] *human soul*, derived from a woman, trained by a woman, was most truly *womanly* in its characteristics. Examine the doctrines he taught, the duties and virtues he enforced, the examples he set—where, in any of these, are the distinctive traits men vaunt as proofs of masculine greatness? Physical strength, earthly honours, riches, worldly wisdom, even the gifts of intellect and the pride of learning, our Saviour put all these down far, far beneath *meekness*, mercy, purity, patience, charity, humility; qualities and graces always considered peculiarly feminine… (*Women's Record*, p. 129)

This example may suggest that men can be trained to think like women, but as it is Jesus, the exceptional nature of the case suggests that this is unlikely. The second comes in the United States with the individual liberty protected in constitutional laws. This accelerates the ability of women to shape the character of men in moral ways, and delivers results that are evident to all: '[t]he result is before the world,—a miracle of national advancement. American mothers train their sons to be Men!' (*Women's Record*, p. 564).

Hale's belief in women is unfailing, leading her to question the portraits of women like Cleopatra, Delilah, Xantippe, Zenobia and even Agrippina—the mother of Nero—as bad. Her approach is to contextualise, noting that their views and deeds paled in comparison to the actions of their fathers, sons and male contemporaries. They were of their time, but their underlying nature as women made them less prone to extreme behaviour (*Women's Record*, pp. 21–2; 32; 63;150). In short, history proves that women are needed to make general sense of things. The gendering of metaphysics is a theme I will return to in chapter eight, but for the moment I simply want to observe that the combination of metaphysics and history does not necessarily lead to the celebration of the achievements of white men.

Thinking history as wonder for the first time

Hale, Howitt, Defoe and Ranke all present history as a means for testing whether we are making the best use of our powers of mind to make sense of the world, which for them has the purpose of appreciating God. Moreover, for all but Defoe, that activity of sense making is identified with intuition, a mental power that appears to leap the gap between the material and the spiritual worlds that they assume to exist. Successful application of intuition accords with the achievement of progress both on an individual and on a world historical level. Retraction from intuition, Howitt warns us, sets the world into a degenerative spiral.

Were it not for their interest in intuition and the supernatural, they probably would have already featured in histories of history. That historiography commonly stresses the important contributions of Kant and Hegel in calling upon philosophical reasoning to outline progressive world histories. Yet as we shall see, both offer more expansive notions of reasoning than we might first credit.

Kant's *Idea for a Universal History with a Cosmopolitan Aim* (1784, hereafter *Idea for a Universal History*) is very different to the histories discussed in the previous section. That difference is evident most in the length of Kant's work: around ten pages versus the 300–900 pages of the other works reviewed. That length is a function of Kant's determination not to intuit the universal in a mass aggregation of historical particulars, but to set forth nine logical propositions which explain all of the details in those other works. The universal proceeds to the particular, not the other way around. In this way, it is the inverse of the example-based approach to explanation of historical principles we saw in Polybius' *Histories* in Chapter One. Aristotle is acknowledged as the primary inspiration for this approach, with Kant making it clear in his *Critique of Pure Reason* (1781) that 'our primary purpose is the same as his [Aristotle's], although widely diverging from it in manner of execution' (A80/B105).[16] Kant agreed with Aristotle's aim in writing the *Categories*—which we encountered in the previous chapter—to describe the kinds of being that cannot be further reduced. But he also thought Aristotle's method of arriving at them to be largely an accident of his empirical observations (*Critique of Pure Reason,* hereafter *CPR*, A81/B107). No doubt, he could have levelled the same criticism against Polybius, or many of the historians that feature in this book. Kant's 'copernican revolution' in philosophy (*CPR*, Bxvi–xviii), and in history, was to insist that categories might be logically derived from a systematic analysis of the forms of human judgement that structure our understanding of the sensible world. On this view, the categories are *a priori*: justification for them is not dependent on empirical observation or experience, but they explain how we make sense of empirical observations.

Human reason gives shape to all of our experiences of the world, including the writing of history, and experiences over historical time. Kant's first and second propositions in *Idea for a Universal History* suggest that it is natural for all organisms to develop, and that human beings are distinctive not only because they develop rational capabilities, but also because the development of that rationality plays out at species rather than at individual level. This means that if we are to understand the ongoing development of rationality, we will need to think about history, and not just about things like psychological observations (*Idea for a Universal History*, p. 11). Quite distinctively, too, Kant proposes that the engine of the development of rationality is the antagonism or 'unsocial sociability' of human beings (*Idea for a Universal History*, p. 13). In simple terms, this is the adage of not being able to live or live without others. We have a propensity to want to live in community, but we also want to assert our independence and superiority over others. This drives a competitiveness of mind that results in the innovations that gradually improve all of our lives.

As to the nature of this unsocial sociability, and therefore on how it contributes to our structuring of the sensible world, we have to look beyond *Idea for a Universal History* to works such as *Religion Within the Boundaries of Mere Reason* (1793). In his account of the predispositions to humanity, Kant makes it clear that unsociability requires reason, but that the comparing of self love at its heart generates a predisposition towards the vices of jealousy, envy, hostility and superiority (*Religion Within the Boundaries of Mere Reason*, 1.2). This may suggest that unsocial sociability is a form of *akrasia*, which in chapter two we learned about as the idea of weakness of will. In simple terms this means that when we are selfish or adopt a stance of superiority towards others, we act against our own better judgement. We know we can act selflessly or with kindness towards others, but we do not. This way of thinking about weakness of will suggests its potential connection with moral choice, which Kant picks up on in his third predisposition in *Religion Within the Boundaries of Mere Reason*. Weakness of will is weakness of moral will because it leads to harm towards others. The paradox of this account of weakness of will is that short-term exercise of the vices can lead to innovations which improve the overall wellbeing of humans. Individual bad can lead to community good.

Kant is unclear about how we are to assess the moral wrong and the moral good of individual actions that lead to good outcomes in the long run. Nor is it clear from his account whether we know these longer term outcomes will come; it took Hegel to present our lack of awareness of these outcomes in his phrase 'the cunning of reason'. Kant's key emphasis is on the way that the application of rational choice shapes our experience of the world. That he connects rational choice with the exercise of the vices suggests, however, a broader aetiology of 'reason' than we might assume. That is confirmed in accounts of ideas such as the 'noble sublime' in *Observations on the Feeling of the Beautiful and the Sublime* (1764). On Kant's account, the spontaneous experience of pleasure, or pain—or as he suggests in later works, sense of admiration or respect—we get when we contemplate phenomena such as a massive mountain range, the Egyptian pyramids or poetry or art is accompanied by 'quiet wonder' (*Observations on the Feeling of the Beautiful and the Sublime*, 2:209; 48; *Critique of Pure Judgement*, 1790, 5:245). That 'quiet wonder', we learn in the *Critique of Pure Judgement*, is a sense of astonishment or mental shock that arises when we experience a phenomenon that runs against our expectations (5: 272).

The reconciliation of Kant's ideas across the full range of his writings should not be assumed. What we can note, though, is an openness to the idea that our understanding of the world is shaped by more than the rational choice of the best course of action. His explanation of our mental world sees the potential of good arising from vice-driven actions over the long term, and of moral contemplation being accentuated by wonder at phenomena that do not fit with our notions of how the world is or how it might be. In so arguing, he makes a case for the writing of history, and for wonder in the writing of history.

What Kant does not offer us, though, is an account of how the mind comes to be able to operate in these ways. That task, it is well known, became one of the key contributions of Hegel.

Hegel's *Philosophy of History* sets out the story of the realisation of Spirit. In a manner akin to Kant, Hegel argues that Spirit is universal and that it cannot be detected in an investigation of the actions of particular individuals. Rather, the rationality in individuals contributes to the development of Spirit over time and cannot necessarily be seen by them. This suggestion that the realisation of Spirit is not apprehended by individuals, we recall from above, is described in the phrase 'the cunning of reason'. But Hegel also takes it a step further than Kant, arguing that the *development* of rationality in individuals contributes to the development of Spirit. This stems from his insistence in seeing the Spirit as immanent, which of course includes people. And as the immanent develops, Spirit develops. This fundamental point in Hegel's philosophy is expressed well in this passage from the *Philosophy of Mind*:

> Spirit was treated as a thing; [its] categories were regarded, in the general manner of the abstractive intellect, as inert, fixed; as such they are incapable of expressing the nature of Spirit. Spirit is not an inert being but, on the contrary, absolutely restless being, pure activity ... not an essence that is already finished and complete before its manifestation, keeping itself aloof behind its host of appearances, but an essence which is truly actual only through the specific forms of its necessary self-manifestation [and] ... inwardly bound to [the body] .... The entire development of mind else but the raising of itself to truth, and the so called psychic forces have no other meaning than to be the stages of this ascent (*Philosophy of Mind*, §378; §397).

This double story of freedom unfolding through history, and the historical unfolding of thought as philosophy stands as the reason for Heidegger's appraisal—noted in the introduction of this chapter—of Hegel as thinking the philosophy of the Greeks for the first time. By this he explains that '[t]o this day there has been no experience of history that, seen philosophically, could respond to this history'.[17] And this thinking, Heidegger notes repeatedly throughout his writings, pays heed to Aristotle's invitation for us to see philosophy as beginning with wonder. It is not simply that Hegel saw Spirit as being realised both in history and in the individuals that are a part of history. He also saw individuals and histories retaining the vestiges of what comes before the present. The idea of history is needed for us to see this, and as we recall from the introduction, Hegel perhaps overextended in his argument that only history can capture this. We cannot make sense of our own and the world's development in advance; we can only make sense of them by looking to history. As he writes in *Lectures on the Philosophy of World History*:

> Thought is of a universal and of a collective nature, so that it cannot die, but always retains its identity. Each determinate form which the spirit assumes does not simply fade away naturally with the passage of time, but is preserved in the self-determining, self-conscious activity of the self-consciousness. Since this preservation is an activity of thought, it is both a conservation and a transfiguration. Thus while the spirit on the one hand preserves the reality and the continuity of its own nature, it is at the same time enriched by the essence, the thought, the universal aspect of what was formerly its mere existence. (*Lectures on the Philosophy of World History*, p. 61)

The logical consequence of this view for Hegel—and thus Heidegger—is that if philosophy *begins* with wonder, then wonder must still be present in our mental operations and metaphysical sense making today.

This is not obvious from a consideration of the work that is best known to historians, *Lectures on the Philosophy of World History*. In that work we see individual and disciplinary development in the manifestation of three successive forms of historical thought and action, which he labels original, critical, and philosophical. According to Hegel, original historians 'primarily [describe] the actions, events, and conditions which they [have] before their own eyes and whose spirit they [share]' (*Philosophy of History*, pp. 1–3). This view of history does not hold because historians realise that their own views and those of the people they write about may not be in agreement. Moreover, the use of forms of evidence in addition to eyewitness accounts does not restrict history to the description of contemporary events.

In critical history, which succeeds original history, surveys of a people, a country or even the known world are offered. This represents an advance on the restriction of original history to contemporary witness accounts of phenomena but they struggle to provide a rationale for the restriction of their works or to accommodate views of the world that differ from their explanations. Philosophical historians acknowledge that different historical ideas and events are all part of the one reality that is Spirit, that those ideas differ over time, and that they need to contemplate their own activities of mind in laying out that history. In this way, Hegel signals that history is philosophy, and philosophy history, and that bringing the two together promises the reward of self-knowledge of ourselves as in a state of becoming free individuals in local and global communities.

To see wonder, we have to acknowledge Hegel's work as a whole, including part three of *The Philosophy of Mind*, which Sallis treats as something of an empirical ancillary to the main metaphysical game. It is not, as recognised not only by Heidegger, but also by his contemporary, R.G. Collingwood. Collingwood argued in works such as *Speculum Mentis* (1924) that in order to explain historical thought, you also needed to explain artistic thought.[18] This is because the vestiges of artistic thought are a part of historical thought. In our world grown old, wonder is not left behind; it remains as part of a more and more complex and nuanced operation of mind that is needed to catch intimations of the Spirit.

Philosophy as history

For Hegel, it was never a case of either rationality *or* wonder. Both, in unity, are needed to apprehend the universal in the immanent. So too, we see the same comingling of the rational, wonder, intuition and the 'spiritual eye' of eighteenth and nineteenth century historians such as Ranke, Defoe, Howitt, and Hale. None present the case for that comingling in as sophisticated a manner as Hegel, but their attempts probably still made sense to their readers. And the combined force of their cases needed to be made in order for the diversity of a growing world of readers to appreciate the enduring value of history in revealing the universal. Men, women and children all read history,[19] and history made sense to them in multiple, non-collapsible ways: in the revelation of Spirit/Mind (e.g. Hegel), the unfolding of the good (e.g. Kant), proof of multiple, permeable realms (e.g. Defoe), in expressing a case for a return to an old way of 'seeing' (e.g. Howitt) or the revelation of women as the world's future (e.g. Hale).

Yet as we shall see from the last chapter in this book—which focuses on Heidegger and Hannah Arendt—those cases might not have been made persuasively enough to generate awareness of the power of metaphysics and wonder in twentieth-century historiography and philosophy. Somehow wonder was assumed to have been lost in the transposition to rational scientific and philosophical thought at the birth of the twentieth century, and it, like metaphysics, seemed to fall away. This sets the stage for Heidegger's argument for the protection of the discipline of history from a banal death via a return to metaphysics and to wonder. In the chapters that follow, it will be for us to judge whether the stakes have been that high.

Notes

1 See for example Charles A. Beard, 'That Noble Dream', *The American Historical Review*, 1935, vol. 41(1), pp. 74–87.
2 See for example Rudolf Carnap, 'Überwindung der Metaphysik durch Logische Analyse der Sprache,' ['The Elimination of Metaphysics through Logical Analysis of Language'] *Erkenntnis*, 1932, pp. 60–81; Charlie D. Broad, 'Critical and Speculative Philosophy', in *Contemporary British Philosophy: Personal Statements (First Series)*, ed. J.H. Muirhead, London: G. Allen and Unwin, 1924, pp. 77–100; and William H. Walsh, *An Introduction to Philosophy of History*, London: Hutchinson, 1951.
3 For a reading of metaphysics as shorthand for the presentation of a progressive Western narrative, see Francis Fukuyama, *The End of History and the Last Man*, London: Free Press, 1992, and critical response to Fukuyama in Samuel P. Huntington, *The Clash of Civilizations and the Remaking of World Order*, New York: Simon and Schuster, 1996.
4 Michael Bentley, *Modern Historiography*, London: Routledge, 1999, p. vii.
5 Ernst Breisach, *Historiography: Ancient, Medieval, Modern*, 3rd edn, Chicago, IL: University of Chicago Press, 2007, p. 232. See also Eileen K.-M. Cheng, *Historiography: An Introductory Guide*, London: Bloomsbury, 2012, p. 61.

6 Georg G. Iggers, Introduction, in *Leopold von Ranke, The Theory and Practice of History*, London: Routledge, 2011, pp. xix–xx. See also Richard Evans, *In Defence of History*, New York: W.W. Norton, 2000, p. 14.
 7 Peter Novick, *That Noble Dream: The 'Objectivity Question' and the American Historical Profession*, Cambridge: Cambridge University Press, 1989.
 8 Lorraine Daston and Katharine Park, *Wonders and the Order of Nature: 1150–1750*, New York: Zone, 1998, p. 329.
 9 John Spencer, *A Discourse Concerning Prodigies [1663]*, 2nd edn., London: J. Field, 1665, as quoted in Lorraine Daston and Katharine Park, *Wonders and the Order of Nature*, p. 335.
10 Ernst Breisach, *Historiography*, p. 232.
11 John Sallis, 'Imagination, Metaphysics, Wonder', in *American Continental Philosophy: A Reader*, Bloomington, IN: Indiana University Press, 2000, p. 32.
12 Martin Heidegger, 'Hegel and the Greeks', trans. R. Metcalf, in *Pathmarks*, W. McNeill ed., Cambridge: Cambridge University Press, 1998, p. 324.
13 Georg G. Iggers, 'Introduction', p. xxvii.
14 Michael McKeon, *The Origins of the English Novel, 1600–1740*, 2nd edn, Baltimore, MD: Johns Hopkins University Press, 2002, p. 83; and Jayne E. Lewis, 'Spectral Currencies in the Air of Reality: A Journal of the Plague Year and the History of Apparitions', *Representations*, 2004, no. 87, pp. 82–101.
15 Jayne E. Lewis, 'Spectral Currencies in the Air of Reality', p. 90. In making the argument she refers to M. McKeon, *The Origins of the English Novel*, p. 83.
16 The *Critique of Pure Reason* was published in two editions, which are commonly called A and B. The numbers cited refer to the line numbers in each of these editions.
17 Martin Heidegger, 'Hegel and the Greeks', in *Pathmarks*, ed. W. McNeil, Cambridge: Cambridge University Press, 1998, p. 333.
18 Robin G. Collingwood, *Speculum Mentis, or, The Map of Knowledge*, Oxford: Oxford University Press, 1924.
19 On the growth of mass literacy, see for example Martyn Lyons, 'New Readers in the Nineteenth Century: Women, Children, Workers', in *A History of Reading in the West*, eds. G. Cavallo and R. Chartier, Cambridge: Cambridge University Press, 1999, pp. 313–44.

References

Aristotle, *Categories*, in *The Complete Works of Aristotle* trans. J.L. Ackrill and ed. J. Barnes, Princeton, NJ: Princeton University Press, vol. 1, pp. 3–24.

Aristotle, *Nicomachean Ethics*, in *The Complete Works of Aristotle* trans. J.L. Ackrill and ed. J. Barnes, Princeton, NJ: Princeton University Press, vol. 2, pp. 1729–1867.

Aristotle, *Rhetoric*, in *The Complete Works of Aristotle* trans. J.L. Ackrill and ed. J. Barnes, Princeton, NJ: Princeton University Press, vol. 2, pp. 2152–2269.

Defoe, D., *Essay on the History and Reality of Apparitions. Being an account of what they are and what they are not*, London: J. Roberts, 1727.

Defoe, D., *The Secrets of the Invisible World Disclosed: or, an Universal History of Apparations Sacred and Profane, Under all Denominations; whether Angelical, Diabolical, or Human Souls Departed*, London: J. Clarke, 1729.

Hale, S.J., *Women's Record, or Sketches of all Distinguished Women from "The Beginning" till AD 1850*, New York: Harper and Brothers, 1853.

Hegel, G.W.F., *Lectures on the Philosophy of World History*, trans. H.B. Nisbet, Cambridge: Cambridge University Press, 1981.

Hegel, G.W.F., *The Philosophy of History*, trans. J. Sibree, Mineola, NY: Dover, 1900.

Hegel, G.W.F., *Lectures on the History of Philosophy: Plato to the Platonists*, vol. 2, Lincoln, NE: University of Nebraska Press, 1995.

Hegel, G.W.F., *The Philosophy of Mind: Part Three of the Encyclopedia of the Philosophical Sciences* [1830], trans. W. Wallace, Oxford: Oxford University Press, 2007.

Howitt, W., *A Popular History of Priestcraft in all Ages and Nations*, London: John Chapman, 1845.

Howitt, W., *Labour, Land, and Gold, or Two Years in Victoria, 2 vols*, London: Longman, Brown, Green, Longmans, and Roberts, 1858.

Howitt, W., *The History of the Supernatural in all Ages and Nations, and in all Churches, Christian and Pagan: Demonstrating a universal faith*, London: Longman, Green, Longman, Roberts, and Green, 1863.

Kant, I., *Critique of Pure Reason*, trans. and ed. N. Kemp-Smith, London: Macmillan, 1958.

Kant, I., *Observations on the Feeling of the Beautiful and Sublime*, trans. J. Goldthwait, Berkeley, CA: University of California Press, 1960.

Kant, I., *Critique of the Power of Judgement*, trans. P. Guyer and E. Matthews, Cambridge: Cambridge University Press, 2000.

Kant, I., 'Idea for a Universal History with a Cosmopolitan Aim', in *Kant's Idea for a Universal History with a Cosmopolitan Aim: A Critical Guide*, ed. A.O. Rorty and J. Schmidt, Cambridge: Cambridge University Press, 2009, pp. 9–23.

Kant, I., *Religion within the Bounds of Bare Reason*, trans. W.S. Pluhar, Indianapolis, IN: Hackett, 2009.

Kant, I., *Logic*, trans. W. Schwarz, Mineola, NY: Dover, 2014.

Von Ranke, L., *The Theory and Practice of History*, trans. and ed. G.G. Iggers and W.A. Iggers, London: Routledge, 2011.

Von Ranke, L., *Universal History: The Oldest Historical Group of Nations and the Greeks*, New York: Charles Scribner's and Sons, 1884.

7

SEEING THE WONDER TRICK IN HISTORIES OF THE MOVING IMAGE

Lynne Kirby | Tom Gunning | Walter Benjamin | Roland Barthes | Jonathan Crary | Mary Anne Doane |

A train rushes towards you. Do you dodge in fear? Or do you dodge in knowing, performing an act of fear because that is what people do when they watch the film *The Arrival of a Train at Le Ciotat Station* (1895)? Whether the first film audiences were astonished or in on the act with what they saw is one of the core questions posed in film histories. That we do not have a definitive answer to this question is partly a reflection of the sheer technical difficulty of writing film viewers into history. Watching a film does not tell you how people might have looked at it in the past: other sources such as diaries, media reports, scrap books, photo albums and even cinema blueprints can help us to build up some sense of that. But it also turns out that the metaphysical assumptions that researchers draw upon to explain film and film audiences can make a big difference to their judgements of viewer knowing or credulity, and therefore to their appraisal of whether film was an act of, as film historian Tom Gunning puts it, 'I know, but yet I see' in an age when the marvellous purportedly waned.

Welcome to what some commentators would see as the sideshow of this book. Research on the history of film, and on historical films, has burgeoned over the last 40 years. Yet it still seems like early days in understanding how film might contribute to the history of history. This is because film is sometimes seen as prioritising entertainment over an understanding of our world and its past, or even contributing to the creation of a world in which nothing is real and everything is a show.[1] In an endeavour to take film seriously, Hayden White coined the term 'historiophoty'—as distinct from historiography—in order to denote the 'representation of history and our thought about it in visual images and in filmic discourse'.[2] I argued a while back that I do not find this distinction between the two 'historios' helpful, not least because it may contribute to the sense that written history is the default approach to articulating the idea of history, and that other forms of historical expression are ancillary or secondary.[3] This chapter sees my view unchanged, but for different reasons. My reasoning in this case reflects my scepticism about historiophoty as a 'most general' kind of thing. Moreover, in thinking about the study of film as distinctive from written texts, I believe we might have overlooked a question shared by all forms of historical sense making.

What if the literal ways in which historians make general sense of things change? Here we contemplate the idea that historians might see and hear differently over time. The implications of granting this idea, as we shall see in this chapter, are important in considering the role of history in, say, discerning the immanent. A change in perception may improve our discernment of the immanent, or it may make that discernment impossible. Moreover, any change in the nature of perception might have a knock-on effect with wonder, and position it as an aid or an inhibitor in making general sense of things. This chapter charts the rise of scepticism about perception as a universal in written and filmic histories, and tests whether there was a knock-on effect to wonder. The mixed answer that I find—perception changed, but wonder didn't—leads to a new way of thinking about the historicization of metaphysics ushered in by Hegel, where the speed of change for immanent universals may vary.

Making sense of film, making sense of sight

We recall from chapter five Aristotle's provision of what he saw as a systematic categorisation of the most general, distinct kinds of things in *Categories* and in *Metaphysics*. In general, these are taken to be categories that describe the actual structure of the world, rather than grammatical or conceptual categories.[4] His categories are therefore a manifest of what is. A comparison of his list of categories with those of later writers suggest that articulating such a manifest might be difficult, and even impossible. A double test for categories is suggested in the use of the words 'most general', and 'distinct'. Various philosophers have suggested that the most general and distinct kinds of things are mutually exclusive, with their definitions and methods of what that means varying.[5] These approaches have not produced altogether reassuring results, and that has led other philosophers to take a different tack in suggesting that categories could be thought of as differences in linguistic structures rather than an expression of commitment about the way that the world really is. This means that even if we do believe that a list of categories describing the world has been articulated, we can still, as Daniel Nolan suggests, recognise the value of questioning the concepts and relations and distinctions between concepts.[6] Thinking about categories in these ways makes it difficult to justify the treatment of historiophoty as distinctive from historiography. They share at least some of the same technical vocabulary, methods and approaches to the presentation of research results. More significantly, researchers of written and filmic histories share the same propensity to make general sense of things, whether that is via thinking about their results as real, or assuming the existence of boundaries between, for example, what is and is not knowable. It was for similar reasons that I argued in chapter one that it is not possible to draw a solid boundary between history and literature.

Yet film histories may bring assumptions to the forefront that are relatively taken for granted in the analysis of texts. Film is a visual medium, and it invites us to give more attention to the nature of sight. Moreover, significantly, it challenges us to consider whether sensory perception has been stable over time. I need to be clear at the outset that film historians are not alone in this thinking. The last decades of the twentieth century saw a wave of publications on the historical experience of the senses. Typically, they took the form of histories of single senses. John E. Crowley's *The Invention of Comfort* (2001), for example, looks at how people thought about and experienced light and dark in early modern Britain and early North America; Alain Corbin's *The Foul and the Fragrant* (1986) provides a vivid account of senses of smell, and smells, in eighteenth and nineteenth century France; Constance Classon's *The Deepest Sense* (2012) offers a western history of touch; and Ana María Ochoa Gautier has tracked in *Aurality* (2014) changing patterns of sound consumption in nineteenth-century Colombia.[7] A smaller number of works provide more ambitious accounts of entangled senses, or multi-sensory histories, as with Alex Holcombe, Matej Hochel and Emilio Mílan's short history of synaethesia (2008), Robert Jütte's *A History of the Senses* (2004) and David Howes' *Ways of Sensing* (2013).[8] Yet film history has not just argued for the recognition of these sensory shifts, it has also noted the implications of them for the general attempt to make sense of things.

If seeing changes, our ability to discern the immanent may change. Our discernment may improve, or take a backward step, or it may become impossible. Consequently, the role of wonder may change too. It may aid the discernment of the immanent, as Aristotle claimed, or it may block it. All of the thinkers canvassed in this chapter— Lynne Kirby (1952–), Tom Gunning (1949–), Jonathan Crary (1951–), Mary Ann Doane (1952–), Walter Benjamin (1892–1940) and Roland Barthes (1915–1980)—argue that modernity ushered in seismic shifts in seeing and knowing. At first glance, though, their opinions vary on whether there was a knock-on change in wonder. In the case of Benjamin and Barthes, as we shall see, it helps us to restore the real senses of depth perception—which relate to space, time and the emotions—that they believed were extinguished or at least diminished with the onset of the modern. In the case of Crary and Doane, it abets attention, which they characterise as a mental function that protects—and thereby keeps—us from the raw experience of stimuli that might provoke an exploration of the truths of the modern, capitalist world. For Doane it is simply a device for making sense, but for Crary it serves the more sinister function of rendering us as individual, manipulable consumers. At closer inspection, though, we see wonder as stably presented across these four authors' writings as being metaphysically important, as an aid or a barrier to discernment and therefore as on the cusp of the particular and the general. Moreover, wonder is metaphysically conservative: it helps or hinders us in seeing the world as it was, prior to modernity. Seeing might have changed, but the long held idea of wonder as a threshold to making general sense of things did not.

What we arrive at with the suggestion that seeing changed but that wonder did not is an intimation of a different way of thinking about the historicisation of metaphysics. Hegel, we recall from the last chapter, saw immanent universals as realising over time, as our minds realise over time. What went without saying in his account is whether the pace of realisation is constant. It may not be. We therefore close this chapter by noting that while the role of history in discerning universals persists, those universals may come to be understood differently over time, and the pace at which that understanding takes place may also vary across universals and across time. It may be that our understanding of some basic ways of thinking about the world improves or regresses, or the reality of that world may change. Our chapter rounds out with the radical historicisation of metaphysics by Rorty, Collingwood, Wittgenstein and Braudel, who argued in different ways that our general sense making moves in the manner of a river or a wave.

Seeing double

We begin our analysis with what appears to be a simple example from film history. In 1896, the writer Maxim Gorky documented his first experience of watching some Lumière films, with one of them very likely being *The Arrival of a Train at Le Ciotat Station*. One paragraph of that account provides us with some sense of Gorky being shocked—and perhaps even frightened—by what he saw:

> Suddenly something clicks, everything vanishes and a train appears on the screen. It speeds straight at you—watch out! It seems as though it will plunge into the darkness in which you sit, turning you into a ripped sack full of lacerated flesh and splintered bones, and crushing into dust and into broken fragments this hall and this building, so full of women, wine, music and vice.

But that paragraph is part of a longer text in which it appears clear that Gorky did not labour under the illusion that what he saw was real. Here is the paragraph again, with other parts of that larger body of text, highlighted by my use of italics:

> Last night I was in the Kingdom of the Shadows.
> *If only you knew how strange it is to be there. It is a world without sound, without colour. Everything there… is dipped in monotonous grey* ….
> Suddenly something clicks, everything vanishes and a train appears on the screen. It speeds straight at you—watch out! It seems as though it will plunge into the darkness in which you sit, turning you into a ripped sack full of lacerated flesh and splintered bones, and crushing into dust and into broken fragments this hall and this building, so full of women, wine, music and vice.
> *But this, too, is a train of shadows.*[9]

This example shows that very little additional information is needed to render an historical source complex. Gorky opens by acknowledging that his experience is with a 'kingdom of shadows' that is *strange*. That strangeness arises from rendering the everyday world—the familiar—without sound and colour. This might be read as a precondition for wonder in the Aristotelian sense. Yet his use of the word shadows may also indicate a judgement of us being in Plato's cave, so to speak, and therefore that our encounter with film is not with 'this hall, this building', or universals, or the *real*. His 'watch out!' might therefore have been a knowing expression: I know that the film is not real, but I might call out 'watch out!' to go along with the performance.

On balance, Gorky's account of his experience suggests that he did not experience wonder, and therefore that we should consider it as an example of Gunning's 'I know, but yet I see'. Put more simply, Gorky is assumed to be a sophisticated, rational viewer. But we have to stop at this point, and remind ourselves that Gorky did not write his account as he watched the film. He wrote it afterwards. The gap between the two might have been a matter of hours or days, but that gap is large enough for the possibility of any transitory experience of wonder being explained by rational thought, or being checked, constrained or constructed by the verbal and non-verbal responses of others. Moreover, it is important to acknowledge that Gorky took into that screening his prior experiences of visual images, and of other forms of entertainment. In short, Gorky does not provide us with an isolated 'of the moment' account of his experience that would allow us to judge whether he was astonished or not.

There is at least a double reading of Gorky's experience. The first puts his film viewing into the context of anterior, contemporary, and successor experiences. The second, which is implied in the idea of 'going along with the performance', suggests that Gorky's physical response to the film might have been shared with others as a cultural experience. Both readings historicise. The first historicises 'Gorky', and might suggest at its most radical interpretation that there is no stable sense of self that should be denoted with his proper name. The second historicises perception, and it can also imply the historicisation of Gorky. It suggests that the act of making sense might belong to a particular place and time. Put crudely, the way that the first film audiences displayed wonder, or awe, may differ from the ways that we might display wonder and awe. And their displays might have been deliberative, and shared. I did that simply by saying that Gorky 'went along with the performance'. Just like that, and perhaps without realising it, I raised a question about whether there is a stable notion of 'making sense' that may help us to contemplate universals. I questioned the idea of a stable, universal approach to making general sense of things.

Seeing the trick: shocked, or in on the act in film histories?

The same question seems to be at play in histories of the moving image from the last half century. Early histories of film appear to have assumed that viewers were genuinely shocked and awed by what they saw.[10] With the appearance of the writings of Tom Gunning, however, that assumption came to be slowly unravelled via a close reading of a wide range of cinematic and pre-cinematic evidence. Gunning noted, quite rightly, that the first film viewers took their experiences of other attractions to screenings. And those experiences, he notes, refracted the rise of the modern and the apparent loss of the marvellous that followed as a consequence of a far-reaching change in the way that people saw the world.

Today, Tom Gunning's name is synonymous with the history of early cinema, yet he generously acknowledges the inspiration of other writers like Lynne Kirby. At the same time, he repeatedly makes the case for seeing film viewers in a different way to Kirby. This is a reasonable assessment, given that Kirby and Gunning draw upon two very different pre-cinematic precedents to support their claims about viewer experiences: the railroad, and visual attractions respectively. Yet I hold that they have more in common than might be first thought, and as we shall see, that commonality is the assumption that perception was a cultural construct, and as so subject to historical change.

Cinema emerged at a time of rapid rail expansion. We should therefore not be surprised, Kirby argues in her 1988 *Camera Obscura* article 'Male Hysteria and Early Cinema', that trains featured in so many early films. Indeed, legend has it that Albert E. Smith, one of the founders of Vitagraph, solved the problem of film flicker by considering how the rapid procession of telegraph poles he saw as a rail passenger might be transposed into film cell frames.[11] But the conjoining of film and rail, Kirby further argues, was on an experiential, as well as a technological level. She has in mind the changes in time management that the railways ushered in, such as the standardisation of time zones. Moreover, railway travel also sped up experiences of travelling, leading to a different view of landscapes to that seen by foot or by horse. People looked at the world differently, and that different way of seeing was, to Kirby's mind, seamlessly transposed to the cinema because early production was dominated by travel and scenic films (*Parallel Tracks*, pp. 7, 19, 44–5).

The acceleration of time and panoramic—wide and shallow—views of landscape made possible by the railways implied sensory overload, which Kirby frames as an 'experience of shock' (*Parallel Tracks*, p. 7). As railway provision expanded, there was an increase in accidents. These accidents not only injured people physically—'railway spine', for example, described accident-induced spinal damage—but also psychologically. In the last decades of the nineteenth century, the condition of 'railway brain' emerged, and its application as a diagnosis soon spread to those who were traumatised but otherwise physically uninjured in an accident. George Drinka even notes that hysteria could be generated by simply being in proximity to a train.[12] Here, Kirby and Drinka gesture towards Freud, whose essay 'The Infantile Sexuality' describes the railway phobia obsession of boys and men.[13]

What intrigues Kirby most about these cases is that they signalled the shift away from the assumption that hysteria afflicted women because they had a more delicate nervous system than men. Moreover, it was also assumed that the stimulus for this hysteria could be proximity to a fairground or a cinematic train, as well as to a real one. Yet exposure to these stimuli was also seen as providing the opportunity for individuals to build up some form of resilience. Fairground attractions such as simulated train rides and staged train collisions turned shock into—as Kirby puts it—'a programmed unit of mass consumption' (p. 121), and Freud assumed that repeated exposure to these units of consumption could help individuals to build up a 'stimulus shield' against the collapse of time and space experienced as a consequence of accelerating mechanisation and urbanisation. The result was '[a]n unstable western subject, embodied concretely in passengers and spectators ... one anticipating, yet immune, to shock' (*Parallel Tracks*, p. 7). But Kirby also holds that the same cultural shift also displaced some men from jobs, and that had a psycho-cultural knock on effect. As she explains:

> ... nineteenth-century mechanisation and urbanisation—railway assisted—made of its traumatized victims something like female hysterics. In other words, it emasculated men, even if only, for some, those of a certain class. Women, proletarian men, and the marginal thus bore the brunt of the shocks of modernity. The 'emasculated' male, the male hysteric, might then be seen as the boomerang of male, technological culture against itself, a vision of the railroad neurotic as a man reduced to a female, or non-male state, like the proverbial woman tied to the tracks and assaulted or traumatized by the train. The paradox: investment, or, overinvestment in the male 'culture of time and space' was emasculating. (p. 7)

Viewer responses to *The Arrival of a Train at Le Ciotat Station* (1896) are therefore not necessarily just physiological, and they are not necessarily knowing. A wealthy male viewer might have viewed films in a knowing fashion, safe from the possibility of mental instability. For the working-class man, on the other hand, watching *Arrival of a Train at Le Ciotat Station* brought with it the risk of hysteria and therefore of being emasculated. He was suggestible, vulnerable, and hypnotizable (*Parallel Tracks*, p. 8). The threat of that emasculanisation could be known, Kirby further argues, because films such as *The Photographer's Mishap* (1901) and *Asleep at the Switch* (1910) co-opted it as their topic. Visual culture played back emotional culture, and there was therefore no guarantee that the working-class, male viewer would be able to resist it. That threat, Kirby concludes, could only be corrected with the rise of narrative films after 1909, when men were shown in relation to women and qualities of 'proper' masculinity and femininity asserted (*Parallel Tracks*, pp. 117–31). Those narratives set hysteria back into association with women.

Gunning's film viewers appear to be very different to those of Kirby. Indeed he argues for such an appraisal, albeit in the footnotes of his 1989 paper for *Art and Text*, 'An Aesthetic of Astonishment: Early Film and the (In)Credulous Spectator'. At base, he agrees with Kirby that cinema prior to the end of the first decade of the twentieth century was not dominated by narrative. Rather, this was the time of the 'cinema of attractions', when the exhibitionist presentation of the 'magical' properties of film technologies in actuality and visual illusion films dominated ('The Cinema of Attraction: Early Film, Its Spectator and the Avant-Garde', *Wide Angle*, 1986). If you look at the films of the Lumière brothers and Georges Méliès, you can see Gunning's point. The Lumière brothers mounted a camera in close proximity to an oncoming train, and Méliès *The Black Imp* (1905)—which runs to just under four minutes—uses around 60 stop-motion cuts to suggest the appearance and disappearance of an imp to a traveller. This is clever camera and post-production editing work, and Gunning believes that film audiences knew that.

His grounds for arguing for the knowing viewer—as distinct from the potentially hysterical viewer in Kirby's analysis—comes from his argument that we need to pay attention to pre-cinematic precedents, and that we have to identify the right precedents. Railway fairground attractions were a precedent for railway films, as Kirby notes. But there is a wider range of precedents to be considered, Gunning argues, if we remember that the form of the earliest films is just as important as their contents. This is not to suggest that narrative is absent from the first films, but Gunning's point is that film technologies themselves were at the forefront of the first screenings. That is, people went to see films as much to admire the equipment used to project them, and the forms of editing used to structure them, as to see the images shown. If we think about film as a foregrounded technological bag of tricks, then other pre-cinematic precedents come into view, such as magic or illusion shows, vaudeville, and fairground attractions. Indeed, as Gunning notes, film was often itself a fair ground or variety show attraction, with tours of the screening apparatus or the enclosure of a film within an amusement ride both being possibilities.

Bringing this range of pre-cinematic precedents into view, Gunning asserts, makes it difficult to sustain any systemic notion of the first film audiences being stupefied, terrified, or credulous about the reality of what they saw. Rather, Gunning characterises them as 'sophisticated urban pleasure seekers', who kept abreast of trends in stagecraft. In short, they were in on the act and they performed wonder and awe in a knowing way because that is what people did when they went to the movies. Seen in that way, we begin to apprehend the logic of Gunning's claims about the appeal of Méliès work, which are captured in this extract:

> Méliès's theatre is inconceivable without a widespread decline in belief in the marvellous, providing a fundamental rationalist context. The magic theatre laboured to make visual that which it was impossible to believe. Its visual power consisted of a *trompe l'oeil* play of give-and-take, an obsessive desire to test the limits of an intellectual disavowal—I know, but yet I see. ('An Aesthetic of Astonishment', p. 35)

Gunning's claims about the waning of the marvellous in the context of a rising rationalism deserve some pause. It is not that he sees the end of the nineteenth century as ushering in the end of magic or illusion. Rather, his claim is that these kinds of attraction flourished in part because they presented 'a conscious focus on the fact that they were only illusions' ('An Aesthetic of Astonishment', p. 117). So the attraction of magic was a double focus on what appeared to be unbelievable, and on the art that it made it possible for a viewer to appreciate something as unbelievable. On this account, the viewer of *The Black Imp*, for example, appreciates both the magic of an appearing and disappearing spirit, and the camera craft that made that possible. Moreover, this double sensibility provides Gunning with the means to explain Gorky's account of *The Arrival of a Train at Le Ciotat Station* as '[b]elief and terror ... larded with an awareness of illusion and even ... the ennui of the insubstantial, the bleak disappointment of the ungraspable phantom of life' ('An Aesthetic of Astonishment', p. 118).

Gunning's idea of the cinema of attractions shifts the locus of shock, awe and wonder from the content of films to their technologies and craft ('An Aesthetic of Astonishment', p. 125). But he also explicitly connects this experience to Augustine's idea of *curiositas*. Gunning's interpretation of *curiositas* sees film viewing characterised as a never-sated, compelling distraction, particularly by unbeautiful or monstrous sights. This accords with the account of Augustine's writings I provided in chapter two. But Gunning's *curiositas* departs from Augustine's account in an important way. While Augustine saw the endless appeal of *curiositas* as an unthinking addiction—therefore rendering it sinful in his eyes—Gunning's curious viewer is knowingly dissatisfied by the limitations of film. He or she experiences ennui; never able to see film overturn the 'drying up of experience and its replacement by a culture of distraction' ('An Aesthetic of Astonishment', p. 126). But he or she also does nothing about it. This is because, Gunning concludes, the distanced, knowing stance of the film viewer is symptomatic of a disempowering alienation which modern, and particularly urban life produces.

Kirby and Gunning appear to disagree about film viewers. Yet they both share an ultimately negative appraisal of what film viewing offers us: hysteria or ennui. This is because when we look beyond the surface of their accounts, we see the same thing: film as abetting the alienation which results from modern, consumerist, urban life. This conclusion is on one level unsurprising, for both openly acknowledge their debt to the work of Walter Benjamin and Roland Barthes, and in particular Benjamin's writings on modernity and shock (*Parallel Tracks*, p. 12). But there is a further commonality in their thinking which turns our attention more directly to the story of wonder narrated in this book. For their arguments to work, it has to be assumed that—as Jonathan Crary puts it—'the ways in which we intently listen to, look at, or concentrate on anything have a deeply historical character' (*Suspensions of Perception*, p. 1).

Seeing as history, wonder as conservative metaphysics

Kirby and Gunning affirm—albeit in different ways—the historicisation of perception. Put simply, this is perception as other than an unmediated physiological phenomenon or as flowing from a universal rationality or from metaphysics. This historicisation is denoted—rather than formally acknowledged—by Kirby's and Gunning's citation of Walter Benjamin (1892–1940). So too, Benjamin's enculturated notion of perception sits at the base of other histories of the moving image such as Roland Barthes' *Camera Lucida* (1980), Jonathan Crary's *Techniques of the Observer: On Vision and Modernity in the Nineteenth Century* (1990) and *Suspensions of Perception: Attention, Spectacle, and Modern Culture* (1999), and Mary Ann Doane's *The Emergence of Cinematic Time: Modernity, Contingency, the Archive* (2002).

Across a range of writings, Benjamin brings into focus the onset, experience, and habituation of the modern. A predominant feature of that habituation is the daily experience of shock brought on by perceptual overload. With a gesture towards Freud's *Beyond the Pleasure Principle*,[14] Benjamin uses the writings of Baudelaire as a lens to describe our acceptance and even need for perceptual stimulation in the modern world:

> Moving through this traffic involves the individual in a series of shocks and collisions. At dangerous intersections, nervous impulses flow though him in rapid succession, like the energy from a battery. Baudelaire speaks of a man who plunges into the crowd as into a reservoir of electric energy. Circumscribing the experience of the shock, he calls this man 'a kaleidoscope equipped with consciousness'. Whereas Poe's passers-by cast glances in all directions which still appeared to be aimless, today's pedestrians are obliged to do so in order to keep abreast of traffic signals. Thus, technology has subjected the human sensorium to a complex kind of training. Then came a day when a new and urgent need for stimuli was met by the film. In a film, perception in the form of shocks was established as a formal principle. ('On Some Motifs in Baudelaire', in *Illuminations*, p. 175)

The more consciousness acknowledges these stimuli by, in effect, date stamping them, the less likely they are to cause trauma in the viewer ('On Some Motifs in Baudelaire', p. 163). Technologies such as photography and film aid this process by providing us with knowing exposure to snippets of stimuli that we can use to build up resilience in the form of what Freud calls a 'stimulus shield' (*Reischutz*) ('On Some Motifs in Baudelaire', p. 161–2). Trauma arises from a breach of this protective shield, undermining a person's ability to navigate everyday life. That breach can occur as a consequence of perceptual overload, where the level of overload might vary as a consequence of a person's prior exposure to, and therefore resilience against, perceptual stimuli.

On Benjamin's view, technologies such as photography and the cinema can have a protective function, and it is not hard to imagine cinematic techniques such as the jump cut—a literal snip in a sequence of snippets—as serving this function well. Moreover, it is assumed that the more consciously the dissonances and stimulation of photography and cinema are acknowledged, the less likely that viewer experience of them will leave behind a lasting memory trace ('On Some Motifs in Baudelaire', p. 160). Yet in engaging with photography and cinema, Benjamin also sees us as paying the price of losing a sense of depth perception of both time and space. This is because they present fast moving panoramic views of phenomena: they offer wide and shallow space, as Kirby suggests. With the spread of photography and film, we are diminished ('A Short History of Photography', pp. 20–21, 23; and 'The Work of Art in the Age of Mechanical Reproduction', in *Illuminations*, p. 220). In essence, then, modernity ushered in a change in the fundamental act of perception, and it was not necessarily good ('The Work of Art in the Age of Mechanical Reproduction', p. 222).

On Benjamin's view, photography and film help us to manage modernity, but that management is within limits. At that limit is what Benjamin calls 'aura', and what Roland Barthes calls 'punctum'. Both writers give us the sense of aura and punctum as a rarity, and as experiences of great value. Benjamin sees the waning of aura at the beginning of photography, when the technology required the subject to hold their pose and gaze for a longer time than is the case now. Writing on Hill's portrait of Elizabeth Johnstone the fishwife, for example, he foreshadows loss:

> ... in that fishwife from Newhaven, who casts her eyes down with such casual, seductive shame, there remains something that does not merely testify to the art of Hill the photographer, but something that cannot be silenced, that impudently demands the name of the person who lived at the time and who, remaining real even now, will never yield herself up entirely into *art* ....
>
> They had an aura about them, a medium which mingled with their manner of looking and gave them a plenitude and a security. ('A Short History of Photography', pp. 7, 18)

The loss of aura means the loss of perceptual depth. That was not to be expected, as it appeared to be one of our 'securest' possessions. And that loss has far reaching implications. Our world is leached of depth to such an extent that it is not even clear that we can communicate with each other anymore:

> ... the art of storytelling is coming to an end. Less and less frequently do we encounter people with the ability to tell a tale properly. More and more often there is embarrassment all around when the wish to hear a story is expressed. It is as if something that seemed inalienable to us, the securest of our possessions, were taken from us: the ability to exchange our experiences. ('The Storyteller', in *Illuminations*, p. 83)

This loss of depth, this extract again makes clear, is not something to have been expected. This was the 'securest of our possessions', Benjamin tells us, thereby underscoring the fundamental change in perception wrought by the modern. Changes in perception pull the ground out from language, leaving us all the poorer.

But the loss of depth is not total. Aura can still be experienced fleetingly, and unintentionally ('The Image of Proust', in *Illuminations*, pp. 201–16). It 'flits by', he expands in 'Theses on the Philosophy of History', and the past, therefore, 'can be seized only as an image which flashes up at the instant when it can be recognised and is never seen again' (*Illuminations*, p. 255). It is not conjured; it comes to us much as Aristotle's experience of wonder does. Aura is conservative in that it returns depth perception to us, unfolding our superficial apprehension of the world. And it is metaphysical in that it restores—albeit fleetingly—our ability to make sense of the world to ourselves and with others.

This, too, is the point of Barthes' account of punctum in *Camera Lucida*. Photography—and to a lesser extent cinema—express meaning when a detail in an image stands out. This is what he calls 'punctum':

> ... it is not I who seek it out ... it is this element which rises from the scene, shoots out of it like an arrow, and pierces me. A Latin word exists to designate this wound, this prick, this mark made by a pointed instrument: the word suits me all the better in that it also refers to the notion of punctuation, and because the photographs I am speaking of are in effect punctuated, sometimes even speckled with these sensitive points; precisely, these marks, these wounds are so many *points* ... punctum is also: sting, speck, little hole—and also a cast of the dice. A photographer's punctum is that accident which pricks me (but also bruises me, is poignant to me). (*Camera Lucida*, pp. 26–7)

Everything about this extract emphases the accident, the 'roll of the dice' of being marked or pricked by punctum. Punctum is something done to me, not something I initiate or seek out. Importantly, too, it is a wound, hurting us and making us feel. Wounds are not necessarily inflicted by those who capture atrocities on film, for someone else has 'shuddered for us, reflected for us, judged for us' (*Camera Lucida*, p. 71). Nor is film a good vehicle for punctum, because of the rapid succession of images and details. It is also not possible to predict which film or image will wound the viewer, even if the maker intends to do so. Rather, punctum is more personal, and more poignant. It is in the eye of the viewer, which in the case of Barthes comes from details of a photograph of his recently deceased mother as a child. The photograph hurts him, reminding him of what he has lost, and thereby makes his mourning all the more acute (*Camera Lucida*, pp. 76–7). That this is a personal experience that might be lost on another reader is underscored by Barthes' exclusion of the photograph from *Camera Lucida*. The highly personal scraps and fragments of *Mourning Diary*, too, underscore Barthes' discontinuous and sporadic experience of being reminded of what he has lost, and of his own mortality (pp. 67, 95). One day it is a word; the next day it is a cake; on another it is an image or a sound. Again, he emphasises that none of these triggers are things that he sought out. The pain of loss comes to him suddenly and with a crippling intensity. He writes variously of 'a violent crying jag', of being 'overwhelmed, on the verge of tears', and of experiencing 'an onset of grief. I cry' (pp. 83; 107; 141). At the same time, he does not want to lose the intensity of his grief; he resists encapsulating his experiences in a time stamped narrative in order to protect it and to experience its depths for longer (pp. 50, 75). With punctum we feel again in ways that the modern denies us. Depth of feeling is restored to each of us.

Barthes' notion of punctum is far more personalised—and therefore idiosyncratic—than Benjamin's idea of aura. Nothing would seem to be further from the contemplation of universals, therefore. But as his notes on mourning show us, depth of feeling is something that we want to hold on to, to protect from diminution or disappearance over time. We want to halt time, and to hold on to the pain forever, thereby rendering it a permanent feature of our mental world. This is also a metaphysical move, as our discussion on Rorty in the final part of this chapter will highlight.

Neither Benjamin nor Barthes use the term wonder to describe the fleeting, intense moments in which the diminution of modernity is resisted. Time, depth and pain are reclaimed, but all too rarely. Conceptually, though, 'aura' and 'punctum' share much in common with earlier ideas of wonder canvassed in this book: they are something we experience, rather than consciously call upon, and they are an aid to escape from habitual ways of thinking about the world.

Quite a different account of wonder appears to be at play in the writings of Jonathan Crary, even though he shares Benjamin's view that perception changed with the onset of the modern. *Techniques of the Observer* does so via the argument that post eighteenth-century biological sciences and technologies such as the camera obscura presented observation as subjective rather than as passive and universal. That is, the mind and the self saw the world; the world did not impress itself upon viewers in the same way across time and space. To this point, there is a rough alignment with Benjamin on modernity. With *Suspensions of Perception*, though, we see an argument that potentially forces us to rethink the ascription of wonder to Benjamin's notion of aura and Barthes' notion of punctum.

From the mid-nineteenth century, Crary argues, new forms of perception and attention—'a fixation, or holding something in wonder'—served institutional constructions of 'a productive and manageable subjectivity' (*Suspensions of Perception*, p. 2). Rather than being a liberator, wonder was part of a body 'that could be captured, shaped, or controlled by a range of external techniques' (*Suspensions of Perception*, pp. 3, 5, 10). As with *Techniques of the Observer*, it is argued that for this to have happened, understandings of seeing had to shift from it being understood as *a priori* and unmediated towards that of being contingent upon the complex physiology of the observer. Seeing and perception came to be entangled in the body. At the same time, modernity gave rise to a burgeoning group of seeing technologies such as photography and film. The intersection of the two was seen in the aim—or the worry—that exposure to technology would foster distraction and a mind overwhelmed by contingency rather than an agentic attention. Here wonder is not fleeting; it is an immersive experience from which one might not be able to escape. This accords with concerns about *curiositas, 'aja'ib* and obsession in chapters two and three of this book. An individual's weakness of will were assumed to be the cause of irreversible absorption in those chapters. This is not argued in Crary's book, at least explicitly. What is implied is that technologies are developed to take advantage of viewer subjectivities; rendering them as manageable, individual *consumers*. This was aided and abetted by mores in which distraction and free association were presented as socially, politically and mentally destructive. People needed to pay attention—and thereby render themselves susceptible to wonder—in order to avoid the chaos that would arise from an unstructured, open mind (*Suspensions of Perception*, p. 14, 17–18). Moreover, they needed to pay attention as individuals; it was a mental burden that all needed to carry. Again, this meant a 'logic of spectacle [which prescribe[d] the production of separate, isolated, but not introspective individuals' (*Suspensions of Perception*, p.79). Crary's conclusion is thus that the subjectivisation of vision—assisted by technologies which stimulated wonder—made possible the subjection and discipline of people in modernity.

So too, Mary Ann Doane sees pre-cinematic technologies—including photography—as being seen as structuring and representing time. Indeed, she sees them, along with cinema, as critical to a 'sea change in thinking' about time, contingency, and indexicality that were part of modernity (*The Emergence of Cinematic Time*, p. 4). Time was standardised, stabilised, depersonalised and rationalised as, for example, people began to travel with greater speed, and work set hours. Moreover, it was visualised: more and more people wore watches, and the movement of workers was captured with the trace of lightbulbs captured in photographs or films called cyclographs and chronocyclographs respectively. Indeed film and photography came to be seen as capturing the moment, as assuring their own indexicality. That is, they were seen as imprints or inscriptions of the real. This is captured well in Doane's use of a quote from the theorist Sigfried Kracauer on the burden of meaning we give to photographs in flattening time: 'A shudder runs through the viewer of old photographs. For they make visible not the knowledge of the original but the spatial configuration of a moment'.[15]

At the same time, however, photography and films such as actualities also promised the chance capture of phenomena in the moment. The Lumière film *Workers Leaving the Lumière Factory* (1895), for example, captured both the regulation of working hours—multiple people leave work at the end of what we assume to be a shift—but also the surprise of a dog entering the bottom right of the screen. In this way, film simultaneously supports both the regulation of time implied in modernity, and resistance against that regulation. Ultimately, however, Doane argues, representations of contingency were both codified and contained as tiny doses and therefore appropriated to modernity. Film may be seen as a form of escapist entertainment, for example, but too much contingency was seen as a threat to individual and social well-being. This is because she, like Gunning and Kirby, acknowledges Benjamin's reading of Freud's *Beyond the Pleasure Principle*. The lure of visual technologies, she argues:

> ... [i]s that of the passing moment, the fascination of the ephemeral, but Walter Benjamin delineates the dark underside of such a relation to contingency as shock or trauma.... Consciousness, for Freud, does not remember. Its most important function is rather to protect the organism against excessive stimuli, to act as a stimulus shield in operation against external energies. According to Benjamin, 'The threat from these energies is one of shocks. The more readily consciousness registers these shocks, the less likely are they to have a traumatic effect.' (*The Emergence of Cinematic Time*, p. 13, see also pp. 31–5).

Thus, Doane's account also provides us with an explanation of why film moves from capturing moments in actualities—the confrontation of the 'cinema of attractions'—towards narratives after the turn of the twentieth century: contingency is contained and appropriated, and that makes the discernment of the immanent impossible.

Through the use of snippets of historical time, cinema builds up what Doane calls 'fictional' time (*The Emergence of Cinematic Time*, p. 143). This is seen particularly in the use of jump cuts to move the film forward in action by removing moments deemed to be less eventful. So too, pan shots of stationary objects might suggest the extension of time. Panorama shots of localities interspersed with action shots might also imply contemporaneity and presence in relation to the event, even though there might have been a considerable gap in filming time. These prefigure the use of jump cuts and fades and dissolves to denote both flashbacks and flashforwards to earlier and later events that are presented as significant. In the process, time 'is rewritten in such a way that contingency and unpredictability are reduced as part of the process, reemerging as the signified' (*The Emergence of Cinematic Time*, pp. 161–2). In this way—the removal of dead moments and the suggestion of an efficient linearity—cinema contributes to the rationalisation of time. It is the negation of unorganised, unstructured time and the threat of the contingent. Thus, ultimately, film might be seen as supporting the wonder-captured individual consumer set out in Crary's vision of modernity.

Crary's and Doane's views of wonder seem to be far removed from Benjamins' and Barthes' views of aura and punctum respectively. One is seen to manage perception in the service of the modern; the other resists it. Both see wonder as associated with the particular and contingent, however, albeit either as facilitating openness to it, or preventing access to it. But they also share in common a conservative function: one sees us return to lost notions of depth; the other protects modern perceptions of the world. And in seeking grounding in depth (Benjamin and Barthes) or in stable notions of the modern (Crary and Doane) they both support the project of metaphysics. So while it is fair to say that these histories of the image assert the historicisation of perception, they simultaneously convey a relatively stable, conservative and metaphysical notion of wonder.

Historicising metaphysics, contingency within limits

At the opening of this book, I confessed that writing a book on making general sense of things in the discipline of history seemed a very odd thing to do. The expectation was that, like oil and water, the two things—history and metaphysics—could not mix, and that they would undoubtedly come into conflict with one another, or at least exist in tension. This chapter appears to confirm that expectation. If sense making is an historical activity, thus not universal, can we assume continuing discernment of immanent universals? As this chapter has intimated, the answer to this question depends on the extent to which we accept historicisation as affecting sense making and its outcomes, and the seemingly associated concept of contingency.

An interesting starting point for us to consider—albeit briefly—are the claims of Richard Rorty (1931–2007), who appears to veer towards the very hard end of contingency and historicisation. Rorty's 'ironist' is committed to the end of metaphysics and to the beginning of the search for new contingencies. That commitment is pretty unapologetic, as it entails sloughing off both the effort 'to achieve universality by the transcendence of contingency' and any 'inherited contingencies'.[16] It is a project against assuming that everyday, 'commonsense' beliefs should be secured and defended as necessary for others to use when thinking about the world. At the end of metaphysics and in the embrace of the contingent, history becomes a possibility. He writes, using language as an example:

> It begins when somebody says 'maybe we don't have to talk the way we do,' meaning not just 'maybe we should call this Y rather than X' but maybe the language-game in which 'X' and 'Y' occur is the wrong one to be playing—not for any particular reason, not because it fails to live up to some familiar criterion, but just because it is, after all, only one among others.[17]

In short, words, languages and forms of communication are open to change. History is not just about being aware of the possibility of change, but actively seeking it out. That only happens when new contingencies are created, when the ironist:

> … is trying to get out from under inherited contingencies and make [their] own contingencies, get out from under an old final vocabulary and fashion one which will be all [their] own.[18]

The ironist does not want to subscribe to the categories posited by Aristotle, and will also question the necessity of even having categories to understand the world. Metaphysics was Aristotle's contingency, writ universal.

Yet Rorty's ironist is an ironist within limits. Treating all vocabularies as 'optional descriptions' might be understood as a universal claim.[19] So too, the autonomy sought from the recognition of beliefs and claims as contingent might also be thought of as something to be desired by everyone. And there is one more claim that might look like a reach for universality, which is highly relevant to this and all chapters in this book. *Contingency, Irony, and Solidarity* returns to the beginning of Aristotle's metaphysics, and sees that:

> The wonder in which Aristotle believed philosophy to begin was wonder at finding oneself in a world larger, stronger, nobler than oneself. The fear in which [Allen] Bloom's poets begin is the fear that one might end one's days in such a world, a world one never made, an inherited world.[20]

At the beginning of the world there is wonder, and at its end there is fear. Wonder is the means by which the real and the rational are asserted; fear is the means by which the world becomes an open question again.

It is right to ask the obvious question about whether Rorty posits autonomy, contingency, wonder and fear as universals by stealth. At the least, we can question whether there are limits to his letting go. And this is a question that we turn back on this chapter, asking why wonder persists in the accounts of Benjamin, Barthes, Crary and Doane. Is it a universal that lurks, passing our notice, in a wider historicisation of perception that they, and Gunning and Kirby, promote? It could be, and serve as, the agent of the modern, keeping us from being positioned as individual consumers. This is Crary's view. Alternatively, it could be, and serve as the liberator from modernity, as Benjamin and Barthes intimate. Either way, as with Rorty's Aristotle, it has a role to play in managing the contingent. It either takes us from the surface fluctuations of modernity—as Benjamin and Barthes suggest—and back to depth of perception, or protects us from being overwhelmed by the rapid succession of sense perceptions that the modern presents. Either way, it is a persistent and conservative feature of how we might make sense of the world, and arguably we should let it go, or at least acknowledge that we need to let it go.

But it could also be a persistent historical mistaken for a universal. As I have written elsewhere, a more stable, yet historical view of metaphysics is to be found in the writings of the historian philosopher R. G. Collingwood, and in those of the philosopher Ludwig Wittgenstein in his collection of notes, *On Certainty*.[21] Wittgenstein, who is not typically associated with metaphysics in any positive sense, provides a very useful analogy in *On Certainty* that explains the idea quite simply and briefly. Different parts of a river move at different speeds. Some parts—such as the water, and small particles or floating objects—may be carried along with great rapidity. Other parts—such as boulders—may move only imperceptibly, generating the impression that they are fixed in place.[22] They are not; they too move. They just do so very slowly. The French historian Fernand Braudel (1902–95) has a similarly evocative analogy concerning the historian's encounter with simultaneous, varying paces of change, which it is useful to recall here:

> history, one might say on the scale not of man, but of individual men, what Paul Lacombe and François Simiand called '*l'histoire événementielle*', that is, the history of events: surface disturbances, crests of foam that the tides of history carry on their strong backs. A history of brief, rapid, nervous fluctuations, by definition ultrasensitive; the least tremor sets all its antennae quivering.[23]

Some events unfold rapidly, as with the crest of a wave, whilst other features of our world persist in the manner of the base of that same wave.

The point of this analogy is to highlight that metaphysics is not an all-or-nothing matter. We may accept the evidence that film historians present which suggest that forms of perception are open to change, and that perception did indeed change at the advent of the modern. But we can also accept that the need for wonder persisted, regardless of whether it served the ends of the modern or not. It is the boulder to the more rapid shifts in perception.

This opens up the intriguing idea of an historicised metaphysics with a varying pace of historicisation implied. Here, some of the ways in which we may make general sense of things may change quickly, whilst other ways may persist or change much more slowly. Hegel intimates as much in his *Philosophy of History*, noting that the realisation of freedom sometimes proceeded slowing, and sometimes quickly. We may quibble—quite rightly—over the details of where and when those changes happened, but the principle at work is still worthy of investigation. It may be seen as delivering us some reprieve from the all-or-nothing notion of ahistorical universals or absolute relativity in our experiences. Where the dispute still lies, though, in whether these historicised approaches to making general sense of things entail ontological commitment. To put it simply, with Wittgenstein's riverbed, or Braudel's base of a wave change, is the real world changing, or just our way of describing it? Hegel would have opted for the former—a descriptive or conservative approach to metaphysics—but it is not clear whether Wittgenstein or Braudel would have agreed. There is much dispute on whether Wittgenstein was consistently or even at all interested in metaphysics, and Braudel never articulated such a view. Regardless, their thought sits at the cusp of revisionary metaphysics—the endeavour of producing a better way of making sense of things—which is the focus of chapters eight and ten.

Notes

1 Jean Baudrillard, *Simulacra and Simulations*, ed. M. Poster, Stanford, CA: Stanford University Press, 1988.
2 Hayden White, 'Historiography and Historiophoty', *American Historical Review*, 1988, vol. 93(5), pp. 1193–99.
3 Marnie Hughes-Warrington, *History Goes to the Movies: Studying History on Film*, London: Routledge, 2007, pp.187–94.
4 Brian Carr, *Metaphysics: An Introduction*, Atlantic Highlands, NJ: Humanities Press, 1987.
5 See for example Roderick Chisholm, *On Metaphysics*, Minneapolis, MN: University of Minnesota Press, 1989; Annie Thomasson, *Fiction and Metaphysics*, Cambridge: Cambridge University Press, 1999; and Michael Dummett, *Frege, Philosophy of Language*, 2nd edn, Cambridge, MA: Harvard University Press, 1981.
6 Daniel Nolan, 'Categories and Ontological Dependence', *Monist*, 2011, vol. 94(2), pp. 277–300.
7 John E. Crowley, *The Invention of Comfort: Sensibilities and Design in Early Modern Britain and Early America*, Baltimore, MD: Johns Hopkins University Press, 2001; Alain Corbin, *The Foul and the Fragrant: Odor and the French Social Imagination*, Cambridge, MA: Harvard University Press, 1986; Constance Classen, *The Deepest Sense: A Cultural History of Touch*, Chicago, IL: University of Chicago Press, 2012; and Ana M.O. Gautier, *Aurality: Listening and Knowledge in Nineteenth-Century Columbia*, Durham, NC: Duke University Press, 2014.
8 Alex Holcombe, Matej Hochel and Emilio Milan, 'Synaesthia: The Existing State of Affairs', *Cognitive Neuropsychology*, 2008, vol. 25(1), pp. 93–117; Robert Jütte, *A History of the Senses: from Antiquity to Cyberspace*, trans. J. Lynn, London: Polity, 2004; and David Howes, *Ways of Sensing: Understanding the Senses in Society*, London: Routledge, 2014.
9 Jay Leyda, *Kino: A History of the Russian and Soviet Film*, London: Allen and Unwin, 1960, appendix 2, pp. 407–8.
10 For a brief account of that early historiography, see Martin Loiperdinger and Bernd Elzer, 'Lumiere's Arrival of the Train: Cinema's Founding Myth', *Moving Image*, 2004, vol. 4(1), pp. 89–118.

11 Terry Ramsaye, *A Million and One Nights*, New York: Simon and Schuster, 1926, pp. 351–2; as cited in Lynn Kirby, 'Male Hysteria and Early Cinema', *Camera Obscura*, 1988, vol. 6(2), pp. 112-132.
12 George F. Drinka, *The Birth of Neurosis: Myth, Malady and the Victorians*, New York: Simon and Schuster, 1984, p. 109; as cited in Lynn Kirby, 'Male Hysteria and Early Cinema'.
13 Sigmund Freud, *Three Essays on the Theory of Sexuality*, London: A.A. Brill, 1920, p. 45.
14 Sigmund Freud, *Beyond the Pleasure Principle and Other Writings*, Harmondsworth, UK: Penguin, 2003.
15 Siegfried Kracauer, 'Photography', in *The Mass Ornament: Weimar Essays*, trans. and ed. Y. Levin, Cambridge, MA: Harvard University Press, 1995, as quoted in Mary Anne Doane, *The Emergence of Cinematic Time*, Cambridge, MA: Harvard University Press, 2002, p. 23.
16 Richard Rorty, *Contingency, Irony, and Solidarity*, Cambridge: Cambridge University Press, 1989, pp. 25, 13.
17 Richard Rorty, *Essays on Heidegger and Others*, Cambridge: Cambridge University Press, 1991, pp. 43–5.
18 Richard Rorty, *Contingency, Irony, and Solidarity*, p. 97.
19 Richard Rorty, *Philosophy and the Mirror of Nature*, Princeton, NJ: Princeton University Press, 1979, p. 379.
20 Richard Rorty, *Contingency, Irony, and Solidarity*, p. 27.
21 Marnie Hughes-Warrington, *'How Good an Historian Shall I be?': R.G. Collingwood, the Historical Imagination and Education*, Thorveton, UK: Imprint, 2003.
22 Ludwig Wittgenstein, *On Certainty*, eds G.E.M. Anscombe and G.H. von Wright, Oxford: Blackwell, 1975, §99.
23 Fernand Braudel, *The Mediterranean and the Mediterranean World in the Age of Philip II*, vol. 1, trans. S. Reynolds, Glasgow: William Collins, 1972, p. 21.

References

Barthes, Roland, *Camera Lucida*, New York: Hill and Wang, 1980.
Barthes, Roland, *Mourning Diary*, trans. R. Howard, New York: Hill and Wang, 2012.
Benjamin, Walter, *Illuminations: Essays and Reflections*, ed. H. Arendt, New York: Harcourt, Brace and World, 1968.
Benjamin, Walter, 'A Short History of Photography' [1931], *Screen*, 1972, vol. 13(1), pp. 5–26.
Crary, Jonathan, *Techniques of the Observer: On Vision and Modernity in the Nineteenth Century*, Cambridge, MA: MIT Press, 1990.
Crary, Jonathan, *Suspensions of Perception: Attention, Spectacle, and Modern Culture*, Cambridge, MA: MIT Press, 1999.
Doane, Mary Anne, *The Emergence of Cinematic Time: Modernity, Contingency, the Archive*, Cambridge, MA: Harvard University Press, 2002.
Gunning, Tom, 'The Cinema of Attraction: Early Film, Its Spectator and the Avant-Garde', *Wide Angle*, 1986, vol. 8(3–4), pp. 56–63.
Gunning, Tom, 'An Aesthetic of Astonishment: Early Film and the (In)Credulous Spectator', *Art and Text*, 1989, no. 34, pp. 31–45.
Kirby, Lynne, 'Male Hysteria and Early Cinema', *Camera Obscura*, 1988, vol. 6(2), pp. 112–132.
Kirby, Lynne, *Parallel Tracks: The Railroad and Silent Cinema*, Durham, NC: Duke University Press, 1997.

8

HISTORY'S OTHERS, HISTORY'S ETHICS

Joan Wallach Scott | Lynn Hunt | Merry Wiesner-Hanks | Luce Irigaray | Jacques Derrida | Hélène Cixous | Marguerite La Caze

Early modern European history (roughly 1500–1800) is weird at the best of times. Although no single historian is responsible for generating this impression, it is hard not to be struck by the late twentieth-century historiographical wave that has delivered us stories of women who gave birth to rabbits or cats, farmers who fought witches in fields with sorghum stalks, a miller who likened the universe to cheese with maggots, and the enacting of political revenge through the killing of cats.[1] No area of historiography, it would seem, is better suited to the study of wonder.

Merry Wiesner-Hanks' *The Marvelous Hairy Girls* sits broadly within this wave, contributing to an important discussion on whether being human implies continuity in identity. As she explains:

> When people looked at the Gonzales sisters, or their pictures, they saw beasts or monsters as well as young women, but this was also true when they looked at most women. The ancient Greek philosopher Aristotle, whose ideas were still powerful in the sixteenth century, had described women as monsters because they were not as perfect as men. Medieval and Renaissance theologians and philosophers placed women between men and animals in the hierarchy of creation, for women, in their view, had less reason than men and were therefore more like animals. The lives of the Gonzales sisters highlight this complex relationship between beastliness, monstrosity, and sex .... This lens brings the world of all women in the sixteenth century into sharper focus, for even among marvels the lives of women and men were very different. (*The Marvelous Hairy Girls*, 2009, pp. 10–11)

In simple terms, we cannot assume that the Gonzales family of *The Marvelous Hairy Girls* saw or experienced the world as you or I do. Their lives were overlaid with traditions and explanations that saw their thick body hair as an expression, for example, of God's will. But Wiesner-Hanks' specific focus on the Gonzales sisters is also deliberate, because she wants to show us that gender and sex are powerful lenses for making sense of the world. Aristotle's framing of woman in *Generation of Animals* (737a) as a 'deformity' which occurs routinely made it possible for subsequent thinkers to see women as incomplete men, and even as monstrous. This was not just a physical appraisal: as we noted in chapter two, Thomas Aquinas' presentation of curiosity as incomplete wonder and rationality offered the opportunity to see women as mentally *and* physically incomplete, and therefore as doubly monstrous. Moreover, the mental and the physical reinforced one another in a cycle of deformity. With their imperfect bodies and minds, women were susceptible to birth the monstrous (*Marvelous Hairy Girls*, ch. 4). The Gonzales sisters were not just doubly monstrous, they were triply monstrous: they had female minds, they had female bodies covered in hair, and they were the descendants of a hairy man from the distant Canary Islands (p. 46). Like their father and brothers, they were kept at the French court. They were never, however, given a courtly role, and they were never taught to read or to write. What trace we have of them is refracted through portraits and through men's writing about them (p. 10).

As with many other Early Modern European historians, Wiesner-Hanks sees the micro histories of the Gonzales sisters as drawing upon and as contributing to wider themes in feminist history, postcolonial theory, queer theory, disability theory, and monster history (p. 224). But on the final page of the book, she halts consideration of the interplay between these theories and the specificities and generalities of history to ask the question 'Is this fair?'. In answering her own question, a connection between historical sense making and ethics is made:

> Are we treating [the Gonzales sisters] simply as objects, just as the marchesa of Soragna appears to have treated Antoinetta? Perhaps. But I have tried as much as possible (and probably more than I should, as an historian and not a novelist) to include some speculations about what they themselves might have thought, how they might have understood the worlds in which they lived. That is as far as we can go, for not one shred of evidence survives from any female member of the family. In that, they are like most girls of humanity's past. But they are more visible than most, and we can do one thing that no one who wrote about them in their own day thought important to do. We can remember them not simply as marvelous hairy girls, but as inviduals with names: Maddalena, Francesca, and Antoinetta Gonzales (p. 225).

This is a theme she expands upon in her more recent reflections on empathy and ethics and history, noting that sometimes imagination and empathy are needed to bring voiceless people like the Gonzales sisters in to history. This may ruffle the feathers of those who see history as strictly circumscribed by the known, but Wiesner-Hanks rightly points out that decisions of exclusion are themselves ethical decisions and in need of scrutiny.[2]

This chapter is about the ethical implications of our attempt to make general sense of things through the idea of history. It picks up from the last chapter in highlighting the interest of various writers in revisionary, rather than descriptive metaphysics. That is, they seek to move from outlining the most basic features of things to making sense of things in new ways, including radically new ways. The driver in this case is the question of how we *ought* to make sense of the world, rather than that we simply make sense of the world. And that driver, in turn, arises from the acknowledgement that metaphysicians might not have done as good a job as they might have in making sense of things, because their claims about the world either do not make sense to whole groups of people, or worse, their claims result in harm against those groups of people. In this chapter, I look to gender history to explore these claims. The intersection of gender and history is at least as old as the first written histories, with Herodotus for example using the interrelations of men and women as a diagnostic for the health of civilisations in his *Histories*. Women and men have continued that tradition to this time, exploring shifting notions of gender identity and gender relations through biographical catalogues that describe the feats of worthy or problematic individuals, historical novels, national and world histories, and children's primers.[3] Yet there is a prevailing perception that gender history is a recent discovery. Work continues to rectify that perception, but its persistence means that gender is often excluded as a topic from introductory historiographical texts, or treated as a late, separate theme. This has meant in practice that women are contained in one chapter, as if the remainder of texts somehow function above gender. Gender is signalled late in this book too, and my signal is deliberate as I want to place it in close proximity to the conclusion of this book. Proximity will emerge as an important theme in this chapter, functioning as it does to remind us of the personal, and 'near miss' nature of making sense of things. Indeed, it will highlight the interaction of history with metaphysics as unsettling, and even deeply unpleasant. But I have also worked to ensure that this chapter is not a leak-proof container for women: my inclusion of Sarah Joseph Hale in chapter six, for instance, locates a gendered metaphysics of history right at the heart of what is often taken to be the beginning and the end of the modern story of history. It is for all of us to see gender in our attempts to make the most basic sense of things, even if we are not sure if gender is a universal itself.

More particularly, this chapter shows how contemporary historians such as Weisner-Hanks (1952–), Joan Wallach Scott (1941–) and Lynn Hunt (1945–) have identified gender and sex as key means for initiating an examination of the assumptions that marginalise, subordinate or render invisible the experiences of individuals or groups in historiography. Scott's suggestion that we should not just stir women in to history, but use their experiences to stir up historiography is anchored primarily in Jacques Derrida's (1930–2004) thoughts on how we should treat others, which—like gender history—are only just gaining traction in the history of history.[4] Ironically, as this chapter will show, Derrida—like the Hamlet he describes—seems to be 'always late'. I will extend Scott's line of thought, showing how Luce Irigaray (1930–) and Marguerite La Caze (1964–) use a gendered reading of Descartes' *The Passions of the Soul*—a key text in chapter five of this book—to show that wonder is indispensable to our hospitable treatment of others. In unpacking those ideas, I will question Irigaray's assumption of a given gender binary, and note La Caze's presumption of wonder needing generosity in order to function as a trigger for their idea of an ethics of difference. Derrida's writings suggest no need of wonder, let alone wonder in connection with generosity. His interest, rather, is in *Unheimlichkeit*—translated generally as the uncanny in English—which I unpack as a key part of his call for us to see the traces of what is not present in our attempts to make sense of the world. This is a deliberate choice of word which conveys our simultaneous attraction and revulsion to being 'un homed' from a world that makes sense; a sensible world that is predicated upon the silencing and exclusion of so many oppressed people, past, present, and future. Additionally, I note his interest in describing our encounters with the *unheimlich* as haunting; encounters with revenants who are neither dead, nor alive, and therefore who confound our sense of how the world is. This drives his call for the conjuration of Marx to usher in 'democracy to come' in *Specters of Marx*, and his reminder of the ultimate impossibility of that democracy, as well as unconditional hospitality in later writings such as *Of Hospitality*. In Derrida's view, as with that of Irigaray and La Caze, we need to take personal responsibility for ethics, but also acknowledge that it cannot be fixed, determined or finalised. A final move in the chapter explores Derrida's concepts of the trace and home in the writings of Hélène Cixous (1937–). Cixous, like Derrida, acknowledges the impossibility of definitive notions of history, hospitality and generosity, but at the same time she sees us as being 'so close' [*si prés*]. Her vision of the *Unheimlich* therefore serves as a reminder that theories which place wonder at the beginning of philosophy, thought, or ethics may imply its dissipation as understanding and 'homing' takes hold. On the contrary, she makes the case for us never really getting hold, of wonder always with us, and therefore for a world in which we are at dis-ease with ourselves, others, and histories.

Stirring in, stirring up

Weisner-Hanks' journey to acknowledging the Gonzales sisters starts with the realisation in *Gender in History* that she—like every other history major—was only taught half the story (*Gender in History*, p. 1). Women were either absent, or minimally present. Yet, as she also acknowledges, 'stirring in women' was not a remedy for this oversight either. This is because women's experiences disrupt the categories and paradigms of history making, such as 'nation', 'social class' or 'religious allegiance'. So too, writing only about women ignores the conditions that have so often rendered them invisible or marginal to history. Stirring up history is, she is clear, not just beneficial for women: questioning and breaking down customary narratives and categories brings into focus the different experiences of individual men. History comes to be about individuals and the particular, not just the abstract universal (p. 1). We cannot assume, for example, that women experienced space in the same way as men or transgendered individuals, as she explains in the introduction to *Mapping Gendered Routes and Spaces in the Early Modern World* (2015):

> Real walls—of houses, convents, churches, courtyards, and market stalls—separated (or were supposed to separate) women and men. Travel and commerce generally involved more men than women, which had an impact on the families left behind on one end of a trade route and on those formed at the other end or somewhere along the way. Voluntary and forced migrations shifted the gender balance, necessitating new forms of marriage and other forms of social and sexual relationships. Gender also figured in understandings of spatialized activities, from dissecting the interior of the body to traveling across the globe.[5]

Yet space is often treated as a universal category established by Aristotelian metaphysics and only in need of philosophical fine-tuning. Sexuality has also assumed to be a given, with Wiesner-Hanks advancing in her *Christianity and Sexuality in the Early Modern World* the merits of Foucault's view of it as discursively written upon the body.[6] Some categories have been kept separate from one another when they clearly do intersect, as with 'global history' and 'gender', and 'The Reformation' and 'women', and others, like 'empire', 'emotions' and 'religious belief' intersect in the fashion of a three set Venn diagram.[7]

Why particular categories take hold, are seen in particular ways or connected to other categories is for Wiesner-Hanks a political matter, and suggestive of a revisionary rather than a descriptive view of metaphysics. There is no doubt for Wiesner-Hanks that the writing of history is clearly shaped by politics and by political domination. For example, research on the experiences of individuals and groups in English-language and European language contexts, she notes in a number of publications, far outweighs the efforts of writers in developing contexts (*Gender in History*, p. 10; see also *The Cambridge World History*, vol. 1, p. xix). This, as Wiesner-Hanks notes, is a reality that we have to acknowledge and a curse for anyone who wishes to write on the experiences of women, men and gender diverse individuals around the globe (p. 11). Yet continue writing history we must, navigating between the acknowledgement of difference and 'telling the story of a past that makes sense'.[8] Like Simone de Beauvoir, she acknowledges, 'no failure, no ethics'.[9]

De Beauvoir's point is that if you measure up to yourself and to God, then life has no meaning. It is in falling short, in missing things, that we learn to live. But that living comes only, as Wiesner-Hanks reminds us, in not mistaking the universal for the particular. Here she echoes the thought of Joan Wallach Scott in understanding the far-reaching consequences of applying Jacques Derrida's philosophical insights on deconstruction to the making of history. Scott's understanding of deconstruction emphasises unravelling the idea of fixed categories, beginning with the idea that the creation or assertion of a category implies the negation or the repression of that which is antithetical to it. In her view, the fixed opposition between ideas such as man and woman:

> conceal[s] the heterogeneity of either category, the extent to which terms presented as oppositional are interdependent ... Furthermore, the interdependence is usually hierarchical, with one term dominant, prior, and visible, the opposite subordinate, secondary, often absent or invisible. Yet precisely through this arrangement, the second term is present and central because required for the definition of the first. ('Introduction', *Gender and the Politics of History*, p. 7)

Subjecting categories to inspection means being open to the idea of new categories, new oppositions, and to the inversion of hierarchies. Again, this suggests a revisionary purpose for those interested in making general sense of things, not a descriptive one. For all of these reasons, Scott prefers to talk of gender history rather than women's history because it connotes a focus on the relationship between men and women over time, rather than one group in isolation ('Introduction', *Gender and the Politics of History*, p. 2; see also *The Fantasy of Feminist History*, p. 5).

Scott's motivation for writing gender history is like that of Wiesner-Hanks, political: her words stem from the desire to change the inequalities between women and men. But she also notes the applicability of her ideas to addressing inequalities that stem from race, ethnicity and class ('Introduction', *Gender and the Politics of History*, p. 3). This is a commitment that plays out with strength in her argument against the reductionist treatment of the intersection of gender and class as the study of 'words' in 'Language and Working-Class History' (*Gender and the Politics of History*, pp. 53–65). Words, treated as a data set, have little or no potential to transform the discipline of history in ways that are needed to better help us to understand gender and class (p. 54). What we need, as she argues on the basis of Michel Foucault's thought, is a more challenging exercise in which the conditions of knowledge are illuminated and contested. If history making is to change, it needs to be thought about epistemically ('Introduction', *Gender and the Politics of History*, p. 2). On this reading, knowledge is particular and historical rather than transcendent and abstract, but it is also descriptive of the real world. So particular epistemologies are useful for recasting history, not just epistemology as a universal. Foucault, for example, views the meaning of words to be both unstable and reflective of power and relational dynamics ('Language and Working-Class History', *Gender and the Politics of History*, p. 59). Scott's analysis of work in nineteenth-century Paris, for example, highlights how the shop came to be associated with skilled, male labour, and how work at home was gendered female and treated as relatively unskilled ('Work Identities for Men and Women: The Politics of Work and Family in the Parisian Garment Trades in 1848', *Gender and the Politics of History*, pp. 93–112). So too, she highlights the ambiguity of the term *femmes isolées*, which in nineteenth-century France was used to describe both independent working women and clandestine prostitutes ('"L'ouvrière! Mot impie, sordide…"'- Women Workers in the Discourse of French Political Economy, 1840–1860', *Gender and the Politics of History*, pp.139–63).

But which epistemologies to focus on? The trigger for epistemic illumination is identified in Scott's later work *The Fantasy of Feminist History* (2011) as psychoanalysis because it emphasises the unknowability of sexual difference and therefore the uncertainty of any claims to knowledge about it. Hers is not an epistemology in which the unknowable is tamed as the knowable, and therefore there is not a sense that we have with earlier writings on wonder that the shock of the strange can be overcome through rational operation. In short, there is no recommended epistemology. This, however, implies a valuation of openness over satisfaction with the known. We assume that her grounds for that derive from the views of Derrida and Foucault, but it is not expressed in a way that stretches beyond an interest in epistemology.

Lynn Hunt shares an interest with Scott in contesting seemingly immutable knowledge claims, but her writings also intimate at our need to contend with metaphysics—as well as epistemology—in order to revise the discipline of history. Her 2008 Natalie Zemon Davis Lectures, *Measuring Time, Measuring History*, are a good case in point. As the title suggests, the topic is time, and more specifically historical time. Arguably, there is no other 'category' that is so essential to how we make sense of the idea of history (p. 48). History making without time would not seem to make sense; its role seems to be beyond question. But question it we must, because our understanding of historical time is an historical artefact that has flow on effects which perpetuate the exclusion or minimisation of some phenomena. Like Wiesner-Hanks, Hunt sees time as gendered.[10] As she writes:

> The power of a universal, homogenous, and deep notion of time is incontestable. The notion undergirds Western science, Western imperialism, globalisation, and the current vogue of world history, which some might consider all facets of the same phenomenon. (*Measuring Time, Measuring History*, p. 39)

Historical time is contestable for Hunt. Her grounds for thinking that are not simply a logical step from considering those whose experiences are marginal to or excluded by contemporary historiography towards additive categories of thinking that might acknowledge them. She also hints at the need to work backwards to reveal the sense making that set the course for that marginalisation. Revising history means unravelling it and resetting in upon a new course. That unravelling reaches back to ancient Greek thought, as she notes in a discussion on the 'tenacious' concept of modernity:

> Although there is some question as to whether modernity, as Aristotle said of time more generally, belongs to the class of things that exist or to that of things that do not exist, it does function as a category of our thinking, to judge only by the number of times the word appears in book and article titles …. Of

particular interest is the way the modern came to be seen as a distinct, and eventually superior, category of time. (*Measuring Time, Measuring History*, p. 48; see also p. 118)

She then passes on, leaving us to consider whether calling out the invention of time is enough to think about it differently. In other works such as *Writing History in the Global Era* (2014) and the book she co-authored with Joyce Appelby and Margaret Jacob—*Telling the Truth about History* (1994)—the opportunity to square up against Aristotle and rethink his very approach to metaphysics also appears to be curtailed by her conflation of metaphysics with progress (*Telling the Truth About History*, p. 246; *Writing History in the Global Era*, p. 125). Yet she—like Scott—also reminds us of Derrida's work to unravel 'the binary categories of Western metaphysics' by showing how opposites indicate each other (*Telling the Truth About History*, p. 212).

There is more to metaphysics than the notion of opposites, but Hunt and Scott usefully call out the logic that leads opposites to be seen as relations of centre to periphery, and of dominate to subordinate. And Hunt takes yet another step beyond Scott in calling out the epistemic function that sets that logic in train: empathy. This is most clearly seen in her analysis of the origin of the idea of human rights. Eighteenth-century novels, she argues, fuelled the idea that we can take the 'leap of faith' to achieve the psychological identification that renders someone else like us (*Inventing Human Rights*, ch.1). So too, in their own way, pornographic works from the eighteenth century onwards transgressed mores and downplayed specificities of time, place, history and even language in order to create an imagined community of male readers (*The Invention of Pornography*, introduction).

Wonder's other

In Hunt's world, empathy creates affiliation and therefore has the function of subordinating those who are different. How, then, might difference be illuminated in order for metaphysics to be reconsidered? In contemporary feminist philosophy, wonder has that role.

Luce Irigaray's rereading of Descartes' *The Passions of the Soul* positions wonder as the departure point for an ethics of sexual difference ('Wonder: A Reading of Descartes, *The Passions of the Soul*', in *An Ethics of Sexual Difference*, pp. 72–82). Her claim is twofold: first, that sexual difference between male and female is fundamental to our making sense of the world (p. 74); and second, that wonder awakens our surprise, curiosity and attraction to that difference (p. 75). How that surprise or curiosity leads to an appreciation of the other derives from her agreement with Descartes that as the first of all passions, wonder is prior to judgement and comparison. It is a visceral openness, if you like, that leads to a direct acknowledgement of another's difference rather than a likening of that person to ourselves or a possession of them (pp. 75, 82). As she explains:

> This first passion is indispensable not only to life but also or still to the creation of an ethics. Notably of and through sexual difference. This other, male or female, should *surprise* us again and again, appear to us as *new, very different* from what we knew or what we thought he or she should be. Which means that we would look at the other, stop to look at him or her, ask ourselves, come close to ourselves through questioning .... Wonder goes beyond that which is or is not suitable for us. The other never suits us simply. We would in some way have reduced the other to ourselves if he or she suited us completely .... Before and after appropriation, there is wonder (p. 74).

Wonder halts hierarchical assimilation, functioning as a bridge between two worlds, marking 'the advent of the other' (pp. 75, 81).

Whether this openness is enough to sustain Irigaray's vision of ethics is an active question for writers like Elizabeth Grosz, Iris Marion Young and Marguerite La Caze. Grosz, quite rightly, questions whether Irigaray's vision of wonder rests upon the assumption of a clean division of male and female, and the marginalisation of other kinds of gender identity.[11] Young has an even stronger objection, arguing that Irigaray's claims are insufficient protection against subordination. As she explains in *Intersecting Voices* (1997):

> The concept of wonder is dangerous. It would not be difficult to use it to imagine the other person as exotic. One can interpret wonder as a kind of distant awe before the Other that turns their transcendence into a human inscrutability. Or wonder can become a kind of prurient curiosity. I can recognise my ignorance about the other person's experience and perspective and adopt a probing, investigative mode toward her. Both stances convert the openness of wonder into a dominative desire to know and master the other person.[12]

Young's solution lies in our adoption of moral humility, and an assumption that our relationship with others is asymmetrical. That is, I should have enough respect for others that I do not assume that they will see the world as I do. If I do adopt that stance, she contends, then there is no reason why Irigaray's view of wonder cannot be applied to any significant social difference, such as race, gender, religion or class.[13]

La Caze agrees with Young's extension of an ethics of difference to social structures other than sexual difference. Yet she also notes Young's move in arguing for a particular kind of wonder, one that is combined with respect. Wonder, because of its being prior to judgement, is ultimately inadequate on its own as a basis for ethics. Wonder may allow me to see the difference between my actions and those of a person who harms others, but not judge that person. Wonder is an initial response, as Aristotle noted. To realise the ethics that Irigaray suggests, La Caze sees us as needing to step from wonder to other dispositions such as respect, generosity, humility and compassion (*Wonder and Generosity*, pp. 24–5). Astutely, she notes that analyses of Descartes' view of wonder typically extract it from his wider discussion on generosity—an esteem that arises from the resolution to use our free will well—as the means to achieving a good life (*The Passions of the Soul*, pp. 103, 107). Generosity, to Descartes' estimation, springs from the combination of wonder with joy and love. And people of generous disposition are 'easily convinced' that others have the capability to use their free will well too (p. 104).

How wonder and generosity combine or work together is not clearly spelled out in either Descartes' or La Caze's writings, but we do get a sense of their complementary relationship from La Caze, particularly in this passage:

> Generosity can provide the limit that prevents wonder from falling over into exoticizing, crass curiosity, or contempt since curiosity is an acceptance of a fundamental sense in which we are all of worth, regardless of the differences that exist between us. Generosity involves a proper judgement of both self and other that forms the background against which we respond to others with wonder .... Conversely, wonder can prevent the presumption that others will think and act like oneself and desire the same kinds of things as oneself, such that one could make decisions and judgements on their behalf. It helps us to recognise the limitations on our own power and on our imaginations. Wonder allows for openness to difference and change in the other. (pp. 31–2)

What this excerpt suggests is that generosity circumscribes wonder, and wonder circumscribes generosity. Moreover, while wonder appears to need to precede generosity to generate the openness upon which an ethics of difference turns, generosity involves what La Caze labels 'proper' judgement, which lays the groundwork for the possibility of wonder at others. Wonder and generosity are distinct dispositions—each can exist without the other—but in La Caze's combination they assume a circular relationship, the beginning and end of which is unclear. Not knowing where wonder and generosity begin and end in relationship with one another is philosophically perplexing. But it might also be thought of as constraining when we recall Scott's invitation for us to remain open to the shifting and unstable nature of concepts.

Scott's interest in concepts reflects Jacques Derrida's challenge to the view of linguistic structures such as words, scriptive symbols or sounds as stable and reflective of the mind, reality, the transcendent or the abstract (*Positions*, pp. 26–7). Rather, he sees texts as referring to other texts in an endless chain of signification that he calls *différance*. Thus there is nothing inherently superior about any single view of wonder, or of generosity. Rather, the various views of wonder that have been advanced reflect particular contexts and viewpoints, much as Scott highlighted different views of work in nineteenth-century France, and Wiesner-Hanks detailed the particular experience of monstrousness for the Gonzales sisters.

Derrida argues for the deconstruction of concepts like wonder on the grounds of it being an 'unconditional ethical demand' of openness to the other.[14] Deconstruction achieves this by illuminating the 'blind spots' of metaphysics, and by showing how our activities of sense making may be subject to change. It is an ethical exercise because there is no God or transcendent to take responsibility for decisions about concepts, truths and knowledge, as was suggested in chapters two and three. And this responsibility lasts our lifetime, because we cannot believe that our decisions will fix meaning for all time. This is not caprice, it is ethics, as he explains in 'Remarks on Deconstruction and Pragmatism':

> I absolutely refuse a discourse that would assign me a single code, a single language game, a single context, a single situation; and I claim this right not simply out of caprice or because it is to my taste, but for ethical and political reasons.[15]

In Derrida's view, the possibility of ethical and political action requires individual choice. This is not neo-liberal individualism, because his writings on the ideas of 'self' and 'other' point to a view of identities as fluid, and even porous. That is, as with concepts, the boundaries of individuals are far from stable or fixed. This is apparent when we consider his writings in particular on hospitality, which he sees as shaping all human interaction and as 'the whole and the principle of ethics'.[16]

Hospitality is both a familiar and a very unsettling idea. Individuals and groups routinely welcome guests and strangers out of charity, civility and what Irigaray would call generosity, and in response to legislated duty or a moral imperative. Moreover, as with ancient and medieval practices, hospitality may serve to validate one's social identity and reputation in public life and thus be valued as a virtue or even used to define humanity. Yet, as Derrida also notes, hospitality is inconceivable and incomprehensible in an unconditional or absolute sense.[17] In the case of absolute hospitality, one gives all that one has to any other person without question, restriction or compensation: it is not circumscribed, subject to 'proper' judgement or needing to be conjoined with other dispositions, as Irigaray sees as necessary for generosity (*Of Hospitality*, pp. 25, 83).[18]

If we draw back from that, then our extension of hospitality is subjected to limitations and a reciprocal exchange of 'violence' ensues (*Of Hospitality*, p. 55). Inviting or giving gifts implies reciprocation, which is to Derrida's mind inhospitable. Here we may think of this situation as introducing the kind of symmetry that Young sees as potentially dangerous for wonder.[19] Must we, he explains, 'ask the foreigner to understand us, to speak our language… in all its possible extensions, before being able and so as to be able to welcome him into our country?' (*On Cosmopolitanism and Forgiveness*, p. 15; *Of Hospitality*, p. 15). Conversely, in inviting the stranger in, host becomes the hostage of the guest and the guest becomes the one who is master. This introduces a dimension not seen in Irigaray's notion of generosity, that of divided authority: 'As soon as I speak to the other, I submit to the law of giving reason(s), I share a virtually universalizable medium, I divide my authority'.[20] It is the tension between the unconditional and conventional and between the host and guest that keeps the idea of hospitality alive. It is 'to come': that is, there is no fixed or final state of hospitality, no end to its history because openness to the event is openness to others. This is his basis for his call for us to acknowledge ethics.

Derrida does not look to wonder to trigger the rejection of metaphysics in favour of a personal ethics. Yet Genevieve Lloyd holds that there is consonance between the idea of wonder and Derrida's sustained interest in the Socratic idea of *aporia*, which he revisits both as the experience of us being stopped in our tracks and as the possibility of thinking the impossible in texts such as *Memoires of Paul de Man*:

> I believe that we would misunderstand it if we tried to hold it to its most literal meaning: an absence of path, a paralysis before roadblocks, the immobilisation of thinking, the impossibility of advancing, a barrier blocking the future. On the contrary, it seems to me that the experience of the aporia, such as de Man deciphers it, gives or promises the thinking of the path, provokes the thinking of the very possibility of what still remains unthinkable or unthought, indeed, impossible. The figures of rationality are profiled and outlined in the madness of the aporetic.[21]

Passages like this make the assimilation of *aporia* to wonder tempting, because terms like 'paralysis', 'roadblock', 'unthought' seem to ring true with the various ways in which wonder has been described throughout this book.

Derrida, however, was a deliberative wordsmith, and it should not pass our attention that he does not use the term and does not rework it as he does *aporia*. Rather, he opts for terms and phrases such as 'haunting', 'time out of joint', and *Unheimlichkeit*. The last of these has the standard English translation of 'uncanny', an experience that is simultaneously familiar and unfamiliar and which generates feelings of both attraction and revulsion, and which leaves a sense of unease, eeriness, and even of being haunted. The appeal of this word over wonder would seem to arise from it being a strongly visceral experience, and of it simultaneously entailing attraction and repulsion by something that is both familiar and strange. Moreover, the combination of the familiar and the unfamiliar would seem on the face of it to address Meno's paradox—if you don't know what you are looking for, inquiry about it is impossible—without recourse to the Socratic idea that the human soul has a vision of the transcendent forms before birth.[22] We might assume that we see the familiar as unfamiliar, and not the other way around.

Unheimlichkeit suggests a strongly affective experience, yet it is also ambiguous, and unstable. Wonder, however, might also bear the same characteristics. Plato's Theaetetus might have experienced the uncanny when his head swam. But there is also something to note about the German phrase that Derrida chooses—like Freud and Heidegger—to use: the *heim* in *Unheimlichkeit* signals to us an estrangement from, denial of or unsettling from *home*.

Aristotle's example triggers for wonder were, we recall from chapter one, all changes in natural phenomena. Plato reports on Socrates' use of social and political concepts as triggers for wonder. Derrida's use of *Unheimlichkeit* gestures at experiences that are far more personal: the home is pulled from under our feet. This makes sense if we note the discussion above that ideas such as hospitality implicate us as responsible for ethics. Unsettling is not 'out there'; it is with us. Moreover, his suggestion of *Unheim*—un-homing—connotes the idea that what was might not be. The past is implicated in our unsettling, as Derrida's *Specters of Marx* and his wider thoughts on Heidegger's notion of the metaphysics of presence so persistently indicate.

Heidegger's writing—as we will see more fully in the final chapter—takes aim at our undue focus on what is, and our forgetting of the conditions and specificities that make what is present to us possible. Derrida takes this cue from Heidegger to prompt us to think not only about what is absent, but also the trace of what is not present within what is.[23] A key example suggested by this chapter, for example, is thinking about the trace of 'woman' in contexts where the thought of 'man' is ever present. This is also one of Derrida's examples of ideas that in being present do not seem to suggest the possibility of alternatives:

> It could be shown that all the names related to fundamentals, to principles, or to the centre have always designated an invariable presence—*eidos, archē, telos, energeia, ousia* (essence, existence, substance, subject), *alethēia*, transcendentality, consciousness, God, man, and so forth.[24]

The *Unheimlichkeit* of the trace becomes apparent in Derrida's writing when it appears as the ghost, the spectre, and the revenant. Ghosts are neither present nor absent, living nor dead, past nor present, and somehow they are also both of these pairs as well. He explains:

> It is a proper characteristic of the spectre, if there is any, that no one can be sure if by returning it testifies to a living past or to a living future, for the *revenant* may already mark the promised return of living being. Once again untimeliness and disadjustment of the contemporary (*Specters of Marx*, p. 123).

They ought not appear, but they do, and they haunt us. As Katherine Withy explains: ghosts ' ... straddle the gaps between the joints in our ways of making sense of the world and in doing so reveal that these joints do not match up perfectly'.[25] Withy's use of the word 'joint' points us to the opening of Derrida's *Specters of Marx*, in which we are reminded of Hamlet being haunted by his father's ghost and his declaration that 'The time is out of joint' (*Hamlet*, 1.4; *Specters of Marx*, p. 1). This presages Hamlet's tortured acknowledgement of the need to do justice, the path to which will be violent and which will ultimately cost him his life. This may seem too high a price to pay, but as Derrida reminds us, metaphysics disguises its violence in presence, reducing difference to the 'totalitarianism of the same'.[26] The queasy responsibility for justice is also ours, and that justice is in the name of those past, present, and not yet born. We must take upon ourselves the opening up of ethics, even though we know that—as with hospitality—it may be impossible, or it may also cost us. We are to be un-homed, as Derrida's invocation in the preface to *Specters of Marx* makes clear, and in that, we may learn to live, finally:

> If I am getting ready to speak at length about ghosts, inheritance, and generations, generations of ghosts, which is to say about certain *others* who are not present, nor presently living... it is in the name of justice .... No justice ... seems possible or thinkable without the principle of some *responsibility*, beyond all living present, within that which disjoins the living present, before the ghosts of those who are not yet born or who are already dead, be they victims of wars, political or other kinds of violence, nationalist, racist, colonialist, sexist, or other kinds of exterminations, victims of the oppressions of capitalist imperialism or any of the forms of totalitarianism (*Specters of Marx*, p. xviii).

Historians are not excused from the need to take responsibility for justice and for ethics. But it should also not be assumed that they are in the best position to achieve it. Their narratives, after all, may suggest a seamless making sense of the world, and contribute to the violence of the metaphysics of present. A key driver for Derrida's *Specters of Marx*, for example, was his twin discomfort with the totalizing and even triumphalist tendencies of those who declared the end of Marxism and thereby of a Hegelian history with a capital 'H', as well as those who see in Marx *the* way of explaining past phenomena. Derrida's response is to take a cue from the first line of *The Communist Manifesto*—'A spectre is haunting Europe'— and to conjure Marx as well as Hamlet's ghost.[27] Marx, stripped of dogmatic assumptions that have pinned his thought down, is needed to cry foul on a world in which liberal democracy is not in evidence and in which the gap between rich and poor grows ever bigger (*Specters of Marx*, pp. 53–4, 63–4, 78, 85). Our world order is that of ten 'plagues': unemployment; the alienation of the homeless, the poor and immigrants; economic wars; the idea and operation of the free market; foreign debt; the influence of the arms industry; nuclear proliferation; the drugs trade and organised crime; and the state of international law (pp. 78–82). The spirit of Marx could illuminate these issues in the ways that *Capital* did for the nineteenth century, although Derrida also notes that the lenses of base/superstructure and class alone will need to be rethought to ensure that the idea of 'democracy to come' might be embraced as a goal (pp. 53–4; 63–4). That democracy is one that sloughs off the ossified and alienating structures of histories, political parties and organisations in favour of bringing the singularity of individuals to the fore (pp. 29, 85, 113–19). So, the spectre haunting the world at the time of *The Communist Manifesto* remains prescient and unrelenting.

So close

Derrida's writing against a metaphysics of presence and in favour of responsibility for ethics is not another metaphysics of presence in disguise. Various commentators have noted that while he returns again and again to the idea of the individual, his dynamic use of concepts and liberal use of neologisms act as reminders of our world being out of joint. But his explorations are also personal and historical, gesturing at the complexity, ambiguity and proximity of his own life experiences with a world of ghosts. Derrida was born to a Jewish family in pre-second world war Algiers, grew up in Vichy Algeria, and moved to France post-second world war. He is at once Jewish, Algerian and French, and also none of those things, unhomed not only by international events that loom large in our histories of the twentieth century, but also never at home with any of the identities that others may have ascribed to him.

Derrida's acknowledgement of his self complexity is interleaved throughout many of his writings. But his writings also refer to, and are intertwined with the trace of others who acknowledge the challenge of learning to live. A great case in point is the counter-trace of Hélène Cixous' writings with those of Derrida on Algeria or what she calls her *Algeriance, Disalgeria* or *malgeria* in works such as 'My Algeriance', *Reveries of the Wild Woman*, and *So Close*. Cixous' life, as she notes, shares many of the features and disjoints experienced by Derrida: she was born to a Jewish family in Oran, Algeria, and relocated to France with her German-born mother after the second world war.[28] But greater emphasis on life writing by Cixous brings the 'so close' aspect of *unheimlichkeit* to the fore: we are haunted not only by the impossibility and ambiguity of a world that we want to simplify and to fix in place, but also how proximate and elusive ethics and justice are to us. Making general sense of things is deeply personal, and not a universal intellectual abstraction.

Cixious' writings on Algeria pick up the Derridian theme of the *Unheimlich*, with 'My Algeriance' setting it out as an adverse reaction to the homliness of others. Her task is not to attach, to build, to settle, unlike 'writers who plot their land, become lord of a manor, search for houses, patrons and identify' ('My Algeriance', p. 74). Cixous' own relationship with any, some or all of identities that she might claim—Algerian, Jewish, French, woman—is an ambiguous bind. She can conjure up any of these identities in the manner of the strange Chinese historians in chapter four, but such an act also means conjuring the trace of what is not present. As she explains in *The Newly Born Woman*:

> there is no *invention* possible, whether it be philosophical or poetic, without there being in the inventing subject an abundance of the other, of variety: separate-people, thought-/people, whose populations issuing from the unconscious, and in each suddenly animated desert, the springing up of selves one didn't know—our women, our monsters, our jackals, our Arabs, our aliases, our frights (p. 84)

The language which describes that alterity—sense of the other—is not pleasant: it is punctuated by the term 'monsters' and culminates in 'frights'. So too, she outlines in painful detail how others dissuade acknowledgement of the other. School in Algeria 'effaces', 'excises', and 'phantomizes' Algerian identity, leaving her unable to 'discern a trace not a single trace of malgeria' (*Reveries of the Wild Woman*, pp. 70–1). More acutely, her mother denies the possibility of trace, as Cixous recounts in *So Close*:

> —What is a tttrace? I was fleeing. I felt my mother's breath on my neck: tttrace! *tttraß!* The word trace was mutating, I felt it hissing in a foreign tongue, it became agonizing, monstrous, we had entered a swampy country, I was floundering. I interrogated my memory, 'what is a trace?' I said, I was ashamed of clinging fast, 'Ouch! ouch! ouch! my memory said, wait! Wait! I have nothing to tell you other than what J[acques] D[errida] told you once and for all, trace, trait, path-breaking .... My mother said: *There's no traces.* She was categorical.—What is a trace!? With what force of annihilation she had struck the word trace with a closed fist. (pp. 58–9)

Trace is variously agonizing, monstrous and swampy, as opposed to both Derrida and her mother telling her *categorically* that it does or it does not exist. So trace is painful, unsettling, monstrous, but it is also elusive to the person who takes responsibility for seeking it. Neither Derrida nor Cixous' mother can act ethically for Cixous, she has to do this for herself.

Derrida signals the impossibility of capturing the trace, for that would fix it as the metaphysics of presence. Cixous, interestingly, sounds out the distance of this gap and overlays it with the pain of us being 'so close', but not quite there. This is not to suggest a quantifiable endeavour, but it indicates something asymptotic: it tends to but does not reach a or the limit. It is a little like Achilles never being able to outrun the tortoise in Zeno's paradox. This is an idea that I will return to in the analysis of Heidegger's various writings on wonder, and its implications for history, in the final chapter of this book. For now, it is simply worth noting that the trace is spectral: it appears real but you cannot touch it. Cixous describes herself variously as living in Algeria but never being 'inside it'; dreaming of arriving in Algeria whilst living there; trying to arrive; 'not quite' belonging; entering if only she had only gotten out of it; separated by an 'almost nothing of steel'; approaching and trying to get closer (*Reveries of the Wild Woman*, p. 1; *So Close*, pp. 7, 8, 37, 38). Finally, there is also the clever play of language in the French version of the title for *So Close: Si près* (so close) sounds the same as *cyprès* (cypress), the elusive trees of her Algeriance (see for example, *So Close*, pp. 58–60).

La Caze's vision of wonder is gendered through the coupling of it with generosity. But her views also continue Descartes' idea—which stems right back to Aristotle—that wonder is at the beginning of thought, of philosophy, of seeing the world anew. This can be interpreted as presenting wonder as a trigger for thought that is dissipated when understanding is achieved. Wonder is fleeting, and as something difficult to analyse because rational consideration may bring it to an end. Derrida and Cixous think otherwise. For them, the *Unheimlich*, the 'uncanny' never ends. We might get close, but we never get to a final destination of thought. This has important implications for history making. We may think of it as focused on the past, but Derrida and Cixious suggest that it may be too much of the present. Any time we fix an historical narrative, tell or show a history, we conjure the traces, the ghosts, of those we do not speak about. Justice and ethics, in their view, demand that we recognise the disjoints in history, conjure its ghosts, and take responsibility for it being unfinished, and unfinishable, business. History is unfinished, and open. This is a painful counter path from which both others and ourselves will seek to depart in order to settle into a 'home' of methods, approaches, categories and identities that we hope will tell the truth about the past. Like Hamlet, we have to reluctantly admit that we need to take responsibility for changing historiography and for conjuring the ghosts that would call out the injustices of the approaches that we set in place. With that admission, we shoulder the terrible burden of accepting that metaphysics is revisionary, rather than descriptive. Wiesner-Hanks' conjuration of the names of the Gonzales sisters, therefore, is not the end of *The Marvellous Hairy Girls*, but, as she notes, its very beginning.

Notes

1 David Cressy, *Travesties and Transgressions in Tudor and Stuart England: Tales of Discord and Dissension*, Oxford: Oxford University Press, 1999; Carlo Ginzburg, *The Night Battles: Witchcraft and Agrarian Cults in the Sixteenth and Seventeenth Centuries*, trans. J. and A.C. Tedeschi, 2nd edn, Baltimore, MD: Johns Hopkins University Press, 2013; id., *The Cheese and the Worms: the Cosmos of a Sixteenth-Century Miller*, trans. J. and A. C. Tedeschi, Baltimore, MD: Johns Hopkins University Press, 1980; and Roger Darnton, *The Great Cat Massacre: And other Episodes in French Cultural History*, London: Vintage, 1985.
2 Merry Wiesner-Hanks and Urmi Engineer Willoughby, *A Primer for Teaching Women, Gender and Sexuality in World History: Ten Design Principles*, Durham, NC: Duke University Press, 2018.
3 Mary Spongberg, Barbara Caine and Ann Curthoys (eds.), *Companion to Women's Historical Writing*, Basingstoke, UK: Palgrave Macmillan, 2005.
4 See for example Ethan Kleinberg, *Haunting History: For a Deconstructive Approach to the Past*, Stanford, CA: Stanford University Press, 2017; Andrew Dunstall, 'The Impossible Dream of History: "History" in Derrida's Of Grammatology', *Derrida Today*, 2015, vol. 8(2), pp. 193–214; and id., *Adventure, Schema, Supplement: Jacques Derrida and the Philosophy of History*, unpublished PhD thesis, Macquarie University, Sydney, 2012.
5 Merry Wiesner-Hanks (ed.), *Mapping Gendered Routes and Spaces in the Early Modern World*, London: Routledge, 2015, p. 1.
6 Merry Wiesner-Hanks, *Christianity and Sexuality in the Modern World*, 2nd edn, London: Routledge, 2010, p. 6.
7 Merry Wiesner-Hanks, *Gender, Church and State in Early Modern Germany*, London: Routledge, 1997, p. 203; id. (ed.), *Mapping Gendered Routes*, introduction; and id., 'Overlaps and Intersection in New Scholarship on Empires, Beliefs, and Emotions', *Cromohs: Cyber Review of Modern Historiography*, 2015–16, vol. 20, pp. 1–24, online at: www.fupress.net/index.php/cromohs/article/view/20132/18764 <accessed 9 January 2017>.
8 Merry Wiesner-Hanks, *Early Modern Europe, 1450–1789*, Cambridge: Cambridge University Press, 2nd edn, 2013, p. 5.
9 Simone de Beauvoir, *The Ethics of Ambiguity*, trans B. Frechtman, New York: Open Road, [1948] 2015, p. 9.

10 Merry Wiesner-Hanks, 'Introduction', in *Gendered Temporalities in the Late Medieval and Early Modern World*, ed. M. Wiesner-Hanks, Amsterdam: University of Amsterdam Press, 2018, p. 7.
11 Elizabeth Grosz, 'The Hetero and the Homo: The Sexual Ethics of Luce Irigaray', in *Engaging with Irigaray: Feminist Philosophy and Modern European Thought*, (eds.) C. Burke, N. Schor, and M. Whitford, New York: Columbia University Press, 1994, pp. 335–50.
12 Iris M. Young, *Intersecting Voices: Dilemmas of Gender, Political Philosophy, and Policy*, Princeton, NJ: Princeton University Press, 1997, p. 56.
13 Iris M. Young, *Intersecting Voices*, pp. 45, 49.
14 Jacques Derrida, *Points… Interviews*, 1974–1994, Stanford, CA: Stanford University Press, 1995, p. 64.
15 Jacques Derrida, 'Remarks on Deconstruction and Pragmatism', in C. Mouffe, ed., *Deconstruction and Pragmatism*, New York: Routledge, 1996, p. 80.
16 Jacques Derrida, *Adieu*, trans. P.A. Brault and M. Naas, Stanford, CA: Stanford University Press, 1999, p. 50.
17 Jacques Derrida, 'Hospitality', in *Acts of Religion*, trans. G. Anidjar, New York: Routledge, 2002, p. 362 [356–420].
18 Jacques Derrida, *Adieu*, p. 82.
19 Jacques Derrida, 'Hospitality', p. 398.
20 Jacques Derrida, *Rogues: Two Essays on Reason*, Stanford, CA: Stanford University Press, 2005, p.101.
21 Jacques Derrida, *Memoires for Paul de Man*, rev. edn., trans. C. Lindsay, J. Culler, E. Cadava, and P. Kamuf, New York: Columbia University Press, 1989, p. 132; as cited in Genevieve Lloyd, 'Derrida and the Philosophical History of Wonder', in *Parrhesia*, 2015, p. 65 [64–82].
22 Plato, *Meno and other Dialogues*, trans. R. Waterfield, Oxford: Oxford University Press, 2009, pp. 80d–e.
23 Jacques Derrida, *Of Grammatology*, trans. G.C. Spivak, Baltimore, MD: Johns Hopkins University Press, 1976, p. 70.
24 Jacques Derrida, 'Structure', in *Writing and Difference*, trans. and ed. A. Bass, London: Routledge and Kegan Paul, 1978, pp. 279–80.
25 Katherine Withy, *Heidegger on Being Uncanny*, Cambridge, MA: Harvard University Press, 2015, p. 17.
26 Jacques Derrida, 'Violence and metaphysics: An essay on the thought of Emmanuel Levinas', in *Writing and Difference*, trans. and ed. A. Bass, London: Routledge and Kegan Paul, 1978, p. 113.
27 Karl Marx and Friedrich Engels, *The Communist Manifesto*, Oxford: Oxford University Press, 2008, p. 1.
28 Hélène Cixous, *Portrait of Jacques Derrida as a Young Jewish Saint*, trans. B. Bie Brahic. New York: Columbia University Press, 2004, p. 5.

References

Appelby, Joyce, Hunt, Lynn, and Jacob, Margaret, *Telling the Truth about History*, New York: W.W. Norton, 1994.
Aristotle, Generation of Animals, in *The Complete Works of Aristotle, vol. 1*, ed. J. Barnes, Oxford: Oxford University Press, 1984.
Cixous, Hélène, 'My Algeriance, in Other Words: to Depart not to Arrive from Algeria', in *Stigmata: Escaping Texts*, trans. E. Prenowitz, London: Routledge, 1998. pp. 153–172.
Cixous, Hélène, *Reveries of the Wild Woman: Primal Scenes*, trans. B. Bie Brahic, Evanston, IL: Northwestern University Press, 2006.
Cixous, Hélène, *So Close*, trans P. Kamuf, Cambridge: Polity, 2009.

Derrida, Jacques, *Positions*, trans. A. Bass, Chicago, IL: University of Chicago Press, 1981.
Derrida, Jacques, *Of Hospitality: Anne Dufourmantelle Invites Jacques Derrida to Respond*, trans R. Bowlby, Stanford, CA: Stanford University Press, 2000.
Derrida, Jacques, *On Cosmopolitanism and Forgiveness*, trans M. Dooley and M. Hughes, London: Routledge, 2001.
Derrida, Jacques, *Specters of Marx: The State of the Debt, the Work of Mourning and the New International*, trans P. Kamuf, London: Routledge, 2006.
Descartes, René, *The Passions of the Soul* [1649], trans S.H. Voss, Indianapolis, IN: Hackett, 1989.
Hunt, Lynn, *Inventing Human Rights: A History*, New York: W.W. Norton, 2008.
Hunt, Lynn, *Measuring Time, Making History*, Budapest: Central European University Press, 2014.
Hunt, Lynn, *Writing History in the Global Age*, New York: W.W. Norton, 2014.
Hunt, Lynn, (ed.), *The Invention of Pornography: Obscenity and the Origins of Modernity, 1500–1800*, New York: Zone Books, 2016.
Irigaray, Luce, *An Ethics of Sexual Difference*, trans C. Burke and G.C. Gill, Ithaca, NJ: Cornell University Press, 1993.
La Caze, Marguerite, *Wonder and Generosity: The Role in Ethics and Politics*, Albany, NY: SUNY Press, 2013.
Scott, Joan Wallach, *Gender and the Politics of History*, 2ndedn, New York: Columbia University Press, [1988] 1999.
Scott, Joan Wallach, *The Fantasy of Feminist History*, Raleigh, NC: Duke University Press, 2011.
Wiesner-Hanks, Merry, *The Marvellous Hairy Girls: The Gonzales Sisters and their Worlds*, New Haven, CT: Yale University Press, 2009.
Wiesner-Hanks, Merry, *Gender in History*, 2nd edn, Oxford: Blackwell, 2010.
Wiesner-Hanks, Merry, 'Preface', in *The Cambridge World History, vol. 1*, ed. D. Christian, Cambridge: Cambridge University Press, 2015, pp. xv–xx.

9

RENEWING WONDER IN POSTCOLONIAL HISTORIES

Ranajit Guha | Gayatri Spivak | Romila Thapar | Rabindranath Tagore | Kalidāsā | Abhinavagupta

Aristotle's thought marks the limit of Indian historiography. This is how we must think about the extensive reach of colonialism, Ranajit Guha (1922–) argues in *History at the Limit of World-History*. Colonialism insinuates itself not only in the everyday ways that people act towards one another, but also in whether they credit each other with ideas, having a past, and histories. In chapter five, we became acquainted with Daston and Park's story of the rise of the discriminating and refined wonder of the connoisseur collector in the early modern world. Their collector, in the spirit of Francis Bacon, challenged existing categories of thought.

Yet Daston and Park's *Wonders and the Order of Nature* was a history of Western thinkers who wondered, rather than those who were the objects of that wonder, or their wonders. In the previous chapter, we began to put a name to those wonders—to the collected, rather than the collector—in the experiences of the Gonzales sisters. We learned that you cannot just 'stir in' the experiences of individuals and groups who have traditionally been marginalised in history and historiography without stirring up the categories and approaches we use to make sense of the world. Metaphysics is exposed, unsettled. Women, for example, are not just objects of thought; a consideration of their experiences in relation to men opens up new opportunities for us to understand and to act upon our ethical responsibilities towards others and to see metaphysics in new ways.

This chapter is not simply an extension of these arguments into the territories of race and colonised peoples. It focuses, rather, on whether the acknowledgement of what some postcolonialists call the subaltern—the traces of peoples 'without history' within the evidence record of the coloniser—implies the need to walk away from historiography as we know it and towards an aesthetic 'historicality' (*aitihasikata*) in which the possibility of *adbhuta, vismaya* or *camatkāra* (wonder) is reclaimed. Ranajit Guha charts this course by showing the affinity of Aristotle's *Metaphysics* with the philosophy of Abhinavagupta (950–1015 CE, also known as Abhinava) in

Rabindranath Tagore's (1861–1941) idea of passing through the threshold limit of wonder to experience the 'historicality of what is humble and habitual' (*History at the Limit of World-History*, p. 94). Romila Thapar (1931–) navigates to a sense of historicality via very different means: her idea of a Western 'scientific' idea of history. As we shall see, the key explanation for this difference of route is her professed need for protection from historiographical interference from the state, violent threats, and colonial portrayals of India as a timeless land of Europeanised wonder. I suggest that the common link between these two writers—and Tagore—could be their refraction of classical Indian metaphysics, and in particular the metaphysics of light developed from various sources such as Kalidāsā (fl. 5th century CE) by Abhinavagupta. That metaphysics argues for immanence in all things, including *itihasa* writings that take in history, and ourselves. Consciousness of the divine light, and the light in ourselves comes via attunement to wonder, which is latent in all experiences and built upon the preconditions of distanciation and universalisation. Consequently, in the metaphysics of light it makes sense to think of history as being in tune with wonder.

Histories of history rarely, if ever, include India. A notable exception to this is George Iggers, Edward Wang and Supriya Mukherjee's *A Global History of Historiography*, which includes a good summary of why it has been a disciplinary blind spot:

> A major problem with including Indian historiography ... is that not only Western historians but also, until recently, Indian historians have maintained that India possessed no history until the British colonizers introduced it in the nineteenth century.[1]

Yet while they offer a detailed appraisal of records, annals and genealogies before the introduction of Western historical forms, even they declare defeat in judging whether India had a classical historiographical tradition in the manner of ancient Greece and China. It is true, they acknowledge, citing Vinay Lal's *The History of History*:

> ... that ancient India did not have a tradition of history writing in the modern form. 'None ... reveal any understanding of causation in history; none demonstrate any familiarity with historical method and rules of evidence,' it has been said of the Sanskrit texts.[2]

More often than not modern Indian historiography is collapsed into the topic of postcolonial historiography, for which there is no shortage of commentary. Alongside summaries by, for example, Christopher Bayly, there are journals, readers and whole conferences devoted to postcolonial ideas and methodologies.[3] Ranajit Guha is credited as the creator of the first postcolonial journal, *Subaltern Studies: Writings on Indian History and Society*, in 1982. As Dipesh Chakrabarty notes, from there, subaltern studies broadened out to postcolonial studies via the broadening of its remit from India to the colonised world, and the successive acknowledgement of work by, for example, Edward Said on orientalism, Gayatri Spivak on deconstruction and Homi Bhabha on colonial hybridity and mimicry.[4] With these developments came detractors, with Arif Dirlik, for instance, arguing that:

> Most of the generalizations that appear in the discourse of postcolonial intellectuals from India may appear novel in the historiography of India but are not discoveries from broader perspectives ... the historical writing[s] of Subaltern Studies historians ... represent the application in Indian historiography of trends in historical writings that were quite widespread by the 1970s under the impact of social historians such as E. P. Thompson, Eric Hobsbawm, and a host of others.[5]

Out of the combination of these arguments we arrive at a very mixed appraisal of Indian historiography: new, now a global force, potentially methodologically parasitic. The result is unfortunate, with the complexities of each of these claims lost in the frame. Guha's postcolonial history is a focus of this chapter, but so is the scientific approach preferred by Romila Thapar. As noted above, I will conjoin their efforts via an exploration of classical Indian metaphysics before asking whether this reading, too, would benefit from Spivek's critical deconstruction in search of subaltern voices.

Return to historicality

When the British colonised India, they colonised history. History making was an instrument of subordination that grafted classical Indian texts onto Western notions of world history. This process, Guha argues in *History at the Limit of World-History*, was aided by the double meaning of the term *purāna* (pp. 51–3). *Purāna* refers to an extensive corpus of mostly Sanskrit texts that cover a wide range of topics, from cosmology to medicine and traditional lore and myths. Additionally, *purāna* can denote the cumulative nature of many Hindu classical texts: they are often the work of multiple hands over centuries. These two features in combination—old, cumulative texts—made it easy for both Indian elites and Western colonisers alike to treat the *Mahābhārata, Ramayana* and story of Śakuntalā, for example, as history that could be incorporated into western world history. Alternatively, others counted pre-colonial India as prehistory and started their narratives with the arrival of the British, thereby rescuing India 'from Prehistory by her own historians and ushered by them across the border into World-history' (p. 54).

To Guha's view the colonisation of history was incomplete because colonial histories carried the trace of those colonised, particularly if they were treated as opposites such as savage versus civilised or rebel versus lawful (*Elementary Aspects of Peasant Insurgency in Colonial India*, 1999, pp. 2, 17; see also *Dominance without Hegemony* and *A Rule of Property for Bengal*). Moreover, even when historians wrote about ruins or seemingly emptied lands, the presence of others was implied. This will be a familiar point from the discussion on gender in the previous chapter, but Guha frames this phenomenon in ways that differ on two counts. First, he describes it as dominance without hegemony, rather than as a haunting. This difference can be explained through an example: you can write about colonisers but the colonised are implied in that writing. They are there in the sense of Derrida's idea of a 'trace'. As ghosts, I may think that they can unsettle me and make me feel 'unhomed', but as those dominated without hegemony, I may sense that there is a potential threat of insurrection. Guha's ideas are not incompatible with those of Derrida, but his use of the terms 'dominance' and 'hegemony' drives home the political force of marginalising or excluding others, and his use of the word 'without' makes it clear that colonial domination is never complete. Second, he talks of world history being 'at the limit' of its meaning, despite the sense that 'scientific' world history prevailed over wonder. He writes:

> ... the battle of paradigms was won for the West. Experience triumphed over wonder. World-history over *itihasa*. ... But that was also the moment of our admission to World-history. Until then we, 'people without history', had been left out in the cold of Prehistory. However, once enfranchised, we outdid our European rulers and teachers in our enthusiasm for the prose of history. The wide open fields of historicality beyond the precincts of statist narrative were all but forgotten by the historians. No one among them paid heed to the alarm sounded once in a while by a creative voice to complain how schooled academic writing on the Indian past had cut itself off from the prose of the world and the stories it had to tell. (p. 72)

It is tempting for us to read this as history having reached a dead end, but Guha wants us to think of it as akin to an Aristotelian threshold in which we experience wonder and then begin to think about history in new ways (pp. 7, 48–9). World history is not a natural feature of our world, and it is not beyond negotiation. Nor, he goes on, are the general metaphysical principles that prompted its birth. It is not, for example, incumbent upon us to read Aristotle's opening edict in *Posterior Analytics* that all teaching and learning come from pre-existing knowledge as binding (p. 50).[6] Teaching and learning are not just conservative activities; they can be generative too.

The generation of new knowledge and new ways of thinking about the world does not need to stem from an encounter with novel phenomena. We can also experience wonder when we are taken aback by the everyday, or on hearing a familiar story again. The perplexities that Aristotle describes need not be such because we sense them in a first encounter. I can note changes in the moon many times before I experience wonder at them, for instance. To help us understand the significance of his claim, Guha reminds us of the opening of the *Mahābhārata*, in which a traveller is asked to tell stories that his audience has already heard, rather than new stories. It is hard to think of a more Indian and less Western beginning to a story, Guha observes (p. 61). He sees Western thought as having fallen into the habitual expectation that novelty generates historical and philosophical knowledge. Novelty is not assumed for the Indian concepts of *adbhuta* or *adbhutarasa*, which Guha translates as an attunement to wonder or mood of wonder (p. 63). It is not an exceptional experience or the experience of a person who has particular training or gifts: it is always present, in every form of life. Consequently, wonder is not tied to any particular experience and never exhausted by retelling (p.67). This embraces the past, and notions of history, as he explains:

> [*Itihasa*] has the past as its essence. But it is a past anchored to no experience in particular. It is precisely such indefiniteness and openness that enables it to produce … an infinite number of stories and the latter to generate wonder without end …. Yet, if they have proved to be an inexhaustible source of wonder for their audience, it is only because they allow language to illuminate what is unusual about the usual in everyday life. There is no reason why they should not be acknowledged as the stuff that constitutes a broad and comprehensive historicality …. The tale of wonder lives happily with the past. Indeed the relationship of time and story there is one of playfulness, each renewing the other in the course of an interaction that can never end if only because it has never been tied to a beginning (pp. 68–9).

By this account, it is possible to experience wonder via the everyday and different retellings of the same story. It renews our sense of the world in an everyday sense of history—*aitihasikata* or historicality—that is in no way confined to a discipline or to a genre of writing. In short, history can be everywhere because wonder is everywhere.

Guha's *History at the Limit of World-History* is an argument for an appreciation of *abhutarasa* and everyday historicality. In arguing for this, Guha takes his cue from Tagore, India's first Nobel Laureate for literature (Tagore, 'Historicality in Literature', in *History at the Limit of World-History*, pp. 95–9). Tagore did not wish to see the end of history, but its renewal, or *suchana*. As Guha explains:

> That word could mean inauguration or commencement or an indication to disclose what is unknown or not quite explicit yet. Whichever way one takes it, to go back to *suchana* is to retrace a development to its source and to let it show up in its history …. Tagore is evidently not interested in taking a stand against history as such but in pleading for a different approach to it (p. 77).

> That different approach, Guha puts it, means 'travelling over the fence' of the existing boundaries of history to neighbouring fields like literature and aesthetics in which wonder is perenially renewed, as with the creative gaze of a child observing dew, clouds, or a cow lick a foal (pp. 5, 78).

Tagore's idea of history is immanent: there is a latent historicality in every gesture, movement, word and action inside every house and across every field in India. This is not the immanent transcendence of Western historians who abstract out linear stories of states, politics and battles. Nor does it take Western historical form, with strict verisimilitude. Poetry, the short story, myth, music and art may express *aitihasikata* as a 'history of human mind and belief' in which the historian is an active participant.[7] It is, for example, this experience by Rabindranath:

> One day I had just come back from school at about four-thirty and found a dark blue cumulus suspended high above the third storey of our house. What a marvellous sight that was. Even now I remember that day. But in the history of that day there was no one other than myself who saw those clouds in quite the same way as I did or was similarly thrilled. *Rabindranath happened to be all by himself in that instance.* Once after school I saw a most amazing spectacle from our western verandah. A donkey—not one of those donkeys manufactured by British imperial policy but the animal that had always belonged to our own society and has not changed in its ways since the beginning of time—one such donkey had come up from the washermen's quarters and was grazing on the grass while a cow fondly licked its body. The attraction of one living being for another that then caught my eye has remained unforgettable for me until today. *In the entire history of that day it was Rabindranath alone who witnessed the scene with enchanted eyes.* This I know for certain. No one else was instructed by the history of that day in the profound significance of the sight as was Rabindranath. *In his own field of creativity Rabindranath has been entirely alone and tied to no public by history.* ('Historicality in Literature', p. 97).

Here we see that which is unforgettable and beautiful in the everyday, and the importance of Tagore as a meaning maker who has no need for the public approval for his efforts. In being alone, Tagore is 'enchanted', open to being with the world and the 'hunger of history'.[8]

The radical nature of Tagore's 'travelling over the fence' to historicality is hard to spot if you interpret as simply being an Indian take on what Western historians have called 'history from below' or the history of everyday people.[9] It is not, as Guha's short discussion of Heidegger's treatment of Aristotle's idea of *thaumazein* or wonder in the *Metaphysics* reveals. Heidegger renders *thaumazein* as *Befindlichkeit*, and Guha renders this in English as attunement. Attunement, as in the mood of wonder captured in *adbhutarasa*. With this line of translation offered, Guha sets down his argument:

> [*Befindlichkeit*] refers not only to a position but focuses on the moment of positing to indicate how one is to find oneself positioned or disposed. Understood thus, certain aspects of a long lost European tradition show up in the light of an unmistakable affinity with the ancient Indian concept of wonder (p. 65).

In two short sentences, Guha unravels historiography back to Heidegger and on to Aristotle, and then interprets their thought—modern German and ancient Greek—

in affinity with ancient Indian thought. Not Indian thought in affinity with European thought—the gesture of the coloniser who harnesses *purāna* to world history—but the other way around. Aristotle's *thaumazein* can make sense in an Indian tradition that celebrates endless renewal in repetition, and in the everyday. The renewal of Indian historiography is therefore a renewal of Western historiography as well.

It is very tempting to argue that Guha's Tagore-led call for 'history as creative writing' exists far away from the day to day complexities of Indian historiography.[10] Consider, as an example, the reflections of the eminent historian of ancient India, Romila Thapar, on the consequences she has faced in not wanting to see history serve Hindu nationalism or any other political agenda:

> If some of us feel that Hindutva history is less history and more mythology we should have the right to say so, without being personally abused, being called 'anti-national', 'academic terrorists worse than the cross-border variety' and 'perverts,' and being threatened with arrest and with being physically put down. Indeed, a leading Hindutva ideologue, Arun Shourie, even sarcastically said we 'eminent historians' all had hymens so thick that we thought that we had retained our virginity even when we published signed articles in publications of the Left. Apart from the sheer crassness and vulgarity of this statement, if men cannot have hymens, even figuratively speaking, presumably this remark was directed at women historians ('In Defence of History', in *The Past as Present*, p. 70).

Thapar's appointment to the Kluge Chair at the US Library of Congress spawned a petition which protested her 'anti-Hinduism' and school texts she produced were edited without her consent by the Indian government to remove references to ancient Indians eating beef ('Writing History Textbooks: A Memoir', in *The Past as Present*, pp. 73–89).

Thapar expresses support for the blossoming of Indian historiography driven by writers like Guha. Across her writings, however, she professes the need for a more pragmatic approach to counter Hindu nationalist historiography and colonialist tendencies to see India variously as gripped by magic; or historically backward or stagnant; or as characterised by a timeless Sanskrit culture ('History and the Public: An Introduction', in *The Past as Present*, pp. 7–8; and *A History of India*, volume 1, pp. 15–16). Her pragmatism sees her argue in favour of a 'scientific' methodology, which would seem to be at odds with Guha's everyday historicality (see for example *History and Beyond*). It may even be argued that hers is the historiographical voice of a coloniser, or an outperformance of the historiographical voice of a coloniser who demolishes myths in order to call out political excesses in the treatment of the past.[11]

Yet her work also arguably bears the imprint of classical Indian philosophical metaphysics, particularly on the preconditions for wonder—which we learn about as distanciation and universalisation later in this chapter—in making general sense of things. This is seen most clearly in her treatment of the Śakuntalā and Somanatha narratives, including purānic versions of these. Śakuntalā (also known as Shakuntala) is a key figure in ancient and modern Indian texts. The earliest account of her story is found in the *Mahābhārata*, with subsequent, varying accounts of her experiences offered, for example, in the play *Abhijnana-sakuntalam* (*The Recognition of Sakuntala*) by Kalidāsā, in paintings by Ravi Varma, the poem 'Sakuntala Its Inner Meaning' by Tagore, through to William Jones' translation *Sacontala* and films like *Anantyatra* (1985). At one glimpse, Śakuntalā is wife of Dushyanta and bearer of his heir, Bharat, and at another she is the focus of a romantic, tragic epic punctuated by seduction, anguish and happiness. Her story has shifted over time to match expectations both about the relations of men and women, and the purpose of writing. The cumulative result is, as Thapar expresses it, akin to the Alice that grew and grew in *Alice in Wonderland* (*Śakuntalā*, p. vii).

It would be fair to expect Thapar to approach the study of Śakuntalā as a winnowing down to the historical basis of the story. This would seem, after all, to be in alignment with her call for a scientific approach to the past. Yet she does not do that. Rather, the intention of *Śakuntalā*, she is at pains to point out:

> Is not to present a definitive study of the narrative and its treatment, but rather to suggest that when a theme changes in accordance with its location at a historical moment, the change can illuminate that moment, and the moment in turn may account for the change (p. vii).

Telling and retelling illuminate the moment, allowing us to appreciate change. A couple of pages on, she reiterates the point at greater length, making her stance as an historian even clearer:

> Historians comb literature for historical facts, references to events or descriptions of a particular historical time: all of which continues to be a legitimate historical exercise. My intention here is to change the focus somewhat. I would like to take a literary item—such as a narrative—retold a few times and treat this repetition as a prism through which to view points of historical change ... Underlying this exercise is the suggestion that an item of literature, as a narrative, relates to history, not for what it says which is anyway fictional, but what it might indicate as being historically significant (p. 1).

Her *Śakuntalā* will be an acknowledgement of the social power of retelling, an echo of the opening idea of the *Mahābhārata* that it is in hearing a story over and again that our minds take flight. Moreover, arguably it evinces Tagore's 'hunger of history' in *aitihasikata*. Linearity and verisimilitude take a back seat to the idea that in repetition we might think and feel about the world in new ways.

This is not an isolated historiographical excursion for Thapar. *Somanatha* is a revisitation of this approach; an exploration of how Turko-Persian, Sanskrit, Jaina,

Colonial and twentieth-century Indian nationalists have written about the 1026 raid on the temple at Somanatha, Gujarat. Her point is that there is no received version of the raid that can be used to justify the politics of Hindu-Muslim relations in contemporary India (*Somanatha*, p. x). As with *Śakuntalā*, this is akin to a negative finding in 'scientific' history. Yet there is also an acknowledgement of the value of multiple tellings beyond that of simply deflating a political claim, as she explains:

> In analysing the various perspectives on Somanatha after the raid of Mahmud, I would like to explore the idea that the historiography and the narratives that grow out of an event are significant to an understanding of the historical complexity of how the event and the space where it occurs is remembered or forgotten by a range of people (*Somanatha*, pp. 3–4).

This is reflected in her generous analysis of a broad range of narratives, including extracts from the relevant texts. This is not the laboured, circuitous route of a scientific historian that has not made up her mind in favour of a single telling of events. Her point—as with her arguments in *Śakuntalā*—is to note that sometimes resolution in favour of a single account is not possible, and that from situations like this, we can learn the value of telling and retelling for driving thoughts and actions.

Thapar's approach is not restricted to individuals, events or even—as she argues in the forward to *Exotic Aliens*—the history of animals such as lions in India (*Exotic Aliens*, pp. 25–61). Her methodological interest in tellings and retellings underpins her complication of the customary punctuation of early Indian history into three periods: Hindu, Muslim and British, or ancient, medieval and modern ('Interpretations of Early Indian History', in *The Past as Present*, pp. 9–28; see also *A History of India, Cultural Pasts*, and *The Past Before Us*). These variations emphasise differences of view within what is now called India, as well as the interest that travellers and explorers had in India in early times. And again, Thapar does not insist on their resolution, allowing the fine-grained differences in accounts of the past to rebut the colonial impression of a nation suspended in timeless thrall like the audience who watches a snake charmer over and over again (*History of India*, p. 15).

Even the most minor, unresolved variations in poetic, literary, historical, filmic and artistic tellings of the same story have the potential to trigger a change in the ways in which we make sense of the world. It is not clear, therefore, whether we need a linear, singular narrative of events in the form of Western histories. This logic underpins both Thapar's and Guha's visions of history, even though their arrival reflects very different routes. Thapar is aware of Guha's writings, but many of her observations pre-date *History at the Limit of World-History*. My view is that classical Indian metaphysics is a touchstone for both of them, even though its influence plays out in very different ways.

The metaphysics of light, wonder in *Itihasa*

The wonder of *itihasa*, Guha tells us in *History at the Limit of World-History*,

> lives happily with the past. Indeed, the relationship of time and story there is one of playfulness, each renewing the other in the course of an interaction that can never end if only because it has never been tied to a beginning. (p. 69)

These are features he claims for the historicality of Tagore, and which we might also claim for Thapar's sustained interest in historical textual variations. At a very general level, what is at play across their writings is the idea of the general sense of things being immanent in the world; of us not needing to abstract or to force an understanding of that sense but of us being open to the experience of it; and of that immanence implicating us but us also managing a distanciated understanding of it.

It is possible to read the works of Guha, Tagore and—at a stretch—Thapar as refractions and renewals of philosophical thought that stretches back at least as far as the first Sanskrit treatises, the Upanisads (c 1000 BCE), and in particular themes valued by the tenth century Kashmir Saivist or Tantric philosopher Abhinavagupta. This particular reading is encouraged by Guha, who writes of the wonder experienced with historicality in this way:

> Disengaged from experience, it does not claim to produce anything out of a given set of causes nor inform anybody of objects attainable by the common means of knowledge. Neither productive nor informative by intention, it is still a knowledge in the most profound sense of the term. For the apprehension of *rasa* is indistinguishable from self-knowledge, and the rapture generated by *camatkara* or wonder approaches *ananda*, the most profound state of spiritual bliss. (*History at the Limit of World-History*, p. 67)

What stands out is Guha's use of three key Sanskrit terms—*rasa, camatkara*, and *ananda*—that all play an important role in the metaphysics that Abhinavagupta sets out in his consideration of aesthetic experiences, including the experience of what Tagore calls historicality.

Abhinavagupta was one of the key progenitors of what Paul Muller-Ortega and Kirk Templeton have called a Saivist metaphysics of light.[12] This metaphysics ranges across ontology, epistemology and cosmology, but also takes in aesthetics. Divine light—Siva—is immanent in all things, including ourselves, but it is immanent without the sense of essentialism that some would see at play in Plato's idea of forms or Aristotle's immanence in things. Without that light, particular things would not 'shine' or exist (*Parātriśikā Vivaraṇa*, p. 31).[13] Here is Abhinavagupta's way of explaining this, from *Tantrasāra*:

> Light, rather than being is the fundamental determinate of reality and existence. The innate nature of all entities is of the nature of Light as that

which is not Light cannot be shown to have an innate nature (that is, self-evidence). (1.55

The reality of that light is understood, and our own selves are liberated, through the pulsing, throbbing light of a supreme, reflective self-consciousness (*prakāsa*). Here the self is both what illuminates and what is illuminated. Consequently, ontology and epistemology are thought of as one in metaphysics. Moreover, they are united in a realist metaphysics: what is illuminated and what illuminates is real in that it is independent of cognition. What the light reveals is a general sense of things about reality, not my thoughts or language describing reality. As Abhinavagupta explains it:

> ... the Highest Lord manifests the universe in diverse forms, the ultimate reality of which consists in shining. The universe is essentially identical with Self. It is real in its nature. Its highest reality lies in its being one with the Light of consciousness, and its oneness with the Light of consciousness is never disrupted (*Īsvarapratyabhijñāvimarśini*, 4.20).[14]

In this world, consciousness is consequently considered active and creative, realizing itself through will (*icchaśakti*), knowledge (*jñanaśakti*), and action (*kriyaśakti*) (*Sri Tantrāloka*, 1.4). It pulses or vibrates outwards into manifestation, and back again from manifestation into the self (*Sri Tantrāloka*, 4.181–7).

Every perception, thought, sensation or emotion is a pulsation of consciousness, an expansion towards the perception of an individual object and contraction back to subjectivity (*Īsvarapratyabhijñāvimarśinī*, 1.5.14). Words, too, have the capability of revealing the most general sense of things as categories (*tattvas*) that are united in the light of consciousness. To see this, consider the way that Abhinavagupta describes the phonemes of Sanskrit as part of metaphysics:

> The letters from '*a*' to *visarga* denote *Śiva tattva*; those from *ka* to *ṅa* denote the five elements from the earth up to the ether; those from *ca* up to *ña* denote the five *tanmātras* from smell up to sound; those from *ṭa* to *ṇa* denote the five *karmendriyas* (organs of action) from the feet up to the tongue; those from *ta* to *na* denote five *jñanendriyas* from the nose up to the ears; those from *pa* to *ma* denote the group of five i.e., *manas, ahaṃkāra, buddhi, prakṛti*, and *puruṣa*; those from *ya* to *va* denote through *raga, vidyā, kalā* and *māyā tattvas* .... The letters from '*śa*' to '*kṣa*'denote the group of five categories, viz., *Mahāmāyā, Śuddhavidya, Īśvara, Sadāśiva* and *Śakti*. (Parātrīśikā Vivaraṇa, pp. 98–101)

This everyday metaphysics also embraces Abhinavagupta's aesthetics, and in particular his philosophy of theatrics, where we find lines of thought on consciousness, pulsation and *camatkara* that run back to the great playwright Kalidāsā, and onwards to Tagore, Guha, and Thapar.

Everything and every experience radiates light, including ourselves. Yet there were some experiences that captured Abhinavagupta's attention as highlighting the pulsation of consciousness well. Words are one example, as we discovered above. Aesthetic experiences such as going to the theatre are another. *Rasa*, the Sanskrit term for aesthetics, captures the idea of the essence of things in the manner of the emanating sap of a plant, and the experience of wonder in aesthetics—*abdhurasa*—can be thought of as tasting that essence or sap cognitively, via perceptions, thoughts and emotions. There is a dynamism here that aligns well with light, the light which shines from everything. Aesthetics, and the theatre in particular, distils the general essence of things in ways that are conducive to our experience of wonder and consciousness of the light. We can see this way of thinking at work in Abhinavagupta's commentary on Bharati Muni's (fl. 300 BCE–100 CE) older work on aesthetics, the *Natyasastra*:

> When we go to the theatre, we do not have any inclination to think: today, I will have to accomplish something real. Rather we feel: I will listen to and see something beyond my everyday experience, something worthy of my attention, whose innermost essence is pure joy. I will share this experience with the whole audience. One's heart becomes like a spotless mirror; for all one's preoccupations have been completely forgotten and one is lost in aesthetic rapture, listening to the fine singing and music. At this moment, we can identify ourselves with joy, with sorrow, in fact with any one of the feelings evoked in us by the performance of the actors. Listening to the dramatic text, looking at the different figures on the stage, we get an intuitive knowledge of what Rama or Ravana, for instance, are. And such a knowledge is not circumscribed by a definite time or place. Our mind, carried away by wondering (*camatkara*), takes for a couple of days the very form of its own Self and sees the whole world through it. (*Natyaśāstra of Bharatamuni*, 1.107)

The potential for wonder is in all of us, and our experiences with all things—even unreal things such as fictional characters—can trigger wonder (*Tantraloka*, 91.1.53). Yet wonder is not the same as more everyday experiences of cognition such as acts of memory and inference. It is a state of immersion in which we taste the light through expansion in perception and contraction back to subjectivity (*Natyaśāstra of Bharatamuni*, 1.279).[15] Moreover, we may experience wonder in some contexts more than others. The generative power of theatre as fuelling consciousness of light stems from two characteristics, all of which are intimated in the extract above.

Abhinavagupta sees the generative power of the theatre at work first in what we might think of as distanciation or depersonalisation. What we see on the stage is disjoined from our everyday experiences, including the expectations and worries that we might have. Theatres support this shift through the use of design features such as curtains and a proscenium that are quite unlike the features of our everyday world. As Abhinavagupta puts it, 'I will listen to and see something beyond my everyday experience'. Second, our experience of the theatre is an experience in universalisation. The play that I see is not a mimetic experience of real life. It promises representations whose 'innermost essence is pure joy', representations that I can share with the whole audience and which give us intuitive knowledge of the human and the divine which are 'not circumscribed by a definite time or place'. Distanciation and universalisation provide the ground conditions for the connection of the self with the light in things and the light in ourselves. We are absorbed by wonder (camatkara) in the world of the players, and in this wonder, we are liberated from our individuality—the 'I'—and the boundaries between me and things (subject-object dualities). By the repeated, and renewing consideration of what we perceive in the theatre and ourselves, achieve the 'bliss which is the true nature of one's own self … the bliss the comes from realising [the light of the self] with the highest Brahman [Divine light]' (*Natyaśāstra of Bharatamuni*, 1.277).[16] We are implicated in the theatre—as with the world—and it is connected back to us.

Wonder as *camatkara* denotes a threshold when I pass beyond the world of dualities and come to appreciate the unity that is light in all things, including myself. This is not to suggest that the experience of the theatre is all about me, for the case of tragedies highlights our active immersion in experiences in which compassion and concern for others, return to reflection on our ourselves and then renewed attention to others is a key part of any serenity that we achieve from apprehension of the light. As he reflects in *Paratrimshikavivarana*:

> … this wondering (camatkara) is present in the very heart of suffering: some sort of internal joy, made of energy, what a wife or a son used to give us in former times blossoms out once again at the view of people who look like them, or on hearing some moaning. We think 'They will never come back,' and that is the very essence of suffering: a particular wonderment made up of despair. As it has been said: 'Even confronted with pain, there is a possibility, thanks to the blossoming forth of consciousness, of gaining access to serenity'.[17]

The source for the quote that rounds out this extract is the poet and playwright Kalidāsā, who reflects in his retelling of the *Śakuntalā* story on how tragedy begets the connection back to consciousness. He writes:

> Often a man, though happy, becomes uneasy of mind on seeing beautiful objects and hearing sweet music. Surely, he remembers in his soul, though vaguely, associations of former births, deeply implanted in him (*The Recognition of Sakuntala*, in *The Theatre of Memory*, 5.2).

I wish to say more on Kalidāsā in just a moment, but for now I want to return to the example of historicality given by Tagore that I included earlier in this chapter—from page 97 of Guha's translation of 'Historicality in Literature'—for it bears the characteristics of theatrical experiences that fuel wonder. We recall that it captures Tagore's perceptions after he has returned home from school. Seen in the light of Abhinavagupta's writings above, we can also sense its conveyance of distanciation. Tagore tells us that he 'happened to be all by himself', alone, and 'tied to no public by history'. Moreover, it captures the general, the universal in his sight of a 'donkey—not one of those donkeys manufactured by British imperial policy but the animal that had always belonged to our own society and has not changed in its ways since the beginning of time' and the universal attraction of one living being for another when the cow licks the donkey. He is not a passive witness to events but is 'in the field of his own creativity', and because of all these elements above in combination, he experiences 'a marvellous sight', an unforgettable thrill. Aesthetic experiences, we learn from this example, need not take place in a specially designed place such as a theatre. Nor are they confined to a single genre or textual format: the range of texts in *itihasa* captures this sense well. Any experience that sees us distanced from ordinary actions and expectations and in which we are open to the contemplation of the universal is grounds for wonder. *Itihasa*, Tagore's history, is grounds for wonder.

Kalidāsā is the common thread between Abhinavagupta and Tagore. At one level this is hardly surprising given that his plays and poems are appreciated in India at a level akin to that of Shakespeare in the UK. My point is, however, that Kalidāsā is more than a reference point for Tagore; he engages with him aesthetically, in the sense of Abhinavagupta's metaphysics of light. We have seen above Abhinavagupta's referencing of *Recognition of Sakuntala* to make the case that tragedies can like other theatrical genres provide the conditions for experiences of wonder. This is just one example not of citation, but of reflection that deepens the author's movement from self to other in seeking the light.

So too, the relation of Kalidāsā to Tagore is rich and iterative, suggestive of a lifetime of excursions out via reading and reflection back on self-practice. A search for, and experience of, wonder. At the opening of Tagore's poem '*The Meghadūta*' ('*The Cloud Messenger*'), for example, we see him address Kalidāsā directly as 'supreme poet' of the first, and 'hallowed' version of the *Meghadūta*' (*Selected Poems*, p. 50).[18] Later in life he returns to describe his first encounter with the *Meghadūta*, emphasising his sense of what Abhinavagupta would call the light of its words:

> I can recollect many things which I did not understand, but which stirred me deeply. Once, on the roof terrace of our riverside villa, at the sudden gathering of clouds my eldest brother repeated aloud some stanzas from *The Cloud Messenger* by Kalidas. I could not understand a word of the Sanskrit, neither did I need to. His ecstatic declamation and the sonorous rhythm were enough for me (*Reminiscences*, in *Tagore Omnibus*, vol. 1, p. 266).

In between, Tagore draws Kalidāsā to *itihasa*, noting that the lack of what the West would call historical information about his life makes it possible to create stories— even theatre—about him in which distance and universality trigger our own search for the unity of light in self and all things. In Kalidāsā's works, there is an 'emotionally rich, learned, strange otherworldliness,'[19] where the 'emotionally rich' is *rasa* and otherworldliness denotes the experience of wonder. In short, Tagore experiences Kalidāsā in the metaphysics of light.

In this historicality, the idea of history is far from the presentation of universals at work, linearly, in the actions of individuals or of communities or nations. Rather, Kalidāsā's works trigger in us an appreciation of our need to engage and to consistently reengage with the categories and the universal that emanate in the world and in ourselves. This will mean an aversion to received history, any singular telling or timeline that attempts to set the record straight. It will also mean distancing ourselves from boundaries that Western notions of the idea of history draw between past and present, fiction and history, and theatre and history.

With this reading of Tagore and Kalidāsā in hand, we return to Guha and to Thapar. As I noted above, Guha's call upon Tagore's idea of historicality is explicit. Moreover, we should now note that he also acknowledges Abhinavagupta for his understanding of *camatkara* or wonder as omnipresent and as a trigger for historicality. It is in acknowledgement of Abhinavagupta that Guha first talks of *itihasa* as wonder, as not tied to any particular experience, and as therefore never exhausted of retelling (*History at the Limit of World-History*, p. 67). This serves as a preface to the description of *itihasa* at pages 67–8 of *History at the Limit of World-History* that I provided earlier in this chapter. As with Tagore's example of historicality, I will revisit it in the context of our discussion on the metaphysics of light. The presence of distanciation is sounded in the past of *itihasa* as not 'anchored' to any particular experience. Universality is denoted in there being no need to be 'tied to a beginning', and in the idea of 'indefiniteness and openness'. Both distanciation and universality come together in wonder to 'illuminate what is unusual about the usual in everyday life', a wonder in which we move outwards to time and to story, and back to ourselves in a course of interaction that forever renews, and which therefore never ends.

The renewing process of *camatkara* takes in all things, which in Guha's case also extends to Western notions of history, philosophy, and metaphysics. We recall my earlier suggestion that *History at the Limit of World-History* was a reading of Aristotle's idea of wonder and metaphysics as being in alignment with the Sanskrit idea of *camatkara*. It turns out that this is not a one off, for he also renews our understanding of Hegel through historicality. Imagine, he asks us,

> If the writing of history were to ground itself in such historicality, it would have a subject-matter as comprehensive as the human condition itself. The world would open up with all of its pasts ready to serve for its narratives. No continent, no culture, no rank or condition of social being would be considered too small or too simple for its prose. On the contrary, we would be ushered into a complex universe 'of finitude and mutability, of entanglement with the relative, of the pressure of necessity from which the individual is in no position to withdraw.' As one can see from this description, it would be the world of the prose of the world itself. And what stories would it have to tell! (*History at the Limit of World-History*, p. 22)

The Hegel cited in this extract, we should note, is the Hegel of *Aesthetics*, not the Hegel of *The Philosophy of History* that is cited elsewhere in Guha's book. Everything emanates light, including ourselves, and in the experience of aesthetics that is the telling of history we have no right to separate ourselves out from it, not even Hegel.

This brings us to Thapar, whom we might see as connected by the longest bow to *itihasa*. In *The Past Before Us: Historical Traditions of Early North India*, Thapar makes an extended case for a conjoined *purāna-itihāsa* tradition. She sees this as contributing to an ancient Indian history in which both history and historical consciousness took shape from a diverse range of historiographies, including those which took the form of historical writing akin to that produced in the West. (p. 701). *Itihasa* has a history, but she also argues that our search for it is the search for a *chimera* because its purpose is to:

> project an earlier age and its ideals, as well as to introduce the different context of the later time when the composition was re-edited.... Thus, the archaeological search for material culture as the counterpart of the epic becomes something of a chimera. The manipulation of time in the epic is too complex for there to be a correlation with archaeological periodization. At most, artefacts may provide tangible forms to some descriptions in the epic. (*The Past is Before Us*, p. 163).

This plays out not just in her words, but in her work with various texts in *Sakuntala* and *Somanatha*. We recall two excerpts from *Śakuntalā*, which I included earlier in this chapter. The first, from the seventh page of the preface, stresses that hers will not be a definitive study, but rather a play between the universal and the specific, and the other way around. A couple of pages on, at page one, she stresses her distanciation from the expectation that the scientific historian will come down in favour of one version of the truth and her predilection instead for repetitions and variations as a 'prism' on change. This universality provides the ground for her delight in the variations of the past, her wish to break away from straightened nationalist histories that alienate the diversity of experiences that constitute India. Hers is a wonder in tune with the metaphysics of light.

Yet Thapar is in one way more metaphysically insistent than Guha in her exploration of *itihasa*. She relocates Tagore and Kalidāsā in a sense of historicality. Neither is a reified, a singular source for her idea of history: they jostle with each other and with versions of the past from the *Mahābhārata*, Monier Williams, Jones and the theatre of the cinema today. These tellings of the past are entwined with one another—East and West—cross over genres and times, and implicate us, as she notes, in our use of them to illuminate how we think the world ought to be. In holding back from distilling them all down, she invites us to reopen our appreciation of the world, including our being in it. In a way, they might contribute to what Tagore called *swadesh*, a non-geopolitical construct, a deterritorialised imagined community in which no single voice speaks and we are open to the world.[20] Her writings are a powerful reminder that *itihasa* comes clothed in many forms.

Can the subaltern speak?

It might not have escaped your attention that, I, a woman from a different settler society which is yet to substantively credit Aboriginal peoples with a notion of historicality, have tidily grounded Indian historiography in a classical Saivist metaphysics of light. That was very tidy of me. Tidy is the problem, Gayatri Spivak argues in key texts such as *Critique of Postcolonial Reason*. In the last chapter, I noted that Jacques Derrida's writings refer to, and are intertwined with, the trace of others who acknowledge the burden of learning to live. In that light, I positioned Hélène Cixous' writings as a counter trace to Derrida, arguing that her exploration of her relationship with Algeria is an acknowledgement of us being 'so close' but never at a final destination of thought. Every attempt at making general sense of things conjures up the trace of those who are denied our hospitality. Those denied haunt us, Derrida's and Cixous' challenge to us was to recognise metaphysics not only as descriptive, but as *prescriptive*, an attempt to fix the world in ways that lifts from us the personal burden of an ethics lived in our openness and hospitality to others.

Spivak is another counter trace to Derrida, literally in her translation of his *Of Grammatology* (1967), but philosophically and historically in her challenge to him and to all of us about whether we will let the subaltern—particularly women—speak. *Critique of Postcolonial Reason* unmasks the legacy of European metaphysics in denying the subaltern humanity and voice, right through to today. For just as the 'three wise men of the Continental (European) tradition'—Kant, Hegel and Marx—stripped humanity down to its European lights, so too postcolonial theorists have not been immune from creating historiography with an elitist bent (pp. 111, 276). Their own privilege—of lives lived, for example, outside of India and inside the well-endowed universities of the US—can be too easily forgotten when we read their history, philosophy and literature. In the case of India, what might result is not a breaking down of the metaphysics of presence, as Derrida called it, but the reinscription and masking of the privilege of Sanskritic Brahmans over dalits, outcastes, yadavs and the various Aboriginal groups of India. The strength and difficulty of Spivak's prose have made her an easy target for critics. But she reminds us of the import of the two phases of deconstruction described in the last chapter. The first focuses on how ideas are defined by their traces; the second moves beyond the positioning and counter positioning of those opposites to a personalised sense of ethics that seeks openness and affirmative relations with the 'other', particularly women. These phases play out in the move from what she calls colonial discourse studies to transnational cultural studies, the complication of economics, philosophy, literature, history and other cultural forms, by the lived experience of women. We cannot escape metaphysics, but we can let the subaltern speak, she urges, if only we are prepared to listen.

Spivak's argument that there is no escape from metaphysics aligns with many of the ideas laid out in my discussion of Derrida and Cixous in the last chapter. But she extends their thinking in laying out the argument that we can encourage multiple, even conflicting attempts, at metaphysics by listening to groups who have formally been cast as the 'native', particularly women. Guha and Thapar would seem to be far from this suggestion, but it is important to consider the implications of their understandings of *itihasa*. Guha opts for the everyday historicality that is latent in all of us. He does so by consciously appropriating Western metaphysics and reading it in the light of Saivism. Thapar holds back from coming down in favour of a single telling of India's early past. Indeed, she complicates it, much to the frustration of those who would wish to harness it more firmly to political ends. These inclinations, I believe, suggest an interest in listening.

Notes

1 George G. Iggers, Edward Q. Wang and Supriya Mukherjee, *A Global History of Modern Historiography*, 2nd edn, London: Routledge, 2016, p. 38.
2 George G. Iggers, Edward Q. Wang and Supriya Mukherjee, *A Global History of Modern Historiography*, pp. 40–1. Quote is from Vinay Lal, *The History of History: Politics and Scholarship in Modern India*, New Delhi: Oxford University Press, 2005, p. 50.
3 C.A. Bayly, 'Modern Indian Historiography', in *Companion to Historiography*, ed. M. Bentley, London: Routledge, 1997, pp. 677–91.
4 Dipesh Chakrabarty, 'Subaltern Studies and Postmodern Historiography', *Nepantla: Views from the South*, 2000, vol. 1(1), pp. 9–32. See also Edward W. Said, Orientalism, New York: Vintage, 1979; Gayatri Chakravorty Spivak, 'Subaltern Studies: Deconstructing Historiography,' in *Selected Subaltern Studies*, New York: Oxford University Press, 1988, pp. 3–32; and Homi Bhabha, *The Location of Culture*, London: Routledge, 1994.
5 Arif Dirlik, 'The Aura of Postcolonialism: Third World Criticism in the Age of Global Capitalism,' *Critical Inquiry*, 1994, vol. 20(2), p. 340.
6 Aristotle, *Posterior Analytics*, trans. J. Barnes, Oxford: Oxford University Press, 1975, p. A1.1.71a.5
7 Rabindranath Tagore, 'Aitihaasik Chitra' [1898], in *Itihaas*, Calcutta: Biswabharati, 1957, p. 138, as quoted in Suvadip Sinha, 'Ghostly Predicament: Narrative, Spectrality and Historicality in Rabidranath Tagore's "The Hungry Stones"', *Interventions: International Journal of Postcolonial Studies*, 2015, vol. 17(5), pp. 728–43. See also Ranjan Ghosh, 'Rabindranath and Rabindranath Tagore: Home, World, History', *History and Theory*, 2015, vol. 54(4), p. 136.
8 Rabindranath Tagore, 'Itihashik Chitra [The Historical Portrait]', in *Rabindra Rachanavali*, 1994, vol. 15, p. 516; as quoted in Ranjan Ghosh, 'Rabindranath and Rabindranath Tagore', p. 137.
9 Edward P. Thompson, 'History from Below', *Times Literary Supplement*, 7 April 1966, pp. 279–80; and see for example Frederick Krantz (eds.), *History from Below: Studies in Popular Protest and Popular Ideology in Honor of George Rudé*, Montreal: Concordia, 1985.
10 Rosinka Chaudhuri, 'The Flute, Gerontion, and Subalternist Misreadings of Tagore', *Social Text*, 2004, vol. 22(1), pp. 103–22.
11 For an example in another colonial context of an historian calling for scientific history as a protection against the political uses of the past, see Theodore W. Moody, 'Irish History and Irish Mythology', *Hermathena*, 1978, pp. 6–24.
12 Paul Eduardo Muller-Ortega, 'Luminous Consciousness: Light in the Tantric Mysticism of Abhinavigupta', in *The Presence of Light: Divine Radiance and Religious Experience*, ed. M. Kapstein, Chicago, IL: University of Illinois Press, 2002, pp. 45–79; and Kirk Templeton, *Suhrawardī, Abhinavagutpa, and the Metaphysics of Light*, unpublished PhD thesis, California Institute of Integral Studies, 2013.

13 See also Mark S.G. Dyczkowski, *The Doctrine of Vibration: An Analysis of the Doctrines and Practices of Kashmir Shaivism*, Albany, NY: SUNY Press, 1987, p. 26.
14 See also Kirk Templeton, *Suhrawardī, Abhinavagutpa, and the Metaphysics of Light*, p. 162.
15 On this point, see also Michel Hulin, 'The Conception of Camatkara in Indian Aesthetics', in *Practices of Wonder: Cross- Disciplinary Perspectives*, Eugene, OR: Pickwick, 2013, p. 229.
16 On this characterisation of theatre, see Geoff Ashton and Sonja Tanner, 'From Puzzling Pleasures to Moral Practices: Aristotle and Abhinavagupta on the Aesthetics and Ethics of Tragedy', *Philosophy East and West*, 2016, vol. 66(1), pp. 13–39; and Adheesh Sathaye, 'The Production of Unpleasurable Rasas in the Sanskrit Dramas of Ārya Kṣemīśvara,' *Journal of the American Oriental Society*, 2010, vol. 130(3), pp. 361–84.
17 Abhinavagupta, Paratrimshikavivarana, p. 49, as quoted in Michel Hulin, 'The Conception of Camatkara in Indian Aesthetics', p. 233.
18 On Tagore's treatment of Kalidāsā as, variously, divine, semi divine or as Siva's court poet, see William Radice, 'Tagore and Kalidāsā', *South Asia Research*, 1996, vol. 16(1), pp. 45–60.
19 William Radice, 'Tagore and Kalidāsā', p. 51.
20 Rabindranath Tagore, 'Satyerahvān,' in Partha Chatterjee (ed.), *Lineages of Political Society: Studies in Postcolonial Democracy*, New Delhi: Permanent Black, 2011, p. 104.

References

Abhinavagupta, *Īśvarapratyabhijñāvimarśinī: Doctrine of Divine Recognition*, 3 vols, eds K. A. Subramania and K.C. Iyer and K.C. Pandey, Delhi: Motilal Banarsidass, 1986.
Abhinavagupta, *Parātrīśikā Vivaraṇa: The Secret of Tantric Mysticism*, trans. J. Singh, Delhi: Motilal Banarsidass, 2005.
Abhinavagupta, *Naṭyaśāstra of Bharatamuni: Text, Commentary of Abhinavabharati by Abhinavaguptacarya and English Translation,3 vols*, trans. M.M. Ghosh, ed. P. Kumar, Delhi: New Bharatiya, 2006.
Abhinavagupta, *Sri Tantrāloka and other works, 9 vols*, trans. S.P. Singh and S. Maheshvarananda, New Delhi: Standard Books, 2015.
Abhinavagupta, *Tantrasāra*, trans. G. Chatterjee, Varasani, India: Indica Books, 2015.
Guha, Ranajit, *Elementary Aspects of Peasant Insurgency in Colonial India*, Durham, NC: Duke University Press, 1983.
Guha, Ranajit, *A Rule of Property for Bengal: An Essay on the Idea of Permanent Settlement* [1981], Durham, NC: Duke University Press, 1996.
Guha, Ranajit, *Dominance without Hegemony: History and Power in Colonial India*, Cambridge, MA: Harvard University Press, 1997.
Guha, Ranajit, *History at the Limit of World-History*, New York: Columbia University Press, 2002.
Kālidāsa, *Theatre of Memory: The Plays of Kālidāsa*, New York: Columbia University Press, 1984.
Kālidāsa, *The Loom of Time: A Selection of his Plays and Poems*, Harmondsworth, UK: Penguin, 2007.
Spivak, Gayatri, *Critique of Postcolonial Reason: Toward a History of the Vanishing Present*, Cambridge, MA: Harvard University Press, 2011.
Tagore, Rabindranath, *Selected Poems*, trans. W. Radice, Harmondsworth, UK: Penguin, 1985.
Tagore, Rabindranath, 'Historicality in Literature', trans. R. Guha, in *History at the Limit of World-History*, New York: Columbia University Press, 2002, pp. 96–99.
Tagore, Rabindranath, *The Tagore Omnibus, 4 vols*, New Delhi: Rupa, 2003–2005.

Thapar, Romila, *A History of India*, vol. 1, Harmondsworth: Penguin, 1966.
Thapar, Romila, *History and Beyond*, Oxford: Oxford University Press, 2000.
Thapar, Romila, *Śakuntalā: Texts, Readings, Histories*, London: Anthem, 2002.
Thapar, Romila, *Cultural Pasts: Essays in Early Indian History*, Oxford: Oxford University Press, 2003.
Thapar, Romila, *Early India: From Origins to AD 1300*, Harmondsworth, UK: Penguin, 2003.
Thapar, Romila, *Somanatha: The Many Voices of History*, London: Verso, 2005.
Thapar, Romila, 'The Lion: From Pride to Metaphor', in Valmik Thapar, Romila Thapar and Yusuf Ansari, *Exotic Aliens: The Lion and the Cheetah in India*, New Delhi: Aleph, 2013.
Thapar, Romila, *The Past before Us: Historical Traditions of Early North India*, Cambridge, MA: Harvard University Press, 2013.
Thapar, Romila, *The Past as Present: Forging Contemporary Identities Through History*, London: Aleph, 2014.

10

THE BANALITY OF HISTORY

Martin Heidegger | Hannah Arendt

I have faced writing this chapter with dread. Dread because Martin Heidegger (1889–76) stands as both accused and accuser. Accused for his unquestionably anti-Semitic remarks and his endorsement of National Socialism, all brought to a head again by the publication in 2014 of his so-called *Black Notebooks* from 1931 to 1941. Accuser as the one who wishes to shake us from our state of sleepwalk and to return to Aristotle's idea of philosophy beginning with wonder so that we might wrestle with the question of what it means to be. You can of course treat the accused and the accuser as two Heideggers, and deal with them separately. Yet Aristotle never suggested that wonder was a pleasant experience, and none of us, Hannah Arendt (1906–75) has argued, are exempt from being overtaken at wonder at the simple and of succumbing to the banality of evil ('Martin Heidegger at Eighty', and *Eichmann in Jerusalem*).

At the limit: the Holocaust

There is no shelter or stillness apart from the Holocaust. The depth and the scale of the individual horrors and collective destruction involved challenge us even today to think about whether any sense can be made of it at all. Representation may seem necessary, but also abhorrent, as Theodor Adorno argues:

> The so-called artistic rendering of the naked physical pain of those who were beaten down with rifle butts contains, however distantly, the possibility that pleasure can be squeezed from it. The morality that forbids us to forget this for a second slides off into the abyss of its opposite …. By this alone an injustice is done to the victims, yet no art that avoided the victims could stand up to the demands of justice.[1]

He is not the only one to see the Holocaust as demanding an invidious choice: Primo Levi recounts the decision of survivors about whether to speak or to remain silent.[2] Their struggle, David Carroll has argued, is due to the Holocaust being 'a limit case of knowledge and feeling, in terms of which all such systems of belief and thought, all forms of literary and artistic expression seem irrelevant or even criminal'.[3] Saul Friedlander has also spoken of the Holocaust as an 'event at the limits', and Berel Lang on how 'certain limits based on a combination of historical and ethical constraints' shape what representations can be made of it as a matter of 'fact and right'.[4] The limit posited in all of these cases is not an outer boundary, beyond which we cannot pass. This much is suggested by Lang when she notes that talk of the impossibility of representing the Holocaust comes with a 'negative rhetoric', but which we might also think of as a 'un rhetoric':

> We hear it referred to as unspeakable, and we usually afterward a fairly detailed description of what is unspeakable, that description intended, of course, to prove that the designation was warranted.[5]

Thomas Tresize takes all of these descriptions of the Holocaust as a limit as suggesting that it is 'taboo'. This means that there will be limits to the evidence about it and what forms of representation of it will be accepted by historians, their readers, survivors and their families, and the wider community. There is nothing to stop people from crossing over the boundaries implied, but it is extremely unlikely that other people will accept their efforts.[6] In this case, the limit is something we will not cross if we wish to remain in good standing with other people.

Dominick LaCapra sees the 'limit event' of the Holocaust differently, as an extreme trauma that makes third person writing by historians unsuitable. Historians can negotiate that limit via the 'empathetic unsettlement'—the blurring of the boundary between the perspective of the historian and the victim of the extreme trauma—which can presage psychoanalytical historiographical 'acting out' and 'working through'. Acting out is seen in the compulsive living out of the trauma, rehearsing its details over and over again; working through on the other hand is an open-ended process seen in getting distance on the trauma, thinking about the experience in the comparative frame of life then and life now.[7] Not everyone agrees with him that the Holocaust can be part of a process of 'normalisation' via working through, even it that process is seen as open ended. So how should we think of this talk of the Holocaust being at 'the limit'?

Dwelling in wonder

In his *Metaphysics*, Aristotle suggests that a limit can be thought of as:

> the last of each thing, and the first point outside which no part of a thing can be found ... it is obvious that 'limit' has not only as many senses as 'beginning' but even more; because the beginning is a kind of limit, but not every limit is a beginning. (*Metaphysics* V.17.1022a4–5)

A limit can be an end, but it can also be a beginning: it is the 'last' and it is the 'first'. Aristotle's logic can be applied to ideas as well as to spatial or topographical considerations. The Holocaust as taboo, for example might be seen as circumscribing socially unacceptable publications, whereas the Holocaust as extreme trauma might be seen as the beginning of 'empathetic unsettlement' and learning to live again. This latter sense of limit as beginning runs through Heidegger's thought, starting in section 12 of *Being and Time* with his interpretation of the 'in' in 'being in' as residing, dwelling in, or a state of familiarity with something, rather than topographical containment. This idea is then played out in his definition of curiosity as 'not dwelling anywhere', as restlessness and excitement at novelty and change in section 36, and then again in the contrasting definitions he offers for curiosity and wonder. The curious, he tells us, have nothing to do with the contemplation 'that wonders at' being, or wondering to the point of not understanding. They know just in order to know and are shaped by idle talk of the kind described in the quote that opens this chapter (1.V.172, p. 166; see also *History of the Concept of Time*, 1925, §29.376–8, p. 273).[8]

Heidegger revisits and expands on the idea of wonder many times across his writings, but the sense of it as dwelling remains. In *Basic Problems of Phenomenology*, we learn that it banishes illusions that 'settle' with stubbornness in philosophy (466–468, p. 328) and in *Introduction to Metaphysics* the philosophical illusions wonder contends with are described as a 'mature sureness' of thought and a 'richness in word and stone' (p. 126). Those illusions are not everyday matters, for in the fifth *Black Notebook*, wonder is described as working on the 'question-worthy', the rare and the essential (*Ponderings II–VI*, V.71.352–3, p. 257) and in 'The Origin of the Work of Art' the historical mistaken for the natural. He writes:

> The way that we talk about the thingness of things may seem natural to us, tradition has simply forgotten the unfamiliar source from which it arose, which struck people as strange and caused them to wonder (*Poetry, Language, Thought*, p. 24).

In summary, wonder opens what is thought to be locked (*Discourse on Thinking*, p. 90). It opens our understanding that the ways in which we make general sense of the world are historical, and therefore that they are open to change.

We should therefore not be surprised to see Heidegger argue for the role of wonder in returning us to Plato's perplexity at the idea of being and to a first beginning in which being is sufficiently unsettled, unconcealed or historicised that we can ask questions about it (*Contributions to Philosophy (Of the Event)*, I. Prospect. 4, 6, 17, pp. 10, 18, 37; *Being and Time*, Int. II.19, p. 18). He is aware of the difficulty of the project, and the limited success of his predecessors in even starting it. Hegel is a rare exception, showing with his illumination of metaphysics as history and history as metaphysics that he was the 'first' to think the philosophy of the Greeks as a whole ('Hegel and the Greeks', p. 324). Yet wonder is not a blanket state of perplexity in that return. Heidegger's Freiburg lecture series from 1937–8, published as *Basic Questions of Philosophy*, provides a fine-grained analysis of the distinction between wonder as *Thaumazein* and the 'ordinary wonder' of curiosity or marvelling (*Verwunderung*), admiration (*Bewunderung*), astonishment (*Staunen*) and awe (*Bestaunen*). Those who are curious are 'bewitched and enchanted' with the novel, exceptional, unexpected, surprising and exciting and eschew the familiar and the ordinary. This description will be familiar from my earlier account of curiosity in *Being and Time*, but Heidegger also adds a coda that the objects of the curious remind him of the endless variety of offerings in the cinema (pp. 136–7). In admiration, the production and nature of objects of curiosity are explicitly acknowledged, evaluated and appreciated (p. 142). Finally *Staunen* and *Bestaunen* are seen in degrees of stupefaction or dumbfoundedness at one extraordinary thing (p. 143). What distinguishes the varieties of ordinary wonder from *Thaumazein* is that the former takes the ordinary for granted (pp. 144–145, 149). *Thaumazein*, as Mary-Jane Rubenstein puts it, 'wonders at the inscrutability of the ordinary'.[9] Moreover, it 'dwells', or as Heidegger argues '[p]hilosophy becomes more wondrous the more it becomes what it really is,' away from the idle talk of those who are unknowingly lodged within the confines of habitual metaphysics; the accelerating domination of technology over nature and people; the treatment of people as objects of consumption; and psychologists who wish to disenchant and to dispossess philosophy of the wondrous (pp. 141, 153–6).

Wonder as *Thaumazein* dwells upon the ordinary, rendering it uncanny (*unheimlich*) and un-homing us in ways that we learned about in chapter eight.[10] It does not dissipate after Theaetetus' head swims. It is the first point at the limit. In extreme wonder, there is no escape because to explain the inscrutable would be to destroy it (*Basic Questions of Philosophy*, pp. 145, 150). But with this disposition, history can begin (p. 147). History, Heidegger tells us in an earlier part of the Freiburg lectures, is not the conservative description of the past through the lens of the present. On Heidegger's terms, this is better called 'historiography'. History, by contrast, is revolutionary: 'an upheaval and recreating of the customary so that the beginning might be restructured' (p. 39). History historicises what we assume is natural, showing us that there are other possibilities. History, in short, is creative metaphysics or the possibility of a new beginning with no metaphysics; historiography is conservative, descriptive metaphysics.

Returning to difference

Heidegger doubted whether dwelling in wonder could be started, let alone sustained (*Basic Questions of Philosophy*, pp. 159–60). Nonetheless, his writing shows persistence with the idea that this disposition is needed if we are to begin to un-home our notions of being. Arendt sees Heidegger's dwelling with wonder as decisive in reflecting on who he was ('Martin Heidegger is Eighty').[11] This, in her view, starts with his idiosyncratic reading of Plato's and Aristotle's ideas of wonder as *dwelling* with the ordinary as strange. It continues with him eschewing the idle talk of the curious—including the academic curious described in the quote at the start of this chapter—in favour of the concealed and the clearing of the solitary thinker. The stage is thereby set for the 'hidden king' to lay down *Holzwege*, 'wood paths' which lead nowhere out of the wood. He is, Arendt concludes, Thales in *Theaetetus*:

> While he was studying the stars and looking upwards, he fell into a pit, and a neat, witty Thracian servant girl jeered at him, they say, because he was so eager to know the things in the sky that he could not see what was there before him at his very feet. The same jest applies to all who pass their lives in philosophy.[12]

What lay before Heidegger's feet was the rise of Hitler and National Socialism, the second world war and the Holocaust. These events, unlike the well that Thales fell into, were not something that he did not see. The publication of his *Black Notebooks* in 2014 dispel any doubts we might have about his involvement with the Nazi Party from 1930–34 and the anti-Semitic nature of some of his writings. He was implicated, and then he withdrew. He wanted no part of 'folkish-racist' slogans and saw universities as having failed to speak beyond their rapidly growing public relations departments (*Ponderings II–VI*, 94, pp. 191; 148). Heidegger withdrew and chose to dwell with wonder, Arendt argues. He lived a long life, during which the scale and the horror of the crimes committed became apparent. He said little about what happened in Germany and across Europe in the 1930s and 1940s. What we are left with, Ingo Farin observes:

> Is the ghostly absence of almost any sympathy for the humiliated, the wronged, and mistreated victims of Nazi violence, the lack of moral or ethical critique of the perpetrators themselves, and the outright contempt with which Heidegger dismisses all moderate or principled voices attempting to hold up traditional standards and values of a Christian or liberal-democratic provenance, all of which he considers hopelessly implicated in the very same modernity that caused the problems in the first place.[13]

This absence is the ghostly trace of Chapter Eight in this book.

Arendt's fable-like story about the hidden king suggests the jagged view of the servant girl who jeered at Thales. Some would say she fell in a well of her own making in having a relationship with Heidegger, and in putting forward the generalisation in *Eichmann in Jerusalem* that Jewish leaders—particularly those on Jewish Councils—abetted Nazi atrocities through their cooperation.[14] Yet she, like Heidegger, argues for a return to the beginnings of philosophy in order to re-set it on a different course. The course that she argues for—the return of the philosopher to a new philosophical-political-historical realm of thought and doing—appears to differ markedly from that of Heidegger's solitary thinker. As we shall see, however, they share a focus on the ordinary, as the determinant of reality. Regardless of whether we agree with Heidegger that the ordinary needs to be unconcealed, or with Arendt that consensus is good, their approaches skew the focus of wonder towards the inscrutability of the ordinary and away from the unusual, the rare, or extraordinary. Even with Arendt's determination to treat humans as ends in themselves, and not means to various ends, neither thinker protects us from the risk of falling down the well of the Holocaust.

As you might expect with a discussion on Arendt, we begin with Adolf Eichmann, but the path of our thought will soon travel beyond the well-worn lines set out in *Eichmann in Jerusalem* and *The Origins of Totalitarianism*, to the origins of Western philosophy with Plato. What unsettled Arendt most about the actions of the Nazi bureaucrat Eichmann was how little mental effort he brought to actions that would result in the extermination of countless men, women and children. He was not Hitler, spouting hate from the top. He wanted job advancement and brought his best to minute keeping, operational targets, business processes and logistical efficiencies. He was a *SS-Obersturmbannführer*—lieutenant colonel—who made sure that the trains ran on time and that ever more efficient means were found to exterminate innocent people. He was not stupid, Arendt stresses:

> It was sheer thoughtlessness—something by no means identical with stupidity—that predisposed him to become one of the greatest criminals of that period. And if this is 'banal' and even funny, if with the best will in the world one cannot extract any diabolical or demonic profundity from Eichmann, that is still far from calling it commonplace. (*Eichmann in Jerusalem: A Report on the Banality of Evil*, pp. 287–88)

Banality arises when we relinquish responsibility and act without thinking or even remembering. We forget to think of others and to treat them with respect, as ends in themselves. Eichmann is not singular in this regard, for the absence of convictions and thoughtlessness, Arendt elaborates in *The Human Condition*, is one of the 'outstanding characteristics of our time', as seen in 'the heedless recklessness and hopeless confusion or complacent repetition of "truths" which have become trivial and empty' (p. 5; see also *The Origins of Totalitarianism*, pp. 473–4). History plays its part in maintaining this world, 'historifying' people as enacting the will of a leader or party or instantiating a scientific theory. In this world there are no contingent acts and no acts due to individual responsibility (*Origins of Totalitarianism*, p. 307). Eichmann is therefore not the cause, but the result of a world gone wrong, but we can address it if we simply think about what we are doing and take responsibility for our actions.

It sounds like simple advice, Arendt suggests, but the return to responsibility and care for one another means dealing with a deep-seated problem, one set in course by Plato in his *Republic*. Socrates noted, Plato tells us, 'that many opinions held by many people about such matters as beauty and justice are floating around somewhere in between reality and unreality' and that '[m]ost people are denizens of that intermediate zone of flux'. Like Heidegger's 'idle talkers', they are content to inspect 'swarms of irrelevancies' instead of seeking the Eternal or the Good (480d). It is for these reasons, Plato records Socrates as saying, that:

the philosopher holds his peace and minds his own business, standing aside and, as it were, seeking a sheltering wall against the storm and blast of dust and rain. Observing others given over to lawlessness, he is content if he can keep himself free of iniquities and evil deeds and depart this life content, at peace, and with blessed hope. (496d)

Similarly, in *Sophist* 263e, Plato defines thought as 'silent inner conversation of the soul with itself'. This 'standing aside' or 'seeking a sheltering wall' lays the ground for what Arendt describes as the 'world alienation' at work in Descartes' philosophy, which Kant's 'enlarged mentality' of dialogue in the presence of others was not enough to remedy. So too, history from the time of Herodotus served this cause by prioritising thoughts and words over the things that people did or made ('The Concept of History', in *Between Past and Future*, p. 54). Philosophy became the generator of ideal types—what Kwame Appiah has described as the 'as if' feature of human thought—and its practitioners revered seclusion.[15]

Moreover, Arendt argues, philosophy came to conflate the idea of an ideal type with that of an abstract individual (*The Promise of Politics*, pp. 76, 123; and 'Philosophy and Politics'). The course of the world was set, a course that would eventually lead to Eichmann. Arendt sums up the current state of affairs by saying:

Our tradition of political thought began when Plato discovered that it is somehow inherent in the philosophical experience to turn away from the common world of human affairs; it ended when nothing was left of this experience but the opposition of thinking and acting, which, depriving thought of reality and action of sense, makes both meaningless. ('Tradition and the Modern Age', p. 25; see also 'Thinking and Moral Considerations', p. 162)

Into the vacuum comes the dictator, who makes it all too easy—banal, indeed—for people to relinquish responsibility.

Resetting the political realm means unwinding the split between philosophy and politics ushered in by Plato. A conjoined philosophy-politics would, Arendt believes, provide a remedy through the study of the 'coexistence and association of different men' (*The Promise of Politics*, p. 93). Her basis for this argument is the point that freedom and equality are nonsensical terms when looked at in the light of the abstract individual: they can only develop in a group because they have no meaning inside individuals but only between them ('Introduction into Politics', p. 170). Arendt's point looks to be political and epistemological, but it also turns out that she also sees it as ontologically, even metaphysically:

The presence of others who see what we see and hear what we hear assures us of the reality of the world and ourselves .... For us appearance—something that is being seen and heard by others as well as ourselves—constitutes reality' (*The Human Condition*, p. 186).

Perceptual consensus constitutes reality, and it is historical. This means that metaphysics is historical: if views on what is seen and heard change, our general ways of making sense of things will also change too. This would appear to run up against her prioritization of the study of 'different men' in the philosophical-political world, but that too functions to underscore reality. As she explains:

> If it is true that a thing *is* real … only if it can show itself and be perceived from all sides, then there must always be a plurality of individuals or peoples and a plurality of standpoints to make reality even possible and to guarantee its continuation. In other words, the world comes into being only if there are perspectives; it exists as the order of worldly things only if it is viewed, now this way, now that, at any given time. (pp. 20–30)

Hence, she sees her new world as allowing for contingency, differences and a 'haphazardness' of facts that philosophy and history have struggled to deal with in the past ('Truth and Politics', in *Beyond Past and Future*, pp. 242–3).

The banality of history

Siobhan Kattago sees in Arendt's visions of metaphysics, epistemology and politics the restoration of 'wonder to the political realm of appearance, opinion, and plurality'.[16] She appears to have a good point. Plato's Theaetetus wondered as a consequence of his interactions with Socrates, not as the apparently sole thinker of Aristotle's *Metaphysics*. I am not convinced, however, that Arendt's conjoined philosophical-political realm protects us from falling down the well of the Holocaust any more than Heidegger's historicisation of being. My logic is as follows. Arendt and Heidegger share an interest in returning to the beginnings of philosophy in order to set it on to a new course. Heidegger saw that beginning in Aristotle's naming of wonder in *Metaphysics*; Arendt in Plato's voicing of Socrates' frustrations with the public, political realm in the *Republic*. They also part company in their respective visions of how philosophy ought to be practiced. Heidegger combines a reading of Aristotle's definition of a limit in *Metaphysics* with Plato's various ideas on thought as a silent conversation with oneself and philosophy as standing aside to argue for wonder as *dwelling* apart with the ordinary. Arendt, on the contrary, calls the philosopher back from their shelter and asks them to engage with a world in which plurality is assumed, freedom and equality are achieved in company, and reality is constituted by consensus. Yet both of their approaches show an interest in the ordinary as the means by which metaphysics is created and potentially recreated, in the notion of *Thaumazein* (Heidegger) and in reality by consensus (Arendt). I am not suggesting that both are the progenitors of idle talk, as Heidegger would put it, but I do wonder, as Arendt did, whether 'it is in the nature of academic quarrels that methodological problems are likely to overshadow more fundamental issues' ('The Concept of History', in *Between Past and Future*, p. 53).

What appears to have got missed here is whether their entangled notions of history and metaphysics is more interested in the ordinary than the extraordinary. Heidegger dismissed the extraordinary as the fleeting focus of the curious in 'everyday wonder'. Arendt argues for plurality yet still insists on consensus, even if that does not mean reduction to a single point. Persistent interest in the strange, the edge case, the minority voice, the little or big change in action, the other, as we have learned in this book, can be seen as the realm of the curious. Curiosity, it has been argued by various thinkers, leads at least to distraction and at worst to eternal damnation. Yet consensus, as Arendt acknowledges in *Eichmann in Jerusalem* can lead to situations where evil happens because '[n]obody ... came to me and reproached me for anything in the performance of my duties' (p. 131). A counter argument for Arendt is her recognition of Kant's 'enlarged mentality' in the treatment of others as ends in themselves. But you have to *notice* others in order to do that. Consensus, the ordinary, as chapters eight and nine stressed, renders people invisible.

So, it is that we return to, and begin with, the Holocaust. It is important to note that this is an umbrella term for a constellation of acts that obliterated entire families and which left tragic gaps in others. You can break it down into those individual acts in recognition of the individuality of the lives extinguished. But you cannot render it ordinary, whether you look at it from the perspective of the present, or you lived with it as Heidegger and Eichmann did. It did not make sense, whether you thought about it metaphysically or as someone just turning up to work. It is no wonder that various historians have therefore talked about it as a limit case. A limit, we recall from our discussion of a section in Aristotle's *Metaphysics* V can denote an end point, particularly in topology. But it can also be a first point. Perplexity takes us to an end point and a first point at the beginning of Aristotle's *Metaphysics*, and at the beginning of philosophy. The strange, the edge case, the minority voice, the little or big change in action, the other are not outside of our writings of history and philosophy as general attempts to make sense of things. As we noted in chapters eight and nine, they can mark its beginning.

Notes

1 Theodor Adorno, 'Commitment,' in *Can One Live after Auschwitz? A Philosophical Reader*, trans. R. Livingstone, ed. R. Tiedemann, Stanford, CA: Stanford University Press, 2003, pp. 240–58.
2 Primo Levi, *The Drowned and the Saved*, [1986] trans. R. Rosenthal, London: Abacus, 1989, p. 121.
3 David Carroll, 'Foreword: The Memory of Devastation and the Responsibilities of Thought: "And Let's Not Talk about That"' in J.-F. Lyotard, *Heidegger and "the Jews"*, trans. A. Michel, Minneapolis, MN: University of Minnesota Press, 1990, p. xi.
4 Saul Friedlander, 'Introduction', in *Probing the Limits of Representation: Nazism and the "Final Solution"*, ed. S. Friedlander, Cambridge, MA: Harvard University Press, 1992, p. 3 [1–22]; and Berel Lang, *Holocaust Representation: Art within the Limits of History and Ethics*, Baltimore, MD: Johns Hopkins University Press, 2nd edn, 2003, p. ix.

5 Berel Lang, *Holocaust Representation*, p. 18.
6 Thomas Tresize, 'Unspeakable,' *Yale Journal of Criticism*, 2001, vol. 14(1), p. 43. In the same issue, see also Imre Kertész, 'Who Owns Auschwitz?', trans. John MacKay, *Yale Journal of Criticism*, 2001, vol. 14(1), pp. 267–72.
7 Dominick LaCapra, *Writing History, Writing Trauma*, Baltimore, MD: Johns Hopkins University Press, 2001; see also id., *Representing the Holocaust: History, Theory, Trauma*, Ithaca, NY: Cornell University Press, 1996; and id. *History and Memory after the Holocaust*, Ithaca, NY: Cornell University Press, 1994.
8 For a discussion on Heidegger's understanding of the concept of limit, see Geoff Malpas, *Heidegger's Topography: Being, Place*, World, Boston, MA: MIT Press, 2006, pp. 75–86.
9 Mary-Jane Rubenstein, 'Heidegger's Caves: On Dwelling in Wonder', in *Practices of Wonder: Cross-Disciplinary Perspectives*, Eugene, OR: Pickwick, 2012, p. 148. See also id., *Strange Wonder: The Closure of Metaphysics and the Opening of Awe*, New York: Columbia University Press, 2009.
10 Katherine Withy, *Heidegger on Being Uncanny*, Cambridge, MA: Harvard University Press, 2015.
11 As support for this argument, Arendt quotes from 'Plato's Doctrine of Truth'. This can be found in *Pathmarks*, trans T. Sheehan, ed. W. McNeill, Cambridge: Cambridge University Press, pp. 155–86. See also Mary-Jane Rubenstein's argument that Heidegger's theaetetus shows a preoccupation with concealment in and dwelling in Plato's cave at the time at which the National Socialists took power in Germany.
12 Plato, *Theaetetus*, trans. H.N. Fowler, London: Heinemann, 1921, p. 174a.
13 Ingo Farin, 'The Black Notebooks in their Historical and Political Context', in *Reading Heidegger's Black Notebooks 1931–1941*, eds. I. Farin and G. Malpas, Cambridge, MA: MIT Press, 2016, p. 305.
14 For a summary of the debate, see Sharon Muller, 'The Origins of Eichmann in Jerusalem: Hannah Arendt's Interpretation of Jewish History,' *Jewish Social Studies*, 1981, vol. 43(3–4), pp. 237–54.
15 Kwame Anthony Appiah, *As If*, Cambridge, MA: Harvard University Press, 2017.
16 Siobhan Kattago, 'Why the World Matters: Hannah Arendt's Philosophy of New Beginnings', *The European Legacy*, 2013, vol. 18(2), pp. 170–84.

References

Arendt, Hannah, *Between Past and Future*, Harmondsworth: Penguin, 1954.
Arendt, Hannah, *The Origins of Totalitarianism*, New York: Harcourt, 1968.
Arendt, Hannah, 'Martin Heidegger at Eighty,' trans. A. Hofstadter, *The New York Review of Books*, October 21, 1971, pp. 50–53.
Arendt, Hannah, *The Human Condition*, 2nd edn, Chicago, IL: University of Chicago Press, 1998.
Arendt, Hannah, 'Thinking and Moral Considerations,' in *Responsibility and Judgment*, ed. J. Kohn, New York: Schoken, 2003, pp. 159–192.
Arendt, Hannah, 'Philosophy and Politics,' *Social Research*, 2004, vol. 71(3), pp. 427–454.
Arendt, Hannah, *The Promise of Politics*, ed. J. Kohn, New York: Schoken, 2005.
Arendt, Hannah, *Eichmann in Jerusalem: A Report on the Banality of Evil*, Harmondsworth, UK: Penguin, 2006.
Heidegger, Martin, *Basic Problems of Phenomenology*, trans. A. Hofstadter, Bloomington, IN: Indiana University Press, 1988.
Heidegger, Martin, *Basic Questions of Philosophy: Selected "Problems" of "Logic"*, trans R. Rojcewicz and A. Schuwer, Bloomington, IN: Indiana University Press, 1994.
Heidegger, Martin, *Being and Time*, trans J. Stambaugh, Albany, NY: State University of New York Press, 1996.

Heidegger, Martin, 'Hegel and the Greeks,' in *Pathmarks*, trans R. Metcalf, ed. W. McNeill, Cambridge: Cambridge University Press, 1998, pp. 323–336.

Heidegger, Martin, 'The Origin of the Work of Art', in *Poetry, Language, Thought*, New York: Harper, 2003, pp. 15–87.

Heidegger, Martin, *History of the Concept of Time: Prolegomena*, trans T. Kiesel, Bloomington, IN: Indiana University Press, 2009.

Heidegger, Martin, *Contributions to Philosophy (Of the Event)*, trans R. Rojcewicz and D. Vallega-Neu, Bloomington, IN: Indiana University Press, 2012.

Heidegger, Martin, *Introduction to Metaphysics*, 2nd edn, trans G. Fried and R. Polt, New Haven, CT: Yale University Press, 2014.

Heidegger, Martin, *Ponderings II–VI: Black Notebooks 1931–38*, trans R. Rojcewicz, Bloomington, IN: Indiana University Press, 2016.

CONCLUSION

I wonder as I wander: everyday historiography, everyday metaphysics?

You can sing a single line many different ways, as John Jacob Niles notes:

> A girl had stepped out to the edge of the little platform attached to the automobile. She began to sing. Her clothes were unbelievable dirty and ragged, and she, too, was unwashed. Her ash-blond hair hung down in long skeins …. But, best of all, she was beautiful, and in her untutored way, she could sing. She smiled as she sang, smiled rather sadly, and sang only a single line of a song.[1]

You can sing it in ways that brings people comfort, makes them sad, or which helps them to think of the divine. You can help people to make general sense of things despite the first impression that you are small, unwashed, ragged and untutored.

This book has wandered through what Foucault would probably have called a 'wild profusion' of existing histories and philosophies.[2] Some of the works featured will have made frequent appearances in histories of history or histories of metaphysics, and they might have been known to you. Others will have made their debut appearance in a historiography book, and you may think that this is long-overdue recognition. Some will have appeared, at first appearance, small, unwashed, ragged and untutored. And some will not have shaken that first impression. What right did I have to include them?

It is true that histories of history, and histories of metaphysics have until recently taken the form of 'great white men' compilations. On that count, I am not without guilt in having written *Fifty Key Thinkers on History*, where the number of women is only just beginning to go up after three editions. I have included more women in this book, and historians and philosophers from different times, and cultural and socioeconomic backgrounds. But I do not want you to mistake this for a work of history or metaphysics 'from below' or what might be called everyday historiography and everyday metaphysics. There are too many thinkers from elite backgrounds to sustain any such claim.

More importantly, however, the wandering path of this book has been an argument against the assumption that the boundaries of the idea of history and the idea of metaphysics are firmly inscribed, both against one another, and against other forms of intellectual enterprise. The authors of the first written histories that we know about engaged with, appropriated and adapted ideas from philosophy, and we also see evidence of engagement, appropriation and adaption in reverse. This set in train an entangled history in which the concept of wonder plays an important role. Similar stories might be told for literature, poetry, science and art.

It is also the case that the use of the word 'everyday' would suggest a distinction from history or metaphysics without an adjective, as if there is an amateur and a professional league, to put it bluntly. It is certainly true that some of the thinkers included in this book—and others that you will no doubt think of—do not appear to do a very good job of writing history or of making general sense of things. They advance contradictions, forget what they are arguing, include masses of details for little apparent reason and set up trails of thought quite like Heidegger's *Holzwege* or wood paths. As I noted in the introduction to this book, there is the Euclidean idea of a triangle, and there is the triangle that someone drew on the plastic seat of a moving bus. That is not the same as saying, however, that there is a firm boundary between the two. Historians and philosophers are often included in histories because we still find their ways of thinking about the world engaging, challenging and even provocative. They help us with our own attempts at sense making. They might not have been professional historians or philosophers as we understand them today.

Still others are included because they have been included in earlier histories, and we may hold an expectation that the history offered will not make sense without them. They help the story to hang together, as is the case with the citation of Leopold von Ranke to support the narrative that historiography took a professional and national turn in the nineteenth century. With a new analytical frame, though, it is still possible to see writers like von Ranke in renewed ways, and as part of wider intellectual movements.

Finally, others may be included to show that there were wider approaches to writing history and philosophy than are generally credited, and these approaches may reflect a creativity that we are only beginning to appreciate. They may also show us that some people produced works under very restrictive conditions: this book includes at least one work written in prison and works by authors who did not enjoy full access to information or to discussion by dint of their social status. It is important to note, too, that some of these writers enjoyed popular success far beyond that of their better-known peers. Their works are important because they remind us that histories and philosophies are not just produced, they are also received. Daniel Defoe's attempt to make general sense of the realms of God, the living and spirits may have been more influential than Immanuel Kant's universal history in their day. Recovering that reception history is no easy matter, as chapter seven has reminded us, but it is a powerful reminder that history and philosophy have never been detached exercises.

As you can see from the above discussion, it is possible to draw the boundaries around activities in many ways. If this history of wonder in history and philosophy has taught us anything, it is that boundaries are there to be transgressed. They mark the limit of our thinking, and as Aristotle taught us, a limit can be both an end and a beginning. You cross boundaries to go from old ways of thinking to new ways of thinking. And when you do cross boundaries, you reinscribe your attempts to make general sense of the world along the way. History and metaphysics are not conservative and purely descriptive enterprises. If you know that boundaries are subject to change over time, then you can think about whether they might be revised or even removed to create better ways of thinking about the past, and thinking and acting in the present, and the future. History and metaphysics can therefore be generative and ethical. Wonder, as I said at the start of this book, marks the beginning of historiography.

Notes

1 Ron Pen, *I Wonder as I Wander: The Life of John Jacob Niles*, Lexington, KY: University Press of Kentucky, 2010, p.150.
2 M. Foucault, *The Order of Things*, London: Vintage, 1994, p. xv.

BIBLIOGRAPHY

Abelard of Bath, *Adelard of Bath, Conversations with His Nephew: On the Same and the Different, Questions on Natural Science and On Birds*, trans. and ed. C. Burnett, Cambridge: Cambridge University Press, 1999.
Abhinavagupta, *Īśvarapratyabhijñāvimarśinī: Doctrine of Divine Recognition, 3 vols*, eds. K.A. Subramania and K.C. Iyer and K.C. Pandey. Delhi: Motilal Banarsidass, 1986.
Abhinavagupta, *Parātrīśikā Vivaraṇa: The Secret of Tantric Mysticism*, trans. J. Singh, Delhi: Motilal Banarsidass, 2005.
Abhinavagupta, *Naṭyaśāstra of Bharatamuni: Text, Commentary of Abhinavabharati by Abhinavaguptacarya and English Translation, 3 vols*, trans. M.M. Ghosh, ed. P. Kumar, Delhi: New Bharatiya, 2006.
Abhinavagupta, *Sri Tantrāloka and other works, 9 vols*, trans. S.P. Singh and S. Maheshvarananda, New Delhi: Standard Books, 2015.
Abhinavagupta, *Tantrasāra*, trans. G. Chatterjee, Varasani, India: Indica Books, 2015.
Adorno, Theodor, *'Commitment,' in Can One Live after Auschwitz? A Philosophical Reader*, trans R. Livingstone, ed. R. Tiedemann, Stanford, CA: Stanford University Press, 2003, pp. 240–258.
Ahmad, Zaid, *The Epistemology of Ibn Khaldun*, London: Routledge, 2002.
Al Qazwini, *Die Wünder des Himmels und der Erde*, trans. A. Giese, Berlin: Goldmann, 1986.
Al Tabari, *The History of Al Tabari, 39 vols*, various translators, New York, State University of New York Press, 1989–1998.
Ames, Roger T., *The Art of Rulership*, Honolulu: University of Hawaii Press, 1983.
Appelby, Joyce, Hunt, Lynn, and Jacob, Margaret, *Telling the Truth about History*, New York: W.W. Norton, 1994.
Appiah, Kwame Anthony, *As If*, Cambridge, MA: Harvard University Press, 2017.
Aquinas, Thomas, *Summa Theologica, prima secundae*, Ottawa, Canada: University of Ottawa Press, 1944.
Aquinas, Thomas, *Summa Contra Gentiles*, trans. V.J. Bourke, Notre Dame, IN: University of Notre Dame Press, 1975.
Arendt, Hannah, *Between Past and Future*, Harmondsworth: Penguin, 1954.

Arendt, Hannah, *The Human Condition*, 2nd edn, Chicago, IL: University of Chicago Press, 1998.
Arendt, Hannah, *The Origins of Totalitarianism*, New York: Harcourt, 1968.
Arendt, Hannah, 'Martin Heidegger at Eighty', trans. A. Hofstadter, *The New York Review of Books*, October 21, 1971, pp. 50–53.
Arendt, Hannah, 'Thinking and Moral Considerations,' in *Responsibility and Judgment*, ed. J. Kohn, New York: Schoken, 2003, pp. 159–192.
Arendt, Hannah, 'Philosophy and Politics,' *Social Research*, 2004, vol. 71(3), pp. 427–454.
Arendt, Hannah, *The Promise of Politics*, ed. J. Kohn, New York: Schoken, 2005.
Arendt, Hannah, *Eichmann in Jerusalem: A Report on the Banality of Evil*, Harmondsworth: Penguin, 2006.
Aristotle, *Categories*, in *The Complete Works of Aristotle* trans J.L. Ackrill and ed. J. Barnes, Princeton, NJ: Princeton University Press, vol. 1, pp. 3–24.
Aristotle, *De Anima*, trans C. Shields, Oxford: Oxford University Press, 2016.
Aristotle, *De Sensu and De Memoria*, trans G.R.T. Ross, Cambridge: Cambridge University Press, 1906.
Aristotle, *Generation of Animals*, in *The Complete Works of Aristotle*, vol. 1, ed. J. Barnes, Oxford: Oxford University Press, 1984.
Aristotle, *Metaphysics*, trans H. Tredennick, London: Heinemann, 1933.
Aristotle, Nicomachean Ethics, in *The Complete Works of Aristotle, vol.* 2, trans J.L. Ackrill and ed. J. Barnes, Princeton, NJ: Princeton University Press, pp. 1729–1867.
Aristotle, On Marvellous Things Heard, in *The Complete Works of Aristotle*, ed. J. Barnes, Princeton, NJ: Princeton University Press, 1984.
Aristotle, *Poetics*, trans M. Heath, Harmondsworth: Penguin, 1996.
Aristotle, *Posterior Analytics*, trans. J. Barnes, Oxford: Oxford University Press, 1975.
Aristotle, Rhetoric, in *The Complete Works of Aristotle*, vol. 2, trans. J.L. Ackrill and ed. J. Barnes, Princeton, NJ: Princeton University Press, pp. 2152–2269.
Ashton, Geoff, and Tanner, Sonja, 'From Puzzling Pleasures to Moral Practices: Aristotle and Abhinavagupta on the Aesthetics and Ethics of Tragedy', *Philosophy East and West*, 2016, vol. 66(1), pp. 13–39.
Augustine of Hippo, Two Books on Genesis against the Manichees, in *Saint Augustine on Genesis*, trans. R.J. Teske, Washington, D.C.: Catholic University of America Press, 1991.
Augustine of Hippo, *City of God Against the Pagans*, trans. R.W. Dyson, Cambridge: Cambridge University Press, 1998.
Augustine of Hippo, *Confessions*, trans. H. Chadwick, Oxford: Oxford University Press, 2009.
Bacon, Francis, *The Oxford Francis Bacon, 15 vols*, Oxford: Oxford University Press, 1996.
Bacon, Roger, *Concerning the Marvelous Power of Art and of Nature and Concerning the Nullity of Magic*, London: Williams and Norgate, 1923.
Barthes, Roland, *Camera Lucida*, New York: Hill and Wang, 1980.
Barthes, Roland, *Mourning Diary*, trans. R. Howard, New York: Hill and Wang, 2012.
Baudrillard, Jean, *Simulacra and Simulations*, ed. M. Poster, Stanford: Stanford University Press, 1988.
Bayly, C. A., 'Modern Indian Historiography', in *Companion to Historiography*, ed. M. Bentley, London: Routledge, 1997, pp. 677–691.
Beard, Charles A., 'That Noble Dream', *The American Historical Review*, 1935, vol. 41(1), pp. 74–87.
Bede, *Ecclesiastical History of the English People*, trans. L. Sherley-Price and R.E. Latham, Harmondsworth: Penguin, 1990.

194 Bibliography

Benjamin, Walter, *Illuminations: Essays and Reflections*, ed. H. Arendt, New York: Harcourt, Brace and World, 1968.
Benjamin, Walter, 'A Short History of Photography' [1931], *Screen*, 1972, vol. 13(1), pp. 5–26.
Bentley, Michael, *Modern Historiography: An Introduction*, London: Routledge, 1999.
Berg, Maxine, 'In Pursuit of Luxury: Global History and British Consumer Goods in the Eighteenth Century', *Past and Present*, 2004, vol. 182(1), pp. 85–142.
Berg, Maxine, and Eger, Elizabeth, (eds.), *Luxury in the Eighteenth Century*, Basingstoke: Palgrave Macmillan, 2003.
Berlekamp, Persis, *Wonder, Image, and Cosmos in Medieval Islam*, New Haven, CT: Yale University Press, 2011.
Bester, James, *Lyric Wonder: Rhetoric and Wit in Renaissance English Poetry*, Ithaca, NY: Cornell University Press, 1977.
Bertolacci, Amos, 'The Arabic Translations of Aristotle's Metaphysics', *Arabic Sciences and Philosophy*, 2005, vol. 15(2), pp. 241–275.
Bhabha, Homi, *The Location of Culture*, London: Routledge, 1994.
Bodin, *Method for the Easy Comprehension of History*, trans. B. Reynolds, London: Macmillan, 1989.
Borrego Sargent, Amelia Lynn, 'Gerald of Wales' Topographical Hibernica: Dates, Versions, Readers', *Viator*, 2012, vol. 43(1), pp. 241–262.
Braudel, Fernand, *The Mediterranean and the Mediterranean World in the Age of Philip II*, vol. 1, trans. S. Reynolds, Glasgow: William Collins, 1972.
Breisach, Ernst, *Historiography: Ancient, Medieval, and Modern*, 3rd edn, Chicago, IL: University of Chicago Press, 2007.
Broad, Charlie D., 'Critical and Speculative Philosophy', in *Contemporary British Philosophy: Personal Statements (First Series)*, ed. J.H. Muirhead, London: G. Allen and Unwin, 1924, pp. 77–100.
Burke, Victoria E., 'Recent Studies in Commonplace Books', *English Literary Renaissance*, 2013, vol. 43(1), pp. 153–177.
Campany, Robert F., *Strange Writing: Anomaly Accounts in Early Medieval China*, New York: State University of New York Press, 1996.
Carnap, Rudolf, 'Überwindung der Metaphysik durch Logische Analyse der Sprache,' ['The Elimination of Metaphysics through Logical Analysis of Language'], *Erkenntnis*, 1932, pp. 60–81.
Bynum, Caroline W., *Metamorphosis and Identity*, New York: Zone Books, 2001.
Carr, Brian, *Metaphysics: An Introduction*, Atlantic Highlands, NJ: Humanities Press, 1987.
Carroll, David, 'Foreword: The Memory of Devastation and the Responsibilities of Thought: "And Let's Not Talk about That" ,' in J.-F. Lyotard, *Heidegger and "the Jews"*, trans. A. Michel, Minneapolis, MN: University of Minnesota Press, 1990, pp. i–xxix.
Chakrabarty, Dipesh, 'Subaltern Studies and Postmodern Historiography', *Nepantla: Views from the South*, 2000, vol. 1(1), pp. 9–32.
Chaniotis, A., 'Travelling Memories in the Hellenistic World', in R. Hunter and I. Rutherford (eds.), *Wandering Poets in Ancient Greek Culture*, Cambridge: Cambridge University Press, 2011, pp. 249–269.
Chappell, T. J. D., *Reading Plato's Theaetetus*, Sankt Augustin, Germany: Academia Verlag, 2004, p. 172.
Chatterjee, Partha, *Lineages of Political Society: Studies in Postcolonial Democracy*, New Delhi, India: Permanent Black, 2011.
Chaudhuri, Rosinka, 'The Flute, Gerontion, and Subalternist Misreadings of Tagore', *Social Text*, 2004, vol. 22(1), pp. 103–122.

Chen, Jack W., 'Blank Spaces and Secret Histories: Questions of Historiographic Epistemology in Medieval China', *Journal of Asian Studies*, 2010, vol. 69(4), pp. 1071–1091.
Cheng, Eileen Ka-May, *Historiography: An Introductory Guide*, London: Bloomsbury, 2012.
Chisholm, Roderick, *On Metaphysics*, Minneapolis, MN: University of Minnesota Press, 1989.
Cixous, Hélène, 'My Algeriance, in Other Words: to Depart not to Arrive from Algeria', in *Stigmata: Escaping Texts*, trans. E. Prenowitz, London: Routledge, 1998. pp. 153–172.
Cixous, Hélène, *Portrait of Jacques Derrida as a Young Jewish Saint*, trans. B. Bie Brahic, New York, NY: Columbia University Press, 2004.
Cixous, Hélène, *Reveries of the Wild Woman: Primal Scenes*, trans. B. Bie Brahic, Evanston, IL: Northwestern University Press, 2006.
Cixous, Hélène, *So Close*, trans. P. Kamuf, Cambridge: Polity, 2009.
Clarke, K., *Making Time for the Past: Local History and the Polis*, Oxford: Oxford University Press, 2008.
Classen, Constance, *The Deepest Sense: A Cultural History of Touch*, Chicago, IL: University of Chicago Press, 2012.
Cline, Erin M., 'Religious Thought and Practice', in *Analects*', *Dao Companion to the Analects*, ed. A. Olberding, New York: Springer, 2014, pp. 259–292.
Collingwood, Robin G., *Speculum Mentis, or, The Map of Knowledge*, Oxford: Oxford University Press, 1924.
Confucius, *Analects*, trans. R. Dawson, Oxford: Oxford University Press, 2008.
Corbin, Alain, *The Foul and the Fragrant: Odor and the French Social Imagination*, Cambridge, MA: Harvard University Press, 1986.
Crary, Jonathan, *Techniques of the Observer: On Vision and Modernity in the Nineteenth Century*, Cambridge, MA: MIT Press, 1990.
Crary, Jonathan, *Suspensions of Perception: Attention, Spectacle, and Modern Culture*, Cambridge, MA: MIT Press, 1999.
Cressy, David, *Travesties and Transgressions in Tudor and Stuart England: Tales of Discord and Dissension*, Oxford: Oxford University Press, 1999.
Crowley, John E., *The Invention of Comfort: Sensibilities and Design in Early Modern Britain and Early America*, Baltimore, NJ: Johns Hopkins University Press, 2001.
Curthoys, Ann, and Docker, John, *Is History Fiction?*, 2nd edn, Ann Arbor, MI: University of Michigan Press, 2015.
Daiber, Hans, *Islamic Thought in the Dialogue of Cultures*, Leiden, Germany: Brill, 2012.
Darnton, Roger, *The Great Cat Massacre: And other Episodes in French Cultural History*, London: Vintage, 1985.
Daston, Lorraine, and Park, Katharine, *Wonders and the Order of Nature 1150–1750*, New York: Zone Books, 2001.
Davies, Martin L., *The Prison-House of History: Investigations into Historicized Life*, London: Routledge, 2009.
De Beauvoir, Simone, *The Ethics of Ambiguity*, trans. B. Frechtman, New York: Open Road, [1948] 2015.
De Groot, Jerome, *The Historical Novel*, London: Routledge, 2009.
De Groot, Jerome, *Remaking Histories: The Past in Contemporary Historical Fictions*, London: Routledge, 2015.
Deckard, Michael F., 'A Sudden Surprise of the Soul: The Passion of Wonder in Hobbes and Descartes', *The Heythrop Journal*, 2008, vol. 49, pp. 948–963.
Defoe, D., *Essay on the History and Reality of Apparitions. Being an account of what they are and what they are not*, London: J. Roberts, 1727.

Defoe, D., *The Secrets of the Invisible World Disclosed: or, an Universal History of Apparitions Sacred and Profane, Under all Denominations; whether Angelical, Diabolical, or Human Souls Departed*, London: J. Clarke, 1729.
Derrida, Jacques, *Of Grammatology*, trans. G.C. Spivak, Baltimore, MD: Johns Hopkins University Press, 1976.
Derrida, Jacques, 'Violence and metaphysics: An essay on the thought of Emmanuel Levinas', in *Writing and Difference*, trans. and ed. A. Bass, London: Routledge and Kegan Paul, 1978, pp. 79–153.
Derrida, Jacques, *Positions*, trans A. Bass, Chicago, IL: University of Chicago Press, 1981.
Derrida, Jacques, *Memoires for Paul de Man*, re5th edn, trans. C. Lindsay, J. Culler, E. Cadava, and P. Kamuf, New York: Columbia University Press, 1989.
Descartes, René, *The Passions of the Soul* [1649], trans. S.H. Voss, Indianapolis, IN: Hackett, 1989.
Derrida, Jacques, *Points... Interviews, 1974–1994*, Stanford, CA: Stanford University Press, 1995.
Derrida, Jacques, 'Remarks on Deconstruction and Pragmatism', in C. Mouffe, ed., *Deconstruction and Pragmatism*, New York: Routledge, 1996.
Derrida, Jacques, *Adieu*, trans. P.-A. Brault and M. Naas, Stanford, CA: Stanford University Press, 1999.
Derrida, Jacques, *Of Hospitality: Anne Dufourmantelle Invites Jacques Derrida to Respond*, trans R. Bowlby, Stanford, CA: Stanford University Press, 2000.
Derrida, Jacques, *On Cosmopolitanism and Forgiveness*, trans M. Dooley and M. Hughes, London: Routledge, 2001.
Derrida, Jacques, 'Hostipitality', in *Acts of Religion*, trans. G. Anidjar, New York: Routledge, 2002, pp. 356–420.
Derrida, Jacques, *Rogues: Two Essays on Reason*, Stanford, CA: Stanford University Press, 2005.
Derrida, Jacques, *Specters of Marx: The State of the Debt, the Work of Wourning and the New International*, trans. P. Kamuf, London: Routledge, 2006.
Descartes, René, *Meditations on First Philosophy*, trans. J. Cottingham, Cambridge: Cambridge University Press, 2016.
Dirlik, Arif, 'The Aura of Postcolonialism: Third World Criticism in the Age of Global Capitalism', *Critical Inquiry*, 1994, vol. 20(2), pp. 328–356.
Doane, Mary Anne, *The Emergence of Cinematic Time: Modernity, Contingency, the Archive*, Cambridge, MA: Harvard University Press, 2002.
Drinka, George F., *The Birth of Neurosis: Myth, Malady and the Victorians*, New York: Simon and Schuster, 1984.
Duan Chengshi, *Chinese Chronicles of the Strange*, trans. C.E. Reed, New York: Peter Lang, 2001.
Dummett, Michael, *Frege, Philosophy of Language*, 2nd edn, Cambridge, MA: Harvard University Press, 1981.
Dunstall, Andrew, *Adventure, Schema, Supplement: Jacques Derrida and the Philosophy of History*, unpublished PhD thesis, Macquarie University, Sydney, 2012.
Dunstall, Andrew, 'The Impossible Dream of History: "History" in Derrida's Of Grammatology', *Derrida Today*, 2015, vol. 8(2), pp. 193–214.
Dyczkowski, Mark S. G., *The Doctrine of Vibration: An Analysis of the Doctrines and Practices of Kashmir Shaivism*, Albany, NY: SUNY Press, 1987.
Eckstein, A. M., *Moral Vision in The Histories of Polybius*, Berkeley, CA: University of California Press, 1995.
Evans, Richard, *In Defence of History*, New York: W.W. Norton, 2000.

Farin, Ingo, 'The Black Notebooks in their Historical and Political Context', in *Reading Heidegger's Black Notebooks 1931–1941*, eds. I. Farin and G. Malpas, Cambridge, MA: MIT Press, 2016, pp. 289–321.

Fehling, D., *Herodotus and his 'Sources': Citation, Invention and Narrative Art*, Leeds: Leeds University, 2000.

Feser, Edward, 'Being, The Good, and the Guise of the Good', in *Neo-Aristotelian Perspectives in Metaphysics*, eds. D. D. Novotny and L. Novák, London: Routledge, 2014, pp. 84–103.

Finucane, Ronald C., *Contested Canonizations: The Last Medieval Saints, 1482–1523*, Washington, DC: Catholic University of America Press, 2011.

Foucault, Michel, *The Order of Things: An Archaeology of the Human Sciences*, trans. Anon, London: Routledge, 1970.

Francis, Sing-Chen L., *What Confucius Wouldn't Talk About: The Fantastic Mode of the Chinese Classical Tale*, unpublished PhD thesis, Stanford University, CA, 1997.

Freud, Sigmund, *Three Essays on the Theory of Sexuality*, London: A.A. Brill, 1920.

Freud, Sigmund, *Beyond the Pleasure Principle and Other Writings*, Harmondsworth: Penguin, 2003.

Friedlander, Saul (ed.), *Probing the Limits of Representation: Nazism and the "Final Solution"*, ed. S. Friedlander, Cambridge, MA: Harvard University Press, 1992.

Froese, Katrin, 'The Art of Becoming Human: Morality in Kant and Confucius', *Dao*, 2008, vol. 7, pp. 257–268.

Fukuyama, Francis, *The End of History and the Last Man*, London: Free Press, 1992.

Gabba, E., 'True History and False History in Classical Antiquity', *Journal of Roman Studies*, 1981, vol. 71, p. 50–62.

Gautier, Ana M. O., *Aurality: Listening and Knowledge in Nineteenth-Century Columbia*, Durham, NC: Duke University Press, 2014.

Gerald of Wales, *The History and Topography of Ireland*, trans. T. Forester and T. Wright, full text available online at: http://www.yorku.ca/inpar/topography_ireland.pdf <accessed 21 September 2014>.

Gervase of Tilbury, *Otia Imperialia*, trans. S.E. Banks and J.W. Binns, Oxford: Oxford University Press, 2002.

Ghosh, Ranjan, 'Rabindranath and Rabindranath Tagore: Home, World, History', *History and Theory*, 2015, vol. 54(4), pp. 125–148.

Giannini, A., (ed.), *Paradoxographorum Graecorum Reliquiae*, Milan: Istituto Editoriale Italiano, 1965.

Ginzburg, Carlo, *The Cheese and the Worms: the Cosmos of a Sixteenth-Century Miller*, trans. J. Tedeschi and A.C. Tedeschi, Baltimore, MD: Johns Hopkins University Press, 1980.

Ginzburg, Carlo, *The Night Battles: Witchcraft and Agrarian Cults in the Sixteenth and Seventeeenth Centuries*, trans. J. Tedeschi and A.C. Tedeschi, 2nd edn, Baltimore, MD: Johns Hopkins University Press, 2013.

Goodrich, M., *Miracles and Wonders: The Development of the Concept of Miracle 1150–1350*, Aldershot: Ashgate, 2007.

Grafton, Anthony, *What Was History? The Art of History in Early Modern Europe*, Cambridge: Cambridge University Press, 2007.

Green, Anna, and Troup, Kathleen, (eds.), *The Houses of History: A Critical Reader in Twentieth-Century History and Theory*, New York: New York University Press, 1999.

Greenblatt, Stephen J., *Marvellous Possessions: The Wonder of the New World*, Chicago, IL: University of Chicago Press, 1991.

Gregory, James D., 'Eccentric Lives: Character, Characters and Curiosities in Britain, c. 1760–1900', in *Histories of the Normal and Abnormal: Social and Cultural Histories of Norms and Normativity*, ed. W. Hurst, London: Routledge, 2006.

Gregory, James D., 'Eccentric Biography and the Victorians', *Biography*, 2007, vol. 30(3), pp. 342–376.

Grosz, Elizabeth, 'The Hetero and the Homo: The Sexual Ethics of Luce Irigaray', in *Engaging with Irigaray: Feminist Philosophy and Modern European Thought*, eds. C. Burke, N. Schor, and M. Whitford, New York: Columbia University Press, 1994, pp. 335–350.

Guha, Ranajit, *Elementary Aspects of Peasant Insurgency in Colonial India*, Durham, NC: Duke University Press, 1983.

Guha, Ranajit, *A Rule of Property for Bengal: An Essay on the Idea of Permanent Settlement* [1981], Durham, NC: Duke University Press, 1996.

Guha, Ranajit, *Dominance without Hegemony: History and Power in Colonial India*, Cambridge, MA: Harvard University Press, 1997.

Guha, Ranajit, *History at the Limit of World-History*, New York: Columbia University Press, 2002.

Gunning, Tom, 'The Cinema of Attraction: Early Film, Its Spectator and the Avant-Garde', *Wide Angle*, 1986, vol. 8(3–4), pp. 56–63.

Gunning, Tom, 'An Aesthetic of Astonishment: Early Film and the (In)Credulous Spectator', *Art and Text*, 1989, vol. 34, pp. 31–45.

Hale, S. J., *Women's Record, or Sketches of all Distinguished Women from "The Beginning" till AD 1850*, New York: Harper and Brothers, 1853.

Hall, David L., and Ames, Roger T., *Thinking Through Confucius*, New York: SUNY Press, 1987.

Hansen, W., (ed.), *Phlegon of Tralles: Book of Marvels*, trans. W. Hansen, Exeter: University of Exeter Press, 1996.

Harb, Lara, *Poetic Marvels: Wonder and Aesthetic Experience in Medieval Literary Theory*, unpublished PhD thesis, New York University, 2013.

Hardy, Grant, *Objectivity and Interpretation in the Shih Chi*, unpublished PhD thesis, Yale University, 1988.

Hartog, F., *The Mirror of Herodotus: The Representation of the Other in the Writing of History*, Berkeley, CA: University of California Press, 1988.

Hegel, G.W.F., *Lectures on the Philosophy of World History*, trans. H.B. Nisbet, Cambridge: Cambridge University Press, 1981.

Hegel, G.W.F., *The Philosophy of History*, trans J. Sibree, Mineola, NY: Dover, 1900.

Hegel, G.W.F., *Elements of the Philosophy of Right*, ed. A.W. Wood, trans. H. B. Nisbet, Cambridge: Cambridge University Press, 1991, p. 23.

Hegel, G.W.F., *Lectures on the History of Philosophy: Plato to the Platonists*, vol. 2, Lincoln, NE: University of Nebraska Press, 1995.

Hegel, G.W.F., *The Philosophy of Mind: Part Three of the Encyclopedia of the Philosophical Sciences* [1830], trans. W. Wallace, Oxford: Oxford University Press, 2007.

Heidegger, Martin, *Discourse on Thinking*, trans J.M. Anderson and E.H. Freund, New York: Harper, 1966.

Heidegger, Martin, *Basic Problems of Phenomenology*, trans. A. Hofstadter, Bloomington, IN: Indiana University Press, 1988.

Heidegger, Martin, *Basic Questions of Philosophy: Selected "Problems" of "Logic"*, trans. R. Rojcewicz and A. Schuwer, Bloomington, IN: Indiana University Press, 1994.

Heidegger, Martin, *Being and Time*, trans. J. Stambaugh, Albany, NY: State University of New York Press, 1996.

Heidegger, Martin, 'Hegel and the Greeks,' in *Pathmarks*, trans. R. Metcalf, ed. W. McNeill, Cambridge: Cambridge University Press, 1998, pp. 323–336.

Heidegger, 'The Origin of the Work of Art', in *Poetry, Language, Thought*, New York: Harper, 2003, pp. 15–87.

Heidegger, Martin, *History of the Concept of Time: Prolegomena*, trans. T. Kiesel, Bloomington, IN: Indiana University Press, 2009.
Heidegger, Martin, *Contributions to Philosophy (Of the Event)*, trans. R. Rojcewicz and D. Vallega-Neu, Bloomington, IN: Indiana University Press, 2012.
Heidegger, Martin, *Introduction to Metaphysics*, trans. G. Fried and R. Polt, 2nd edn, New Haven, CT: Yale University Press, 2014.
Heidegger, *Ponderings II–VI: Black Notebooks 1931–38*, trans. R. Rojcewicz, Bloomington, IN: Indiana University Press, 2016.
Hepburn, Ronald, *Wonder and Other Essays*, Edinburgh: Edinburgh University Press, 1984
Herodotus, *The Histories, 4 vols*, trans. A. D. Godley, London: Heinemann, 1926.
Hobbes, Thomas, *Leviathan* [1668], trans. and ed. E. Curley, Indianapolis, IN: Hackett, 1994.
Hobbes, Thomas, *Human Nature and De Corpore Politico*, trans. and ed. J.C.A. Gaskin Oxford: Oxford University Press, 1994.
Holcombe, Alex, Hochel, Matej, and Mílan, Emilio, 'Synaesthia: The Existing State of Affairs', *Cognitive Neuropsychology*, 2008, vol. 25(1), pp. 93–117.
Howes, David, *Ways of Sensing: Understanding the Senses in Society*, London: Routledge, 2014.
Howitt, W., *A Popular History of Priestcraft in all Ages and Nations*, London: John Chapman, 1845.
Howitt, W., *Labour, Land, and Gold, or Two Years in Victoria, 2 vols*, London: Longman, Brown, Green, Longmans, and Roberts, 1858.
Howitt, W., *The History of the Supernatural in all Ages and Nations, and in all Churches, Christian and Pagan: Demonstrating a UNIVERSAL FAITH*, London: Longman, Green, Longman, Roberts, and Green, 1863.
Hughes-Warrington, Marnie, *'How Good an Historian Shall I Be?': R. G. Collingwood, the Historical Imagination and Education*, Thorveton, UK: Imprint, 2003.
Hughes-Warrington, Marnie, *History Goes to the Movies: Studying History on Film*, London: Routledge, 2007.
Hulin, Michael, 'The Conception of Camatkara in Indian Aesthetics', in *Practices of Wonder: Cross-Disciplinary Perspectives*, Eugene, OR: Pickwick, 2013.
Hunt, Lynn, *Inventing Human Rights: A History*, New York: W.W. Norton, 2008.
Hunt, Lynn, *Measuring Time, Making History*, Budapest: Central European University Press, 2014.
Hunt, Lynn, *Writing History in the Global Age*, New York: W.W. Norton, 2014.
Hunt, Lynn, (ed.), *The Invention of Pornography: Obscenity and the Origins of Modernity, 1500–1800*, New York: Zone Books, 2016.
Huntington, Rania, *Alien Kind: Foxes and Late Imperial Chinese Literature*, Cambridge, MA: Harvard University Press for Harvard University Asia Center, 2003.
Huntington, Samuel P., *The Clash of Civilizations and the Remaking of World Order*, New York: Simon and Schuster, 1996.
Hunzinger, J., 'La notion de θαῦμα chez Herodoté', *Ktèma*, 1995, vol. 20, pp. 47–70.
Ibn Khaldun, *The Muqaddimah, 3 vols*, trans. F. Rosenthal, Princeton, NJ: Princeton University Press, 1958.
Ibn Rushd, *Averroes' Middle Commentary on Aristotle's Poetics*, trans. C. E. Butterworth, Princeton, NJ: Princeton University Press, 1986.
Ibn Sina, *The Metaphysics of Avicenna (Ibn Sina)*, trans. P. Morewedge, London: Routledge and Kegan Paul, 1973.
Ibn Sina, *Avicenna's Commentary on the Poetics of Aristotle*, trans. I.M. Dahiyat, Leiden: Brill, 1974.
Ibn Sina, *Remarks and Admonitions*, trans. S.C. Inati, Toronto: Pontifical Institute of Medieval Studies, 1984.

Iggers, Georg G., and Wang, Edward Q., *A Global History of Modern Historiography*, London: Routledge, 2012.

Irigaray, Luce, *An Ethics of Sexual Difference*, trans. C. Burke and G.C. Gill, Ithaca, NY: Cornell University Press, 1993.

Irving v Penguin Books Ltd and Anor [2001] England and Wales Court of Appeal ((Civil Division) Decision 1197, 20 July 2001), online at: http://www.bailii.org/ew/cases/EWCA/Civ/2001/1197.html <accessed 25 March 2018>.

Isidore of Seville, *Etymologies*, trans. S.A. Barney and W.J. Lewis, J.A. Beach, O. Berghof, Cambridge: Cambridge University Press, 2006.

Jardine, Lisa, *Worldly Goods: A New History of the Renaissance*, London: Macmillan, 1996.

Ji Yun, *Shadows In a Chinese Landscape: The Notes of a Confucian Scholar*, trans. and ed. D.L. Keenan, New York: M. E. Sharpe, 1999.

Jütte, Robert, *A History of the Senses: from Antiquity to Cyberspace*, trans. J. Lynn, London: Polity, 2004.

Kālidāsa, *Theatre of Memory: The Plays of Kālidāsa*, New York: Columbia University Press, 1984.

Kālidāsa, *The Loom of Time: A Selection of his Plays and Poems*, Harmondsworth: Penguin, 2007.

Kant, I., *Critique of Pure Reason*, trans. and ed. N. Kemp-Smith, London: Macmillan, 1958.

Kant, I., *Observations on the Feeling of the Beautiful and Sublime*, trans. J. Goldthwait, Berkeley, CA: University of California Press, 1960.

Kant, I., *Critique of the Power of Judgement*, trans. P. Guyer and E. Matthews, Cambridge: Cambridge University Press, 2000.

Kant, I., 'Idea for a Universal History with a Cosmopolitan Aim', in *Kant's Idea for a Universal History with a Cosmopolitan Aim: A Critical Guide*, eds. A.O. Rorty and J. Schmidt, Cambridge: Cambridge University Press, 2009, pp. 9–23.

Kant, I., *Religion within the Bounds of Bare Reason*, trans W.S. Pluhar, Indianapolis, IN: Hackett, 2009.

Kant, I., *Logic*, trans. W. Schwarz, Mineola, NY: Dover, 2014.

Kattago, Siobhan, 'Why the World Matters: Hannah Arendt's Philosophy of New Beginnings', *The European Legacy*, 2013, vol. 18(2), pp. 170–184.

Kertész, Imre, 'Who Owns Auschwitz?', trans. John MacKay, *Yale Journal of Criticism*, 2001, vol. 14(1), pp. 267–272.

Kirby, Lynne, 'Male Hysteria and Early Cinema', *Camera Obscura*, 1988, vol. 6(2), pp. 112–132.

Kirby, Lynne, *Parallel Tracks: The Railroad and Silent Cinema*, Durham, NC: Duke University Press, 1997.

Kleinberg, A., 'Proving Sanctity: Selection and Authentication of Saints in the Later Middle Ages', *Viator*, 1989, vol. 20, pp. 183–205.

Kleinberg, Ethan, *Haunting History: For a Deconstructive Approach to the Past*, Stanford, CA: Stanford University Press, 2017.

Kracauer, Siegfried, 'Photography', in *The Mass Ornament: Weimar Essays*, trans. and ed. Y. Levin, Cambridge, MA: Harvard University Press, 1995.

Krantz, Frederick (eds), *History from Below: Studies in Popular Protest and Popular Ideology in Honor of George Rudé*, Montreal, Canada: Concordia, 1985.

LaCapra, Dominick, *History and Memory after the Holocaust*, Ithaca, NY: Cornell University Press, 1994.

LaCapra, Dominick, *Representing the Holocaust: History, Theory, Trauma*, Ithaca, NY: Cornell University Press, 1996.

LaCapra, Dominick, *Writing History, Writing Trauma*, Baltimore, MD: Johns Hopkins University Press, 2001.
La Caze, Marguerite, *Wonder and Generosity: The Role in Ethics and Politics*, Albany, NY: SUNY Press, 2013.
Lal, Vinay, *The History of History: Politics and Scholarship in Modern India*, New Delhi: Oxford University Press, 2005.
Lang, Berel, *Holocaust Representation: Art within the Limits of History and Ethics*, 2nd edn, Baltimore, MD: Johns Hopkins University Press, 2003.
Le Goff, Jacques, *The Medieval Imagination*, Chicago, IL: University of Chicago Press, 1988.
Levi, Primo, *The Drowned and the Saved*, [1986] trans. R. Rosenthal, London: Abacus, 1989.
Levine, Joseph M., *The Autonomy of History: Truth and Method from Erasmus to Gibbon*, Chicago, IL: University of Chicago Press, 1999.
Lewis, Jayne E., 'Spectral Currencies in the Air of Reality: A Journal of the Plague Year and the History of Apparitions', *Representations*, 2004, 87, pp. 82–101.
Leyda, Jay, *Kino: A History of the Russian and Soviet Film*, London: Allen and Unwin, 1960.
Li, Wai-Yee, 'The Idea of Authority in the Shih Chi (Records of the Historian)', *Harvard Journal of Asiatic Studies*, 1994, vol. 54(2), p. 345–405
Lloyd, Genevieve, 'Derrida and the Philosophical History of Wonder', *Parrhesia*, 2015, pp. 64–82.
Loiperdinger, Martin and Elzer, Bernd, 'Lumiere's Arrival of the Train: Cinema's Founding Myth', *Moving Image*, 2004, vol. 4(1), pp. 89–118.
Loux, Michael J. and Crisp, Thomas M., *Metaphysics: A Contemporary Introduction*, 4th edn, London: Routledge, 2017.
Lucian, *Selected Dialogues*, ed. C.D.N. Costa, Oxford: Oxford University Press, 2009.
Lyons, Martyn, 'New Readers in the Nineteenth Century: Women, Children, Workers', in *A History of Reading in the West*, eds. G. Cavallo and R. Chartier, Cambridge: Cambridge University Press, 1999, pp. 313–344.
Malpas, Geoff, *Heidegger's Topography: Being, Place, World*, Boston, MA: MIT Press, 2006.
Manson, N., 'Epistemic Restraint and the Vice of Curiosity', *Philosophy*, 2012, vol. 87, pp. 239–259.
Manzo, Silvia, 'Francis Bacon's Nat Hist and Civil History: A Comparative Survey', *Early Science and Medicine*, 2012, vol. 17, p. 32–61.
Marr, A., 'Gentille curiosité: Wonder-working and the culture of automata in the late Renaissance', in *Curiosity and Wonder from the Renaissance to the Enlightenment*, eds. R.J.W. Evans and A. Marr, Aldershot: Ashgate, 2006, pp. 149–170.
Marx, Karl and Engels, Friedrich, *The Communist Manifesto*, Oxford: Oxford University Press, 2008.
McKeon, Michael, *The Origins of the English Novel, 1600–1740*, 2nd edn, Madison: Johns Hopkins University Press, 2002.
Moody, Theodore W., 'Irish History and Irish Mythology', *Hermathena*, 1978, pp. 6–24.
Moore, Adrian W. *The Evolution of Modern Metaphysics: Making Sense of Things*, Cambridge: Cambridge University Press, 2014.
Morgan, J. R., 'Fiction and History: Historiography and the Novel', in *A Companion to Greek and Roman Historiography*, Oxford: Blackwell, 2007, pp. 513–565.
Moss, Ann, *Printed Commonplace Books and the Structuring of Renaissance Thought*, Oxford: Oxford University Press, 1996.
Muller, Sharon, 'The Origins of Eichmann in Jerusalem: Hannah Arendt's Interpretation of Jewish History', *Jewish Social Studies*, 1981, vol. 43(3–4), pp. 237–254.
Muller-Ortega, Paul Eduardo, 'Luminous Consciousness: Light in the Tantric Mysticism of Abhinavigupta', in *The Presence of Light: Divine Radiance and Religious Experience*, ed. M. Kapstein, Chicago, IL: University of Illinois Press, 2002, pp. 45–79.

Ney, Alyssa, *Metaphysics: An Introduction*, London: Routledge, 2014.
Nicolai, R., 'The Place of History in the Ancient World', in *A Companion to Greek and Roman Historiography*, ed. J. Marincola, Oxford: Blackwell, 2009.
Nienhauser, William, 'A Note on a Textual Problem in the Shih chi and Some Speculations concerning the compilation of the Hereditary Houses', *T'uong Pao*, 2003, vol. 89(1–3), pp. 39–58.
Nolan, Daniel, 'Categories and Ontological Dependence', *Monist*, 2011, vol. 94(2), pp. 277–300.
Novick, Peter, *That Noble Dream: The "Objectivity Question" and the American Historical Profession*, Cambridge: Cambridge University Press, 1989.
Orosius, *Seven Books of History Against the Pagans*, trans. A.T. Fear, Liverpool, UK: Liverpool University Press, 2010.
Parsons, Howard, 'A Philosophy of Wonder', *Philosophy and Phenomenological Research*, 1969, vol. 30(1), pp. 84–101.
Phlegon of Tralles, *Book of Marvels*, trans. W. Hansen, Exeter: University of Exeter Press, 1996.
Plato, *Theaetetus*, trans. H.N. Fowler, London: Heinemann, 1921.
Plato, *Republic*, trans. P. Shorey, London: Heinemann, 1930.
Plato, *Parmenides*, trans M.L. Gill and P. Ryan, Indianapolis, IN: Hackett, 1996.
Plato, *Five Dialogues: Euthyphro, Apology, Crito, Meno, Phaedo*, trans. G.M.A. Grube, New York: Hackett, 2002.
Plato, *Meno and other Dialogues*, trans. R. Waterfield, Oxford: Oxford University Press, 2009.
Plato, *Phaedo*, trans. D. Gallop, Oxford: Oxford University Press, 2009.
Polybius, *The Histories, 2 vols*, trans. E.S. Shuckburgh, intro. F.W. Walbank, Bloomington, IN: Indiana University Press, 1962.
Popper, Nicholas, 'An Ocean of Lies: The Problem of Historical Evidence in the Sixteenth Century', *The Huntington Library Quarterly*, vol. 74(3), 2011, pp. 375–400.
Popper, Nicholas, *Walter Ralegh's History of the World and the Historical Culture of the Late Renaissance*, Chicago, IL: University of Chicago Press, 2012.
Priestley, J., *Herodotus and Hellenistic Culture: Literary Studies in the Reception of The Histories*, Oxford: Oxford University Press, 2014.
Pu Songling, *Strange Tales from a Chinese Studio*, trans. H.A. Giles, Rutland, VT: Tuttle, 2010.
Puett, Michael, *To Become a God: Cosmology, Sacrifice, and Self-Divinization in Early China*, Cambridge, MA: Harvard University Asia Center for the Harvard-Yenching Institute, 2000.
Radice, William, 'Tagore and Kalidāsā', *South Asia Research*, 1996, vol. 16(1), pp. 45–60.
Ralegh, Walter, *The Works*, Oxford: Oxford University Press, 1829, vols. 2–7.
Ramsaye, Terry, *A Million and One Nights*, New York: Simon and Schuster, 1926.
Robinson, A., *Narrating the Past: Historiography, Memory and the Contemporary Novel*, Basingstoke: Palgrave, 2011.
Robinson, Chase, *Islamic Historiography*, Cambridge: Cambridge University Press, 2002.
Rorty, Richard, *Philosophy and the Mirror of Nature*, Princeton, NJ: Princeton University Press, 1979.
Rorty, Richard, *Contingency, Irony, and Solidarity*, Cambridge: Cambridge University Press, 1989.
Rorty, Richard, *Essays on Heidegger and Others*, Cambridge: Cambridge University Press, 1991.
Rubenstein, Mary-Jane, *Strange Wonder: The Closure of Metaphysics and the Opening of Awe*, New York: Columbia University Press, 2009.

Rubenstein, Mary-Jane, 'Heidegger's Caves: On Dwelling in Wonder', in *Practices of Wonder: Cross-Disciplinary Perspectives*, Eugene, OR: Pickwick, 2012, pp. 144–165.

Rüth, A., 'Representing Wonder in Medieval Miracle Narratives', *Modern Language Notes*, 2011, no. 126, pp. 89–114.

Said, Edward W., *Orientalism*, New York: Vintage, 1979.

Sallis, John, 'The Place of Wonder', in *Double Truth*, New York: SUNY Press, 1995, pp. 191–210.

Sallis, John, 'Imagination, Metaphysics, Wonder', in *American Continental Philosophy: A Reader*, Bloomington, IN: Indiana University Press, 2000, pp. 15–43.

Sathaye, Adheesh, 'The Production of Unpleasurable Rasas in the Sanskrit Dramas of Ārya Kṣemīśvara', *Journal of the American Oriental Society*, 2010, vol. 130(3), pp. 361–384.

Schaeffer, D., 'Wisdom and Wonder in Metaphysics A: 1–2', *The Review of Metaphysics*, 1999, vol. 52(3), pp. 641–656.

Schepens, G., 'Polybius on Phylarchus' "Tragic" Historiography', in *The Shadow of Polybius: Intertextuality as a Research Tool in Greek Historiography*, eds. G. Schepens and J. Bollansée, Leuven, NL: Peeters, 2005, pp. 141–164.

Scott, Joan Wallach, *Gender and the Politics of History*, 2nd edn, New York: Columbia University Press, 1999.

Scott, Joan Wallach, *The Fantasy of Feminist History*, Raleigh, NC: Duke University Press, 2011.

Sima Qian, *Records of the Grand Historian*, rev. edn., 3 vols. trans. B. Watson, New York: Columbia University Press, 1993.

Sinha, Suvadip, 'Ghostly Predicament: Narrative, Spectrality and Historicality in Rabindranath Tagore's "The Hungry Stones"', *Interventions: International Journal of Postcolonial Studies*, 2015, vol. 17(5), pp. 728–743.

Solinus, *The Excellent and Pleasant Worke of Iulius Solinus Polyhistor contayning the noble actions of humaine creatures, the secretes and providence of nature, the description of countries, the manners of the people: with many mervailous things and strange antiquities, seruing for the benefit and recreations of all sorts of persons*, trans. A. Golding, London: I. Charlewoode for Thomas Hacket, 1587.

Soll, Jacob, 'Empirical History and the Transformation of Political Criticism in France from Bodin to Bayle', *Journal of the History of Ideas*, 2003, vol. 64(2), pp. 297–316.

Southgate, Beverley C., *History Meets Fiction*, London: Routledge, 2009.

Spalding, Roger, and Parker, Christopher, *Historiography: An Introduction*, Manchester: Manchester University Press, 2007.

Spiegel, Gabrielle, *The Past as Text: The Theory and Practice of Medieval Historiography*, Baltimore: Johns Hopkins University Press, 1999.

Spivak, Gayatri, *Critique of Postcolonial Reason: Toward a History of the Vanishing Present*, Cambridge, MA: Harvard University Press, 2011.

Spivak, Gayatri Chakravorty, 'Subaltern Studies: Deconstructing Historiography', in *Selected Subaltern Studies*, New York: Oxford University Press, 1988, pp. 3–32.

Spongberg, Mary, Caine, Barbara and Curthoys, Ann, (eds.), *Companion to Women's Historical Writing*, Basingstoke: Palgrave Macmillan, 2005.

Tagore, Rabindranath, *Selected Poems*, trans W. Radice, Harmondsworth: Penguin, 1985.

Tagore, Rabindranath, 'Historicality in Literature', trans. R. Guha, in *History at the Limit of World-History*, New York: Columbia University Press, 2002, pp. 96–99.

Tagore, Rabindranath, *The Tagore Omnibus*, 4 vols, New Delhi, India: Rupa, 2003–2005.

Templeton, Kirk, *Suhrawardī, Abhinavagutpa, and the Metaphysics of Light*, unpublished PhD thesis, California Institute of Integral Studies, 2013.

Thapar, Romila, *A History of India*, vol. 1, Harmondsworth: Penguin, 1966.

Thapar, Romila, *History and Beyond*, Oxford: Oxford University Press, 2000.
Thapar, Romila, *Śakuntalā: Texts, Readings, Histories*, London: Anthem, 2002.
Thapar, Romila, *Cultural Pasts: Essays in Early Indian History*, Oxford: Oxford University Press, 2003.
Thapar, Romila, *Early India: From Origins to AD 1300*, Harmondsworth: Penguin, 2003.
Thapar, Romila, *Somanatha: The Many Voices of History*, London: Verso, 2005.
Thapar, Romila, 'The Lion: From Pride to Metaphor', in Valmik Thapar, Romila Thapar and Yusuf Ansari, *Exotic Aliens: The Lion and the Cheetah in India*, New Delhi, India: Aleph, 2013.
Thapar, Romila, *The Past before Us: Historical Traditions of Early North India*, Cambridge, MA: Harvard University Press, 2013.
Thapar, Romila, *The Past as Present: Forging Contemporary Identities Through History*, London: Aleph, 2014.
Thomasson, Annie, *Fiction and Metaphysics*, Cambridge: Cambridge University Press, 1999.
Thompson, Edward P., 'History from Below', *Times Literary Supplement*, 7 April 1966, pp. 279–280.
Thornton, J., 'Polybius in Context: The Political Dimension of The Histories', in B. Gibson and T. Harrison (eds.), *Polybius and his World*, Oxford: Oxford University Press, 2013, pp. 213–230.
Thucydides, *History of the Peloponnesian War, 4 vols*, trans. C.F. Smith, London: Heinemann, 1969.
Tresize, Thomas, 'Unspeakable,' *Yale Journal of Criticism*, 2001, vol. 14(1), pp. 38–63.
Van Inwagen, Peter, *Metaphysics*, 4th edn, London: Routledge, 2014.
Von Christ, W., *Geschichte der griechischen Litteratur*, Munich: W. Schmid and O. Stählin, 1920–1924.
Von Ranke, L. *Universal History: The Oldest Historical Group of Nations and the Greeks*, New York: Charles Scribner's and Sons, 1884.
Von Ranke, L. *The Theory and Practice of History*, trans. and ed. G.G. Iggers and W.A. Iggers, London: Routledge, 2011.
Walsh, William H., *An Introduction to Philosophy of History*, London: Hutchinson, 1951.
Wanley, Nathaniel, *The Wonders of the Little World, or A General History of Man, 2 vols*, London: W. J. and J. Richardson et al., 1678.
White, Hayden, 'Historiography and Historiophoty', *American Historical Review*, 1988, vol. 93(5), pp. 1193–1199.
Wiesner-Hanks, Merry, *Gender, Church and State in Early Modern Germany*, London: Routledge, 1997.
Wiesner-Hanks, Merry, *The Marvellous Hairy Girls: The Gonzales Sisters and their Worlds*, New Haven, CT: Yale University Press, 2009.
Wiesner-Hanks, Merry, *Christianity and Sexuality in the Modern World*, 2nd edn, London: Routledge, 2010.
Wiesner-Hanks, Merry, *Gender in History*, 2nd edn, Oxford: Blackwell, 2010.
Wiesner-Hanks, Merry, *Early Modern Europe, 1450–1789*, 2nd edn, Cambridge: Cambridge University Press, 2013.
Wiesner-Hanks, Merry (ed.), *Mapping Gendered Routes and Spaces in the Early Modern World*, London: Routledge, 2015.
Wiesner-Hanks, Merry, 'Preface', in *The Cambridge World History*, vol. 1, ed. D. Christian, Cambridge: Cambridge University Press, 2015, pp. xv–xx.
Wiesner-Hanks, Merry, 'Overlaps and Intersection in New Scholarship on Empires, Beliefs, and Emotions', *Cromohs: Cyber Review of Modern Historiography*, 2015–2016, vol. 20, pp. 1–24, online at: http://www.fupress.net/index.php/cromohs/article/view/20132/18764 <accessed 9 January 2017>.

Wiesner-Hanks, Merry, (ed.), *Gendered Temporalities in the Late Medieval and Early Modern World*, Amsterdam: University of Amsterdam Press, 2018.

Wiesner-Hanks, Merry and Willoughby, Urmi Engineer, *A Primer for Teaching Women, Gender and Sexuality in World History: Ten Design Principles*, Durham, NC: Duke University Press, 2018.

Withy, Katherine, *Heidegger on Being Uncanny*, Cambridge, MA: Harvard University Press, 2015.

Wittgenstein, Ludwig, *On Certainty*, eds. G.E.M. Anscombe and G.H. von Wright, Oxford: Blackwell, 1975.

Young, Iris M., *Intersecting Voices: Dilemmas of Gender, Political Philosophy, and Policy*, Princeton, NJ: Princeton University Press, 1997.

Yuan Mei, *Censored by Confucius: Ghost Stories*, trans. and ed. K. Louie and L. Edwards, New York: M. E. Sharpe, 1996.

Zadeh, Travis, 'The Wiles of Creation: Philosophy, Fiction and the 'Aja'ib Tradition', *Middle Eastern Literatures*, 2010, vol. 31(1), pp. 21–48.

Zeitlin, Judith, *Historian of the Strange: Pu Songling and the Chinese Classical Tale*, Stanford: Stanford University Press, 1993.

INDEX

Abelard of Bath (fl. 1116–42) 36
Abhinavagupta (950–1015 CE) xxi, 158, 167–71
Addiction: curiosity and 23, 75
Adorno, Theodor 178
Al Farabi, Abu Nasr (872–950 CE) 45
Al Qazwini, Abu Yahya Zakariya' ibn Muhammad (1203–83) 53–7
Al Tabari, Muhammad ibn Jarir (838–923 CE) xx, 44, 49–52
Al Tusi, Nasir al-Din (1201–74) 55–7
Ames, Roger 65, 68, 71
Antigonos of Karystos (fl. 240 BCE) 15
Appelby, Joyce 146
Appiah, Kwame 184
Aquinas, Thomas (1225–1275 CE) xix, 27–8, 34–5, 48, 140
Arendt, Hannah (1906–1975) xv, xxi, 178, 181–5
Aristotle (384–322 BCE) 2, 3, 34, 35, 47, 82, 92, 95, 113, 121, 122, 124, 135, 139, 143, 158, 161, 163, 167, 179, 180, 181, 186, 191; *Categories* 82–3; Heidegger's reading of xxii; immanence of universals 4; *Metaphysics* xii–xvii, xix, xxi, 8–10, 45, 102; *Nicomachean Ethics* 83; philosophy as starting with wonder xv; *Poetics* xix, 45–6, 57–60; *Rhetorics* 10
Astonishment 6
Attention 122, 132–3
Augustine of Hippo (354–430 CE) xix, 26, 27–8, 32–4, 90, 128; distinction between curiosity and wonder 32

Aura 130–4
Avicenna *see* Ibn Sina, Abu 'Ali al-Husayn

Bacon, Francis (1568–1621 CE) xx, 84–5, 89–92
Bacon, Roger (1214–94 CE) xix, 27–8, 35–7
Barthes, Roland (1915–1980) xxi, 122, 128
Bayly, Christopher 159
Bede (682–735 CE) xix, 27, 28–30, 38–9
Benjamin, Walter (1892–1940) xxi, 122, 128–32
Bentley, Michael xvii
Berlekamp, Persis 52–3
Bertolucci, Amos 45, 58
Bester, James 84
Bhabha, Homi 160
Biography, collective 110–113
Bodin, Jean (1529/30–1596 CE) xx, 81–2, 85–8
Braudel, Fernand (1902–95) 123, 136, 137
Breisach, Ernst xvii, 1–3, 101
Bynum, Caroline 23, 24

Camatkara see wonder
Campany, Robert 66, 72
Carroll, David 179
Categories xx, 82, 85, 86–7, 89, 113, 121, 143–4
Cheng, Eileen Ka-May xvii
Chengshi, Duan (ca. 800–63 CE) xx, 67, 75–6

Chinese historiography 63: harmony in 71; unofficial and official histories and xx, 71–2
Chinese philosophy 64–6; silence in 63
Chronology 87
Cixous, Hélène (1937–) xxi, 142, 153–5, 174
Classon, Constance 122
Cline, Erin 65
Collingwood, R. G. xv, 116–117, 136
Confucius (551–479 BCE) 64–7
Corbin, Alain 122
Crary, Jonathan (1951–) xxi, 122, 132–3, 136
Crowley, John E. 122
Curiosity 26–7, 93, 128, 180

Daston, Lorraine xvii, 24, 84, 88–9, 92, 101, 158
Davies, Martin xii
De Beauvoir, Simone 143
Defoe, Daniel (1684–1731 CE) xx, 103, 107–9, 190
Derrida, Jacques (1930–2004) xii, xv, xxi, 141–2, 148–53, 154, 161, 174
Descartes, René xvii, xx, 72, 83, 85, 95–8, 142, 146–9; Irigaray's reading of 146–7
Dirlik, Arif 160
Doane, Mary Ann (1952–) 122, 133–4

Early modern historiography 139–46
Early modern philosophy xx
Emotions 82–3
Empathy 140
Epistemology 85, 87–88, 89–94
Ethics: 139–55, 191; Confucian 72; self-responsibility and 8
Evans, Richard xiv

Farin, Ingo 182
Feser, Edward xviii
Film historiography xxi, 120–37
Finucane, Ronald 38
Fortune 4, 10, 26
Foucault, Michel 84, 92, 94, 143, 144, 189
Francis, Sing-Chen Lydia 66, 72, 73, 77
Freedom 115–117
Freud, Sigmund 126–7, 129, 133
Friedlander, Saul 179
Froese, Katrin 65

Gabba, Emilio 17
Gautier, Ana María Ochoa 122
Gay, Peter 85
Gender historiography xx, xxi

Gender metaphysics xxi, 110–113, 139–55
Gerard of Wales (1146–1223 CE) xix, 21, 24–7, 31, 33
Gervase of Tilbury (1150–1228 CE) xix, 30–1
Globalisation xvii, 83–4, 143
Gorky, Maxim 123
Green, Anna xvii
Greenblatt, Stephen 83
Gregory, James 84
Grosz, Elizabeth 147
Gu, Ban (32–92 CE) 71–2
Guha, Ranajit (1922–) xiii, xxi, 158–62, 166–7, 170, 172–5
Gunning, Tom (1949–) xxi, 120, 122, 124–7

Hadith 44, 47, 53
Hale, Sarah Josepha (1788–1879 CE) xx, 103, 110–113, 141
Hall, David 65
Hardy, Grant 63, 67
Hegel, G. W. F. (1770–1831) xv, xx, xxi, 100, 102, 109, 115–117, 172–3, 174, 180; Heidegger's appraisal of 103, 115–117
Heidegger, Martin (1889–1976) xii, xv, xvii, xxi, 102, 178–87; on Hegel 103, 115–117, 163, 190
Hellenistic historiography 1–6
Hepburn, Ronald xvi
Herodotus (484–425 BCE) xii, 3, 11–14, 141, 184; von Ranke on 104
Historians: knowledge claims of xix
Historicality xxi, 158, 159, 162–3, 167, 172, 174, 175
Historiophoty 120
history: as metaphysics 181; defining xiii; ethics and 139–55; film and 120–37; gender and 139–55; general sense making and xviii, 81; generative versus preserving 44; god in 110–113; history of xi–xiv, xvii, 1–3; imperialism and 85; paradoxology and 15–18; perception and 22, 24–6, 28; philosophy and xii–xiii, xviii, xx, xxii, 23, 104, 113–117; poetry and 1–3, 45–6, 49–52, 57–60; politics and xxi, 64, 144, 173–5; rigour in 69; subaltern xxi; time and 145–6; universals and xix
Hobbes, Thomas (1588–1679 CE) xx, 82, 83, 95–8
Hochel, Matej 122
Holcombe, Alex 122
Holocaust xxi–xxii, 63–4, 178–87

Horror 6, 58; horrors and 24
Hospitality 149–50
Howes, David 122
Howitt, William (1792–1879 CE) xx, 103, 107
Hunt, Lynn (1945–) xxi, 141, 145–6
Huntington, Rania 66, 72, 73, 77
Hysteria 125–8

Ibn Khaldun, 'Abd-ar-Rahman Abu Zayd Muhammad (1332–1406) 42, 46–8, 105
Ibn Rushd, Abu I-Walid Muhammad Ibn 'Ahmad (Averroes) (1126–1198) 45, 58–9
Ibn Sina, Abu 'Ali al-Husayn (Avicenna) (980–1037 CE) 45, 58
Iggers, Georg G. xvii, 100, 101, 159
Immanence xx, xxi, 4, 66–7, 69, 78, 79; as made possible by God 105–6; ethics as 72
Indian historiography xxi, 158–75
Indian philosophy xxi, 164, 167–75
Intuition 101–2
Irigaray, Luce (1930–)xvii, xxi, 141–2, 146–7
Irving, David xiv
Isadore of Seville (560–636 CE) 27–8
Islamic historiography xx, 43–6, 91; isnads in 44, 47, 49, 55–7

Jacob, Margaret 146
Jardine, Lisa 83
Jütte, Robert 122

Kālidāsa (fl. 5th century CE) xxi, 159, 165, 170, 171–2, 173
Kallimachos of Cyrene (c. 305–240 BCE) 15
Kant, Immanuel (1724–1804 CE) xx, 101, 113–115, 174
Kattago, Siobhan 185
Kirby, Lynne (1952–) xxi, 122, 125–7
Klein, Esther 62–3
Kleinberg, Aviad 23
Knowledge: beginnings of 9; boundary between knowable and unknowable xix, 2, 8; certain 19, 87; distrust of 7–8; of God 34; legitimate 10, 14, 22, 23; limits of 9, 25, 90–1; nature of in Plato's philosophy 7

LaCapra, Dominick 179
La Caze, Marguerite (1964–)xvii, xxi, 141–2, 147, 154
Lal, Vinay 159
Lang, Berel 179
Laziness 36, 46, 59, 69, 92

Levi, Primo 179
Lewis, Jayne 107
Lipstadt, Deborah xiv
Lloyd, Genevieve 150
Lucian of Samosata (120–192 CE) 17–18
Lumière films 120, 123–4, 133

Mandeville, John (1300–1371) 89, 92
Marvels 34
Marx, Karl 152, 174
McKeon, Michael 107
Medieval historiography 21–2, 39
Mei, Yuan (1716–97 CE) xx, 67
Méliès, Georges 126–8
Memory 88, 89–92
Metaphysics 2; categories and xiii; defining xii–xvii, descriptive xxi; epistemology and xix; ethics and xix, 139–55; generative or revisionary xvii, xxi, 60, 91–4, 139–55, 181, 191; historicisation of xxi, 106, 113–117, 181; Indian xxi; making general sense of things and xiv, 2; new science and 109; ordinary 189–91; progress and 100, 113–117; search for the first things and 34; transcendence and xiv; novelty and xiv; universals and xvi; use of as a rhetorical convention 11
Milan, Emilio 122
Miracles 27, 28–30, 31, 34; narratives of 23
Monsters 34, 139–40
Moore, Adrian W. xiii–xvii
Mukherjee, Supriya 159
Muller-Ortega, Paul 167

New science 89–92, 101–103; connection with metaphysics 109
Nienhauser, William 70
Niles, John Jacob 189
Non-sense 6, 9
Novick, Peter 100, 101

Orosius (385–420 CE) 27–8
Orthodoxy 8

Paradoxology: xiii, xix, 2, 15–18, 22, 26, 52–7, 65, 66, 74; ecclesiastical 23, 38–9; histories xx
Park, Katherine xvii, 24, 84, 88–9, 92, 101,
Parker, Christopher xvii
Parsons, Howard xvi
Particulars xx, 2, 113
Perception: boundaries of 2, 3, 6; consensus in 185; depth 130–4; discernment of particulars 104; discernment of universals via 3, 5, 24; hierarchy of 5, 46–8, 47, 54,

74; history of xx, xxi, 120–37; sense making and 22, 89–92; spiritual 109
Phenomena: liminal 16
Phlegon of Tralles (fl. 2nd century CE) 15–17
Photography 129–34
Plato (c. 427–347 BCE) xvi, xix, 2, 4, 47, 82, 167, 180, 181, 183–4, 186; allegory of the cave 5; *Cratylus*, 7; reception in the Islamic world 45; Theaetetus 6–8
Political and social order 91–2, 96–8, 144, 173–5, 182–5
Polybius (200–118 BCE) xiii, xv, xix, 1–6, 86–7, 113; perception in history making 5–6, 71–2; limits of historical knowledge 6; reading of Plato 5; relationship with Aristotle's thought 8–10; universal history by 3–5
Popper, Nicholas 85, 92
Priestley, Jessica 12
Pu, Guo (276–324 CE) 73
Puett, Michael 65
Punctum 130–4
Purānic texts 160, 165

Qian, Sima (145–86 BCE)xviii, xx, 62–4, 67–71, 75, 78–9

Ralegh, Walter (ca. 1552–1618 CE) xx, 85, 89, 92–4
Rasa (aesthetics) 169–71
Rationality 35, 36, 113–115, 127
Robinson, Chase 43
Rorty, Richard (1931–2007) 134–7
Rubenstein, Mary-Jane 181
Rüth, Axel 23, 38

Said, Edward 160
Sallis, John xvii, 102, 116
Scepticism 13
Scientific thought 37
Scott, Joan Wallach (1941–) xxi, 141, 143–45, 148
Shi, Su (1037–1101) 75
Shock 129–32
Silence 63–70
Social mores 16
Socrates xvi
Solinus, Gaius Julius (fl. 3rd century CE) 27–8
Soll, Jacob 85–6
Songling, Pu (1640–1715) xx, 67, 73, 74, 78
Southgate, Beverley 88
Spalding, Roger xvii
Spencer, John (1630–93) 101

Spiegel, Gabrielle 21–2
Spivak, Gayatri 160, 174
Spirit 115–117
Subaltern studies xxi, 159–160, 174–5
Sublime 114
Supernatural: ghosts and revenants 107, 151–2; relationship with the natural 2
Surprise 42

Tagore, Rabindranath (1861–1941) xiii, xxi, 159, 162–4, 170, 173
Tan, Sima (165–110 BCE) 68, 71
Templeton, Kirk 167
Thapar, Romila (1931–) xxi, 159, 164–6, 167, 172–5
Thaumazein, see wonder
Theaetetus xvi
Thucydides (460–395 BCE) 14–15; von Ranke on 104–5
Time 145–6
topoi xiii, xix, 12, 16–18, 22, 38–9, 59, 91
Tosh, John 100
transcendence 2, 26, 66
Tresize, Thomas 179
Troup, Kathleen xvii

Uncanny 142, 150, 181
Unheimlichkeit (un homing) xxi, 142, 150–2, 153
Universal histories xx, 3, 100–117
Universals xvi, xx, 2, 4–5, 32, 47, 52, 55, 58, 69, 85, 92–4, 113–117; God and 26, 39; history as the study of 3, 85; immanence of xix, 4, 24

Varma, Ravi 165
Von Ranke, Leopold (1795–1886 CE)xviii, xx, 99–106, 190

Wajnrub, Ruth 63
Wang, Edward Q. xvii, 159
Wanley, Nathaniel (1638–80 CE) xx, 85, 89, 93–95
Watson, Burton 70
White, Hayden 120–1
Wiesner-Hanks, Merry (1952–) xxi, 139–44
Will 33–4
Williams, Monier 173
Withy, Katherine 151
Wittgenstein, Ludwig 136
Wonder 132 admiration 94; affective notions of xix, 45, 48–9, 82–3, 94–5; against orthodoxy 8; astonishment and 6, 11, 53, 114, 181; as the beginning of philosophy 2, 9, 90, 96, 135; as the

familiar made strange 7; as the extraordinary 12; as perspectival 23, 53; Aristotle and xv–xvi; attunement to xxi, 163; being overwhelmed and 6; boundaries and xvi; curiosities and xvii; curiosity and xxii, 23, 26, 30, 32–3, 35, 39, 93, 180–1; development of 9; dwelling with xxii, 179–81; ethics and 146–55; everyday 161–2; gender and 147–55; globalisation and xvii; horror and 6; Indian philosophy and xvi; individual responsibility and 42–57; intellectual effort and 27; Islamic philosophy and xvi; limits of knowledge and 6, 14, 22; novelty and 11, 12; physiological notions of xix, 45, 48–9; rationality and 23, 26, 90; scepticism and 13; self and 83; sense making and xvi, xix, xx, xxi; shock and 114; social 23, 34, 39, 83, 96–8, 114; universals and xvi, 48; unknowable and 10

Wonders 24; and imperial possession 84

Xiong, Yang (53 BCE–18 AD)
Xiu, Ouyang (1007–1072) 70, 78

Young, Iris Marion 147
Yun, Ji (1724–1805) xx, 67, 77, 78

Zeitlin, Judith 72–3
Zhang, Xupeng 63